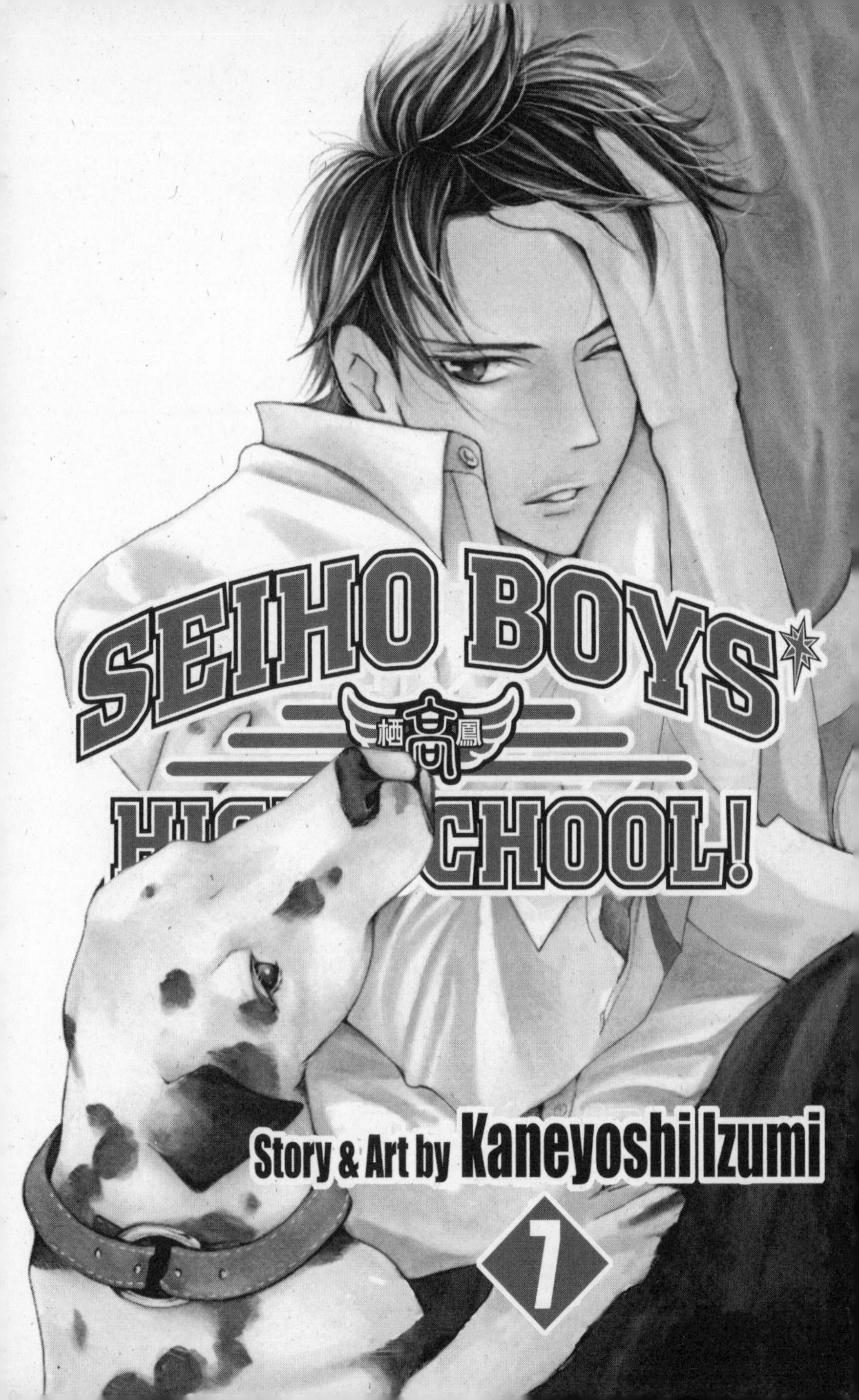
SEIHO BOYS
栖 高 鳳
HIG CHOOL!
Story & Art by Kaneyoshi Izumi
7

SEIHO BOYS' HIGH SCHOOL!

CONTENTS

■Rui Kamiki■ The hottest boy at school. He's going out with the super-average Fuyuka Miyaji.

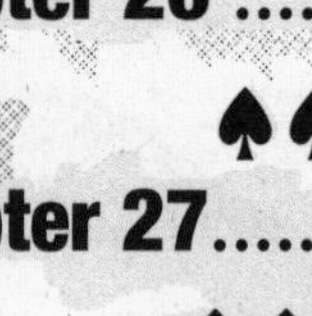

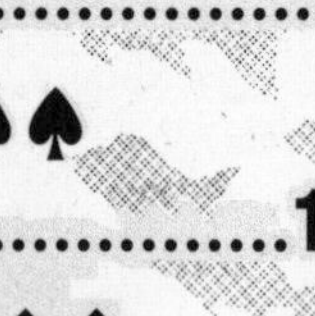

■Chikara Maki■ At first glance, Maki seems like a gentle guy, but he's actually got an aggressive streak. He's dating the beautiful Erika Takano.

■Mamoru Hanai■ A girl trapped in a boy's body, to put it bluntly. He takes photos of his classmates to spread their popularity far and wide.

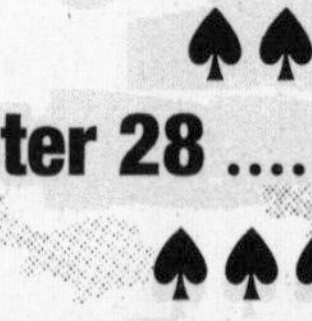

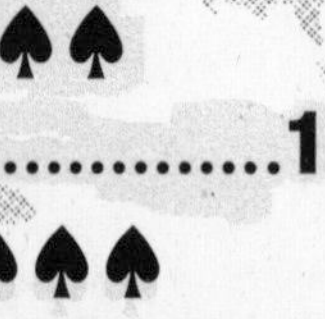

■Hidetoshi Nogami■ Sees himself as far superior to the other students. He is currently involved with the school nurse, Miss Fukuhara.

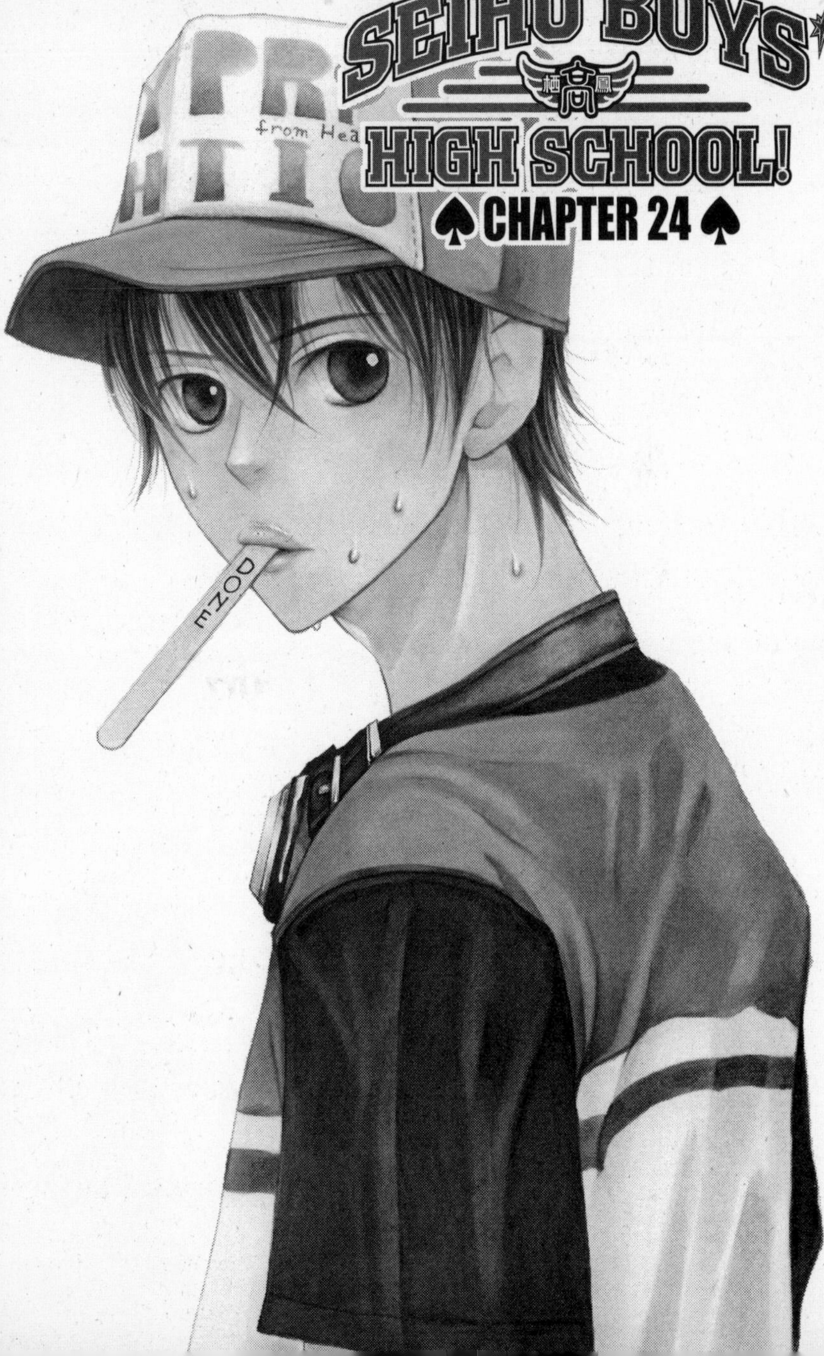
SEIHO BOYS' HIGH SCHOOL!
CHAPTER 24
DOZE

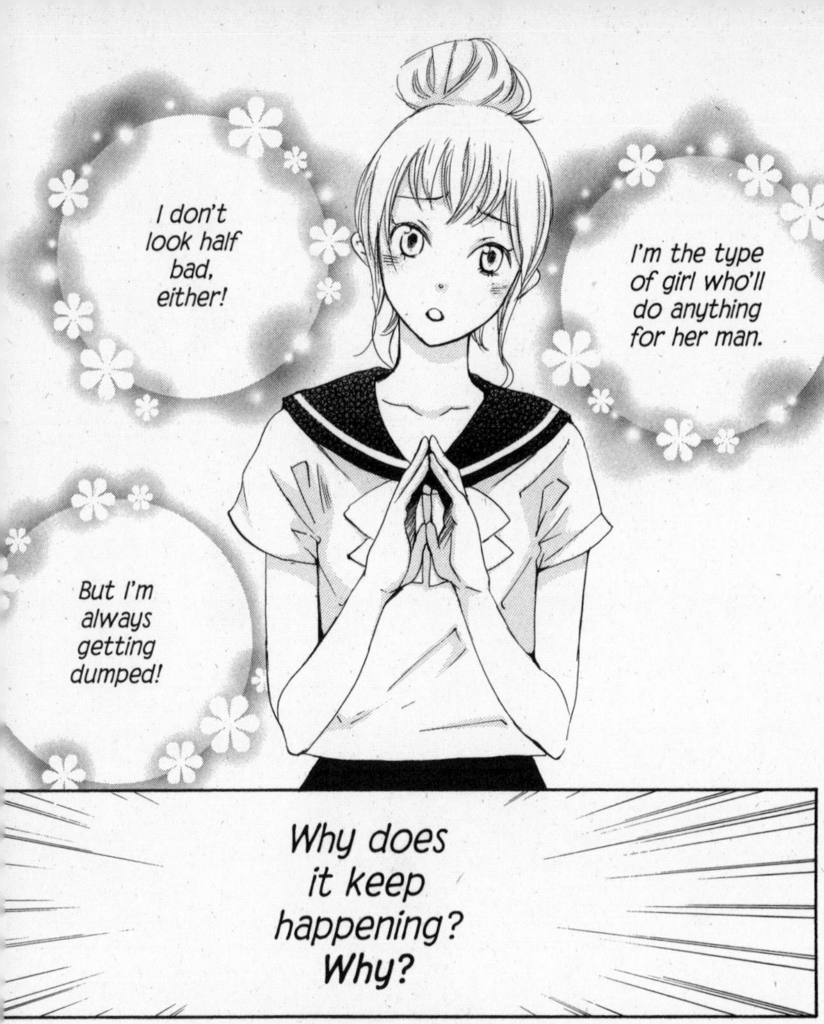
I'm the type of girl who'll do anything for her man.
I don't look half bad, either!
But I'm always getting dumped!
Why does it keep happening? Why?

SEIHO BOYS HIGH SCHOOL!

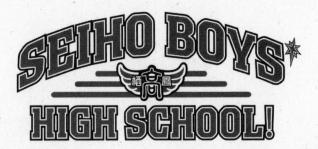

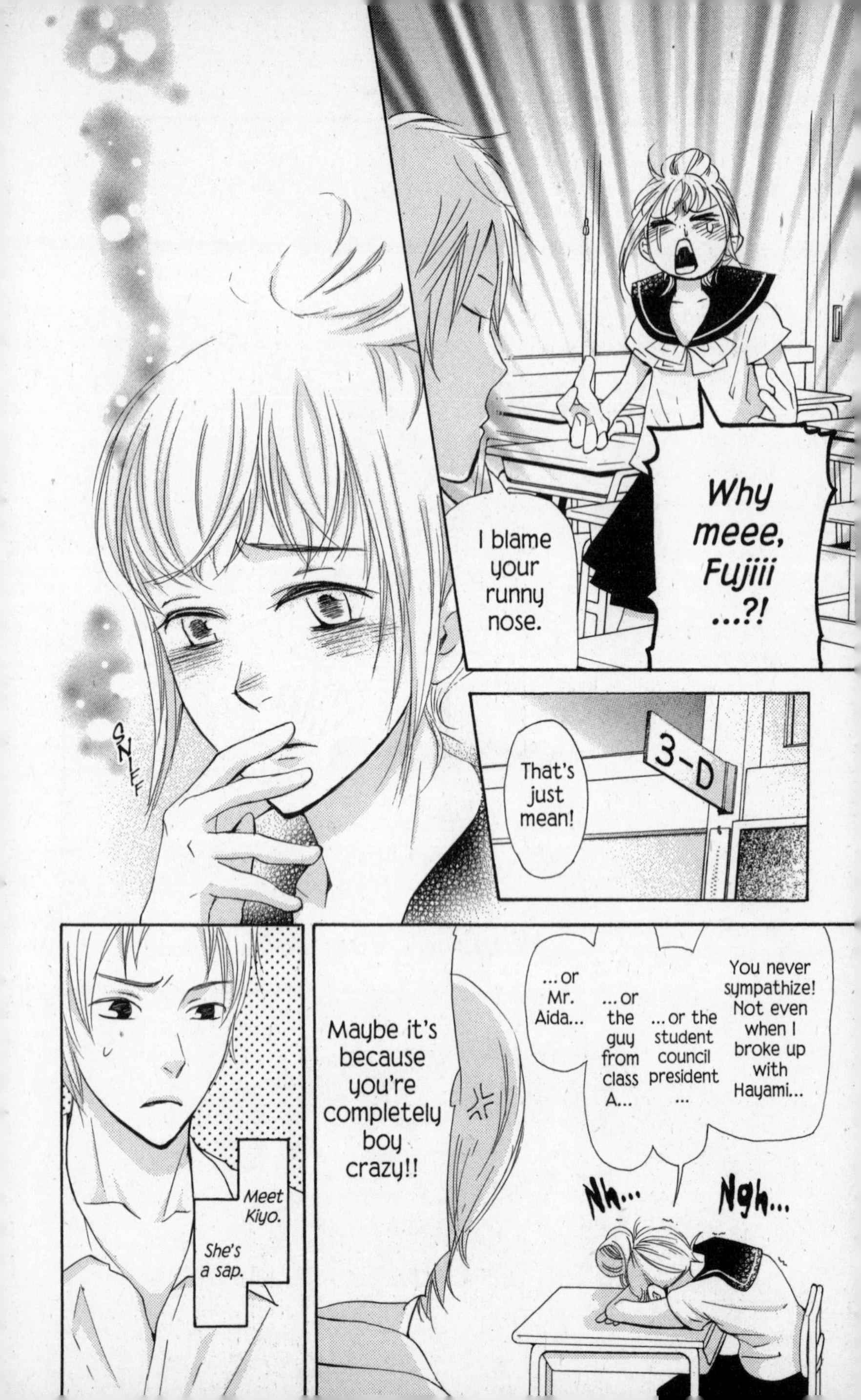
Why meee, Fujiiii ...?!
I blame your runny nose.
3-D
That's just mean!
SNIFF
You never sympathize! Not even when I broke up with Hayami...
...or the student council president...
...or the guy from class A...
...or Mr. Aida...
Ngh...
Nh...
Maybe it's because you're completely boy crazy!!
Meet Kiyo.
She's a sap.

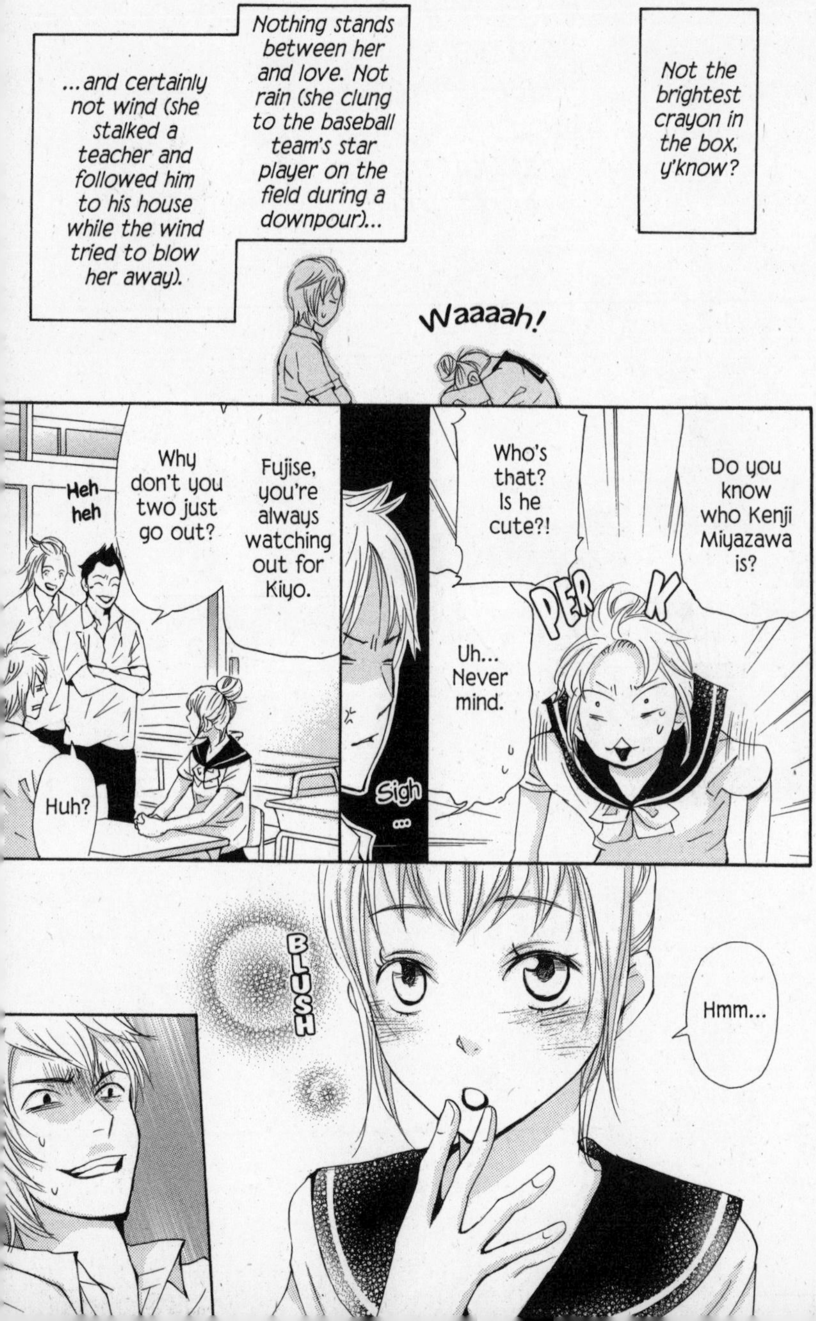
Not the brightest crayon in the box, y'know?
Nothing stands between her and love. Not rain (she clung to the baseball team's star player on the field during a downpour)...
...and certainly not wind (she stalked a teacher and followed him to his house while the wind tried to blow her away).
Waaaah!
Do you know who Kenji Miyazawa is?
Who's that? Is he cute?!
PER K
Uh... Never mind.
Sigh
...
Fujise, you're always watching out for Kiyo.
Why don't you two just go out?
Heh heh
Huh?
Hmm...
BLUSH

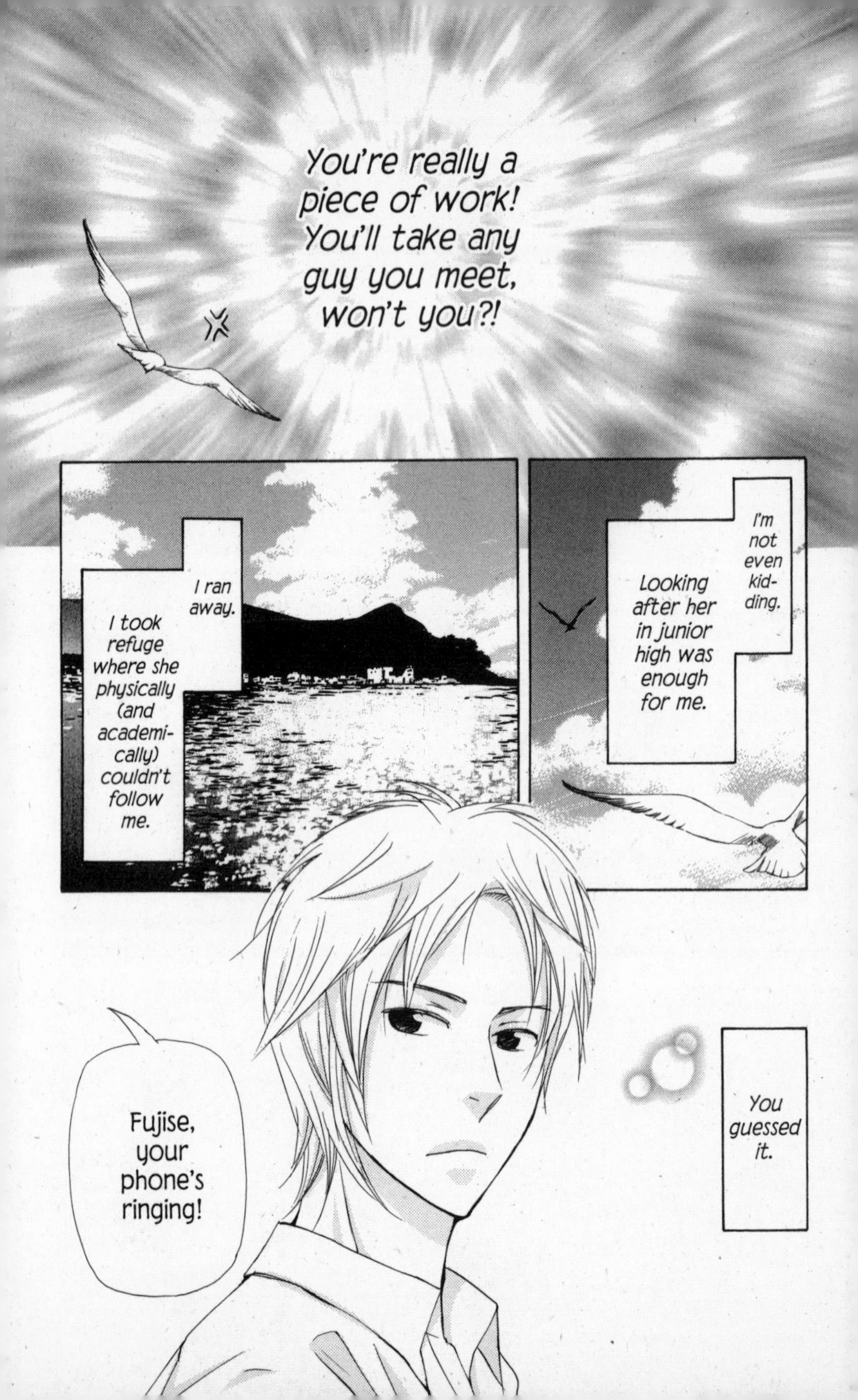
You're really a piece of work! You'll take any guy you meet, won't you?!
I'm not even kid-ding.
Looking after her in junior high was enough for me.
I ran away.
I took refuge where she physically (and academi-cally) couldn't follow me.
You guessed it.
Fujise, your phone's ringing!

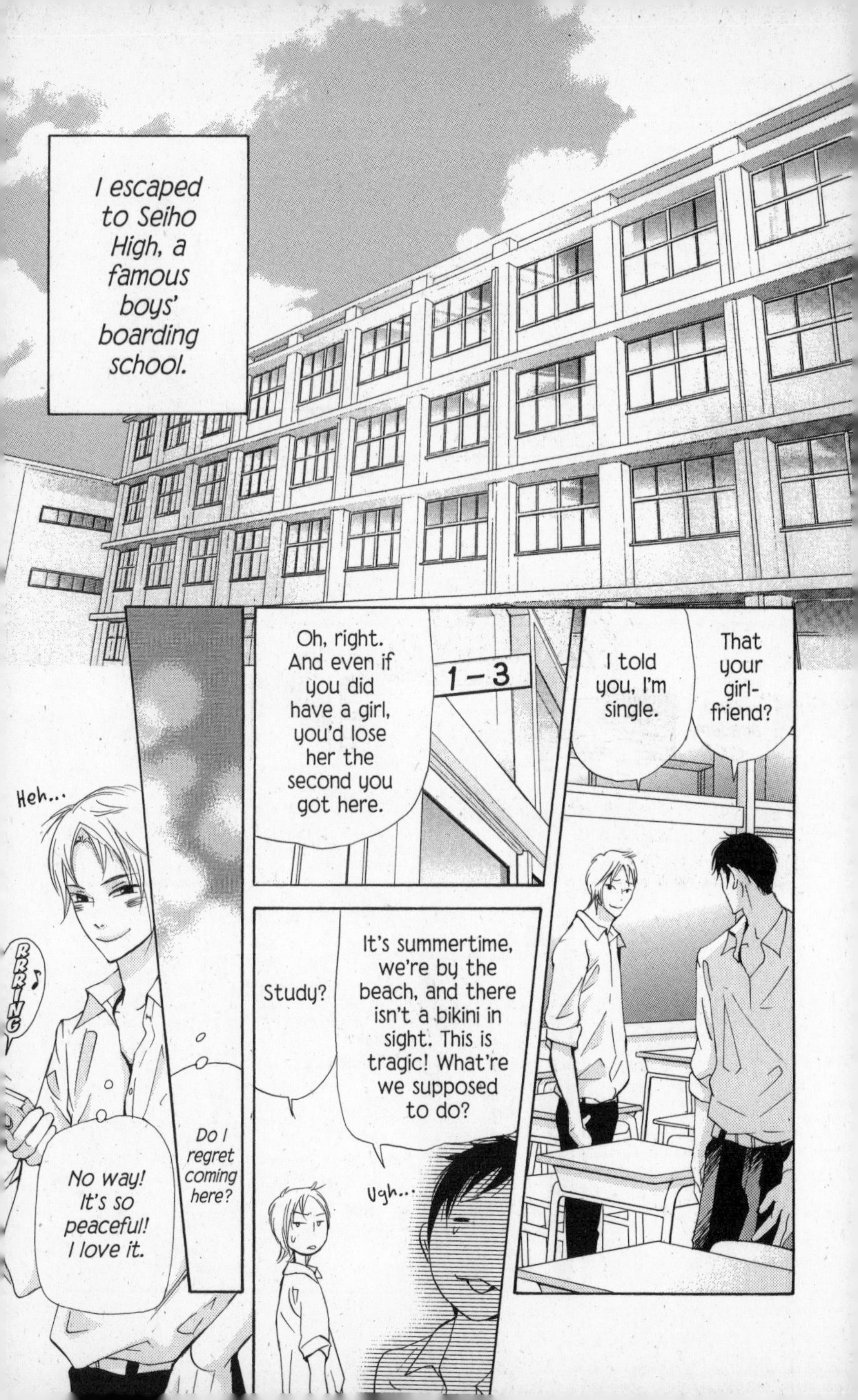
I escaped to Seiho High, a famous boys' boarding school.
1-3
That your girlfriend?
I told you, I'm single.
Oh, right. And even if you did have a girl, you'd lose her the second you got here.
It's summertime, we're by the beach, and there isn't a bikini in sight. This is tragic! What're we supposed to do?
Study?
Ugh...
Heh...
RRRING
Do I regret coming here?
No way! It's so peaceful! I love it.

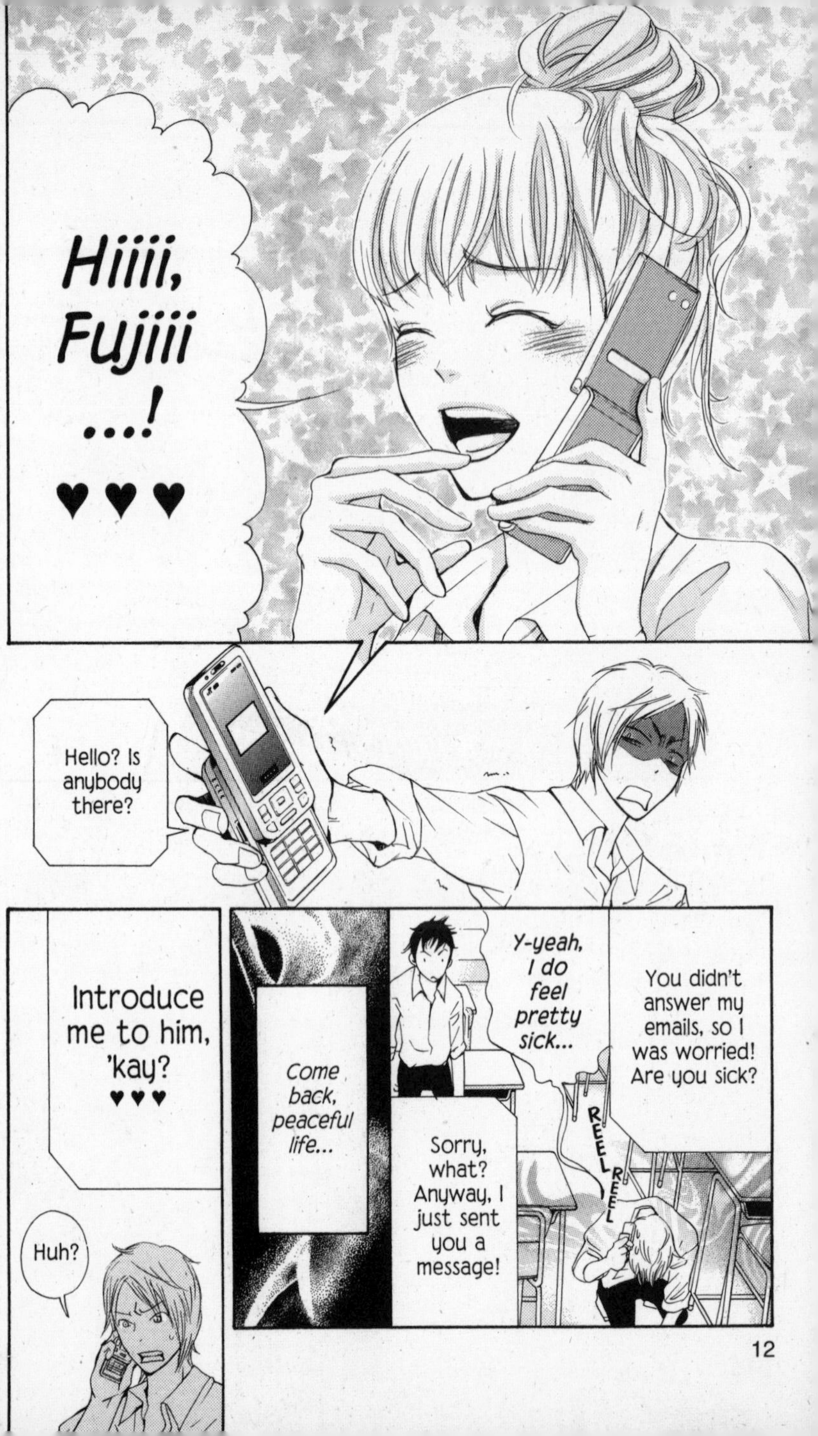
Hiiii, Fujiii ...! ♥♥♥
Hello? Is anybody there?
You didn't answer my emails, so I was worried! Are you sick?
Y-yeah, I do feel pretty sick...
REEL REEL
Sorry, what? Anyway, I just sent you a message!
Come back, peaceful life...
Introduce me to him, 'kay? ♥♥♥
Huh?

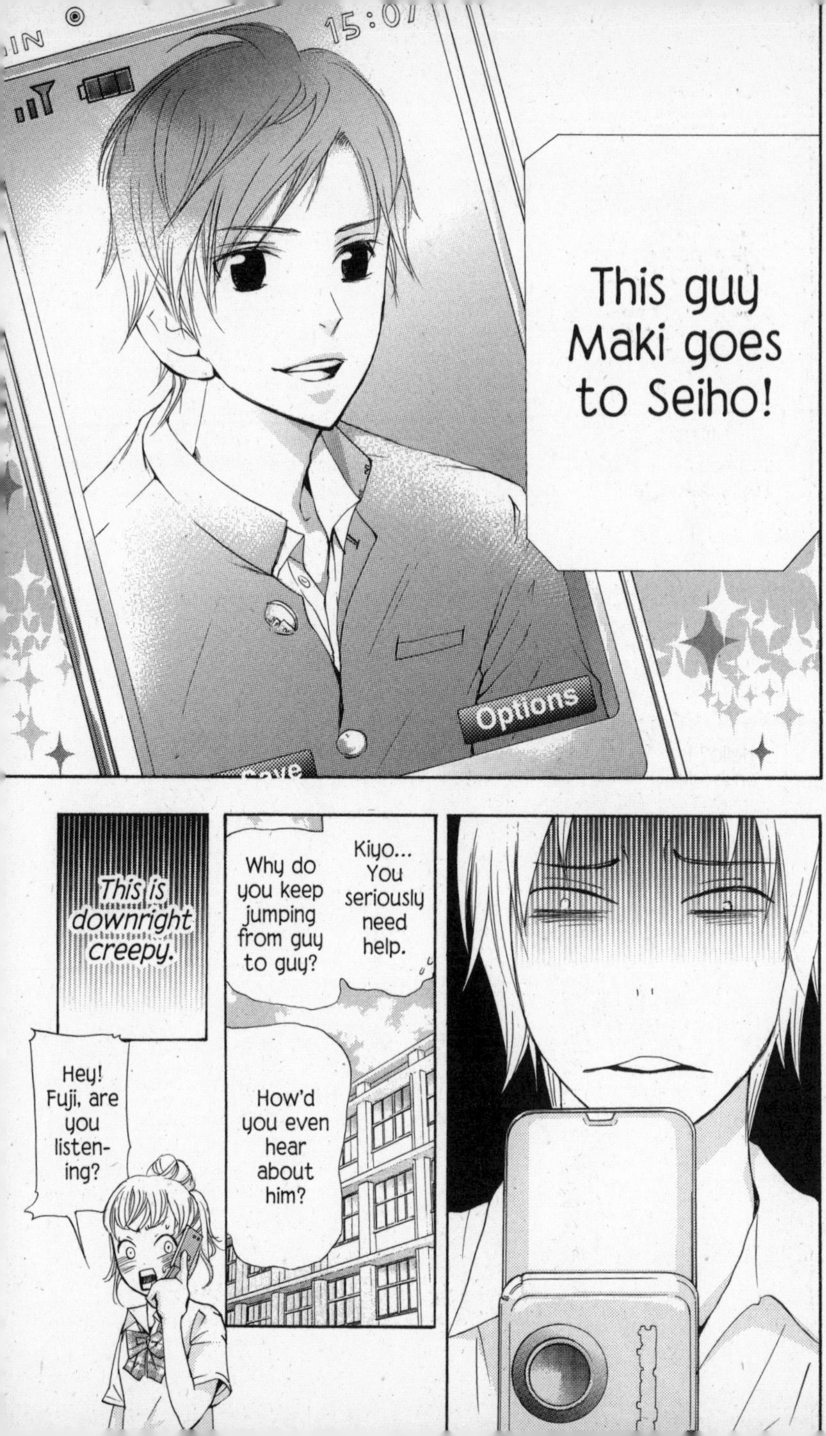
Options
This guy Maki goes to Seiho!
Kiyo... You seriously need help.
Why do you keep jumping from guy to guy?
How'd you even hear about him?
This is downright creepy.
Hey! Fuji, are you listening?

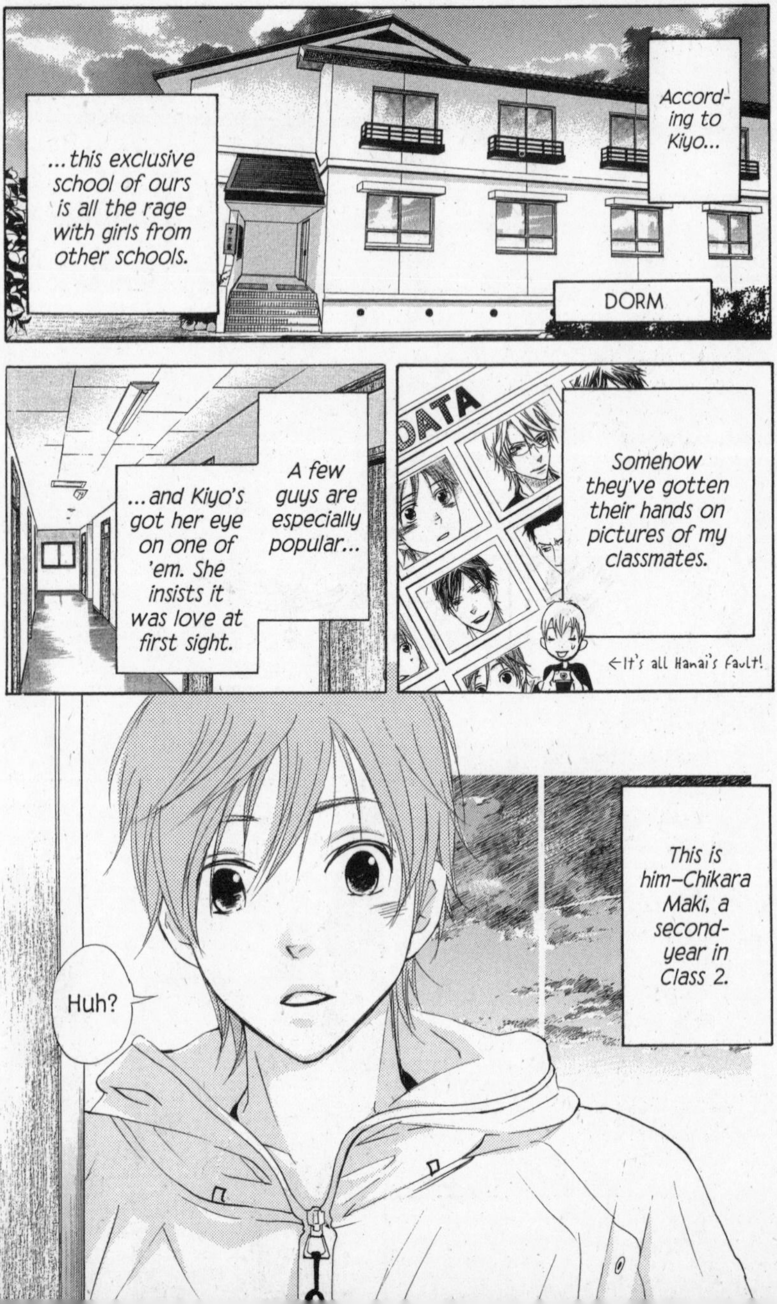
According to Kiyo...
...this exclusive school of ours is all the rage with girls from other schools.
DORM
Somehow they've gotten their hands on pictures of my classmates.
←It's all Hanai's fault!
DATA
A few guys are especially popular...
...and Kiyo's got her eye on one of 'em. She insists it was love at first sight.
This is him—Chikara Maki, a second-year in Class 2.
Huh?

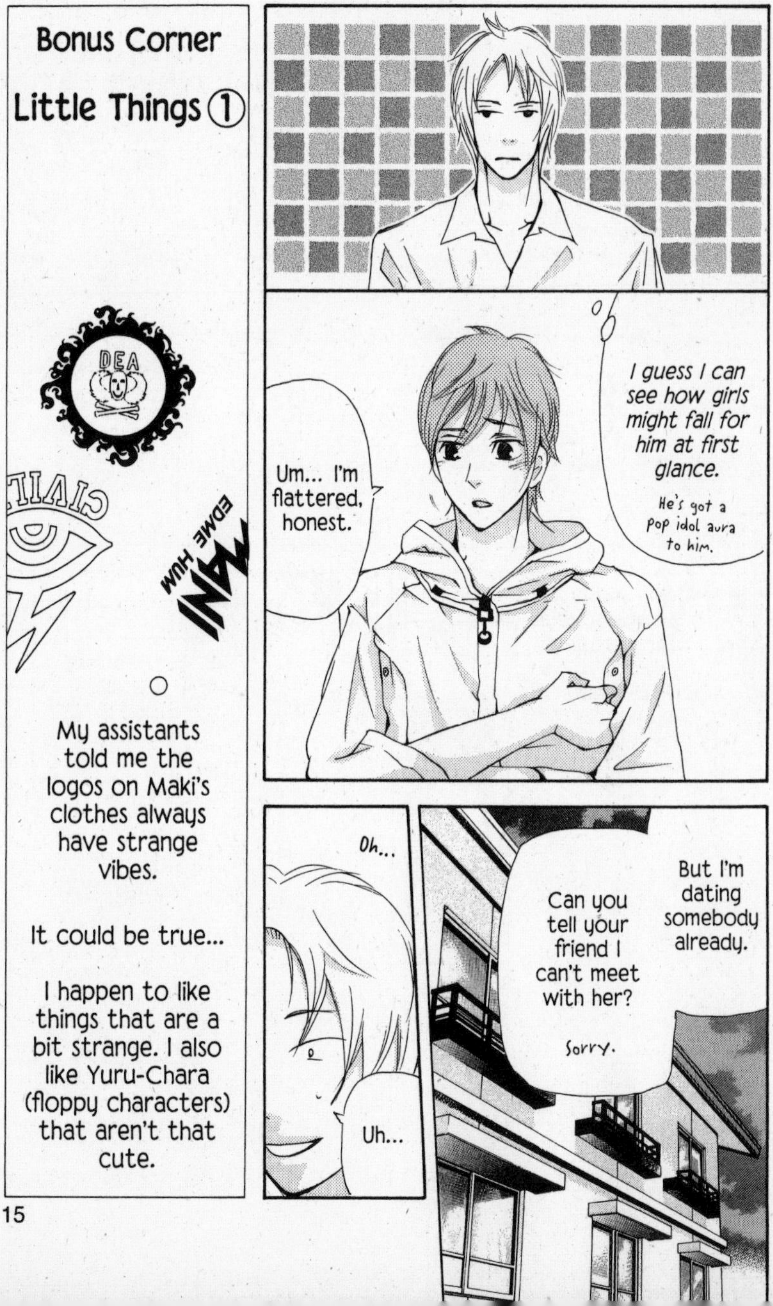
I guess I can see how girls might fall for him at first glance.
He's got a pop idol aura to him.
Um... I'm flattered, honest.
But I'm dating somebody already.
Can you tell your friend I can't meet with her?
Sorry.
Oh...
Uh...

Bonus Corner
Little Things ①

My assistants told me the logos on Maki's clothes always have strange vibes.

It could be true...

I happen to like things that are a bit strange. I also like Yuru-Chara (floppy characters) that aren't that cute.

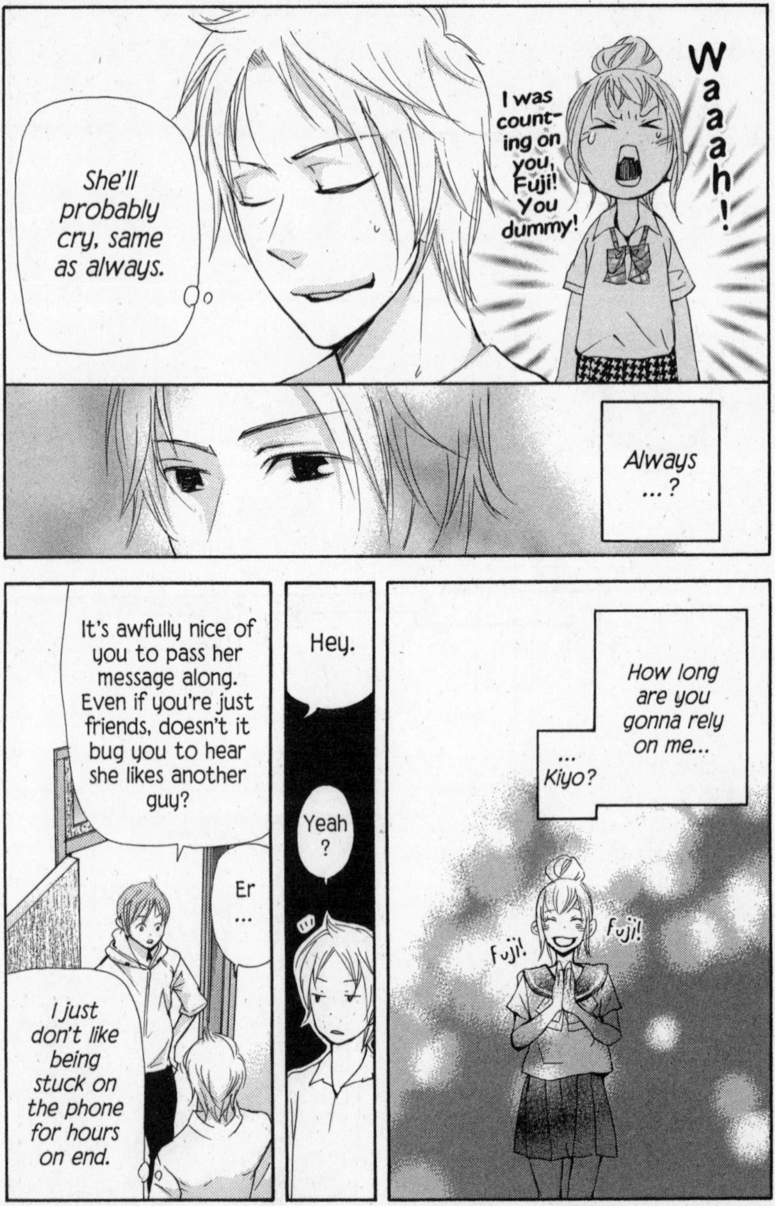
Waaah!
I was counting on you, Fuji! You dummy!
She'll probably cry, same as always.
Always ...?
How long are you gonna rely on me...
... Kiyo?
Fuji!
Fuji!
Hey.
Yeah ?
It's awfully nice of you to pass her message along. Even if you're just friends, doesn't it bug you to hear she likes another guy?
Er ...
I just don't like being stuck on the phone for hours on end.

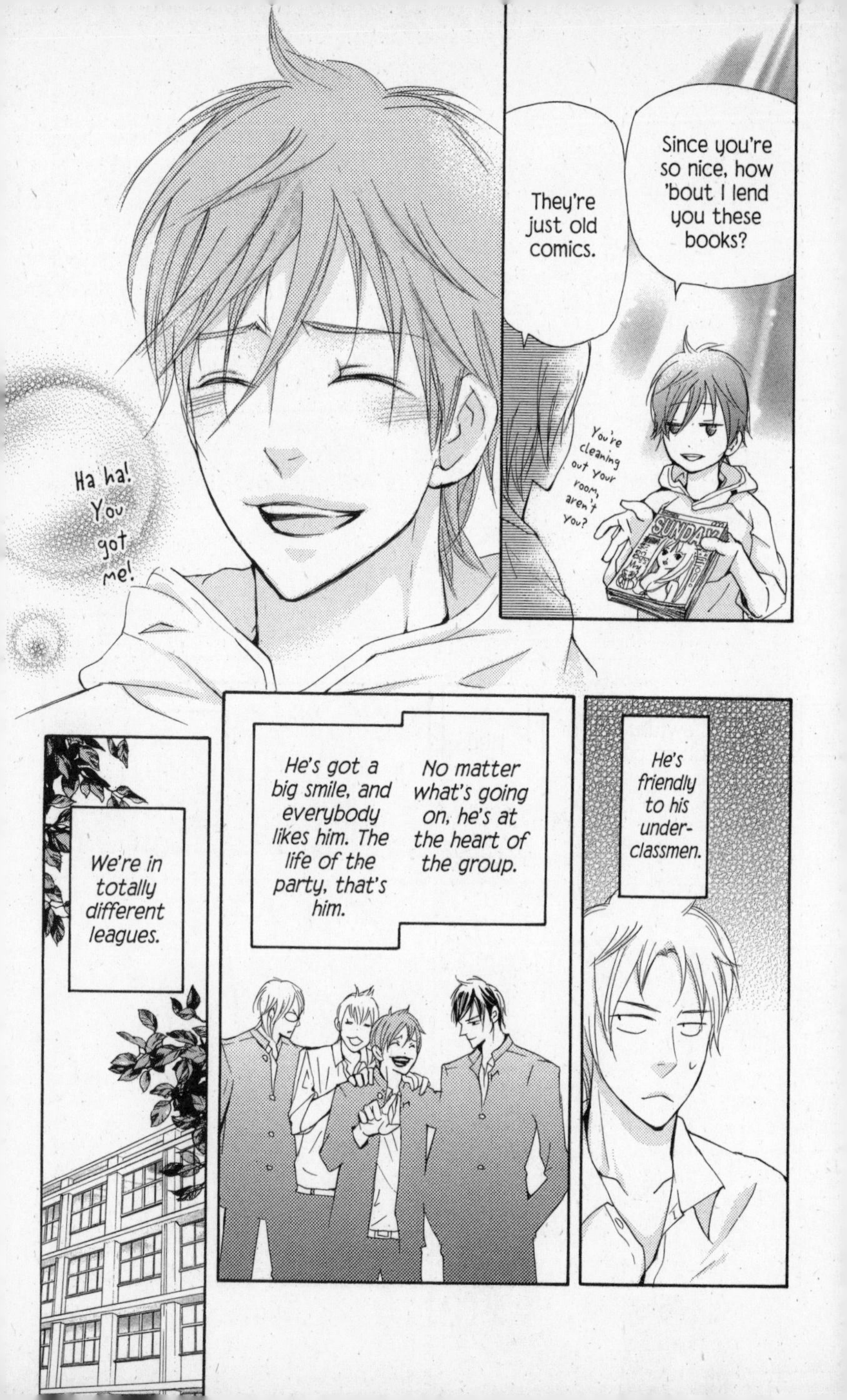
Since you're so nice, how 'bout I lend you these books?
They're just old comics.
You're cleaning out your room, aren't you?
SUNDAY
Ha ha! You got me!
He's friendly to his under-classmen.
No matter what's going on, he's at the heart of the group.
He's got a big smile, and everybody likes him. The life of the party, that's him.
We're in totally different leagues.

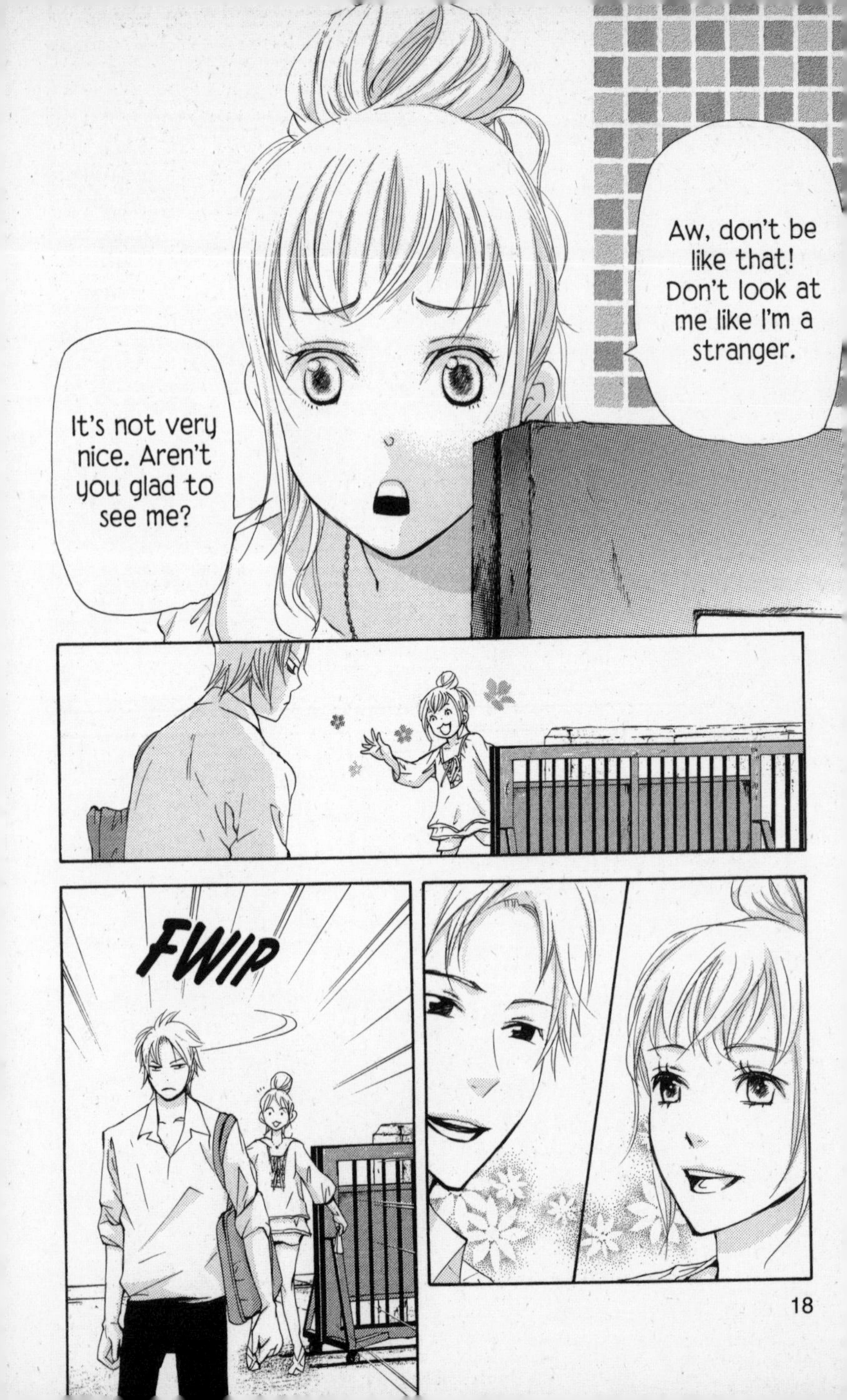
Aw, don't be like that! Don't look at me like I'm a stranger.
It's not very nice. Aren't you glad to see me?
FWIP

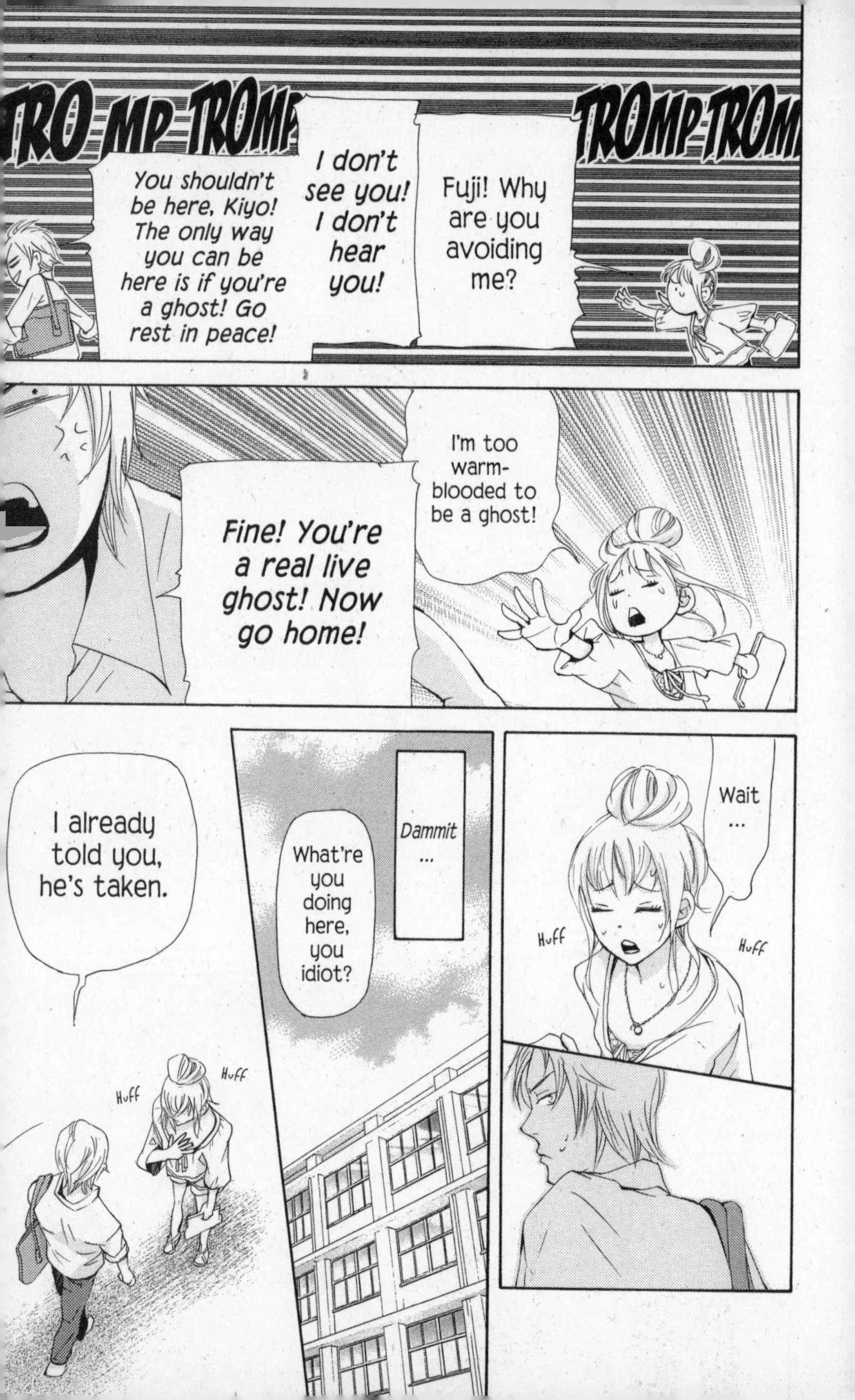
TROMP TROM
Fuji! Why are you avoiding me?
I don't see you! I don't hear you!
You shouldn't be here, Kiyo! The only way you can be here is if you're a ghost! Go rest in peace!
TRO MP TROMP
I'm too warm-blooded to be a ghost!
Fine! You're a real live ghost! Now go home!
Wait ...
Huff
Huff
Dammit ...
What're you doing here, you idiot?
I already told you, he's taken.
Huff
Huff

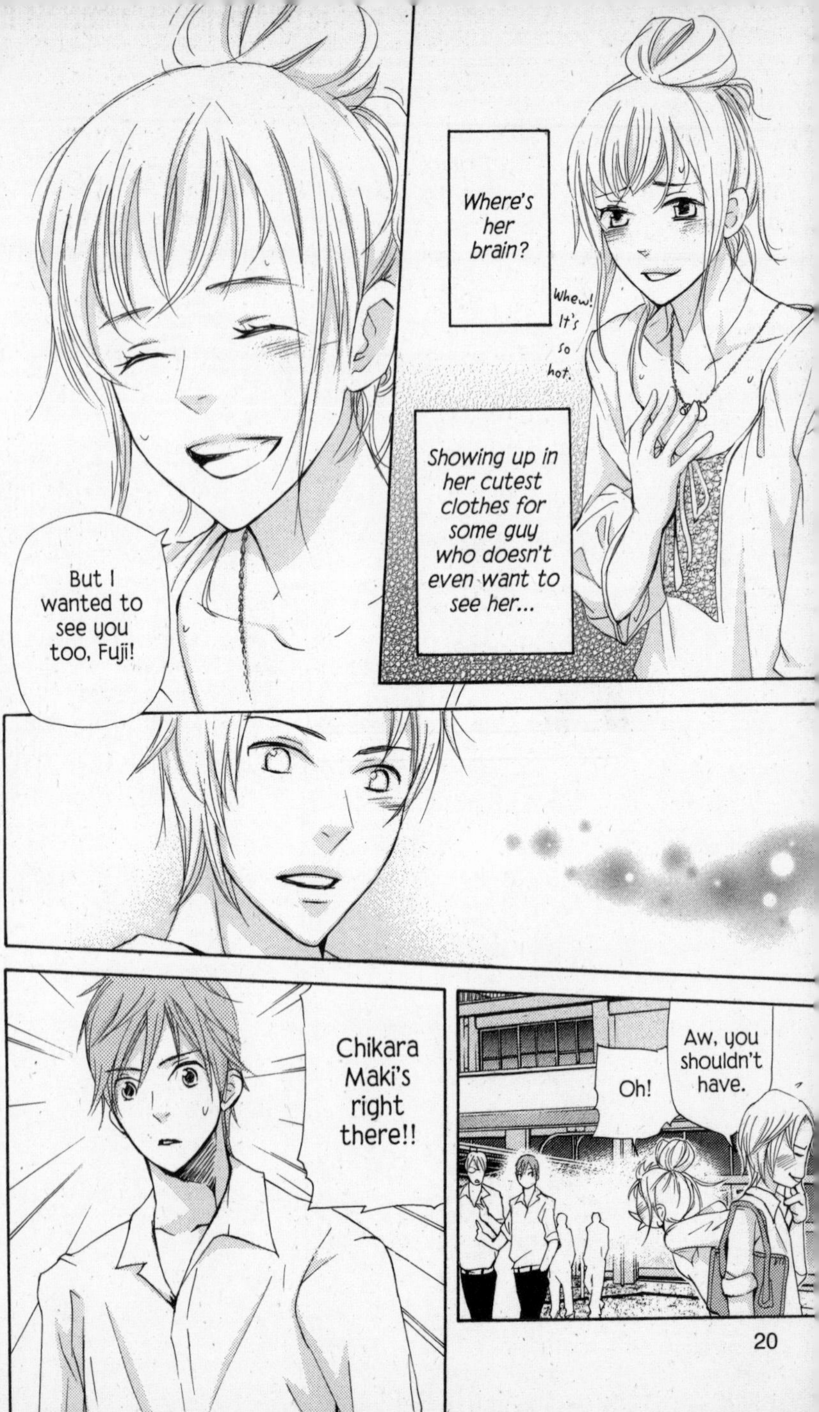
Where's her brain?
Whew! It's so hot.
Showing up in her cutest clothes for some guy who doesn't even want to see her...
But I wanted to see you too, Fuji!
Chikara Maki's right there!!
Aw, you shouldn't have.
Oh!

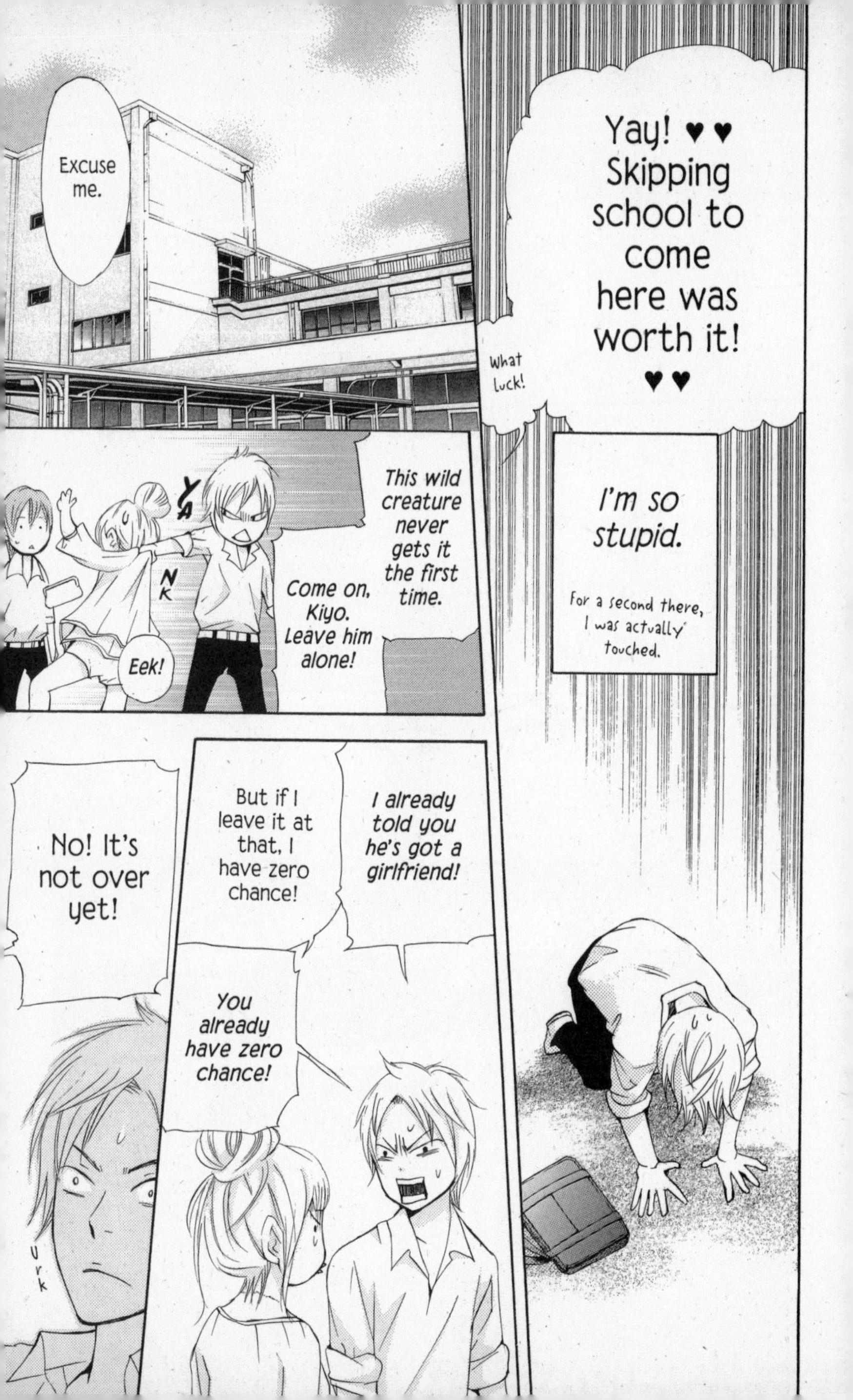
Yay! ♥♥ Skipping school to come here was worth it! ♥♥
What luck!
I'm so stupid.
For a second there, I was actually touched.
Excuse me.
This wild creature never gets it the first time.
Come on, Kiyo. Leave him alone!
YANK
Eek!
I already told you he's got a girlfriend!
But if I leave it at that, I have zero chance!
No! It's not over yet!
You already have zero chance!
Urk

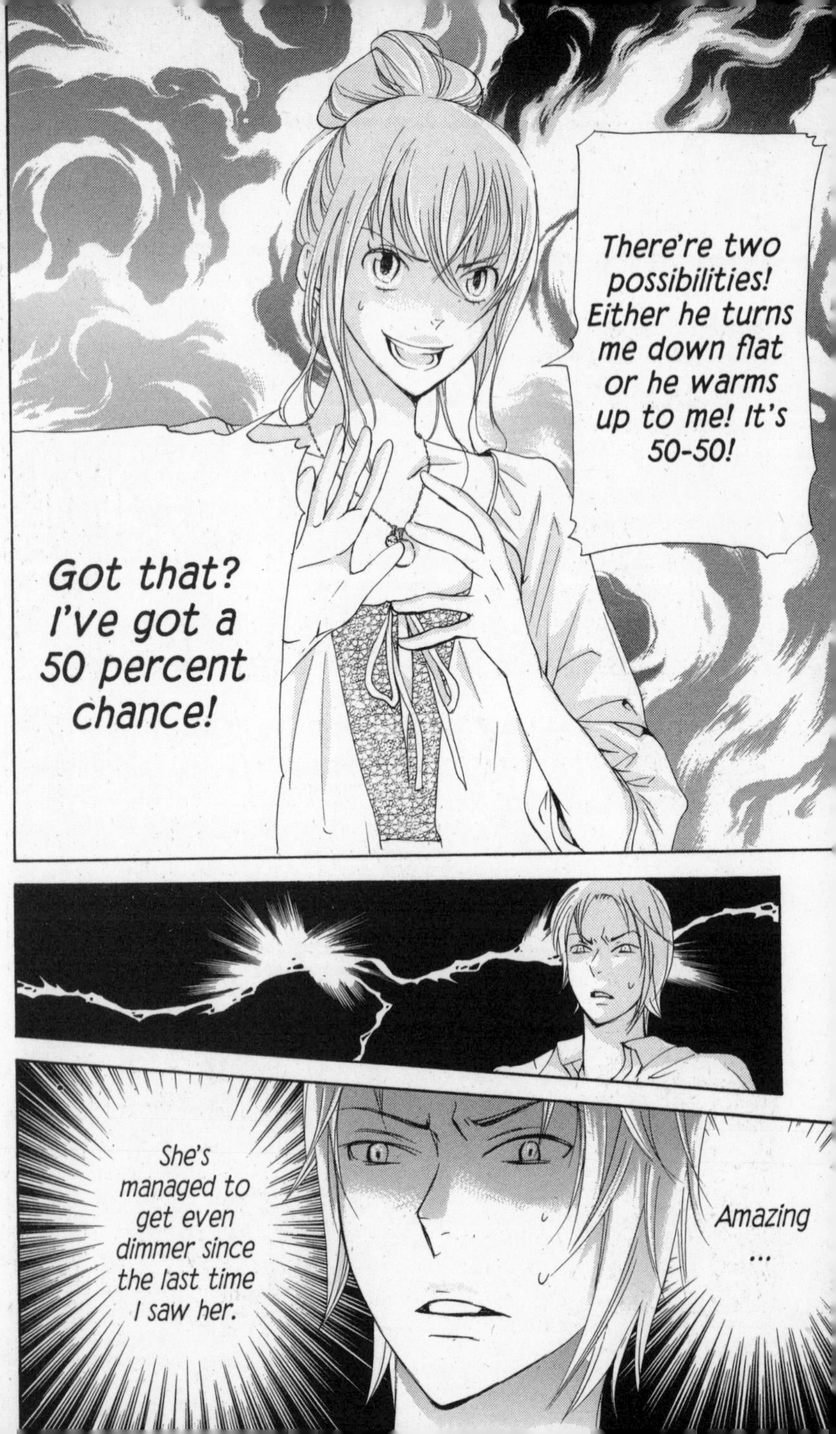
There're two possibilities! Either he turns me down flat or he warms up to me! It's 50-50!
Got that? I've got a 50 percent chance!
Amazing ...
She's managed to get even dimmer since the last time I saw her.

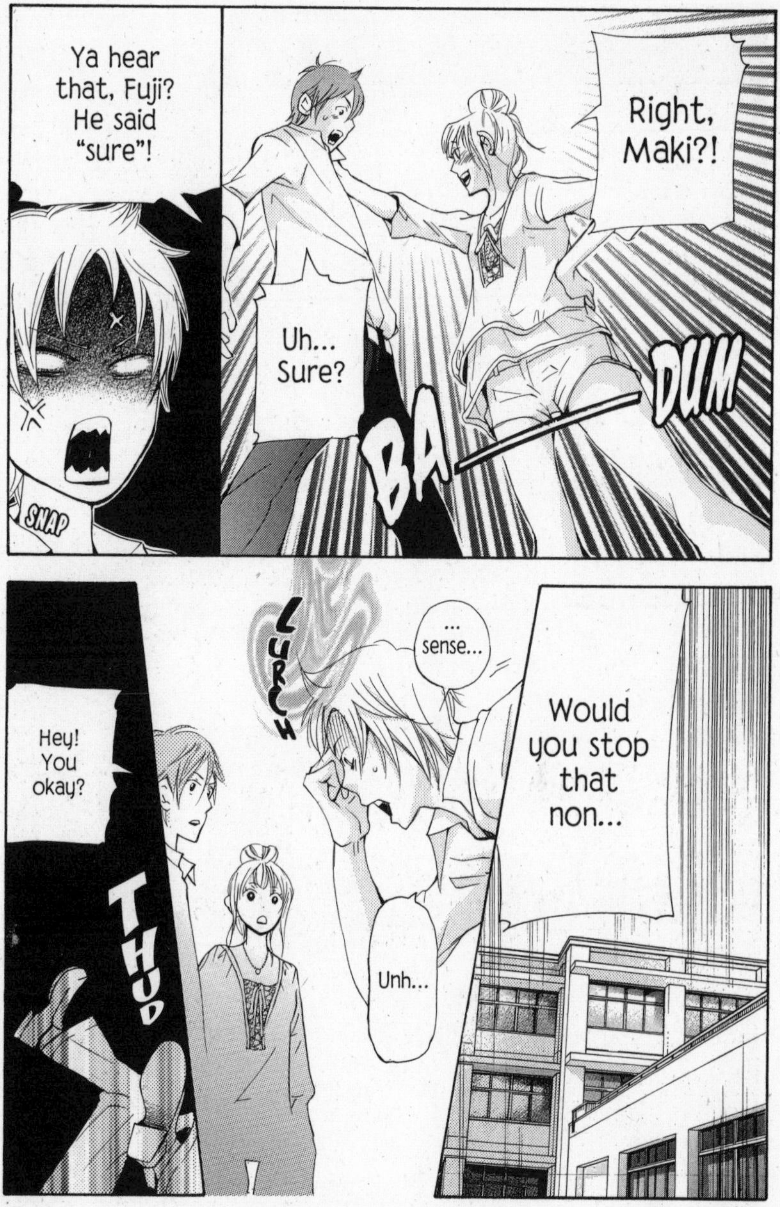
Right, Maki?!
Uh... Sure?
BA DUM
Ya hear that, Fuji? He said "sure"!
SNAP
Would you stop that non...
... sense...
LURCH
Unh...
Hey! You okay?
THUD

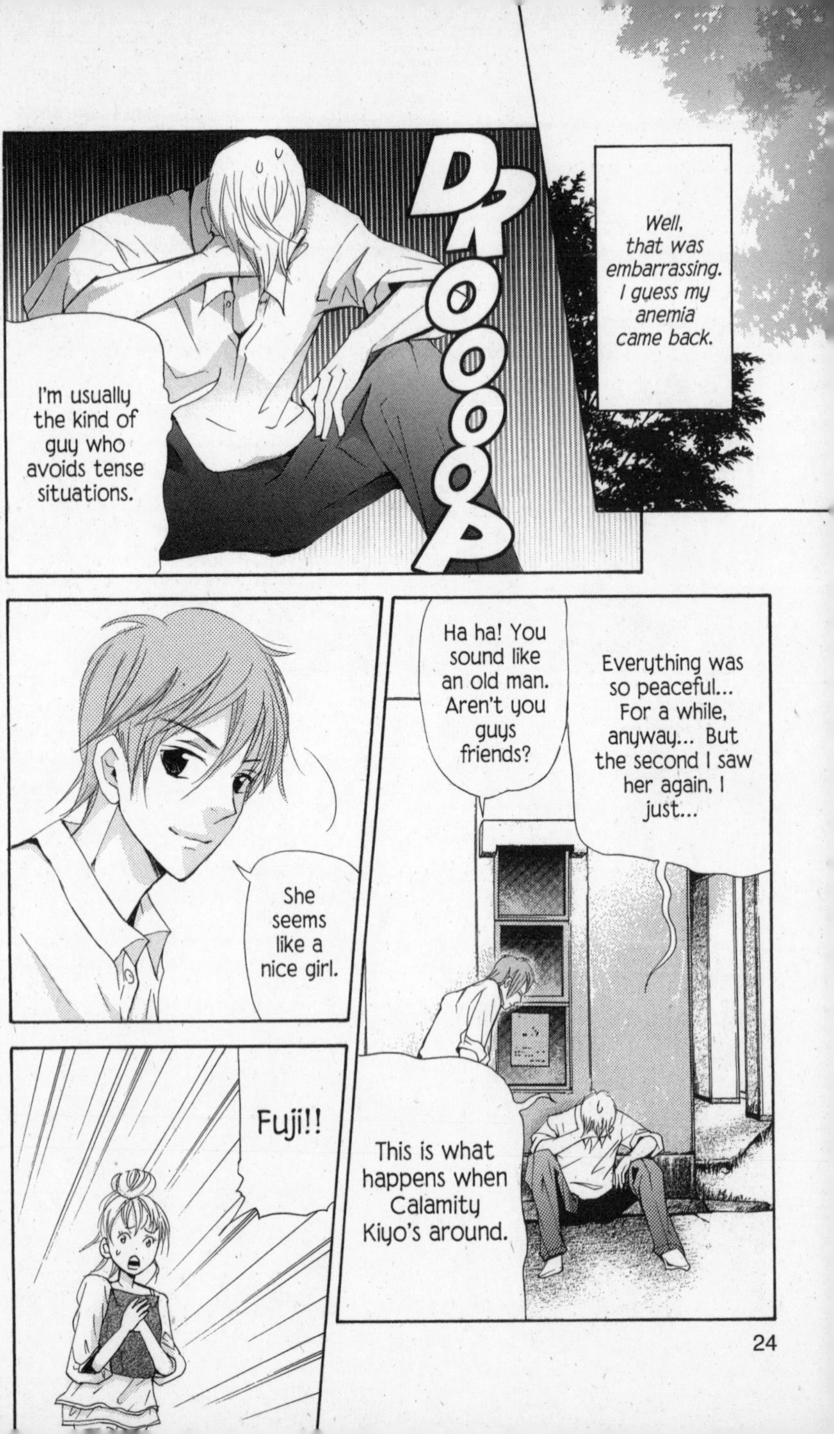
Well, that was embarrassing. I guess my anemia came back.
DROOOOOP
I'm usually the kind of guy who avoids tense situations.
Everything was so peaceful... For a while, anyway... But the second I saw her again, I just...
Ha ha! You sound like an old man. Aren't you guys friends?
This is what happens when Calamity Kiyo's around.
She seems like a nice girl.
Fuji!!

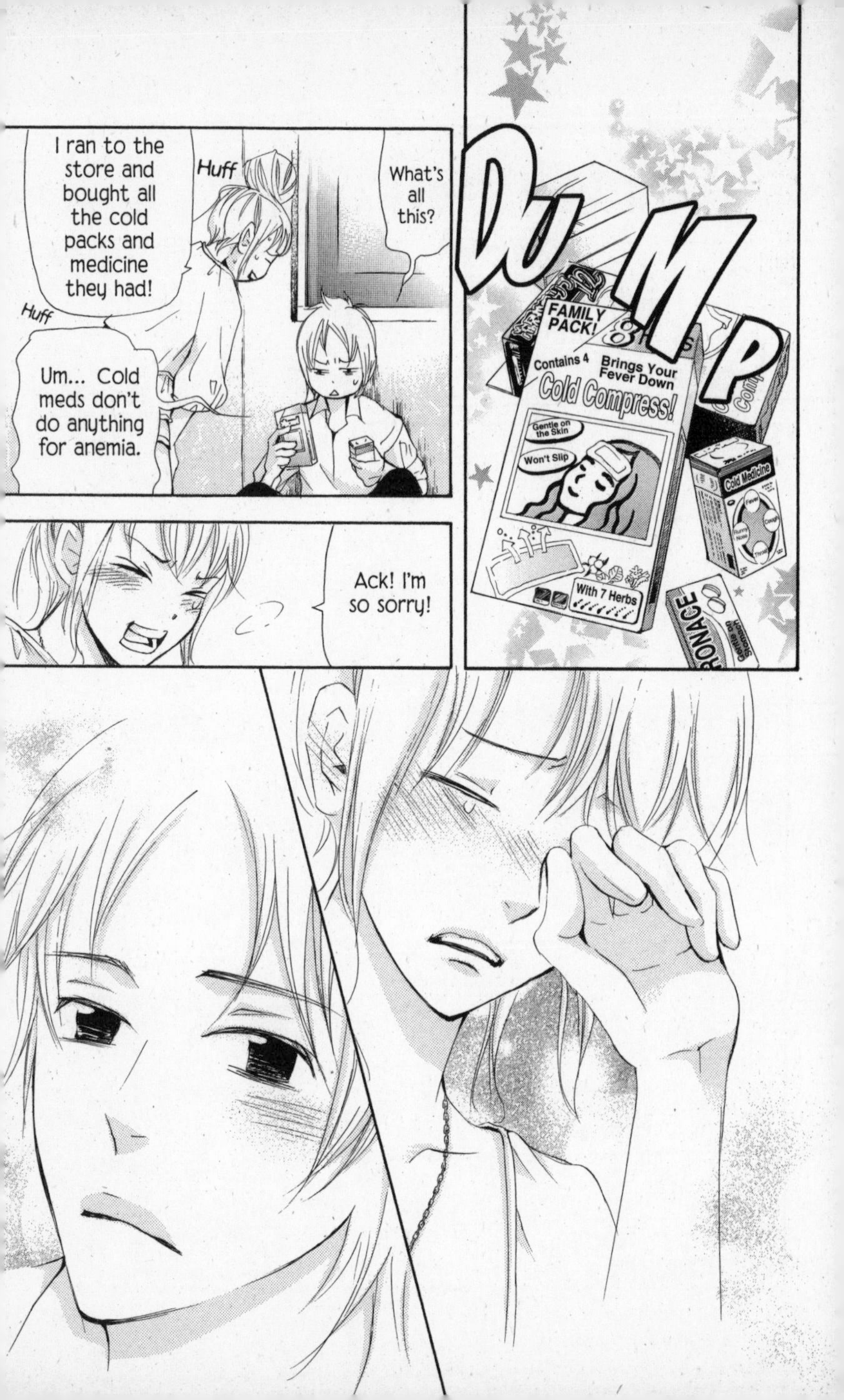
DUMP
FAMILY PACK!
Contains 4
Brings Your Fever Down
Cold Compress!
Gentle on the Skin
Won't Slip
With 7 Herbs
Cold Medicine
RONACE
What's all this?
Huff
I ran to the store and bought all the cold packs and medicine they had!
Huff
Um... Cold meds don't do anything for anemia.
Ack! I'm so sorry!

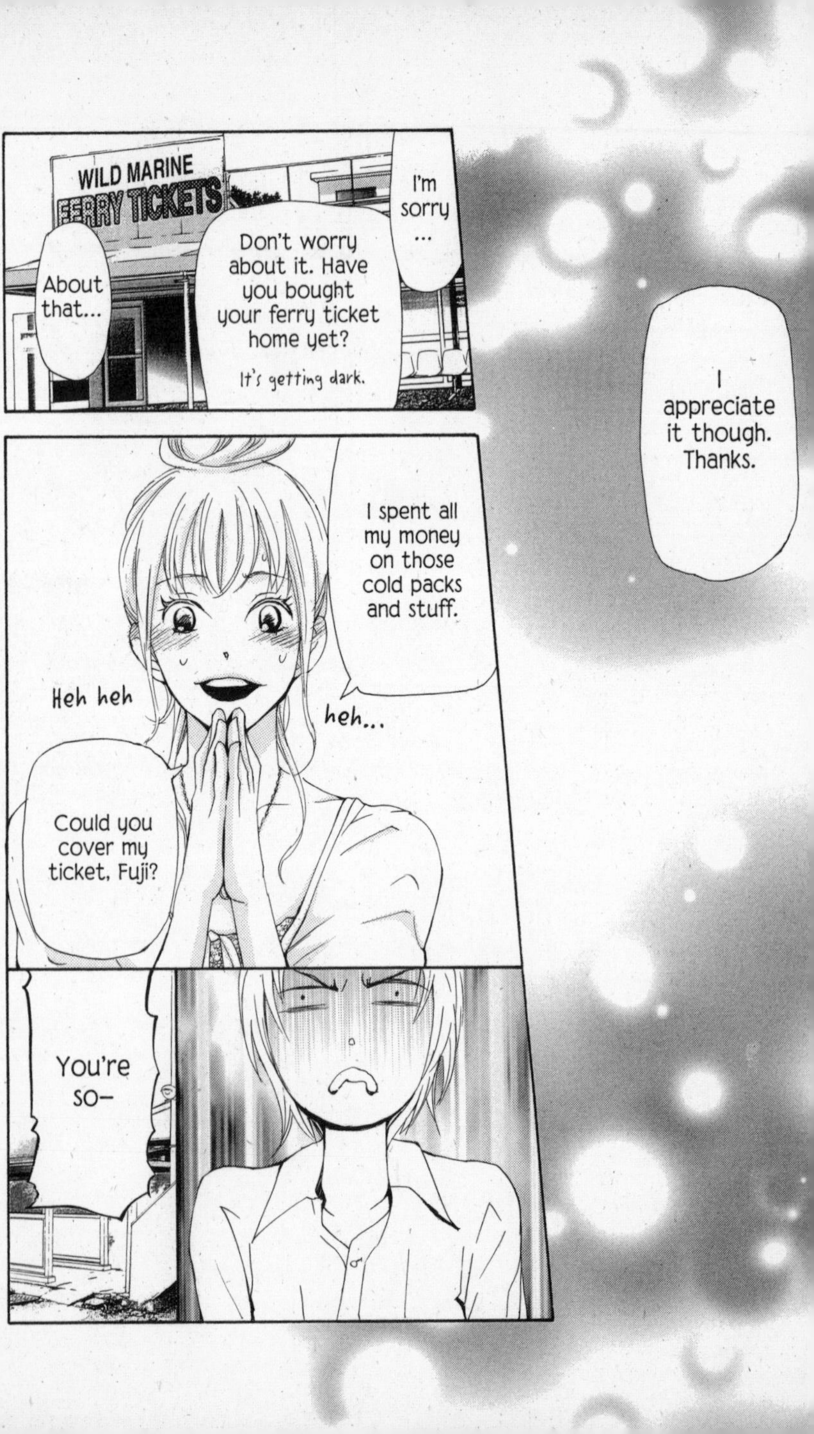
WILD MARINE
FERRY TICKETS
I'm sorry ...
I appreciate it though. Thanks.
Don't worry about it. Have you bought your ferry ticket home yet?
It's getting dark.
About that...
I spent all my money on those cold packs and stuff.
Heh heh
heh...
Could you cover my ticket, Fuji?
You're so–

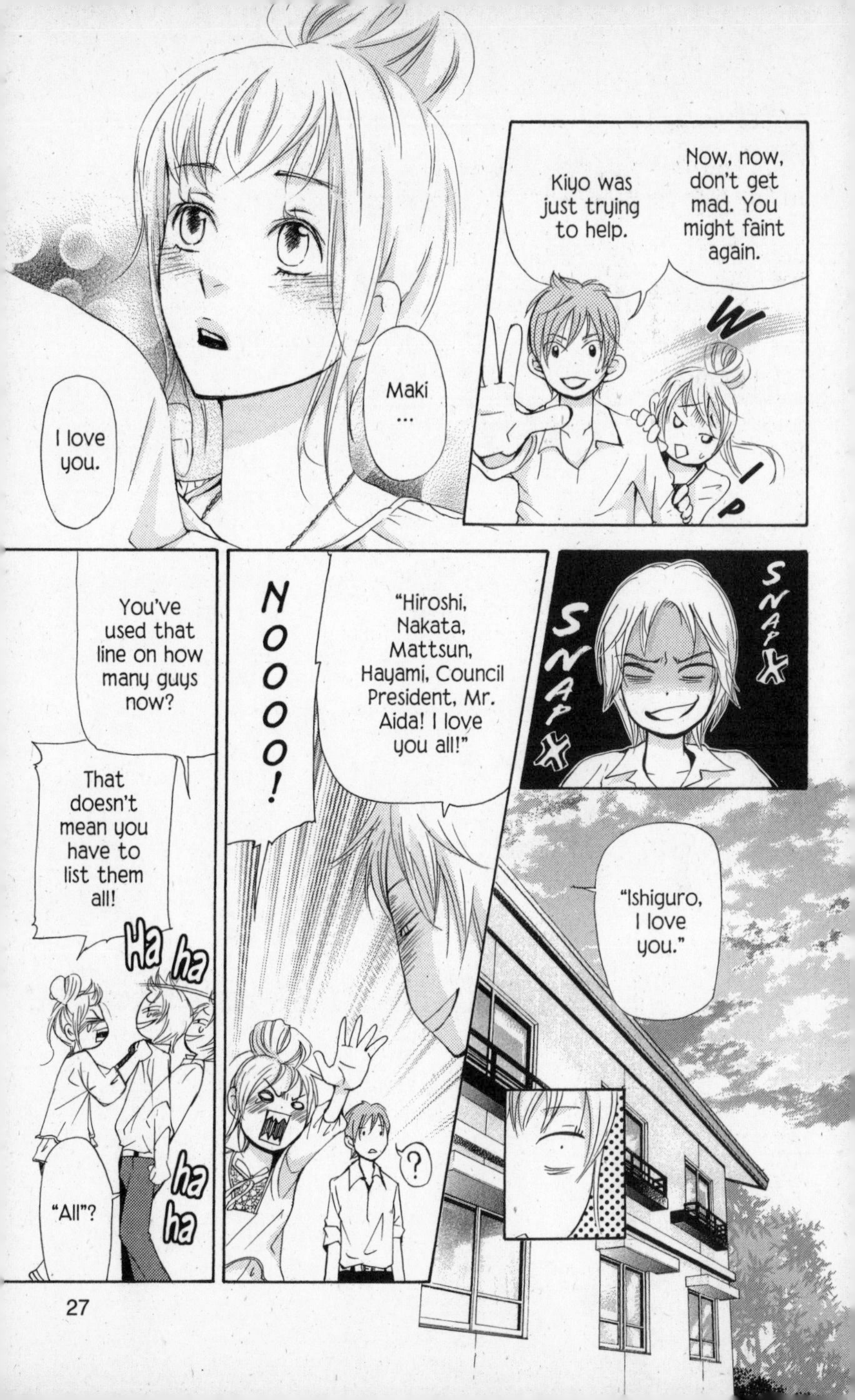
Now, now, don't get mad. You might faint again.
Kiyo was just trying to help.
WHIP
Maki...
I love you.
SNAP
SNAP
"Ishiguro, I love you."
NOOOOO!
"Hiroshi, Nakata, Mattsun, Hayami, Council President, Mr. Aida! I love you all!"
?
You've used that line on how many guys now?
That doesn't mean you have to list them all!
Ha ha
ha ha
"All"?

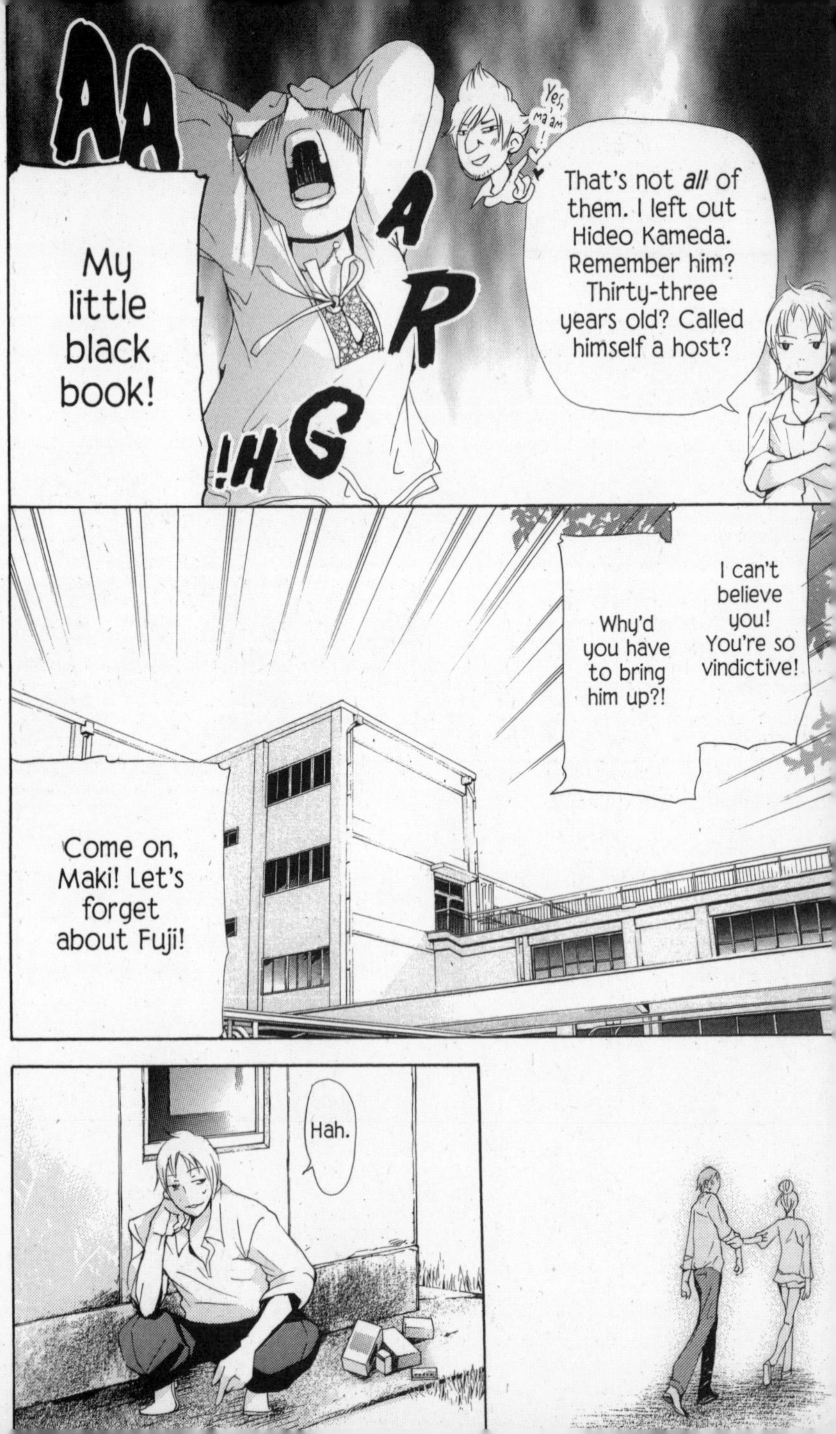

That's not *all* of them. I left out Hideo Kameda. Remember him? Thirty-three years old? Called himself a host?
Yes, ma'am!
AAARGH!
My little black book!
I can't believe you! You're so vindictive!
Why'd you have to bring him up?!
Come on, Maki! Let's forget about Fuji!
Hah.

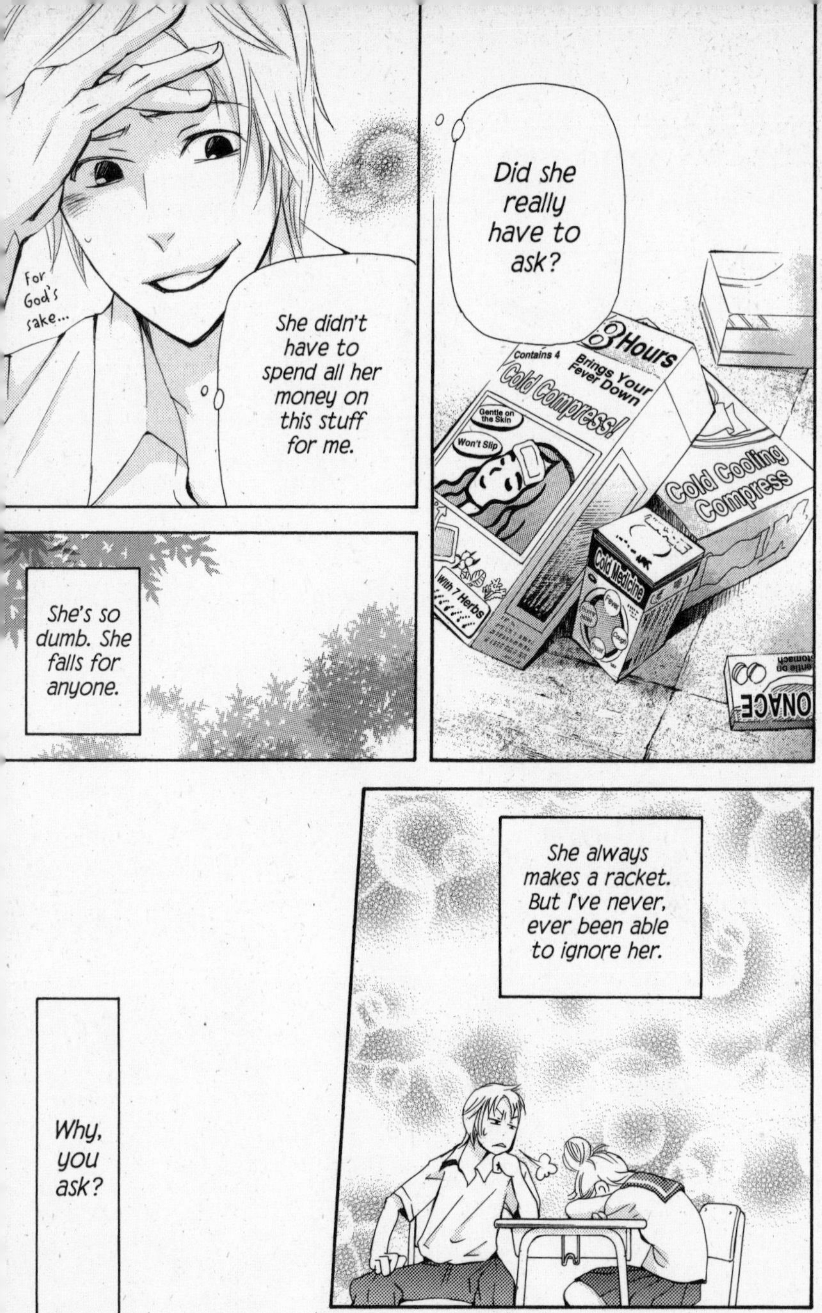
Did she really have to ask?
3 Hours
Contains 4
Brings Your Fever Down
Cold Compress!
Gentle on the Skin
Won't Slip
With 7 Herbs
Cold Cooling Compress
Cold Medicine
For God's sake...
She didn't have to spend all her money on this stuff for me.
She's so dumb. She falls for anyone.
She always makes a racket. But I've never, ever been able to ignore her.
Why, you ask?

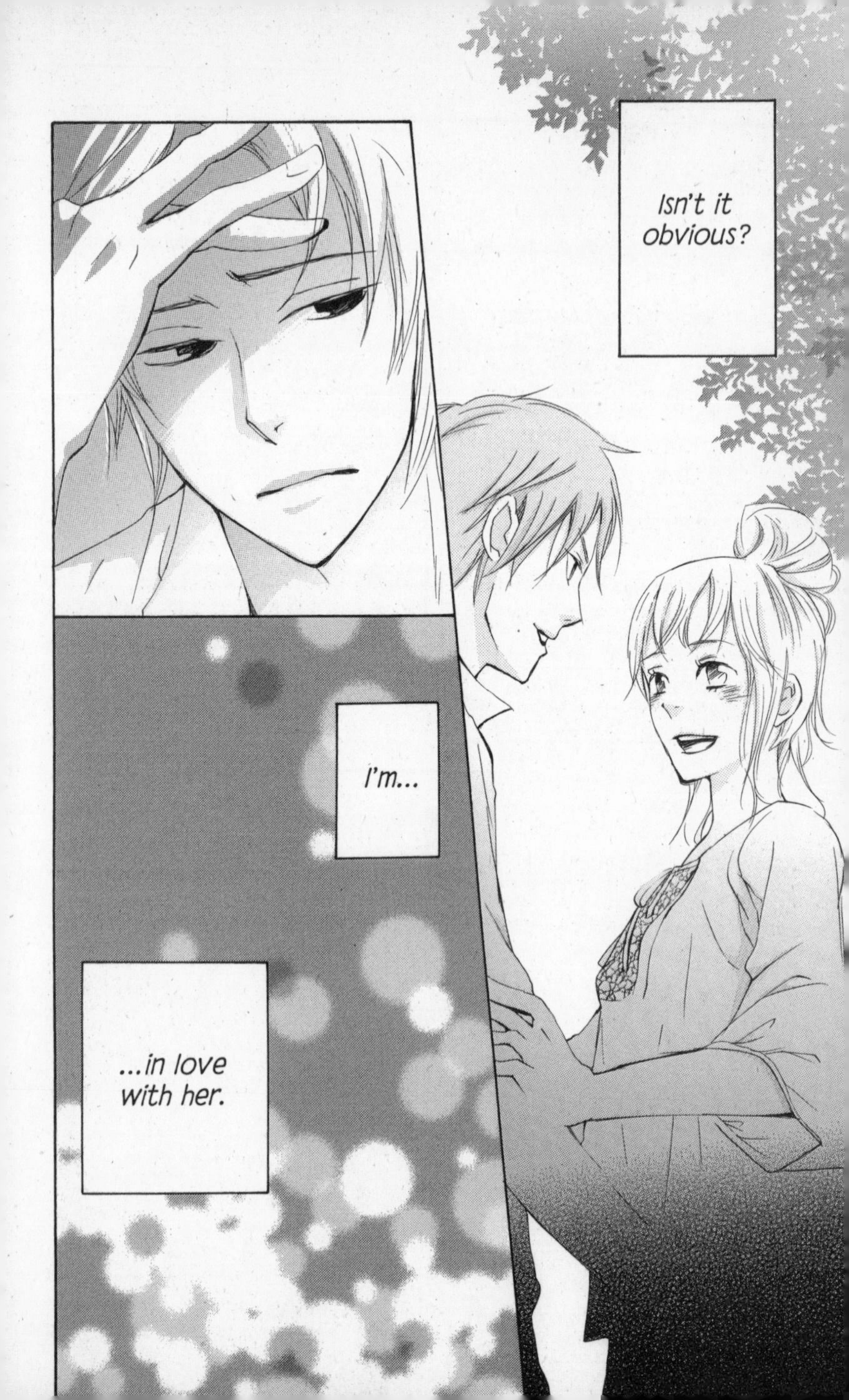
Isn't it obvious?
I'm...
...in love with her.

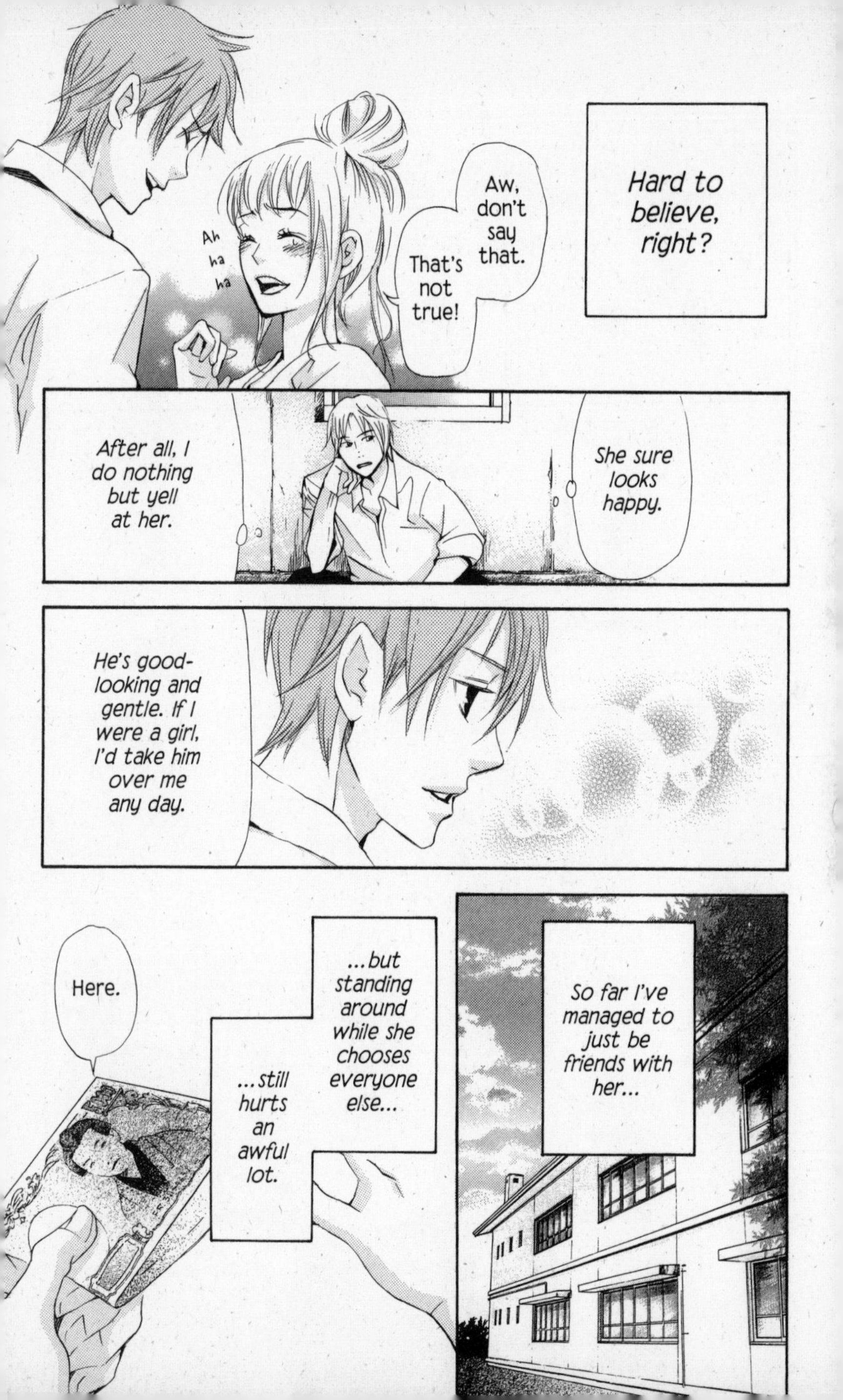
Hard to believe, right?
Aw, don't say that. That's not true!
Ah ha ha
She sure looks happy.
After all, I do nothing but yell at her.
He's good-looking and gentle. If I were a girl, I'd take him over me any day.
So far I've managed to just be friends with her...
...but standing around while she chooses everyone else...
...still hurts an awful lot.
Here.

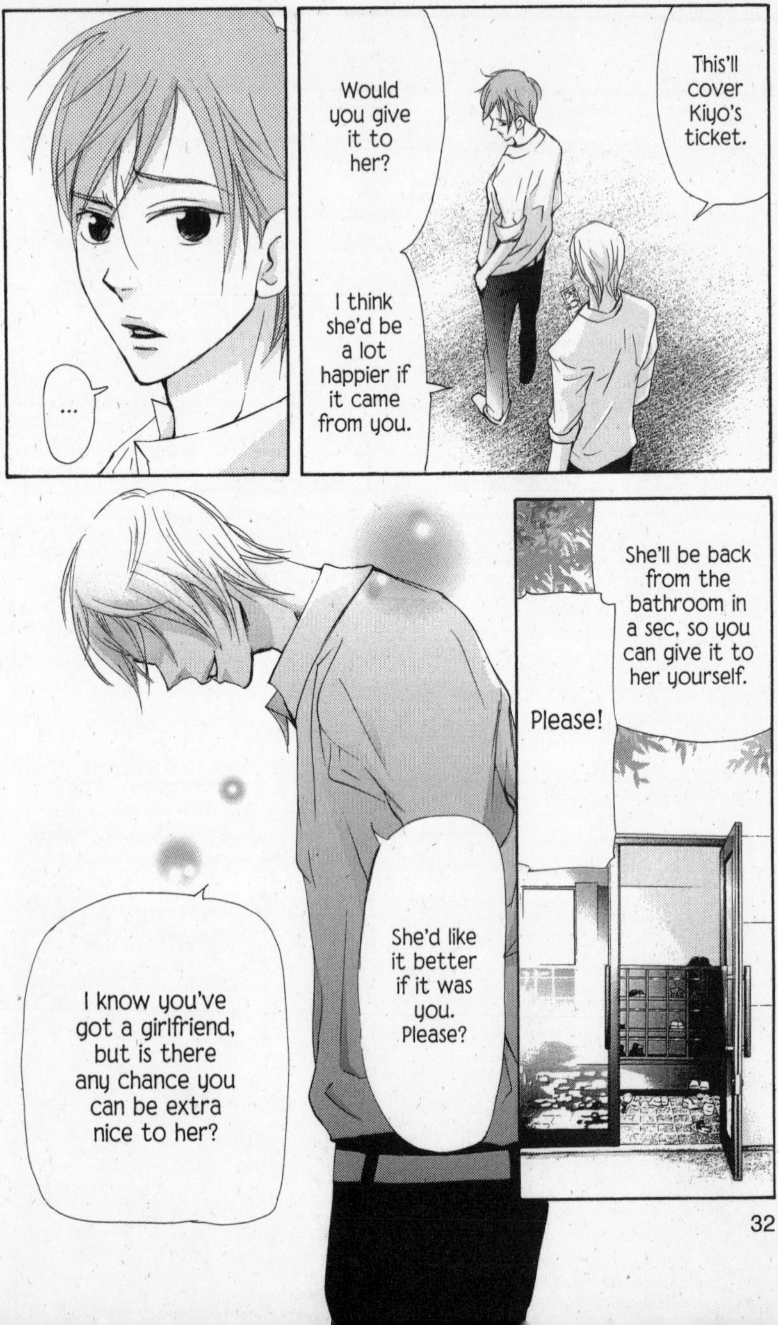
This'll cover Kiyo's ticket.
Would you give it to her?
I think she'd be a lot happier if it came from you.
...
She'll be back from the bathroom in a sec, so you can give it to her yourself.
Please!
She'd like it better if it was you. Please?
I know you've got a girlfriend, but is there any chance you can be extra nice to her?

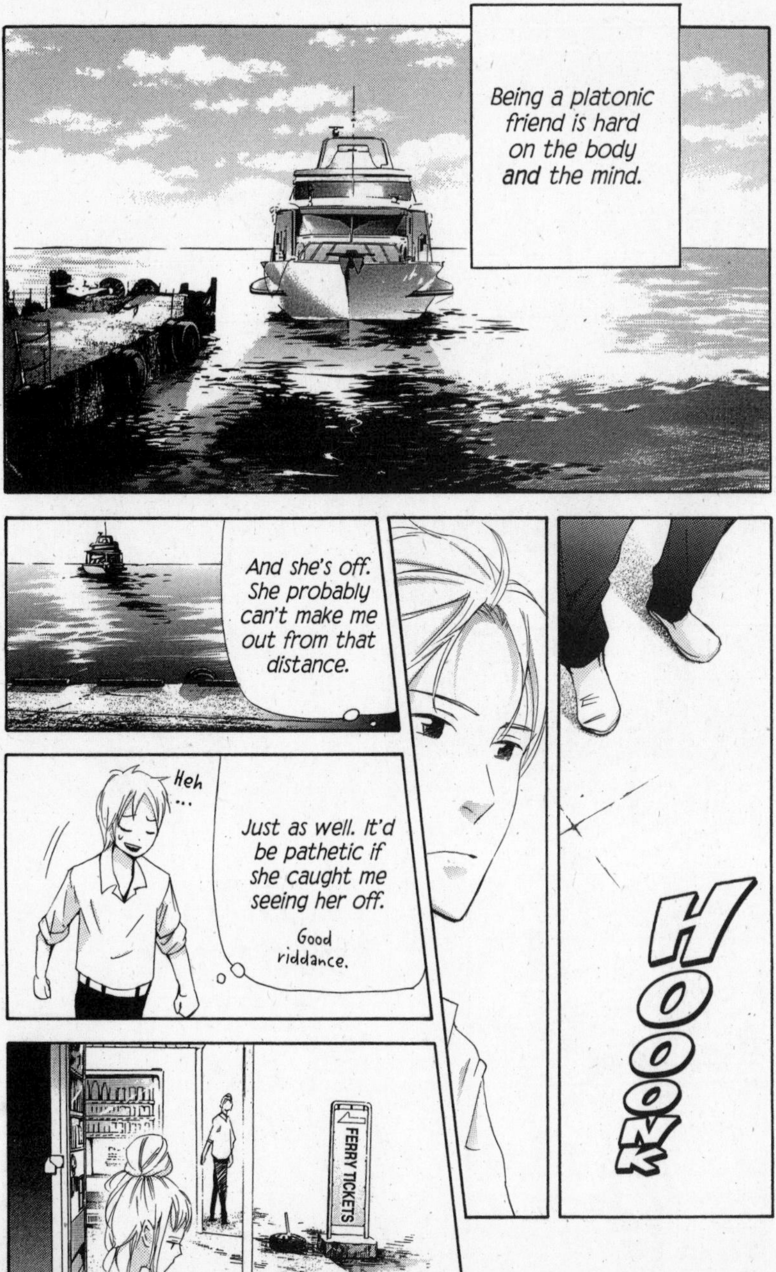
Being a platonic friend is hard on the body and the mind.
HOOOONK
And she's off. She probably can't make me out from that distance.
Just as well. It'd be pathetic if she caught me seeing her off.
Good riddance.
Heh...
FERRY TICKETS

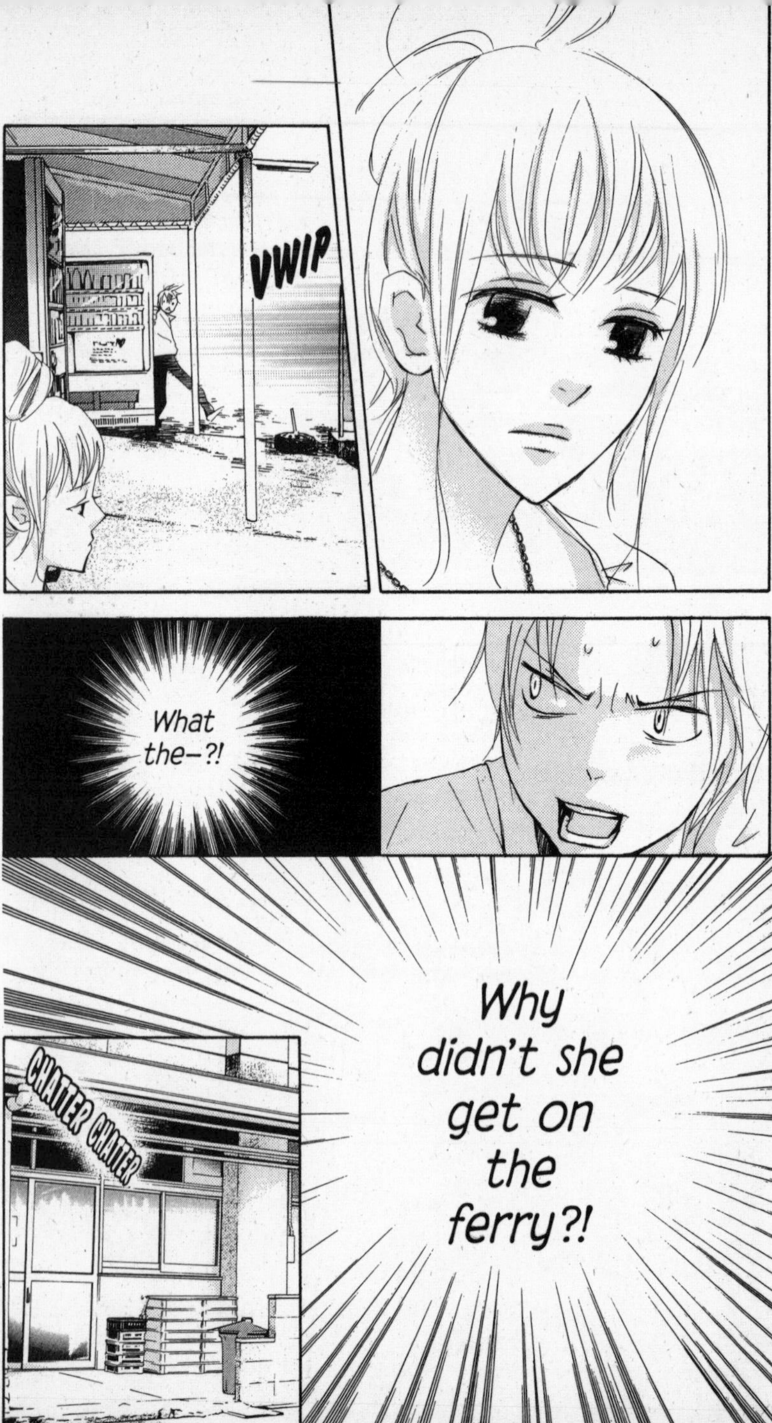
VWIP
What the-?!
Why didn't she get on the ferry?!
CHATTER CHATTER

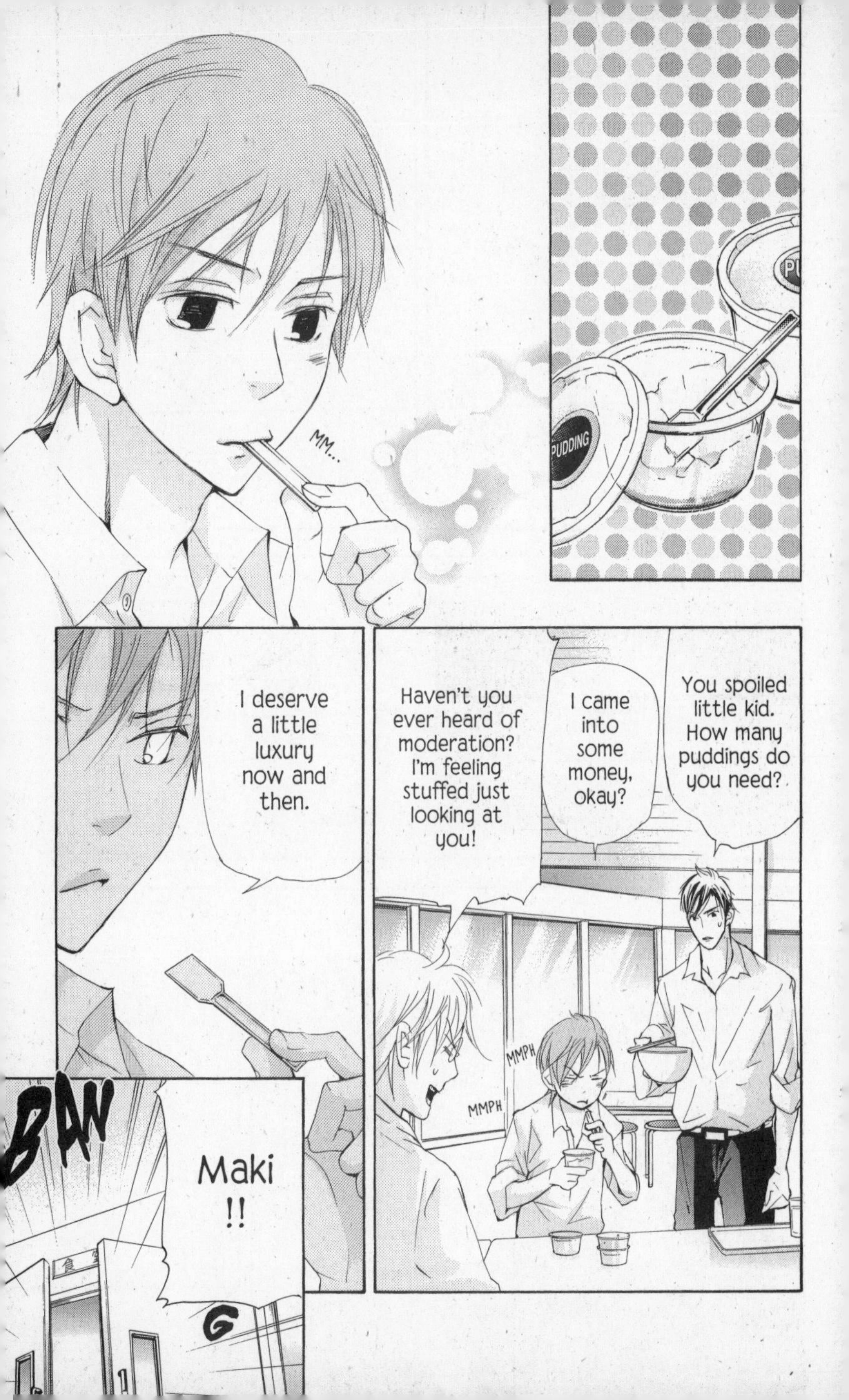
PUDDING
MM...
You spoiled little kid. How many puddings do you need?
I came into some money, okay?
Haven't you ever heard of moderation? I'm feeling stuffed just looking at you!
MMPH
MMPH
I deserve a little luxury now and then.
BAN
Maki !!
G

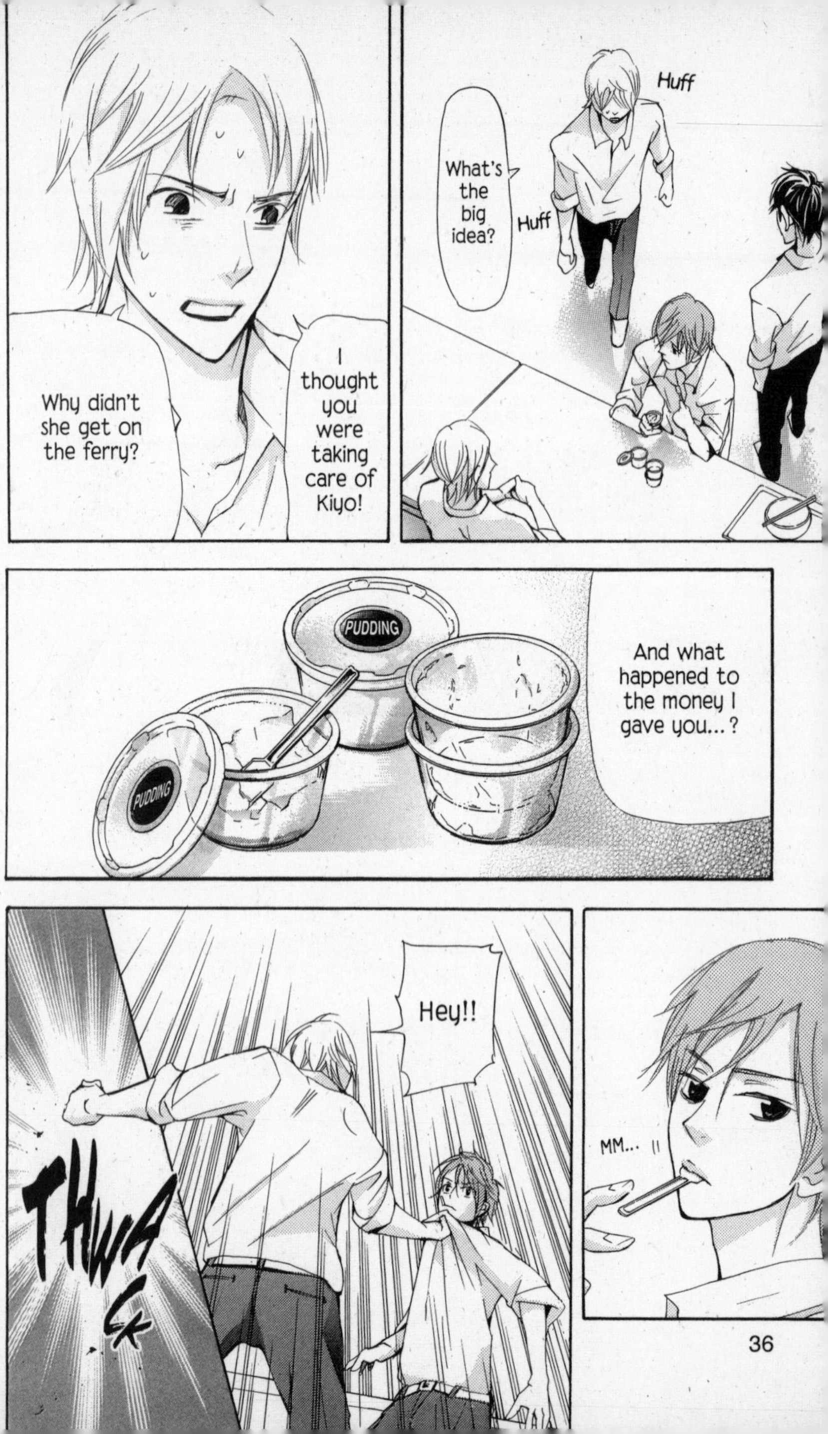
Huff
What's the big idea?
Huff
I thought you were taking care of Kiyo!
Why didn't she get on the ferry?
PUDDING
PUDDING
And what happened to the money I gave you...?
MM... !!
Hey!!
THWA
CK

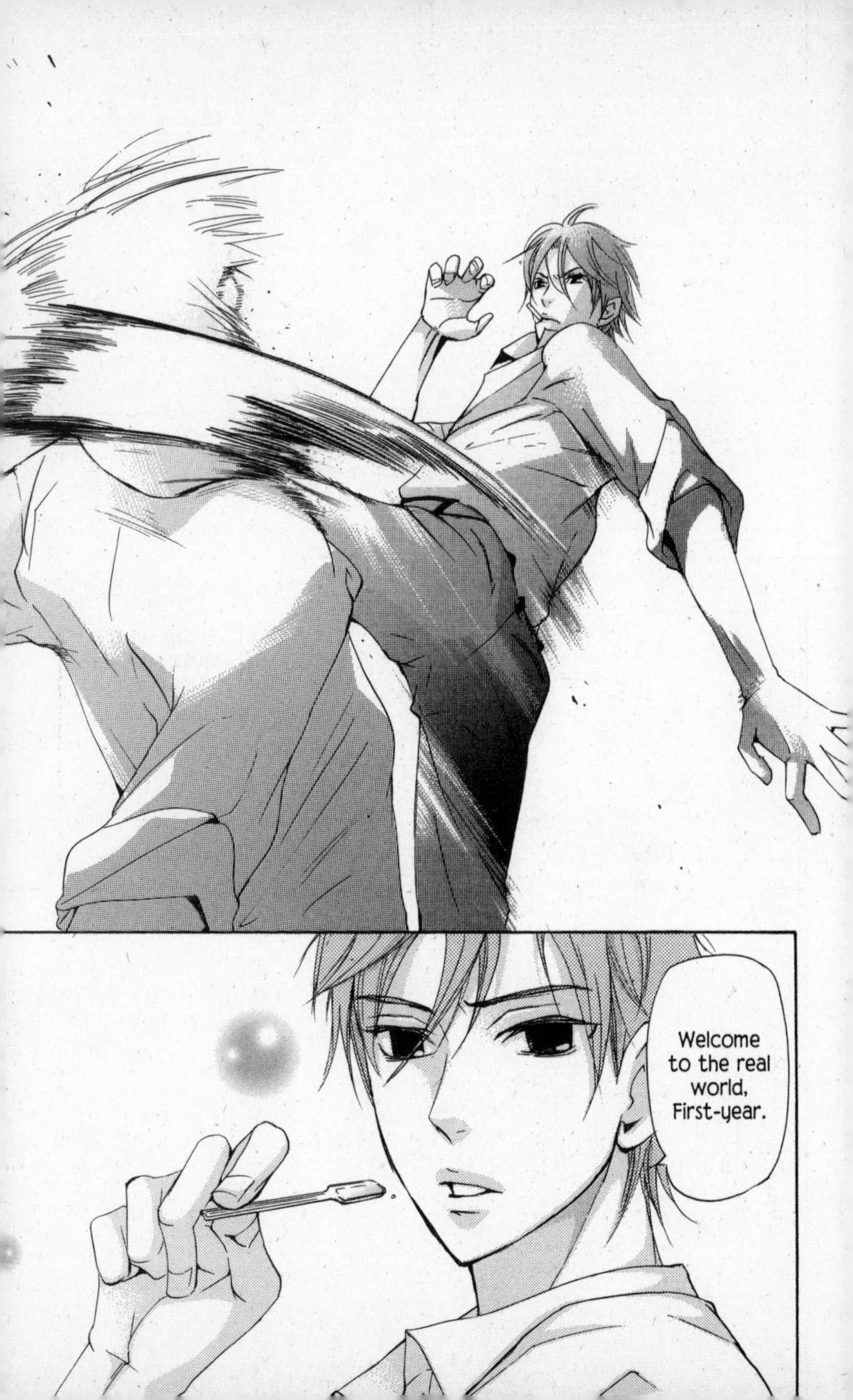
Welcome to the real world, First-year.

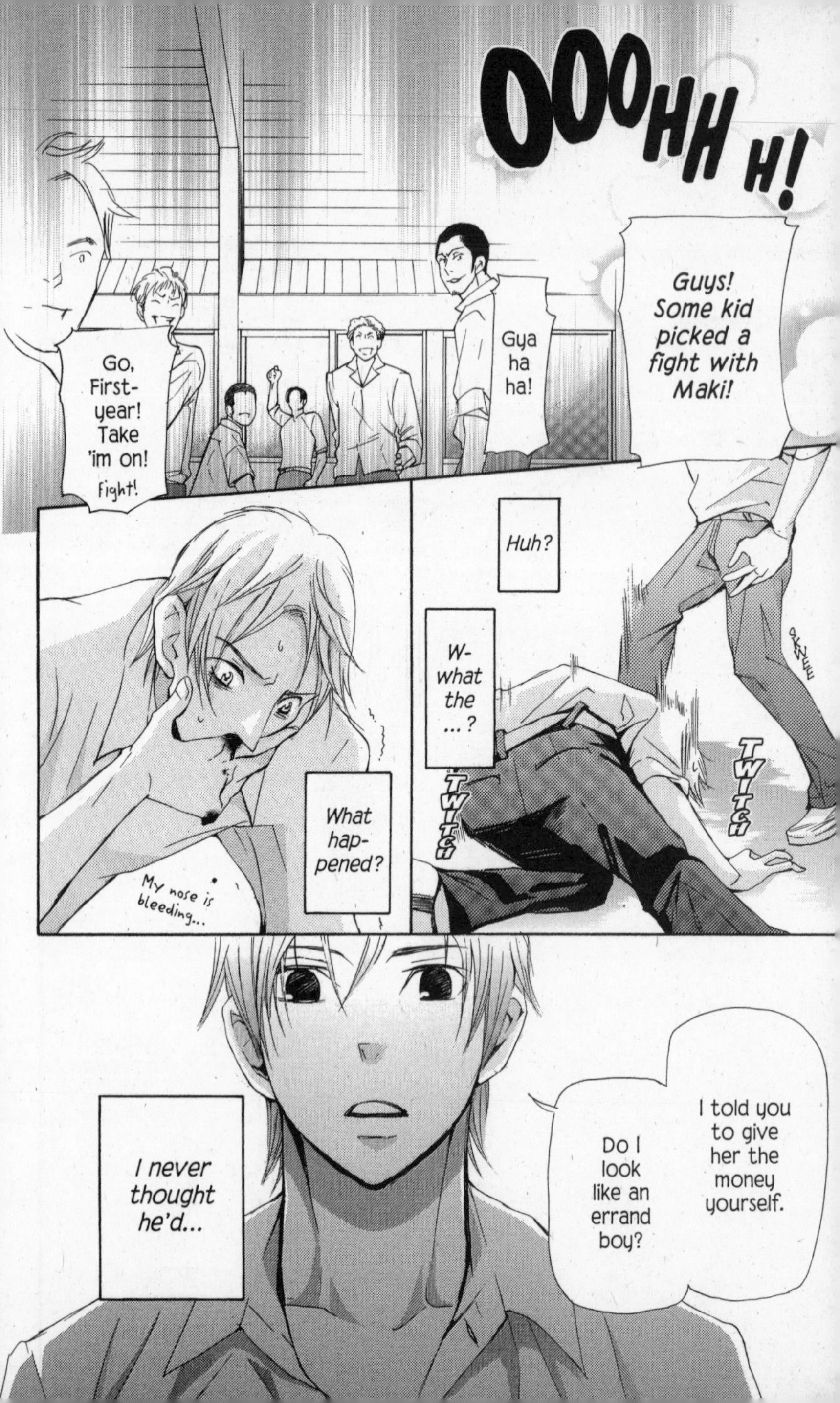
OOOHHH!
Guys! Some kid picked a fight with Maki!
Gya ha ha!
Go, First-year! Take 'im on!
Fight!
Huh?
W-what the ...?
SKWEE
TWITCH
TWITCH
What hap-pened?
My nose is bleeding...
I told you to give her the money yourself.
Do I look like an errand boy?
I never thought he'd...

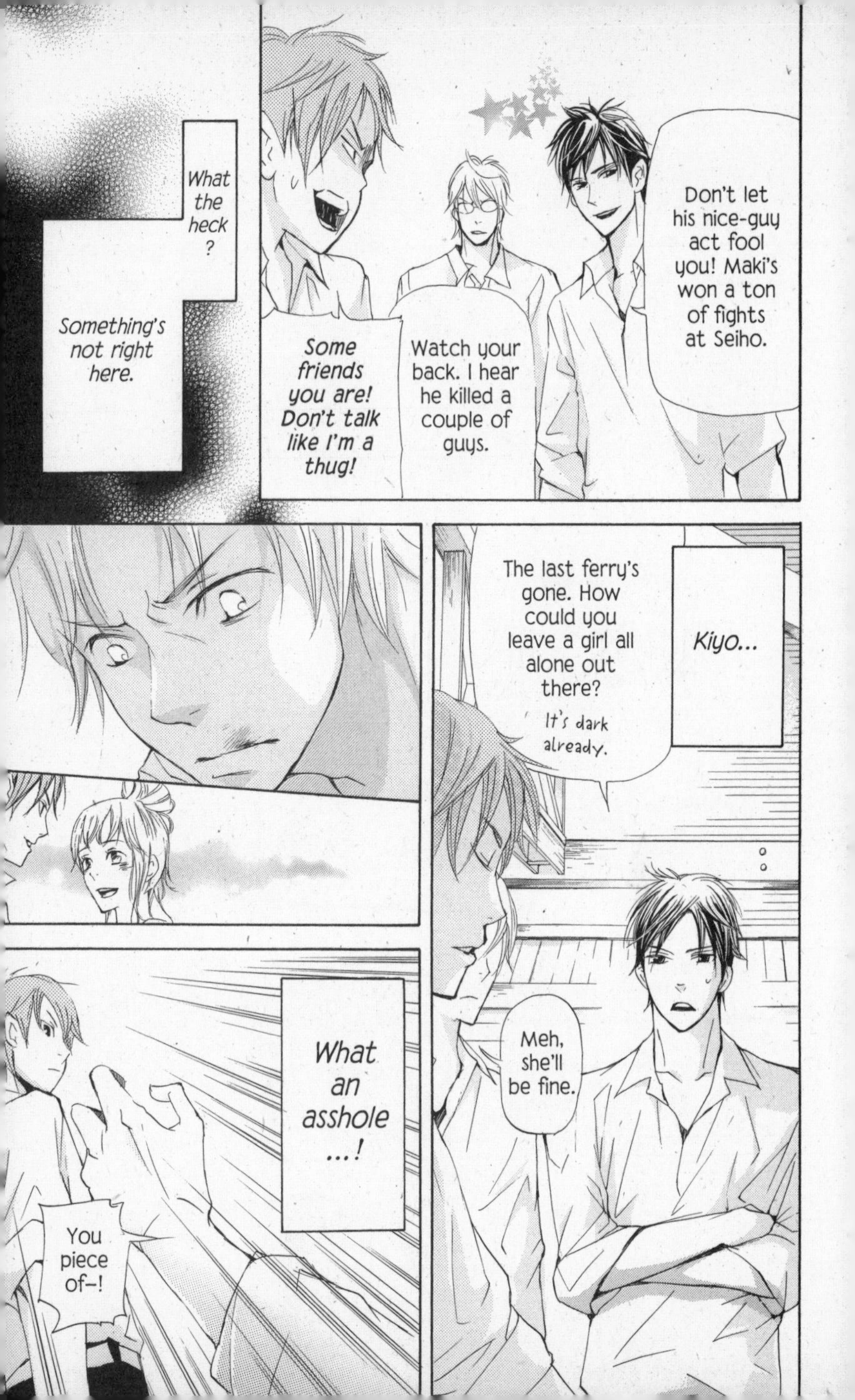
Don't let his nice-guy act fool you! Maki's won a ton of fights at Seiho.
Watch your back. I hear he killed a couple of guys.
Some friends you are! Don't talk like I'm a thug!
What the heck?
Something's not right here.
Kiyo...
The last ferry's gone. How could you leave a girl all alone out there?
It's dark already.
Meh, she'll be fine.
What an asshole...!
You piece of–!

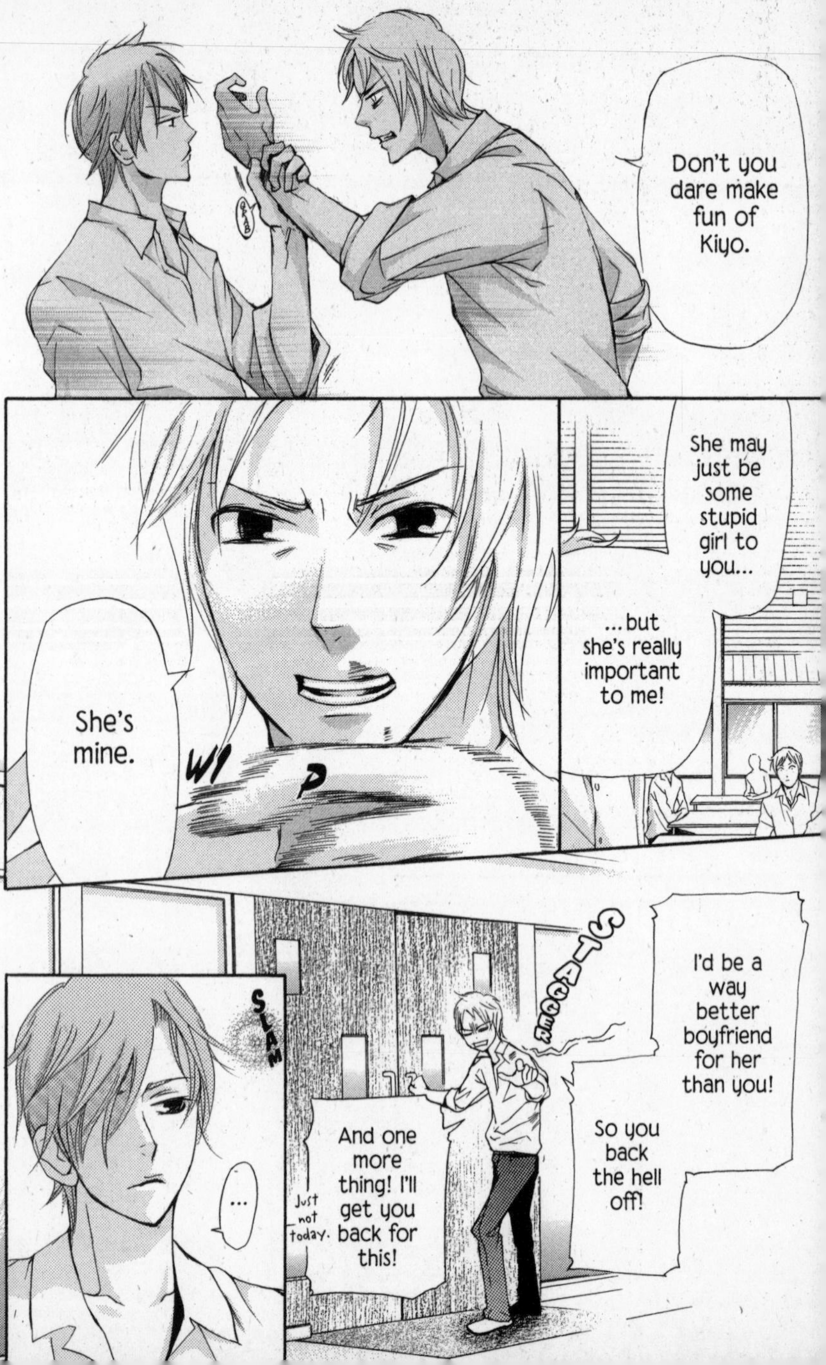
Don't you dare make fun of Kiyo.
She may just be some stupid girl to you...
...but she's really important to me!
She's mine.
I'd be a way better boyfriend for her than you!
So you back the hell off!
STAGGER
And one more thing! I'll get you back for this!
Just not today.
SLAM
...

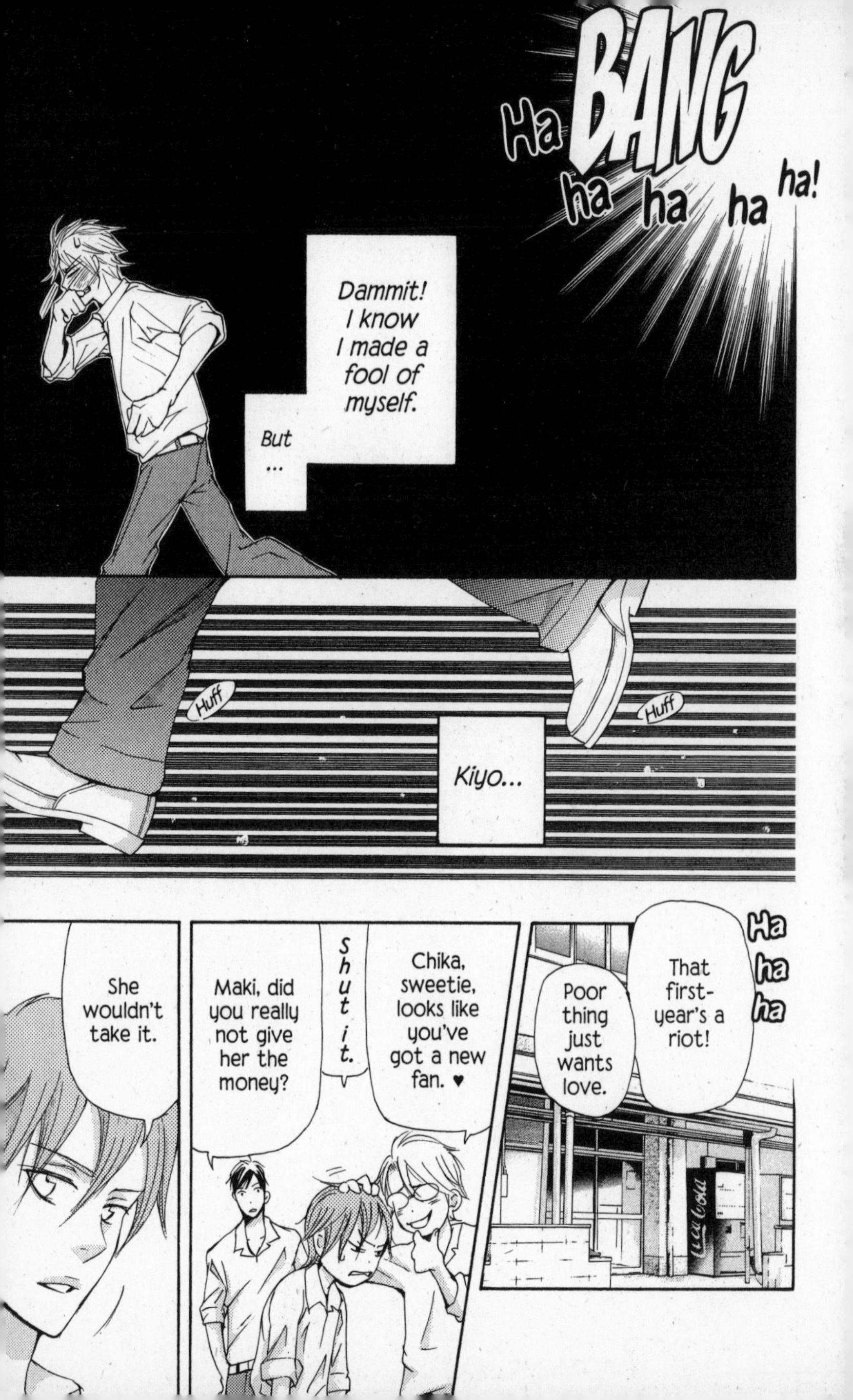
Ha BANG ha ha ha ha!
Dammit! I know I made a fool of myself.
But ...
Huff
Huff
Kiyo...
Ha ha ha
That first-year's a riot!
Poor thing just wants love.
Chika, sweetie, looks like you've got a new fan. ♥
Shut it.
Maki, did you really not give her the money?
She wouldn't take it.

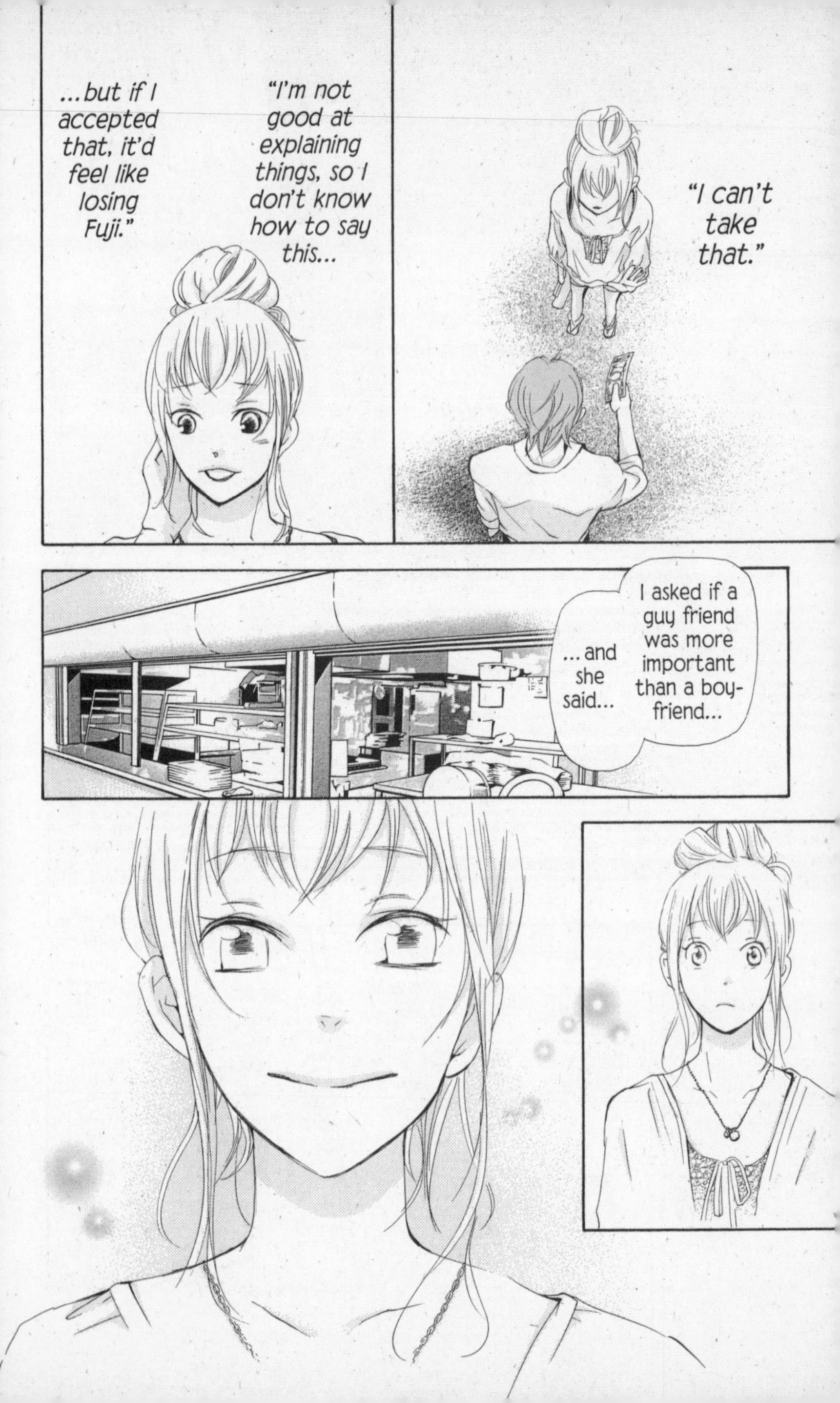
"I can't take that."
"I'm not good at explaining things, so I don't know how to say this...
...but if I accepted that, it'd feel like losing Fuji."
I asked if a guy friend was more important than a boy-friend...
...and she said...

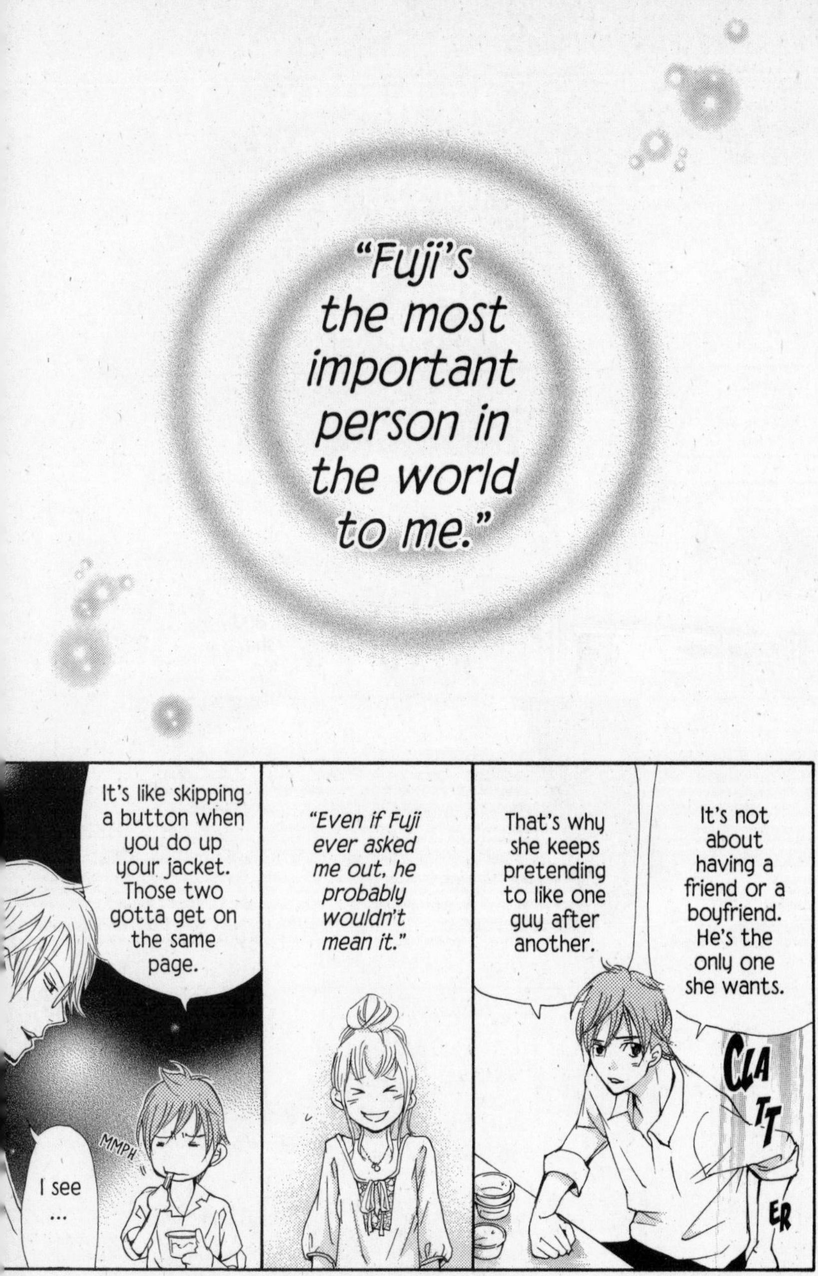
"Fuji's the most important person in the world to me."
It's not about having a friend or a boyfriend. He's the only one she wants.
That's why she keeps pretending to like one guy after another.
CLATTER
"Even if Fuji ever asked me out, he probably wouldn't mean it."
It's like skipping a button when you do up your jacket. Those two gotta get on the same page.
MMPH
I see ...

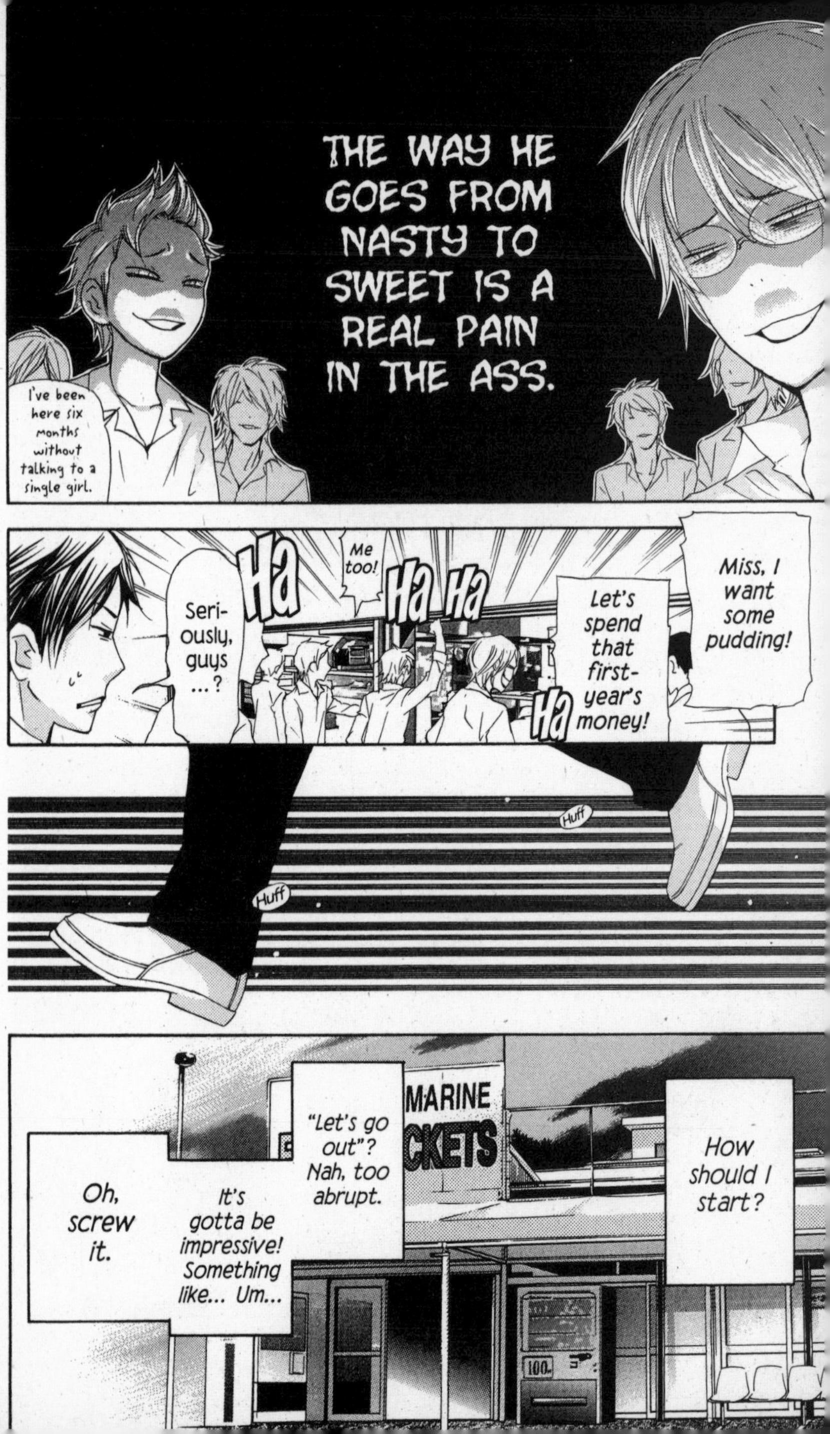
THE WAY HE GOES FROM NASTY TO SWEET IS A REAL PAIN IN THE ASS.
I've been here six months without talking to a single girl.
Miss, I want some pudding!
Let's spend that first-year's money!
Ha
Ha Ha
Ha
Me too!
Seriously, guys...?
Huff
Huff
How should I start?
MARINE
CKETS
"Let's go out"? Nah, too abrupt.
It's gotta be impressive! Something like... Um...
Oh, screw it.
100

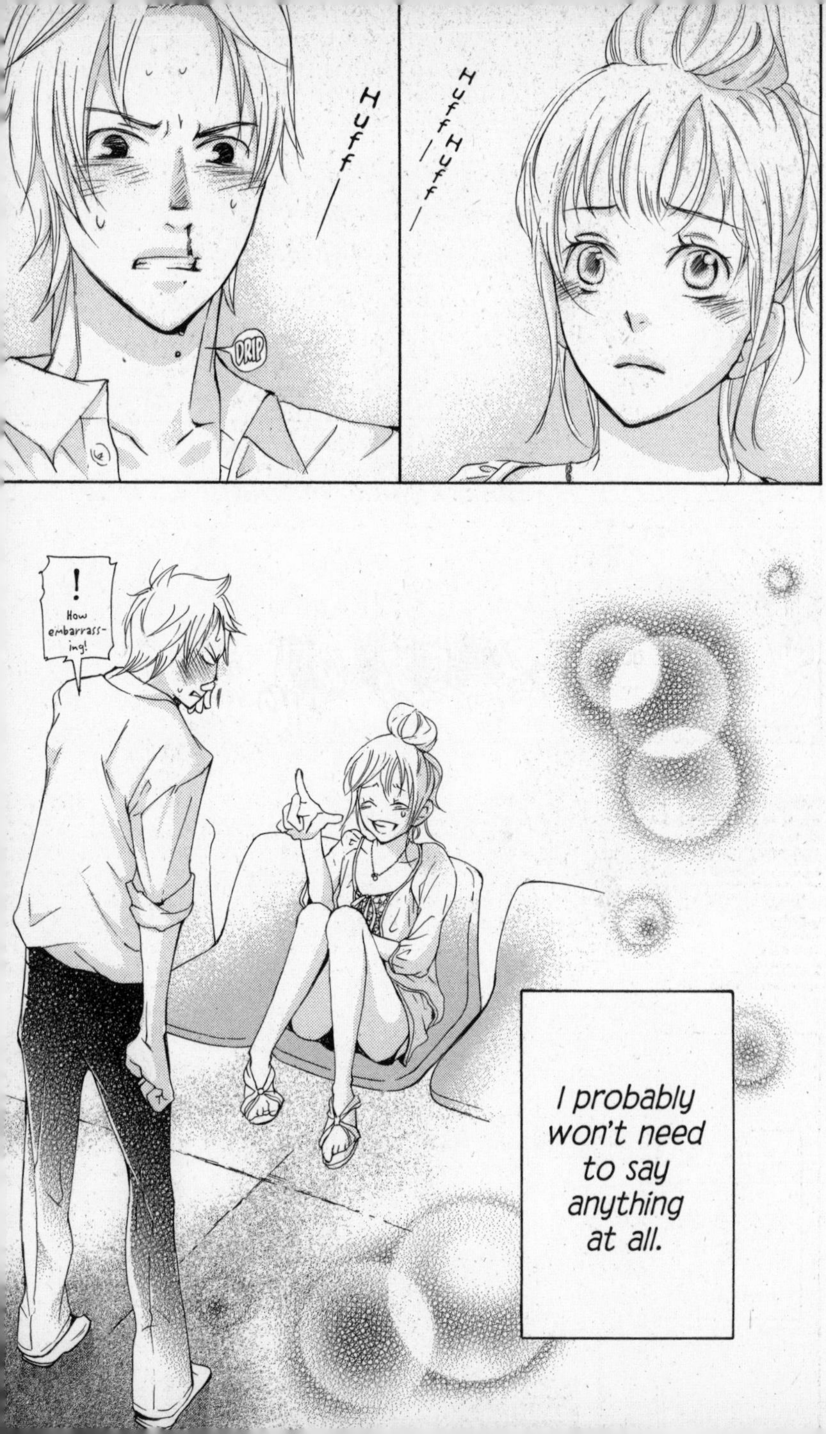
HuffHuff—
Huff—
DRIP
! How embarrass-ing!
I probably won't need to say anything at all.

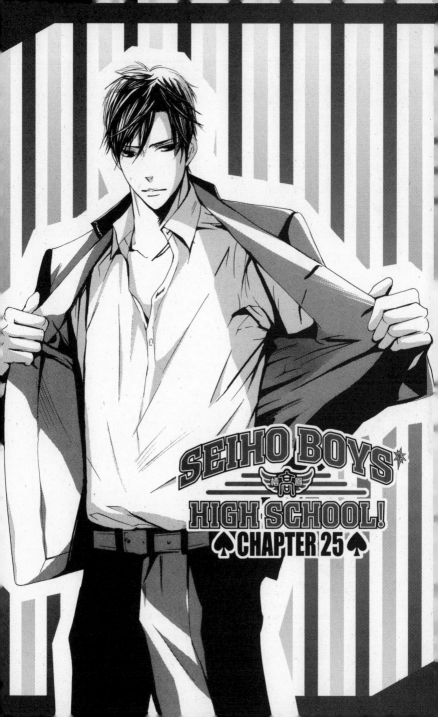

SEIHO BOYS HIGH SCHOOL!

CHAPTER 25

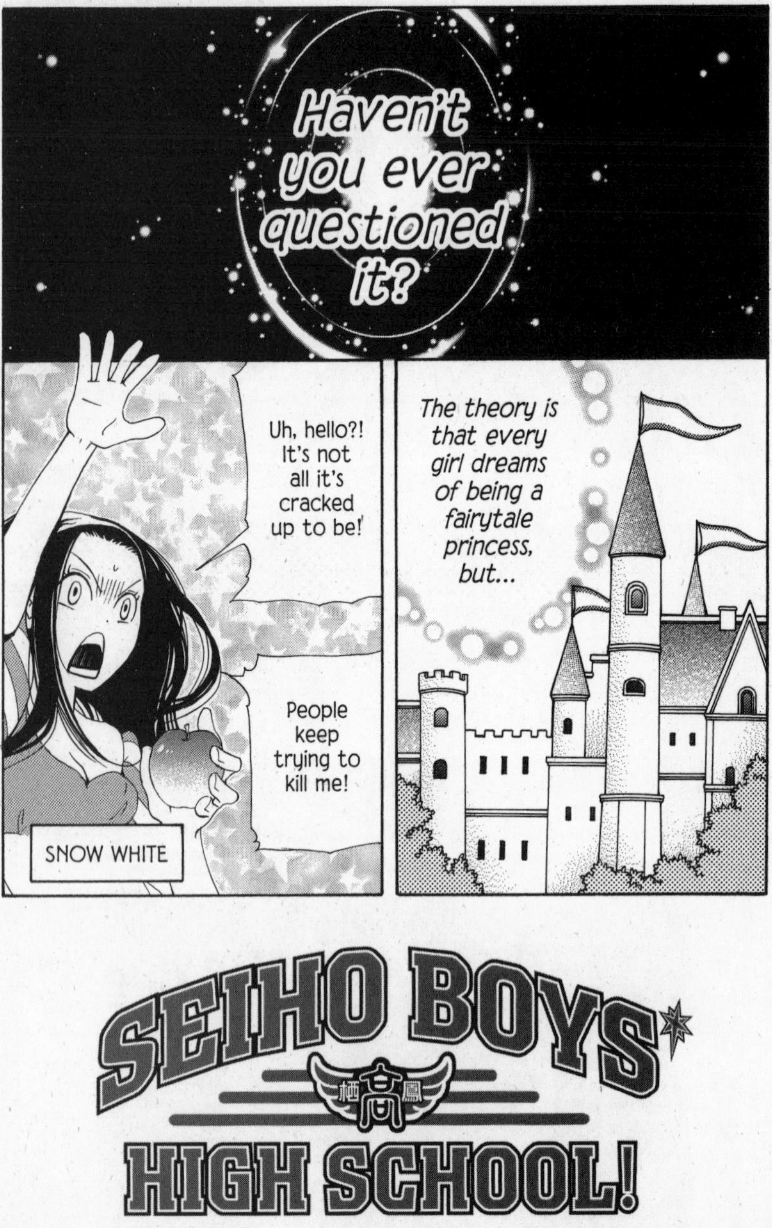
Haven't you ever questioned it?
The theory is that every girl dreams of being a fairytale princess, but...
Uh, hello?! It's not all it's cracked up to be!
People keep trying to kill me!
SNOW WHITE

SEIHO BOYS HIGH SCHOOL!

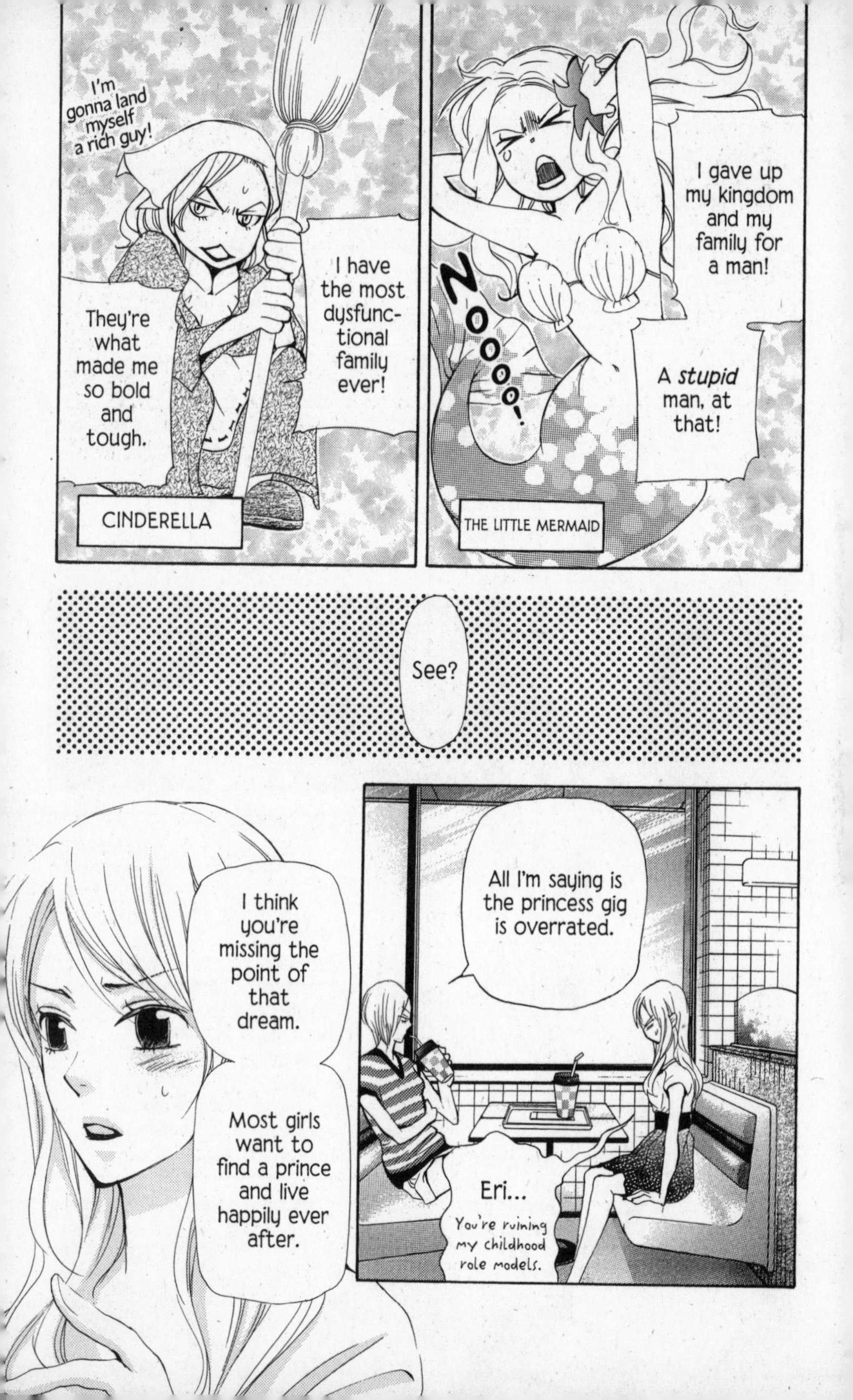
I gave up my kingdom and my family for a man!
A *stupid* man, at that!
NOOOOO!
THE LITTLE MERMAID
I have the most dysfunctional family ever!
I'm gonna land myself a rich guy!
They're what made me so bold and tough.
CINDERELLA
See?
All I'm saying is the princess gig is overrated.
Eri...
You're ruining my childhood role models.
I think you're missing the point of that dream.
Most girls want to find a prince and live happily ever after.

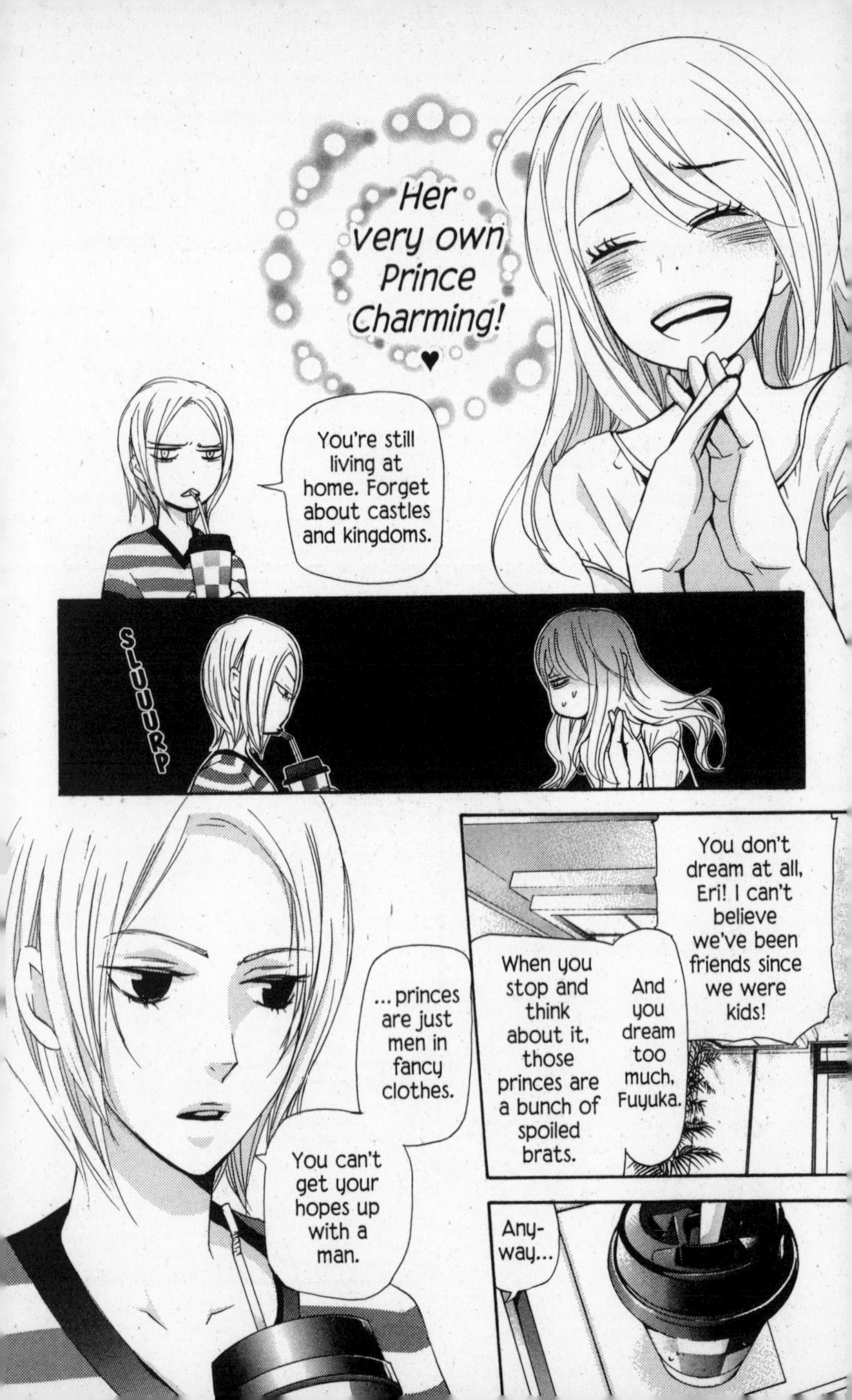
Her very own Prince Charming! ♥
You're still living at home. Forget about castles and kingdoms.
SLUUURP
You don't dream at all, Eri! I can't believe we've been friends since we were kids!
And you dream too much, Fuyuka.
When you stop and think about it, those princes are a bunch of spoiled brats.
Any-way...
...princes are just men in fancy clothes.
You can't get your hopes up with a man.

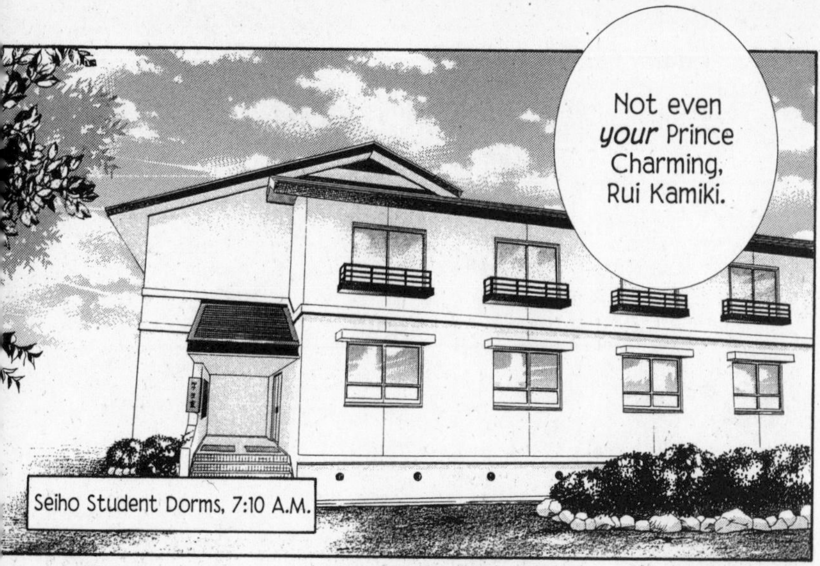
Not even *your* Prince Charming, Rui Kamiki.
Seiho Student Dorms, 7:10 A.M.

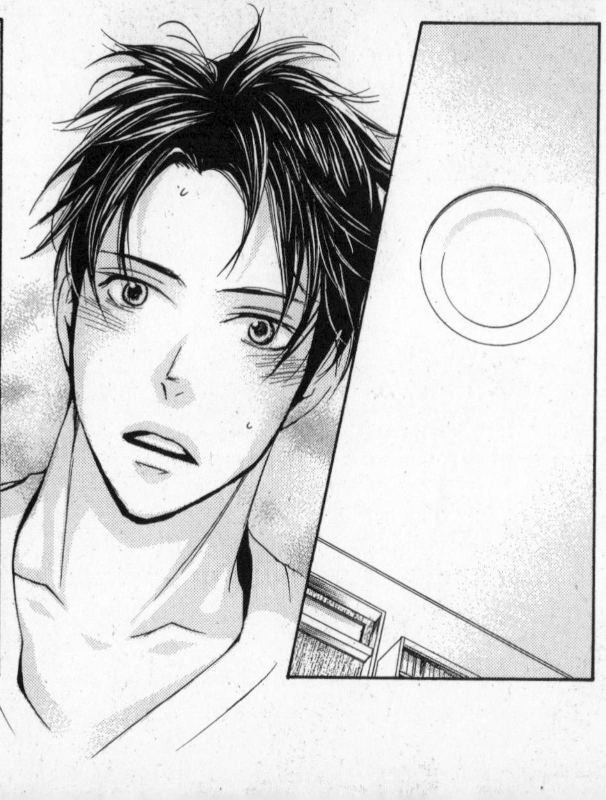

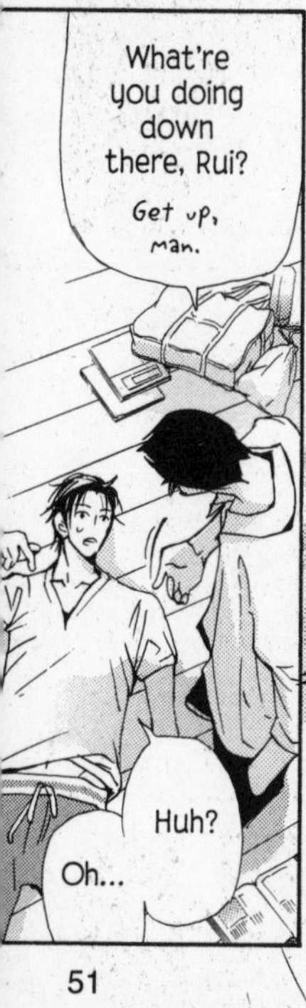
What're you doing down there, Rui?
Get up, man.
Huh?
Oh...

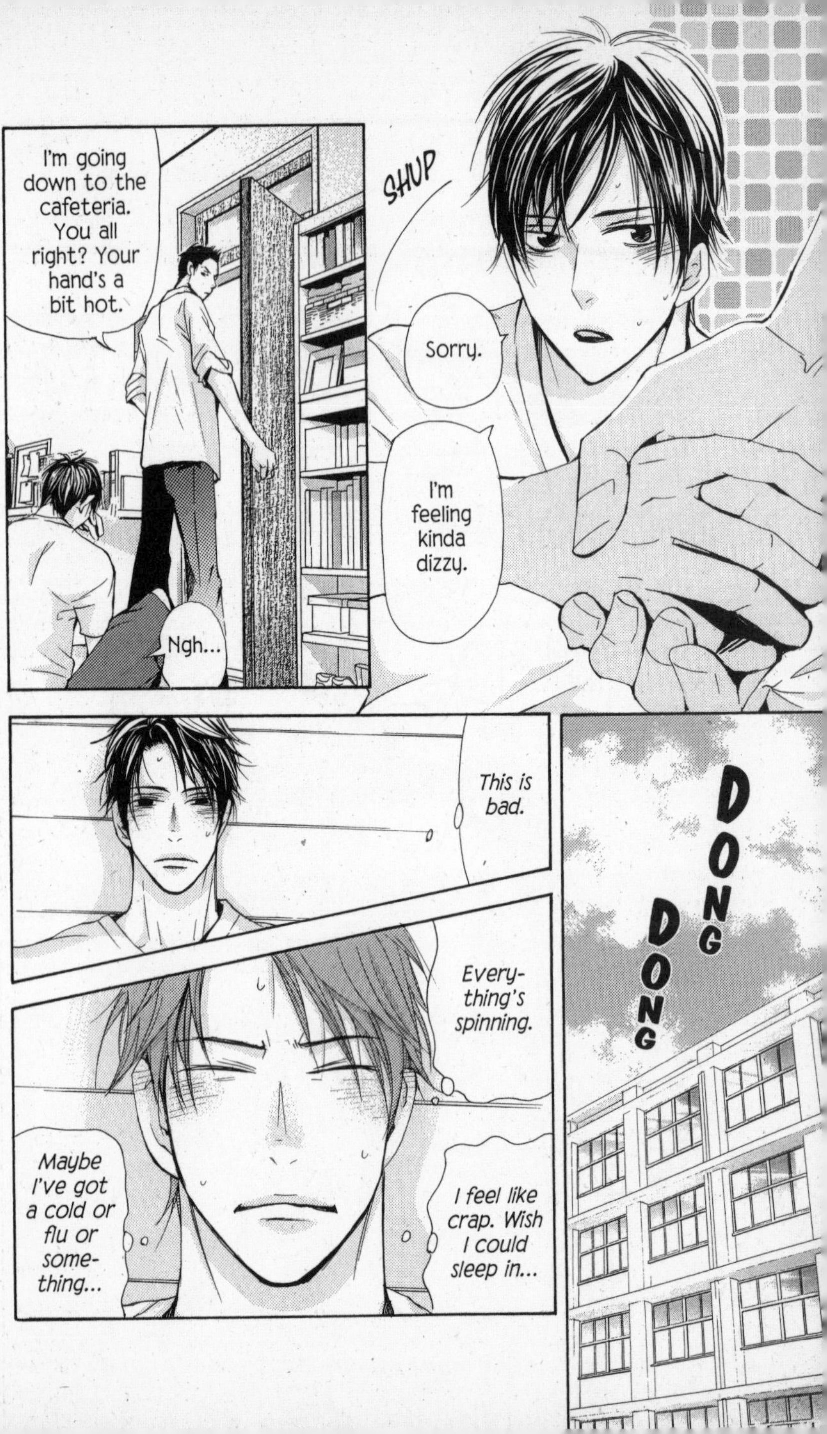
SHUP
Sorry.
I'm feeling kinda dizzy.
I'm going down to the cafeteria. You all right? Your hand's a bit hot.
Ngh...
DONG DONG
DONG DONG
This is bad.
Every-thing's spinning.
I feel like crap. Wish I could sleep in...
Maybe I've got a cold or flu or some-thing...

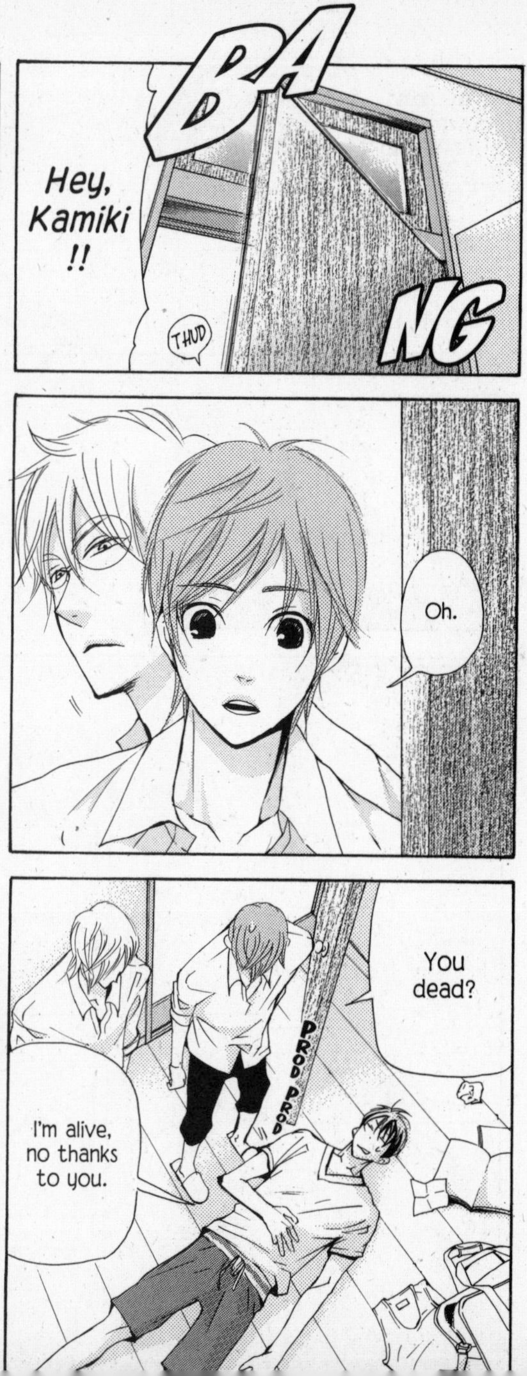
BANG
Hey, Kamiki!!
THUD
Oh.
You dead?
PROD PROD PROD
I'm alive, no thanks to you.

Bonus Corner

Little Things ②

Fuyuka's Cell Phone

I used my old cell phone as the model for this. I almost wish I could give her a newer phone in the manga...! To be honest, drawing cell phones is a pain. They change so quickly...

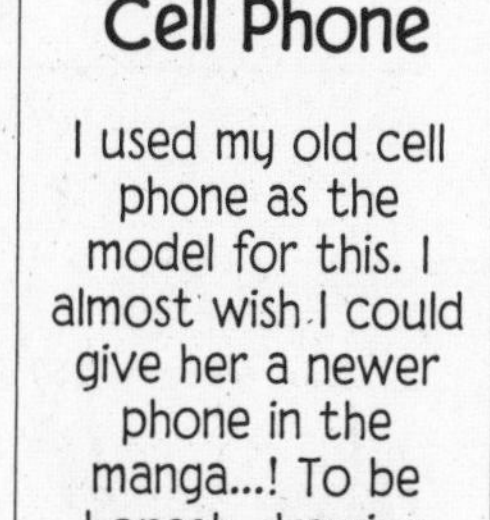

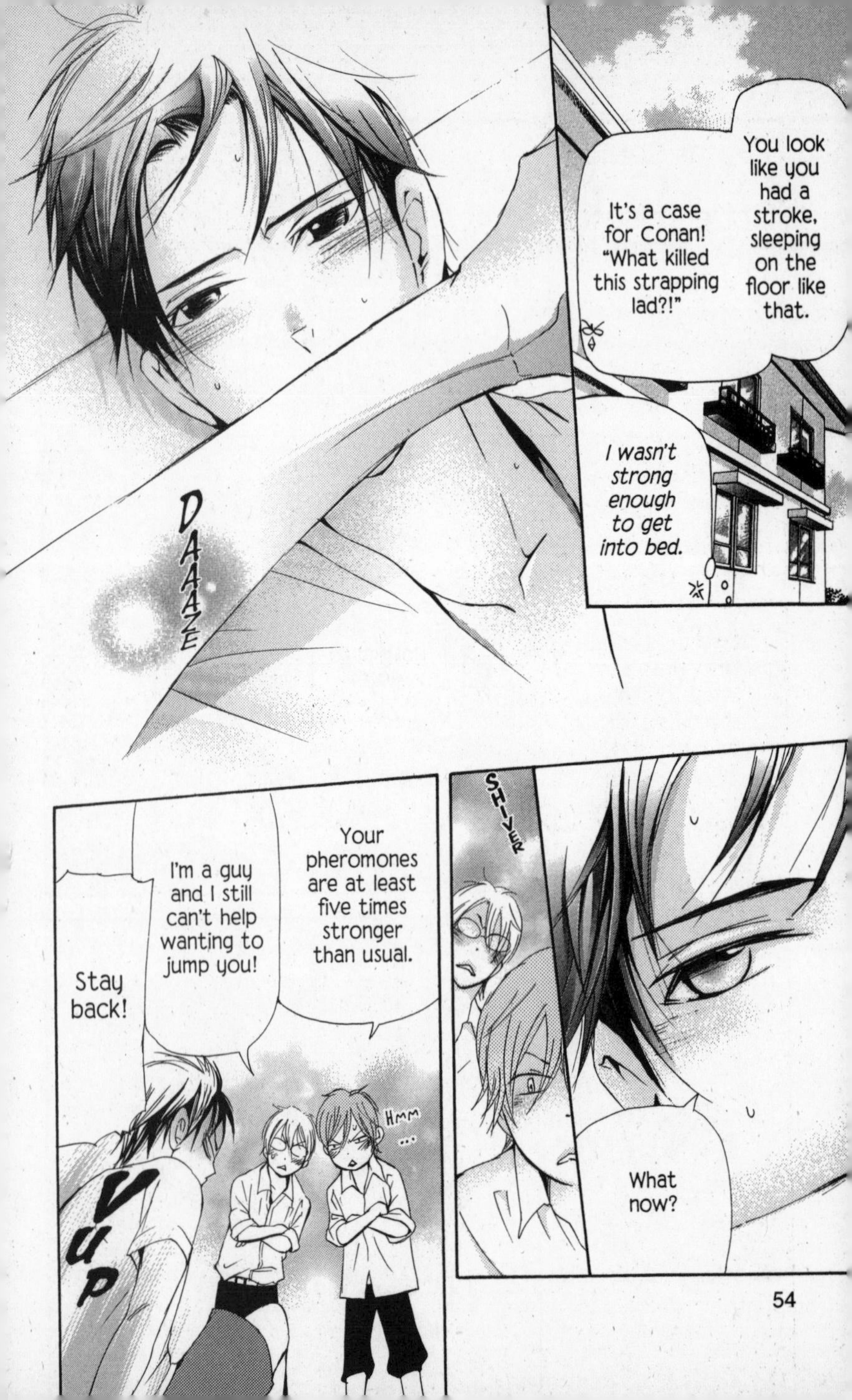
You look like you had a stroke, sleeping on the floor like that.
It's a case for Conan! "What killed this strapping lad?!"
I wasn't strong enough to get into bed.
DAAAAZE
SHIVER
What now?
Your pheromones are at least five times stronger than usual.
I'm a guy and I still can't help wanting to jump you!
Stay back!
HMM...
VUP

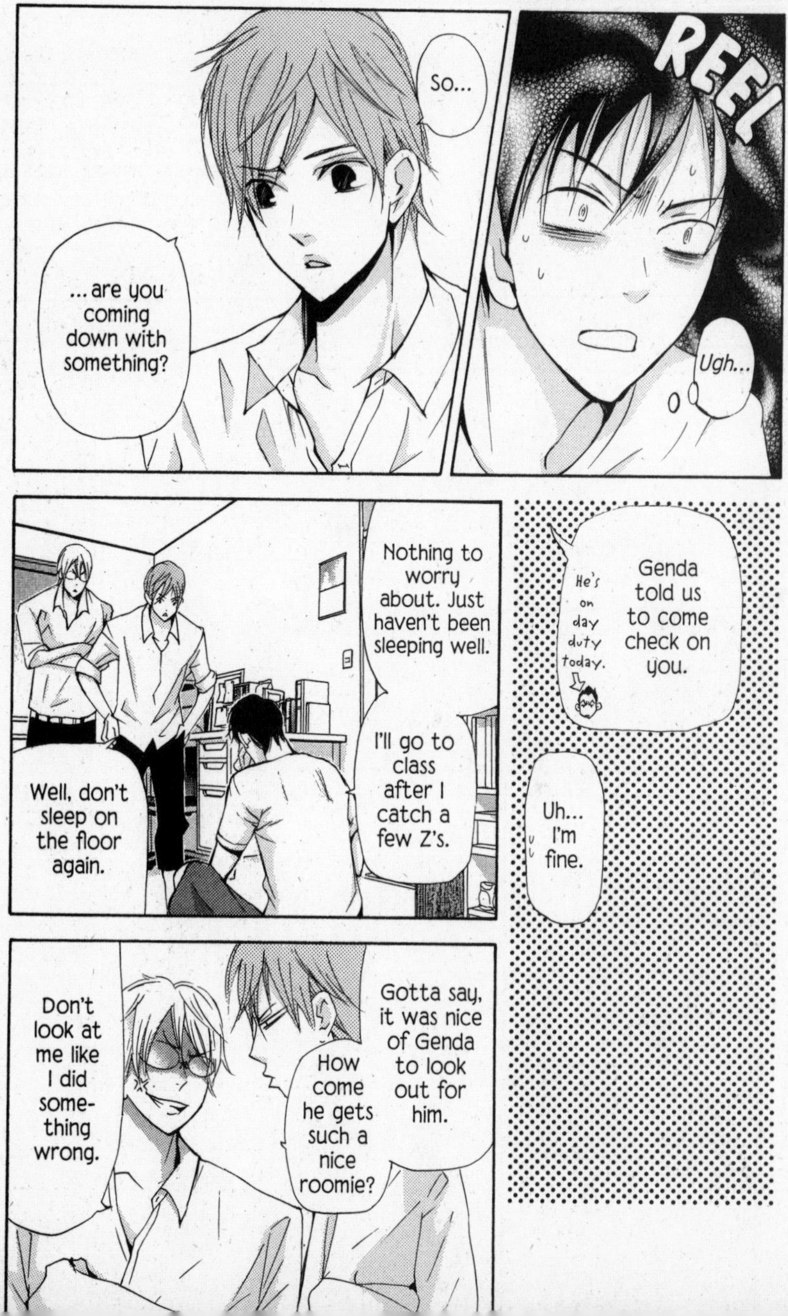
REEL
Ugh...
So...
...are you coming down with something?
Genda told us to come check on you.
He's on day duty today.
Uh... I'm fine.
Nothing to worry about. Just haven't been sleeping well.
I'll go to class after I catch a few Z's.
Well, don't sleep on the floor again.
Gotta say, it was nice of Genda to look out for him.
How come he gets such a nice roomie?
Don't look at me like I did some-thing wrong.

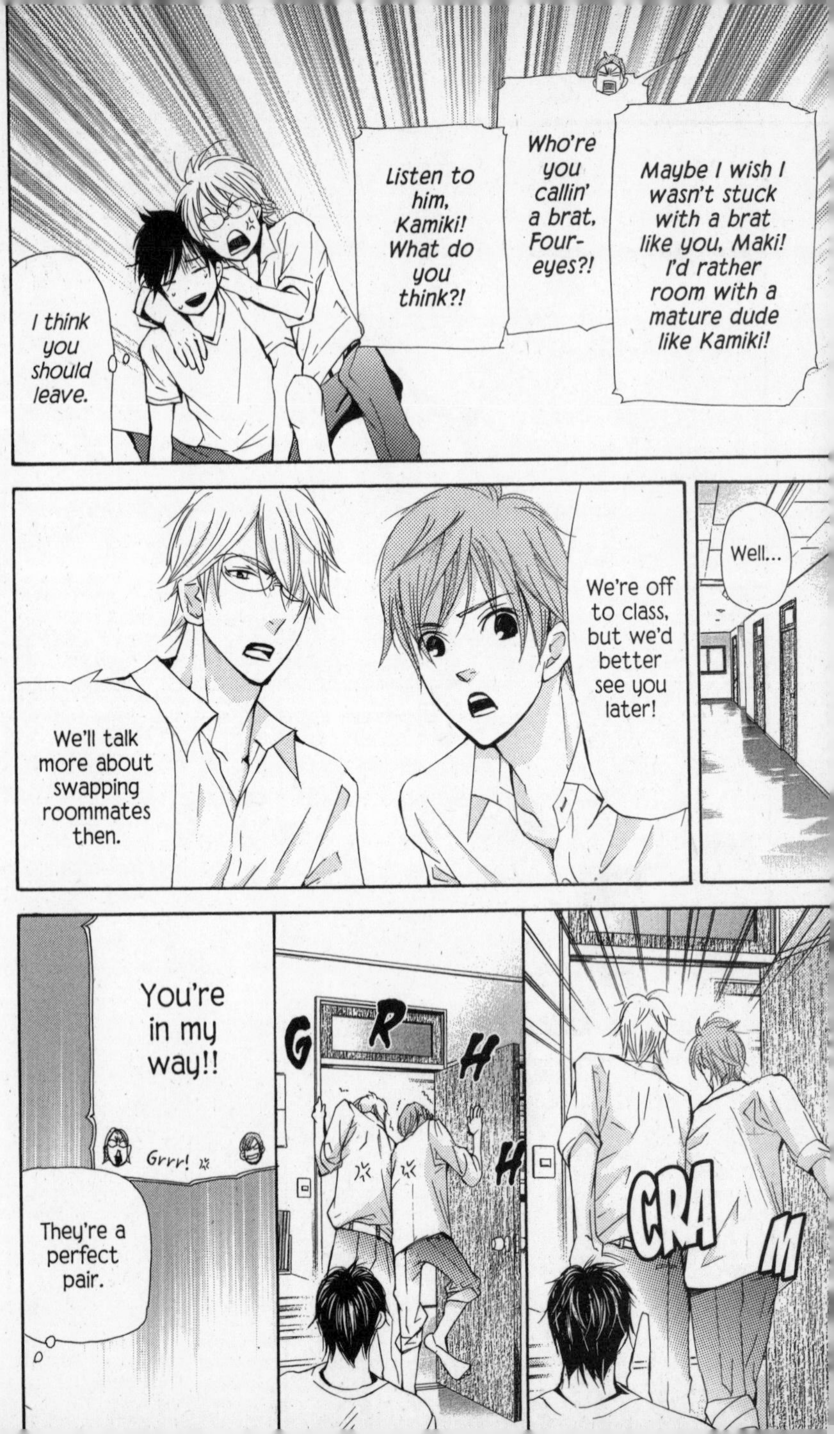
Maybe I wish I wasn't stuck with a brat like you, Maki! I'd rather room with a mature dude like Kamiki!
Who're you callin' a brat, Four-eyes?!
Listen to him, Kamiki! What do you think?!
I think you should leave.
Well...
We're off to class, but we'd better see you later!
We'll talk more about swapping roommates then.
CRAM
GRHH
You're in my way!!
Grrr!
They're a perfect pair.

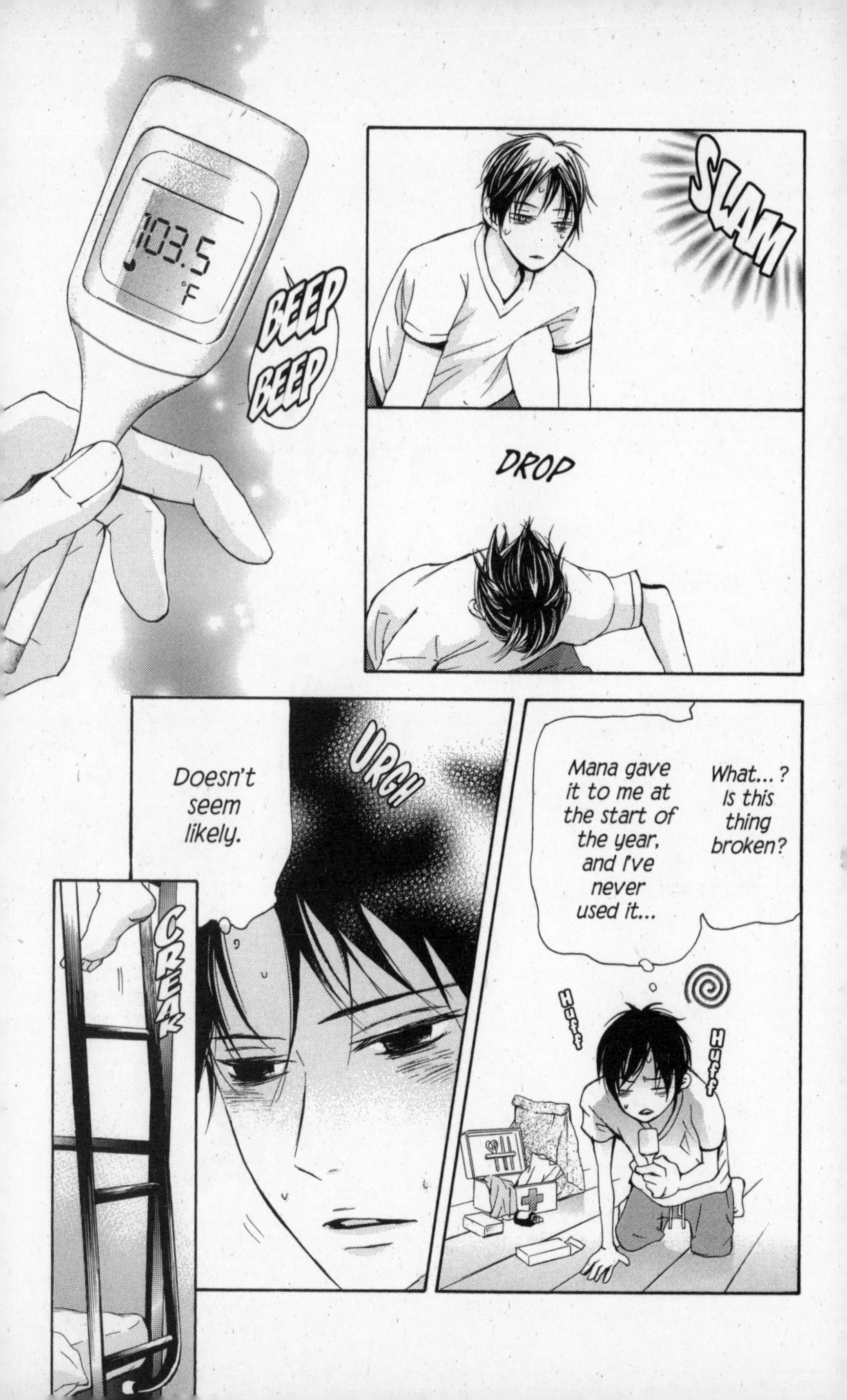
SLAM
DROP
103.5 °F
BEEP BEEP
What...? Is this thing broken?
Mana gave it to me at the start of the year, and I've never used it...
Huff
Huff
URGH
Doesn't seem likely.
CREAK

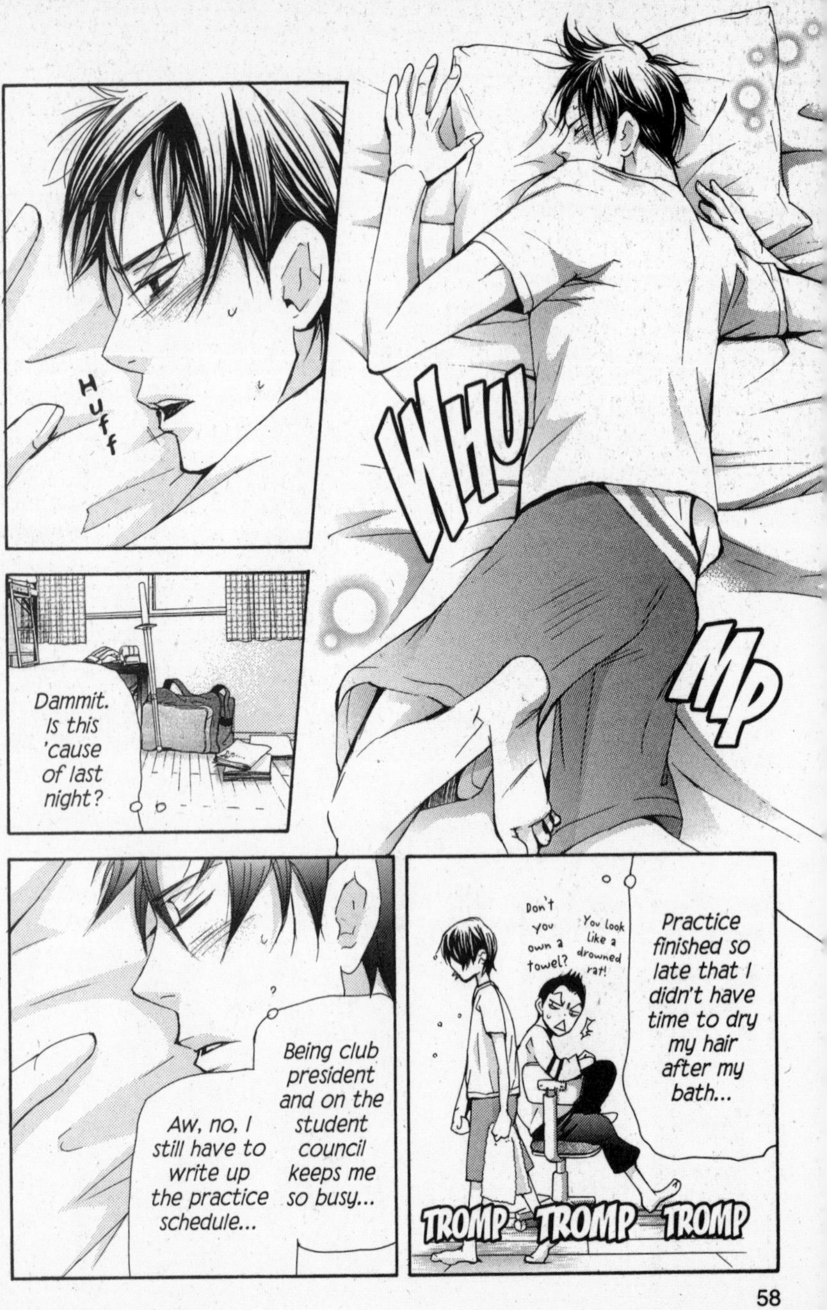
WHU
MP
Huff
Dammit. Is this 'cause of last night?
Practice finished so late that I didn't have time to dry my hair after my bath...
You look like a drowned rat!
Don't you own a towel?
TROMP TROMP TROMP
Being club president and on the student council keeps me so busy...
Aw, no, I still have to write up the practice schedule...

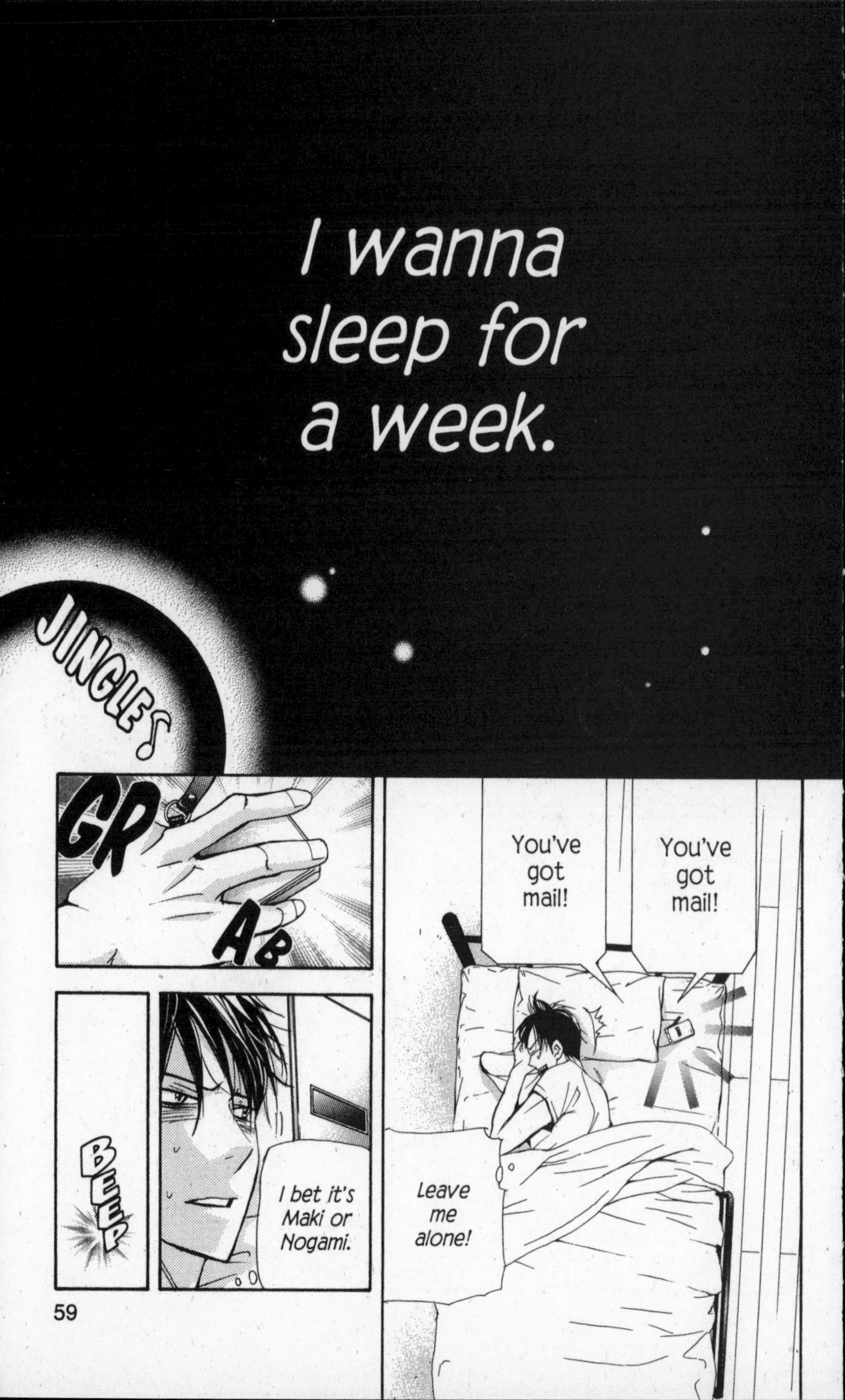
I wanna sleep for a week.
JINGLE♪
You've got mail!
You've got mail!
Leave me alone!
GRAB
BEEP
I bet it's Maki or Nogami.

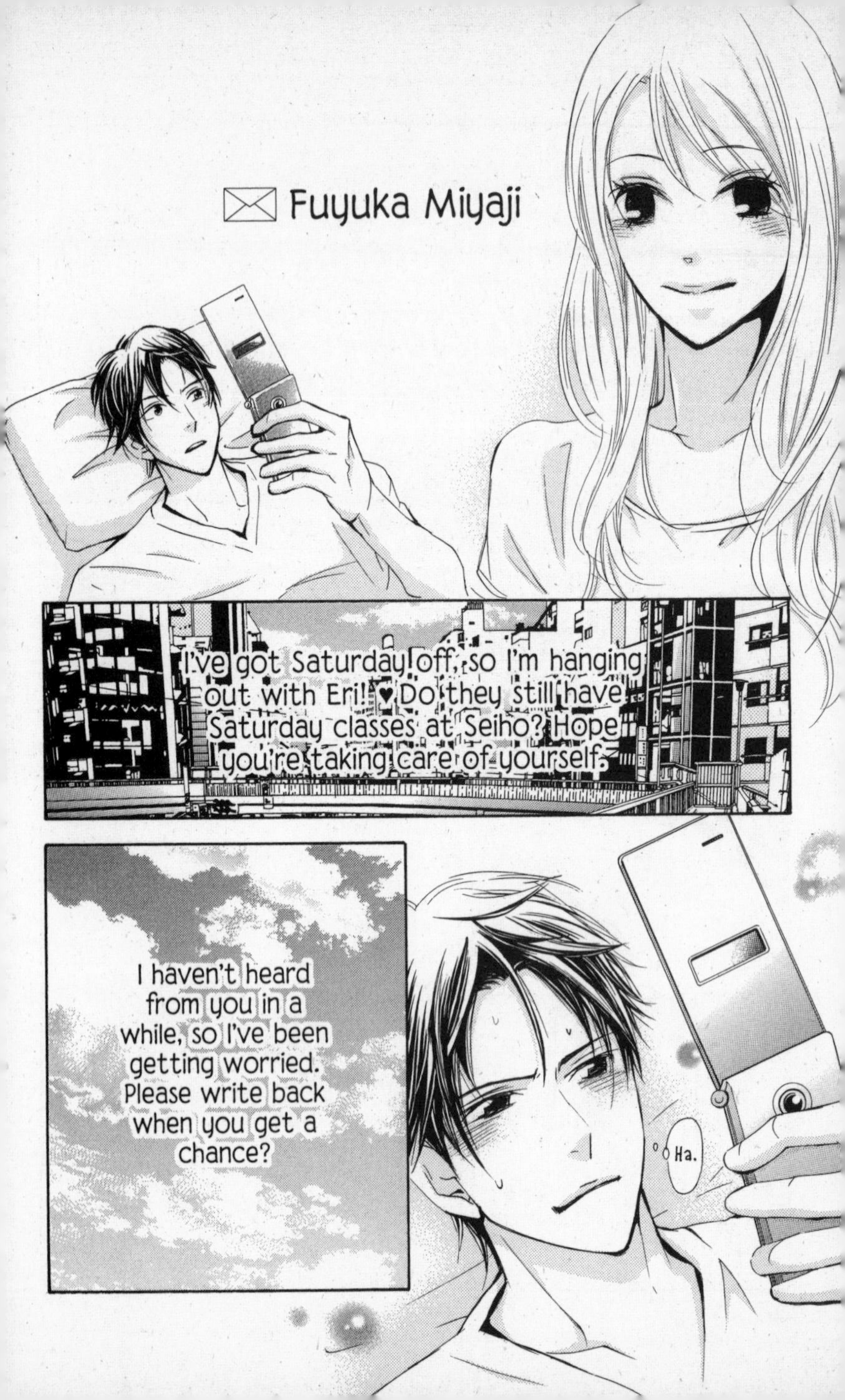
Fuyuka Miyaji
I've got Saturday off, so I'm hanging out with Eri! ♥ Do they still have Saturday classes at Seiho? Hope you're taking care of yourself.
Ha.
I haven't heard from you in a while, so I've been getting worried. Please write back when you get a chance?

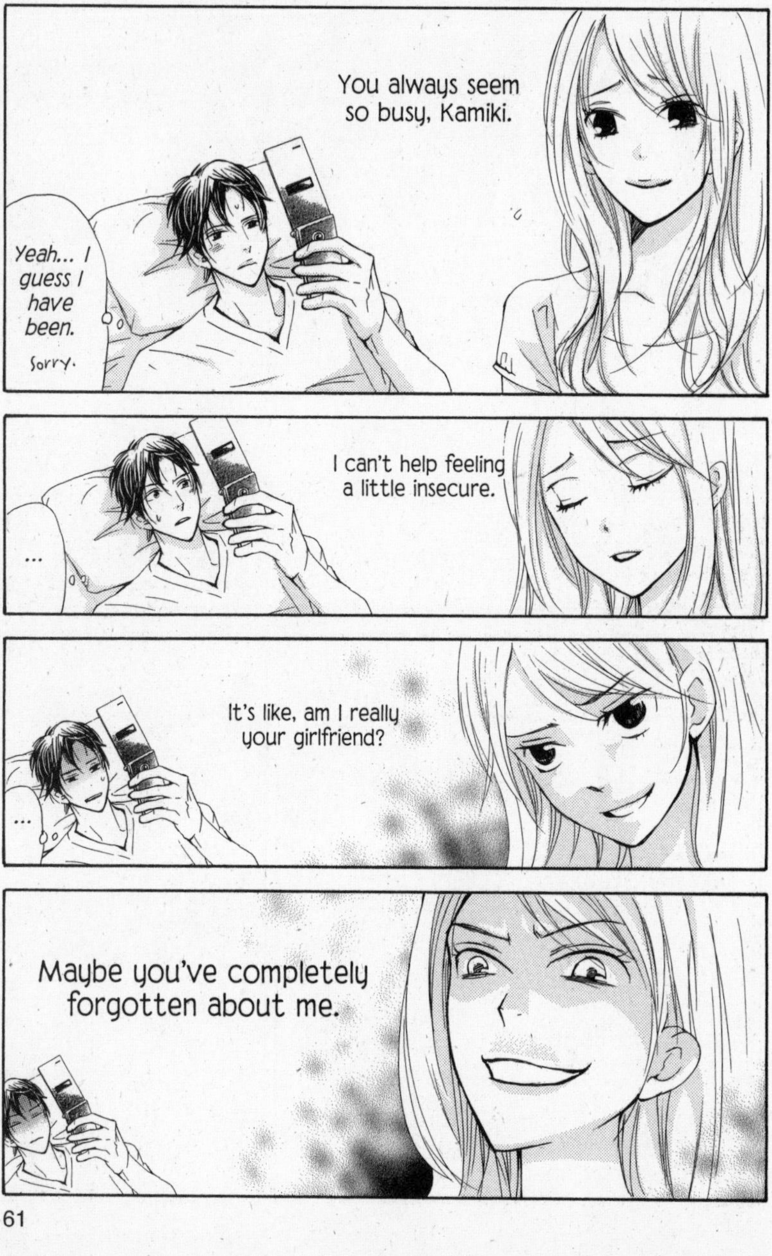
You always seem so busy, Kamiki.
Yeah... I guess I have been.
Sorry.
I can't help feeling a little insecure.
...
It's like, am I really your girlfriend?
...
Maybe you've completely forgotten about me.

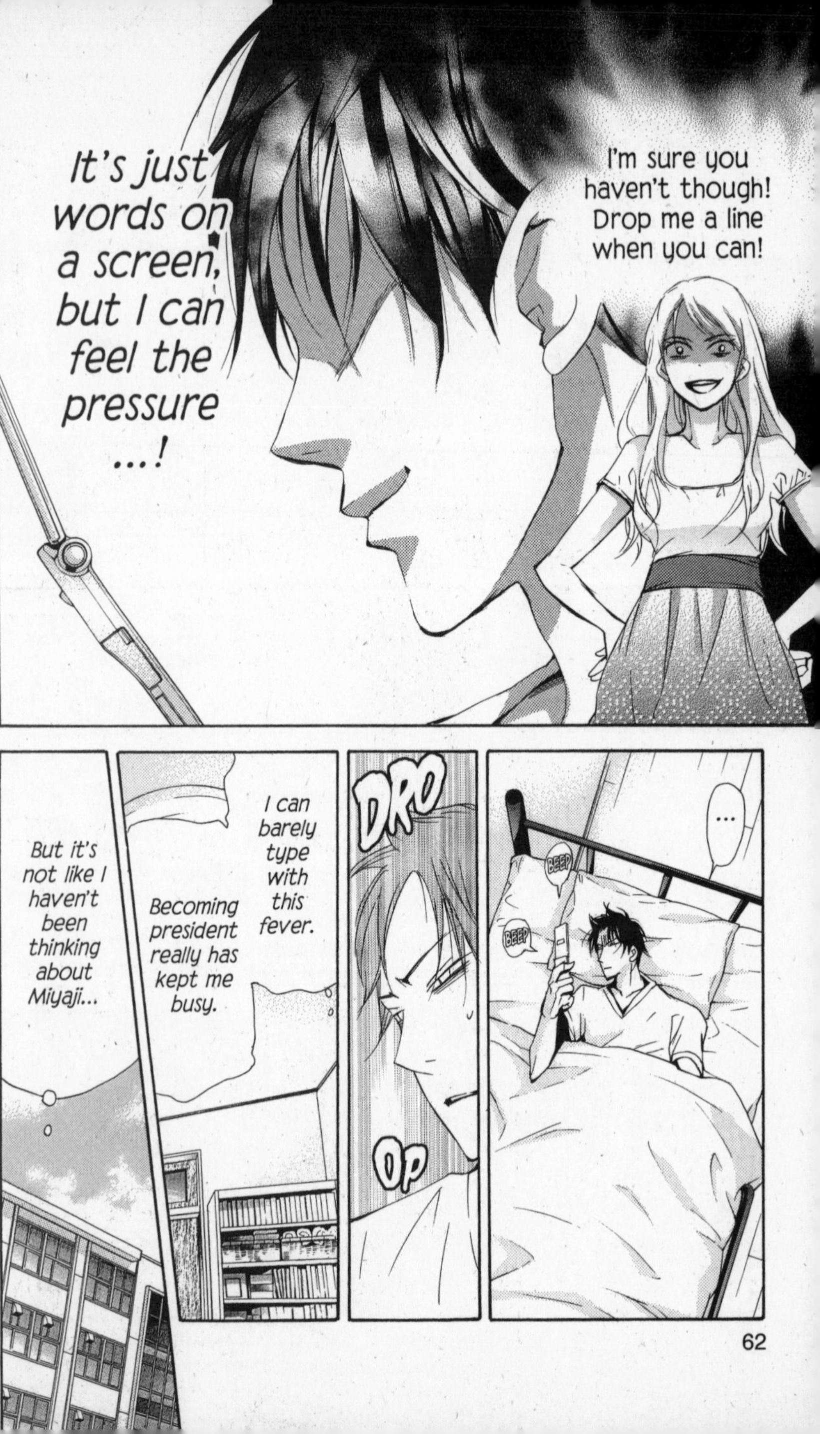
I'm sure you haven't though! Drop me a line when you can!
It's just words on a screen, but I can feel the pressure ...!
...
BEEP
BEEP
DRO
OP
I can barely type with this fever.
Becoming president really has kept me busy.
But it's not like I haven't been thinking about Miyaji...

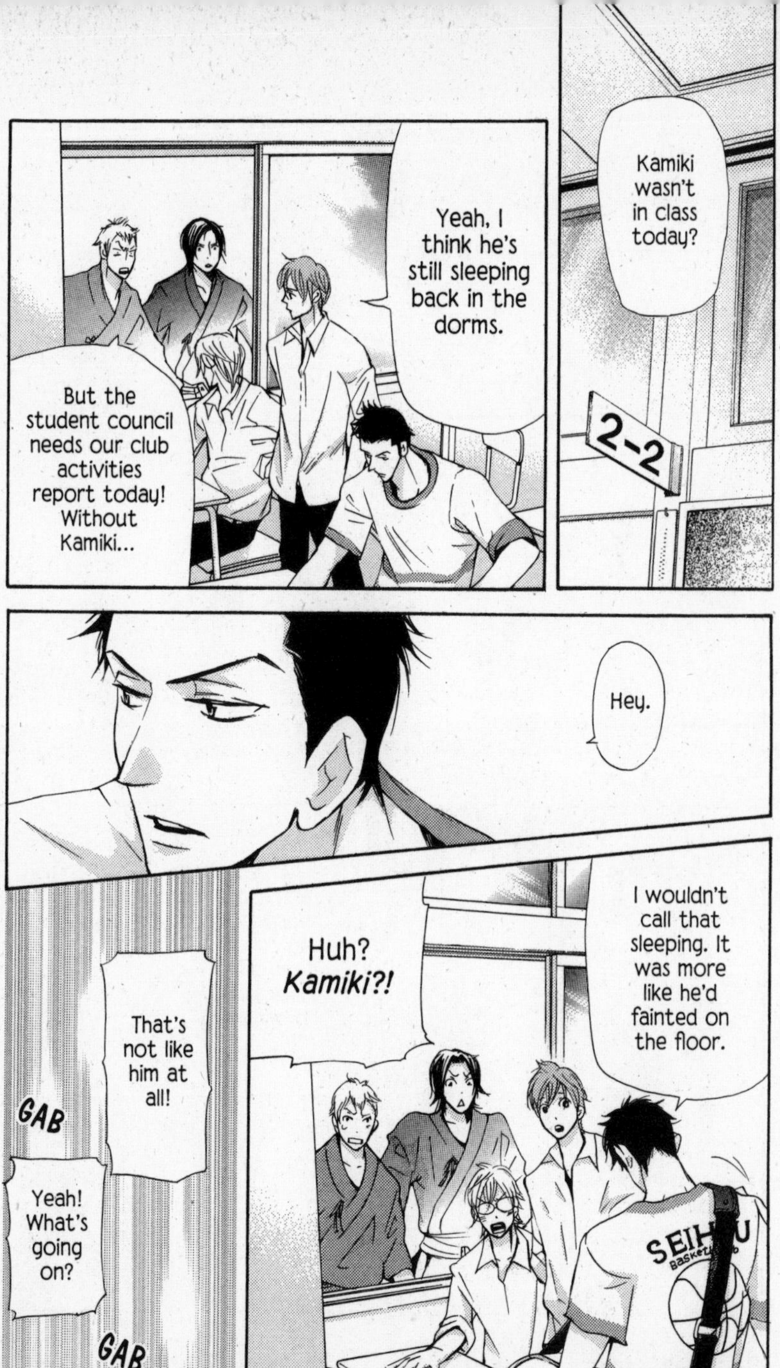
Kamiki wasn't in class today?
2-2
Yeah, I think he's still sleeping back in the dorms.
But the student council needs our club activities report today! Without Kamiki...
Hey.
I wouldn't call that sleeping. It was more like he'd fainted on the floor.
Huh? *Kamiki?!*
That's not like him at all!
GAB
Yeah! What's going on?
GAB

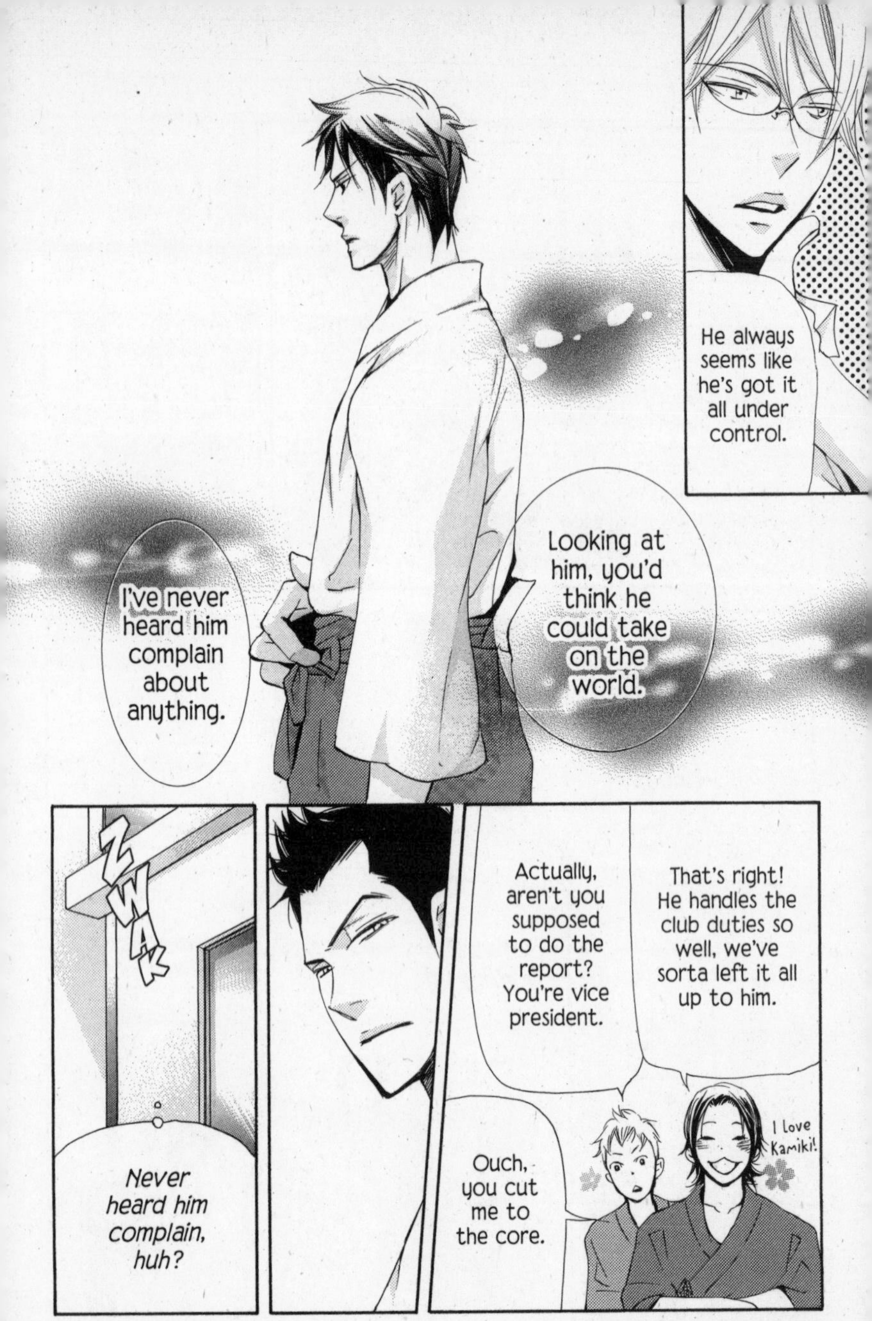
He always seems like he's got it all under control.
Looking at him, you'd think he could take on the world.
I've never heard him complain about anything.
That's right! He handles the club duties so well, we've sorta left it all up to him.
Actually, aren't you supposed to do the report? You're vice president.
I love Kamiki!
Ouch, you cut me to the core.
ZWAK
Never heard him complain, huh?

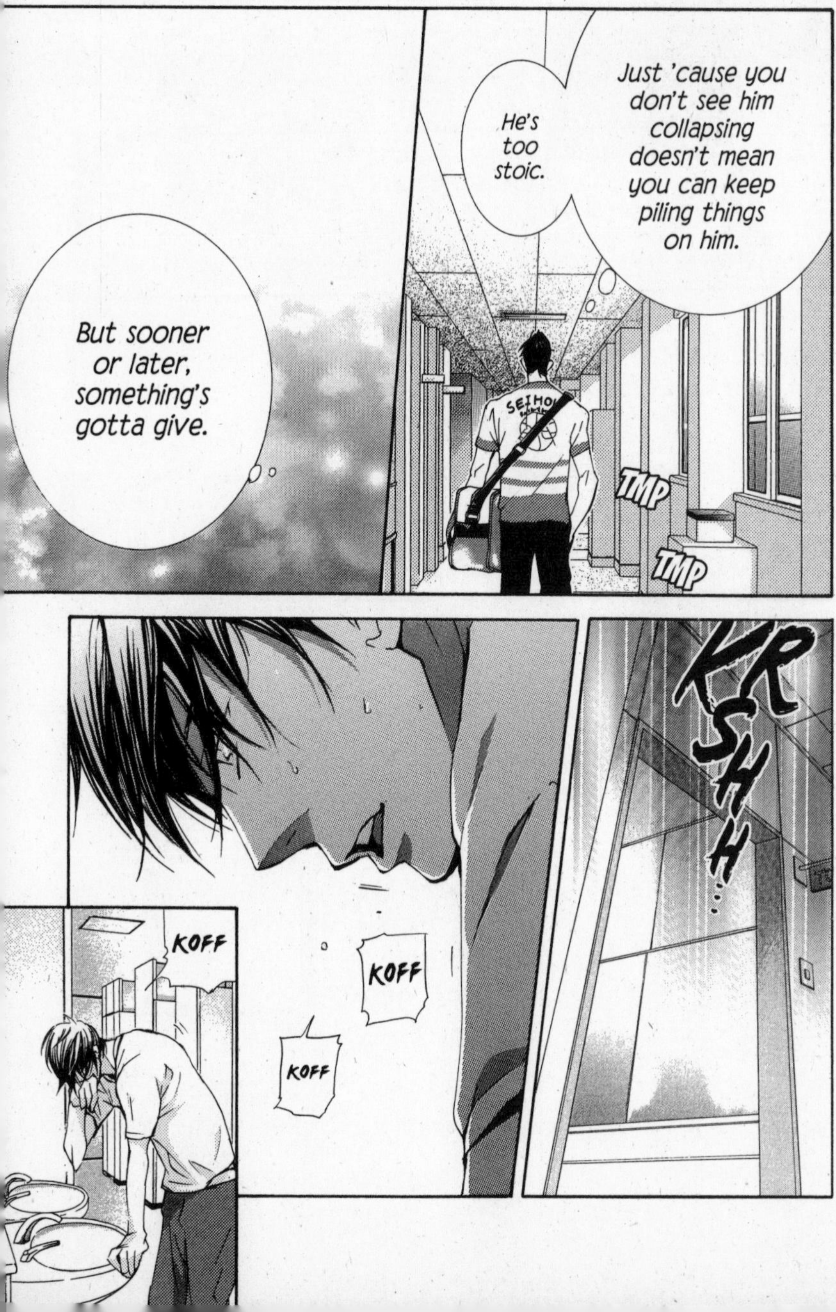
Just 'cause you don't see him collapsing doesn't mean you can keep piling things on him.
He's too stoic.
TMP
TMP
SEIHO
But sooner or later, something's gotta give.
KRSHHH...
KOFF
KOFF
KOFF

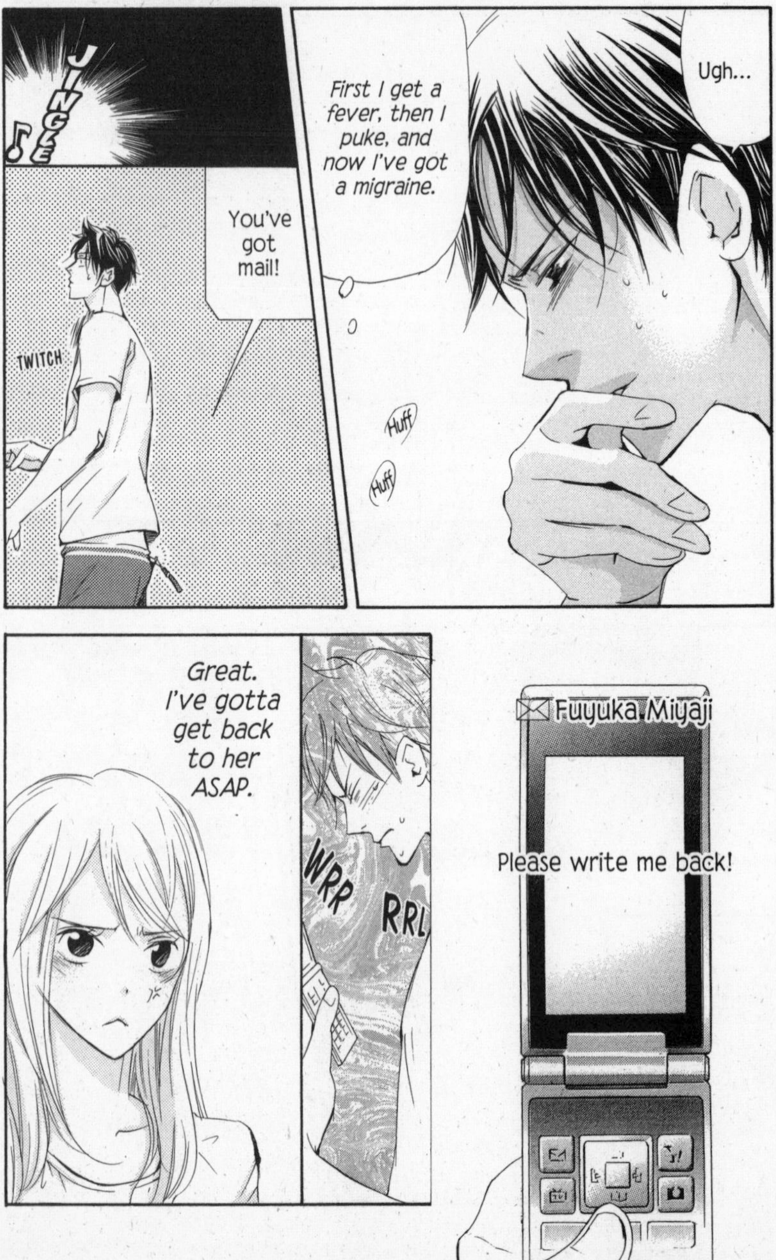
Ugh...
First I get a fever, then I puke, and now I've got a migraine.
Huff
Huff
JINGLE
You've got mail!
TWITCH
Fuyuka Miyaji
Please write me back!
WRR RRL
Great. I've gotta get back to her ASAP.

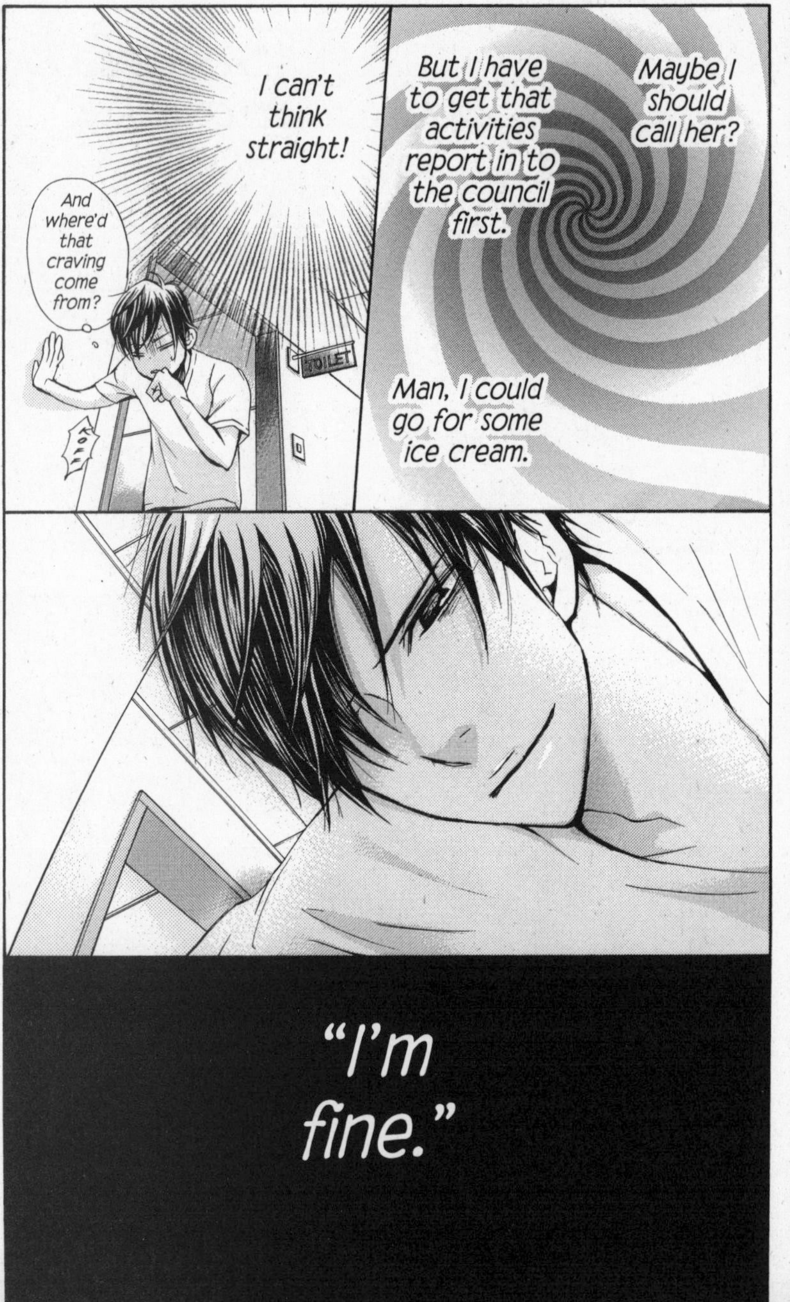
Maybe I should call her?
But I have to get that activities report in to the council first.
Man, I could go for some ice cream.
I can't think straight!
And where'd that craving come from?
TOILET
KOFF
"I'm fine."

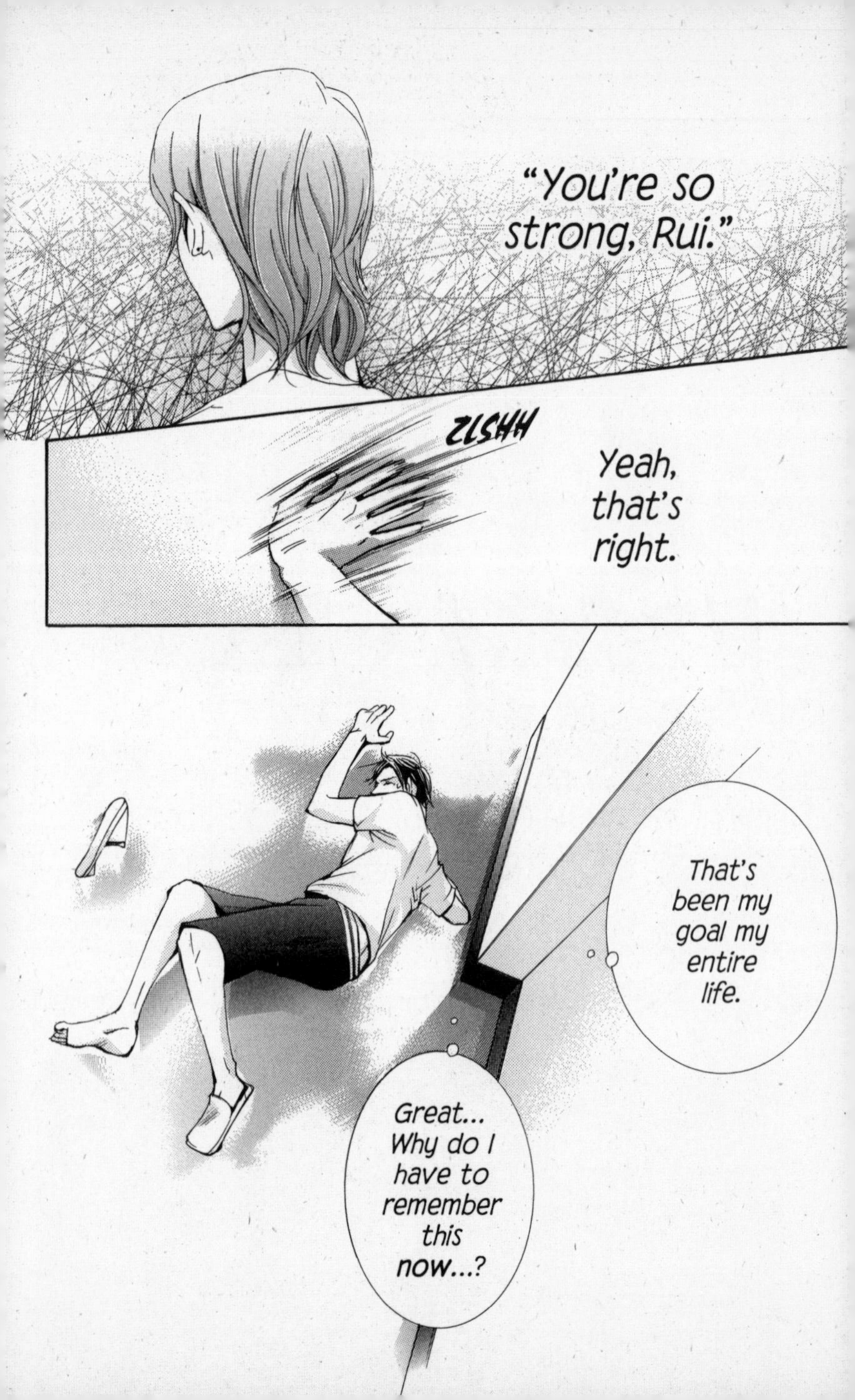
"You're so strong, Rui."
Yeah, that's right.
That's been my goal my entire life.
Great... Why do I have to remember this now...?

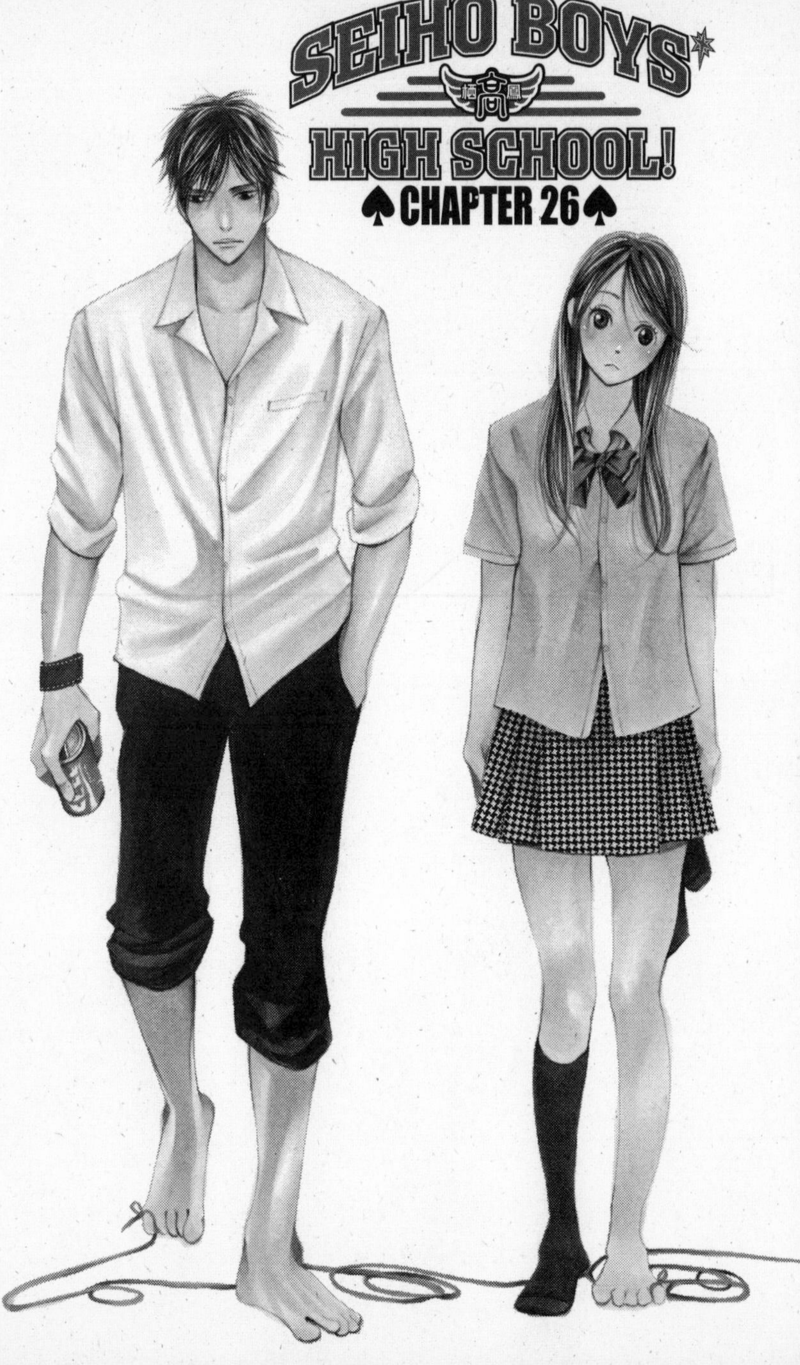
SEIHO BOYS'
HIGH SCHOOL!
CHAPTER 26

Secret Canned-Idea Relief Corner

Fuyuka Miyaji's Cell Phone Strap

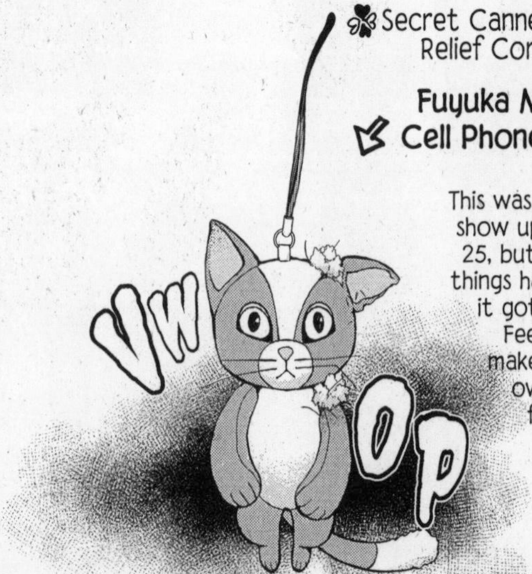
VWOOP

This was supposed to show up in Chapter 25, but a bunch of things happened, and it got dropped. Feel free to make up your own uses for it!

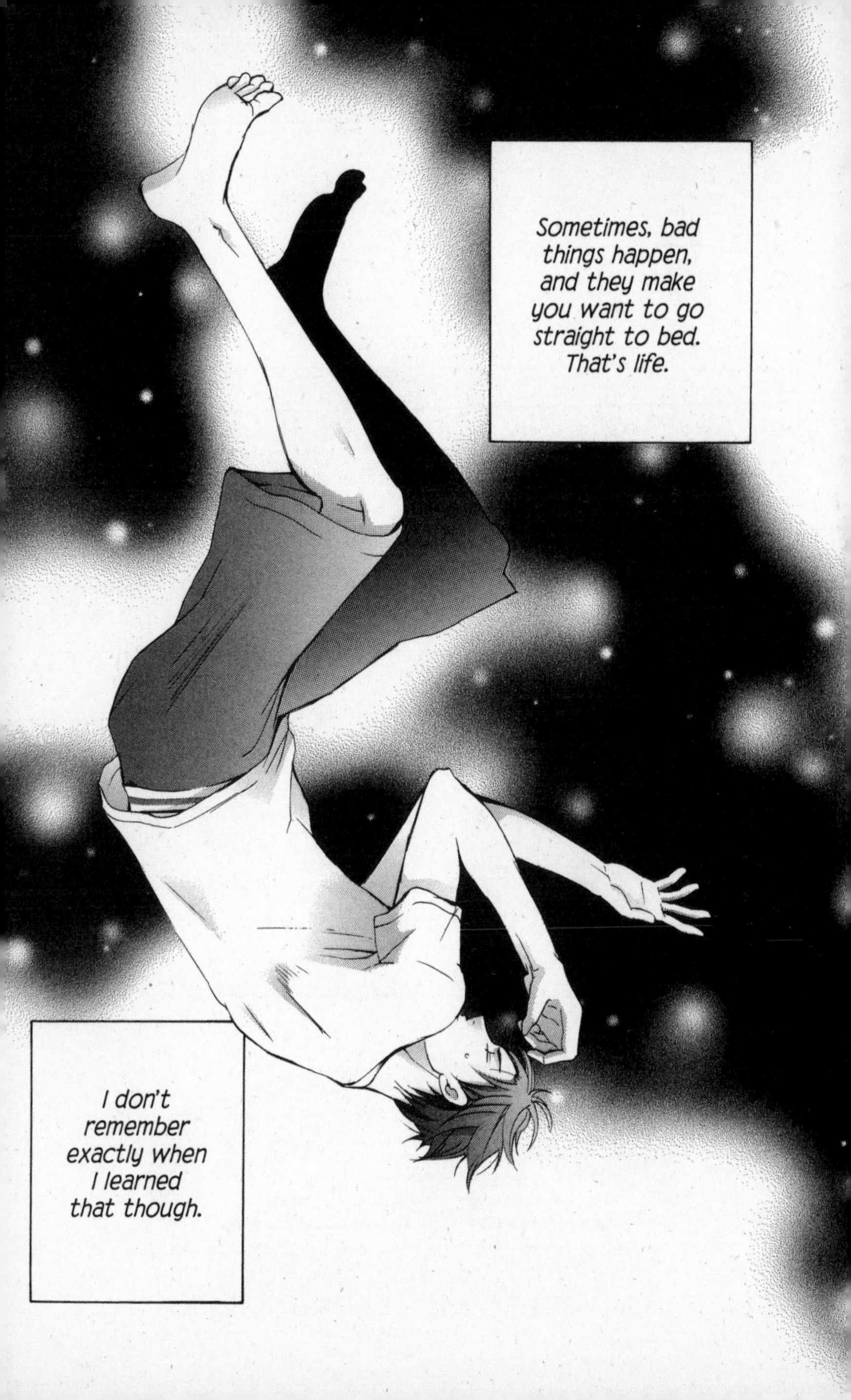
Sometimes, bad things happen, and they make you want to go straight to bed. That's life.
I don't remember exactly when I learned that though.

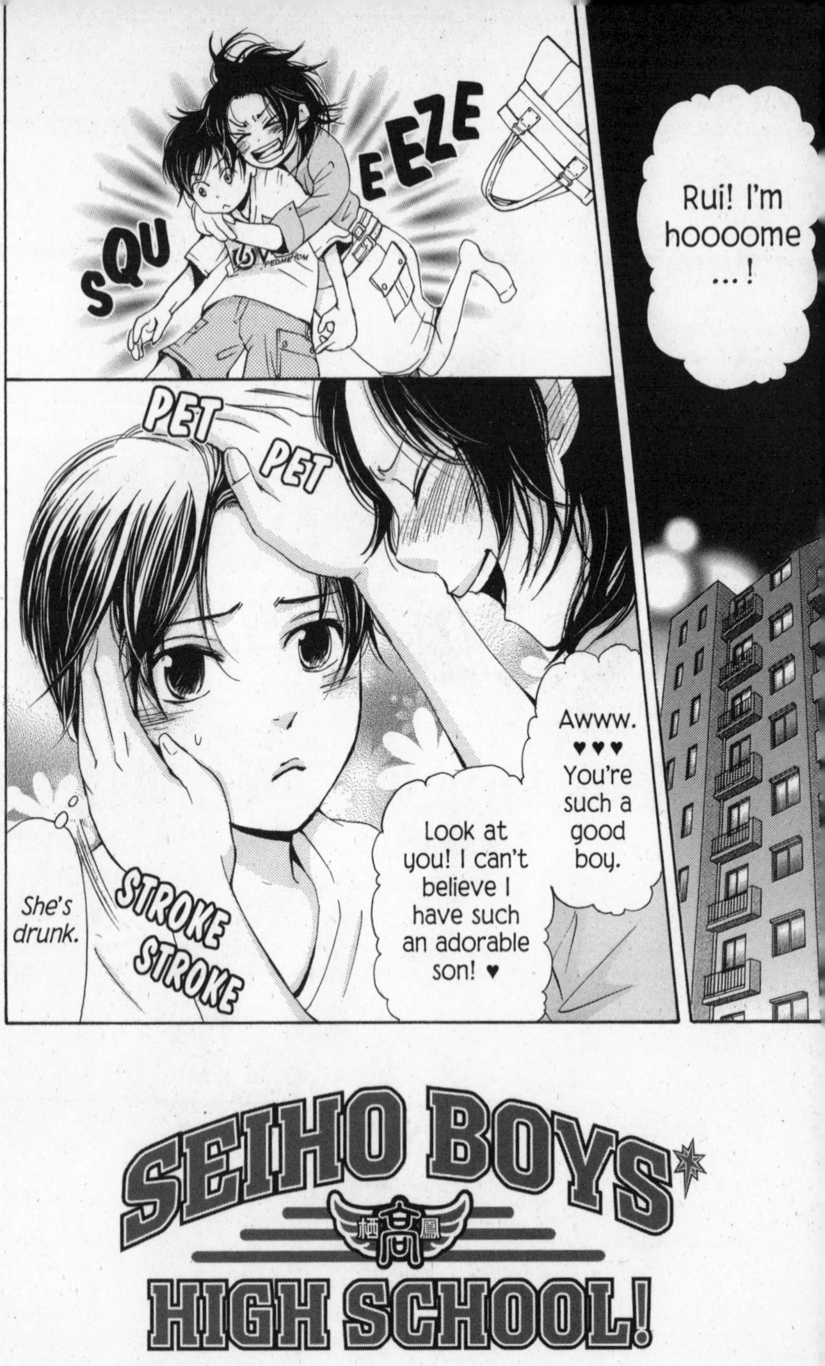
Rui! I'm hoooome ...!
SQUEEZE
PET PET
Awww. ♥♥♥ You're such a good boy.
Look at you! I can't believe I have such an adorable son! ♥
STROKE STROKE
She's drunk.

SEIHO BOYS HIGH SCHOOL!

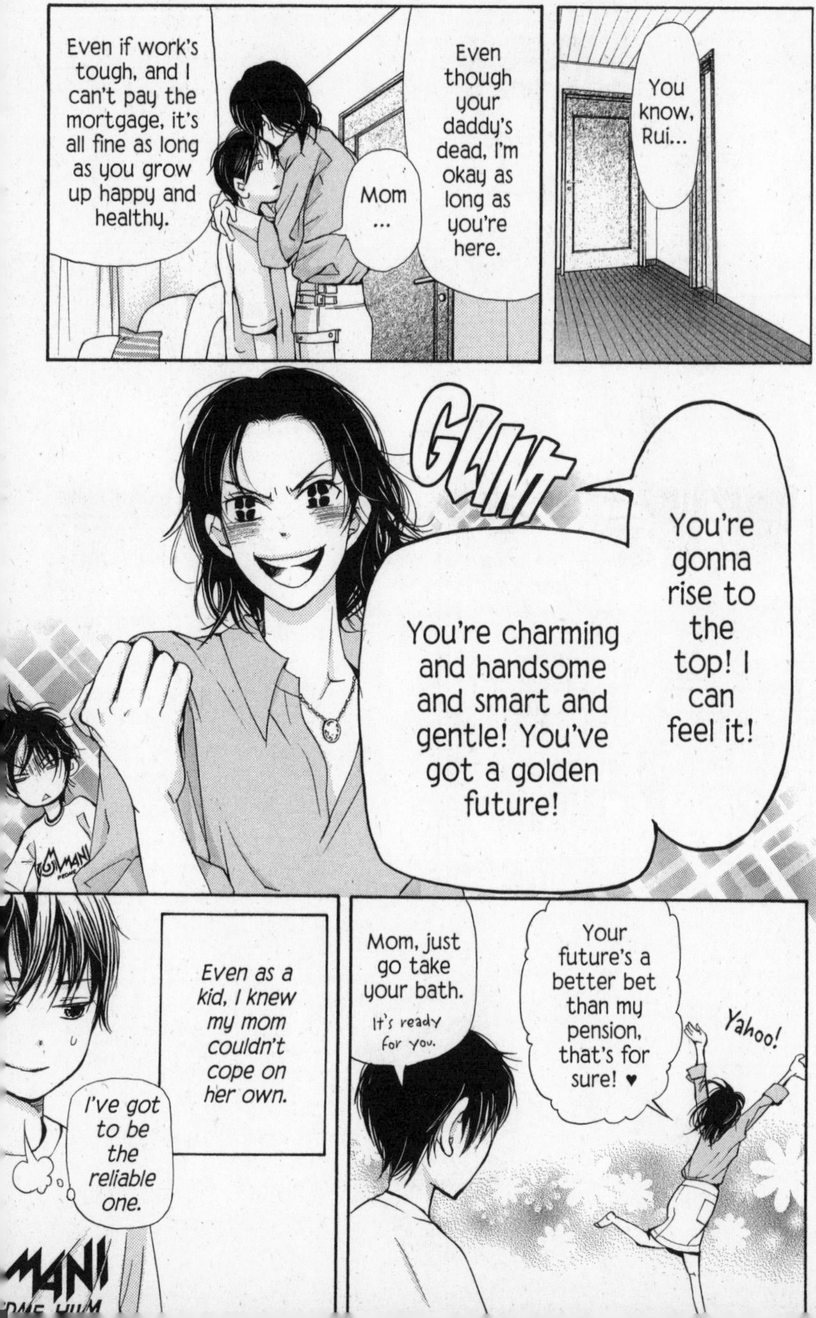
You know, Rui...
Even though your daddy's dead, I'm okay as long as you're here.
Even if work's tough, and I can't pay the mortgage, it's all fine as long as you grow up happy and healthy.
Mom ...
GLINT
You're gonna rise to the top! I can feel it!
You're charming and handsome and smart and gentle! You've got a golden future!
Yahoo!
Your future's a better bet than my pension, that's for sure! ♥
Mom, just go take your bath.
It's ready for you.
Even as a kid, I knew my mom couldn't cope on her own.
I've got to be the reliable one.

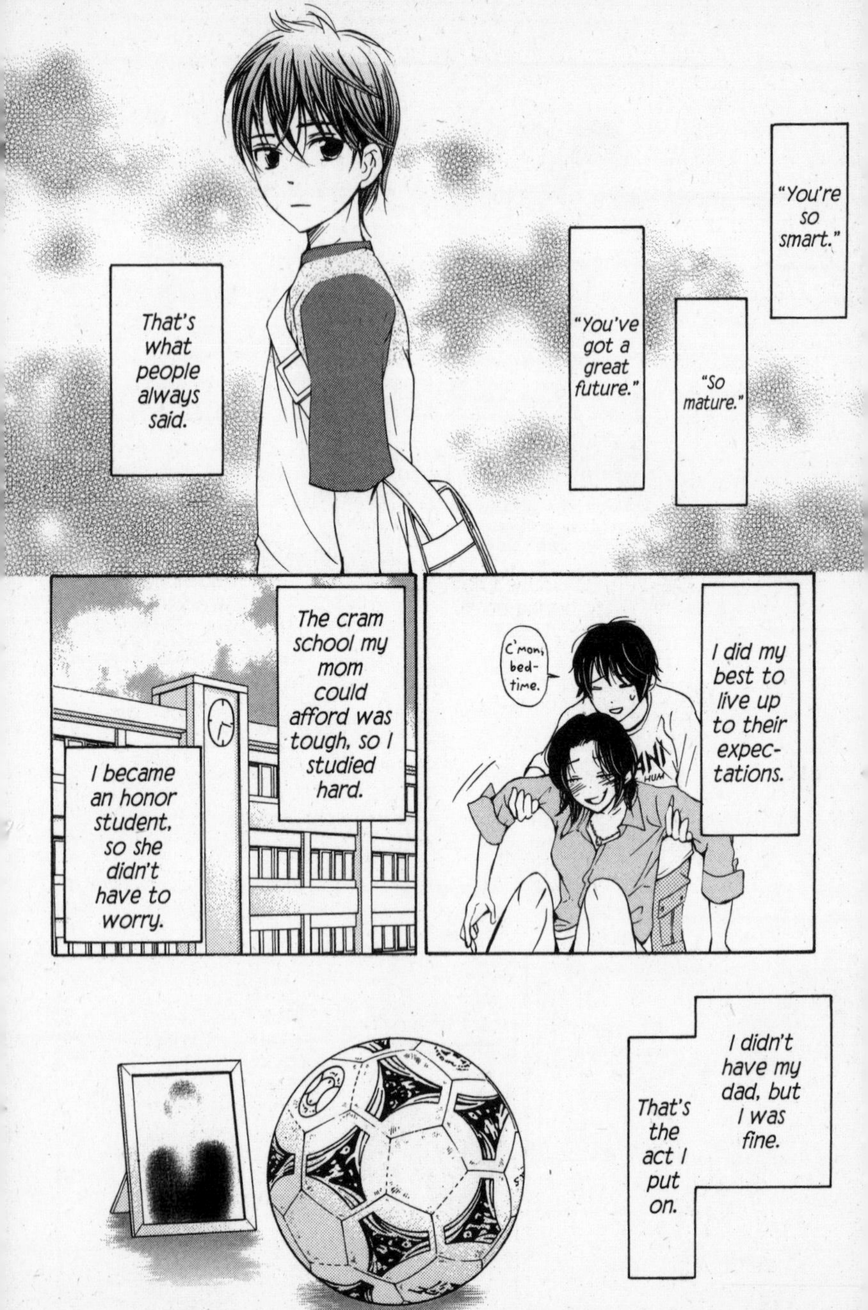
"You're so smart."
"So mature."
"You've got a great future."
That's what people always said.
I did my best to live up to their expectations.
C'mon, bed-time.
The cram school my mom could afford was tough, so I studied hard.
I became an honor student, so she didn't have to worry.
I didn't have my dad, but I was fine.
That's the act I put on.

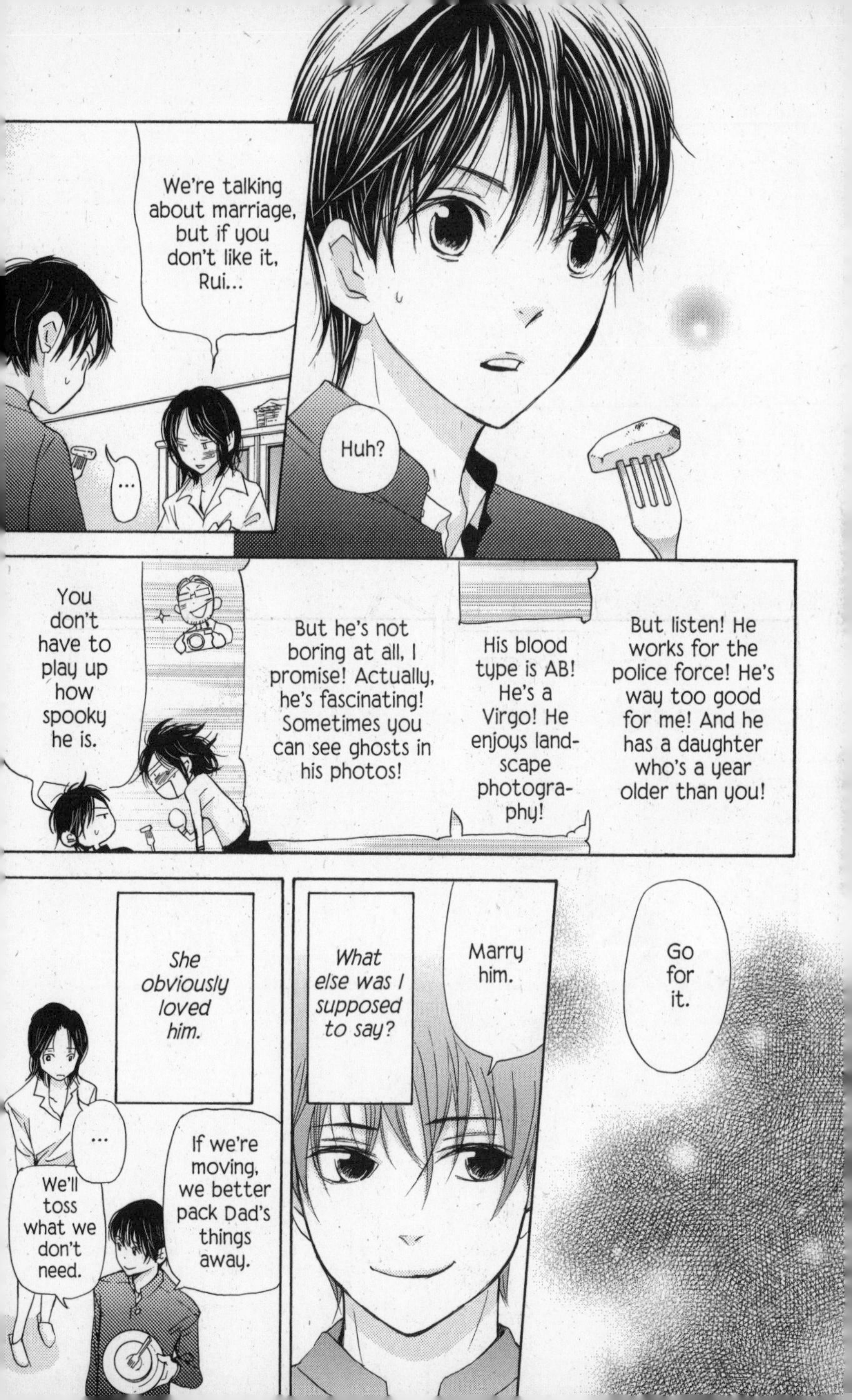
Huh?
We're talking about marriage, but if you don't like it, Rui...
...
But listen! He works for the police force! He's way too good for me! And he has a daughter who's a year older than you!
His blood type is AB! He's a Virgo! He enjoys land-scape photogra-phy!
But he's not boring at all, I promise! Actually, he's fascinating! Sometimes you can see ghosts in his photos!
You don't have to play up how spooky he is.
Go for it.
Marry him.
What else was I supposed to say?
She obviously loved him.
...
If we're moving, we better pack Dad's things away.
We'll toss what we don't need.

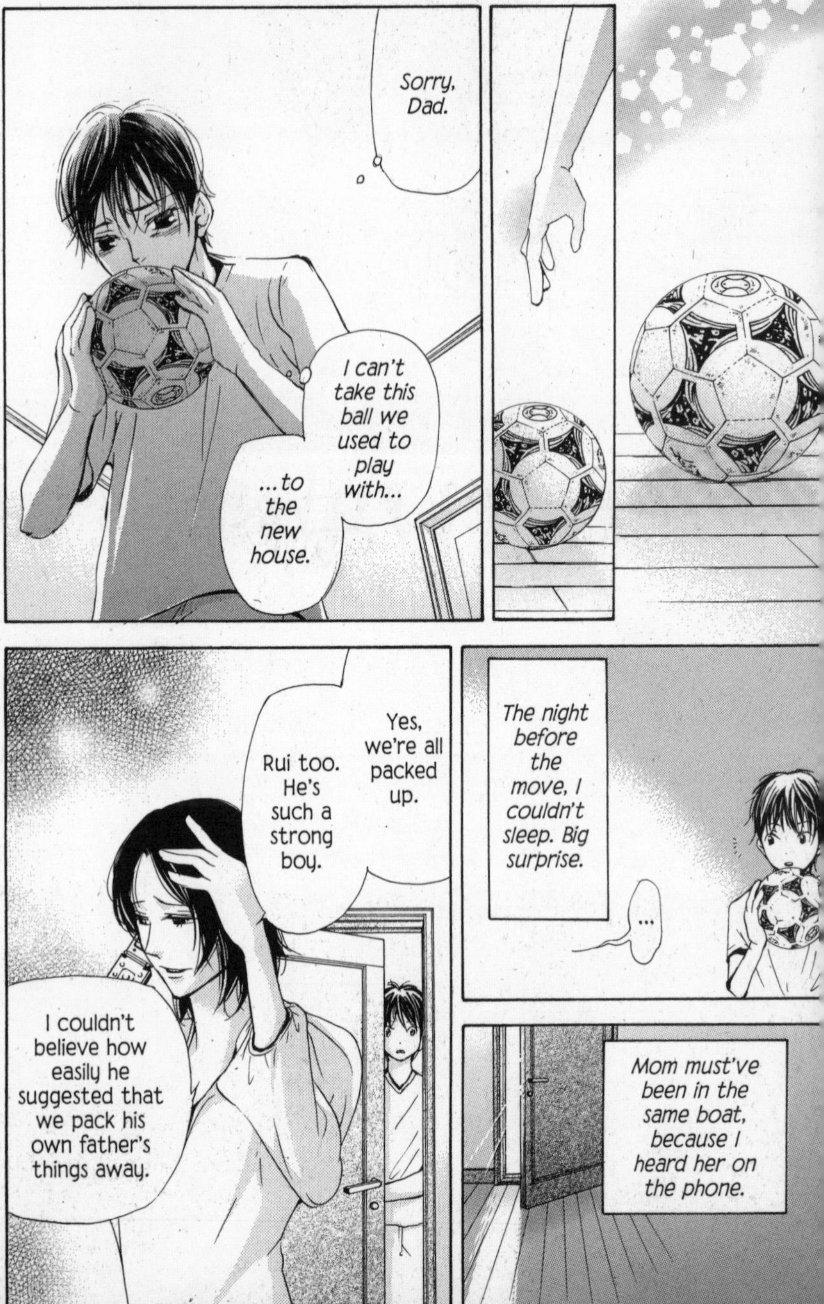

Sorry, Dad.
I can't take this ball we used to play with...
...to the new house.
The night before the move, I couldn't sleep. Big surprise.
...
Mom must've been in the same boat, because I heard her on the phone.
Yes, we're all packed up.
Rui too. He's such a strong boy.
I couldn't believe how easily he suggested that we pack his own father's things away.

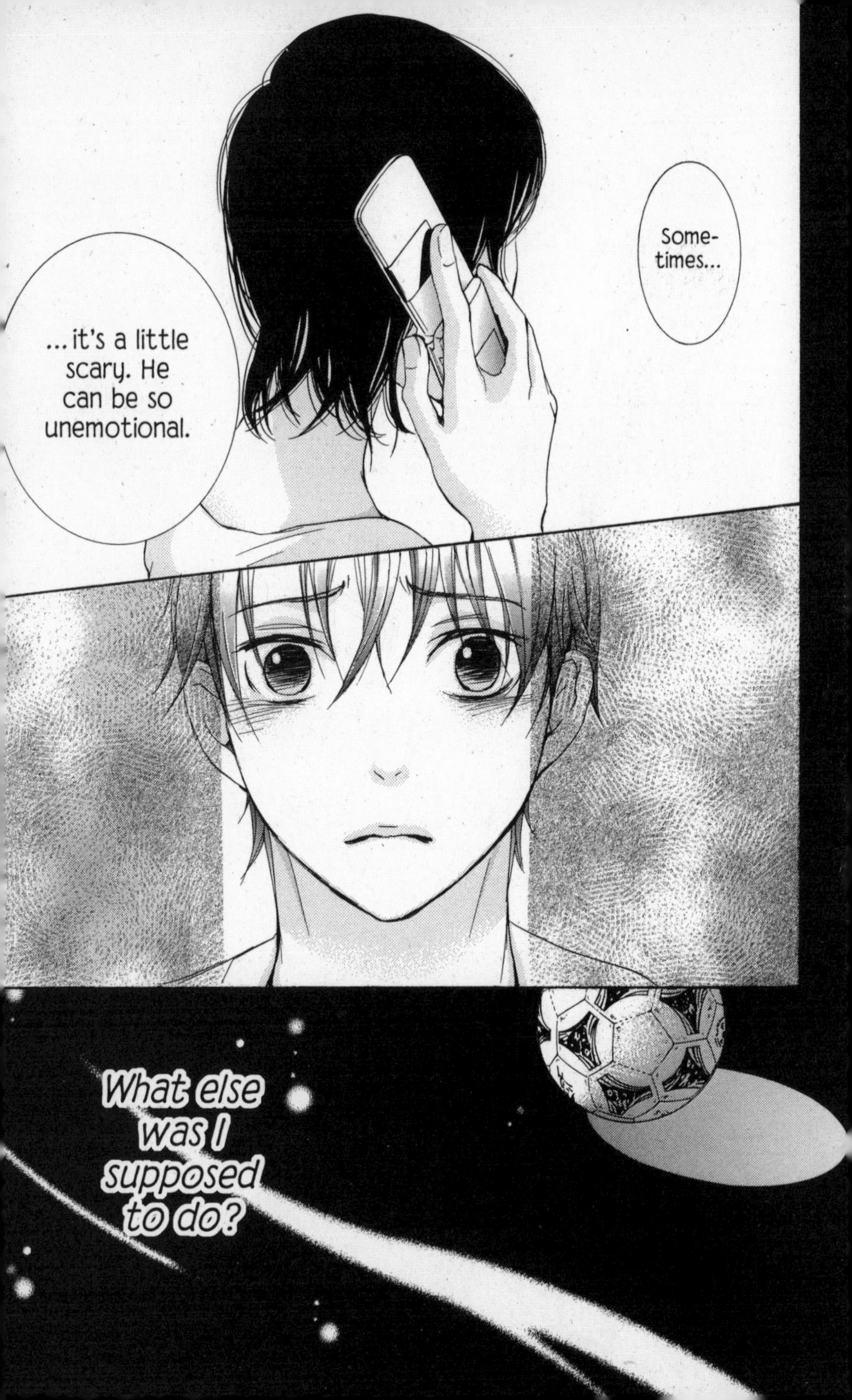
Some-
times...
...it's a little scary. He can be so unemotional.
What else was I supposed to do?

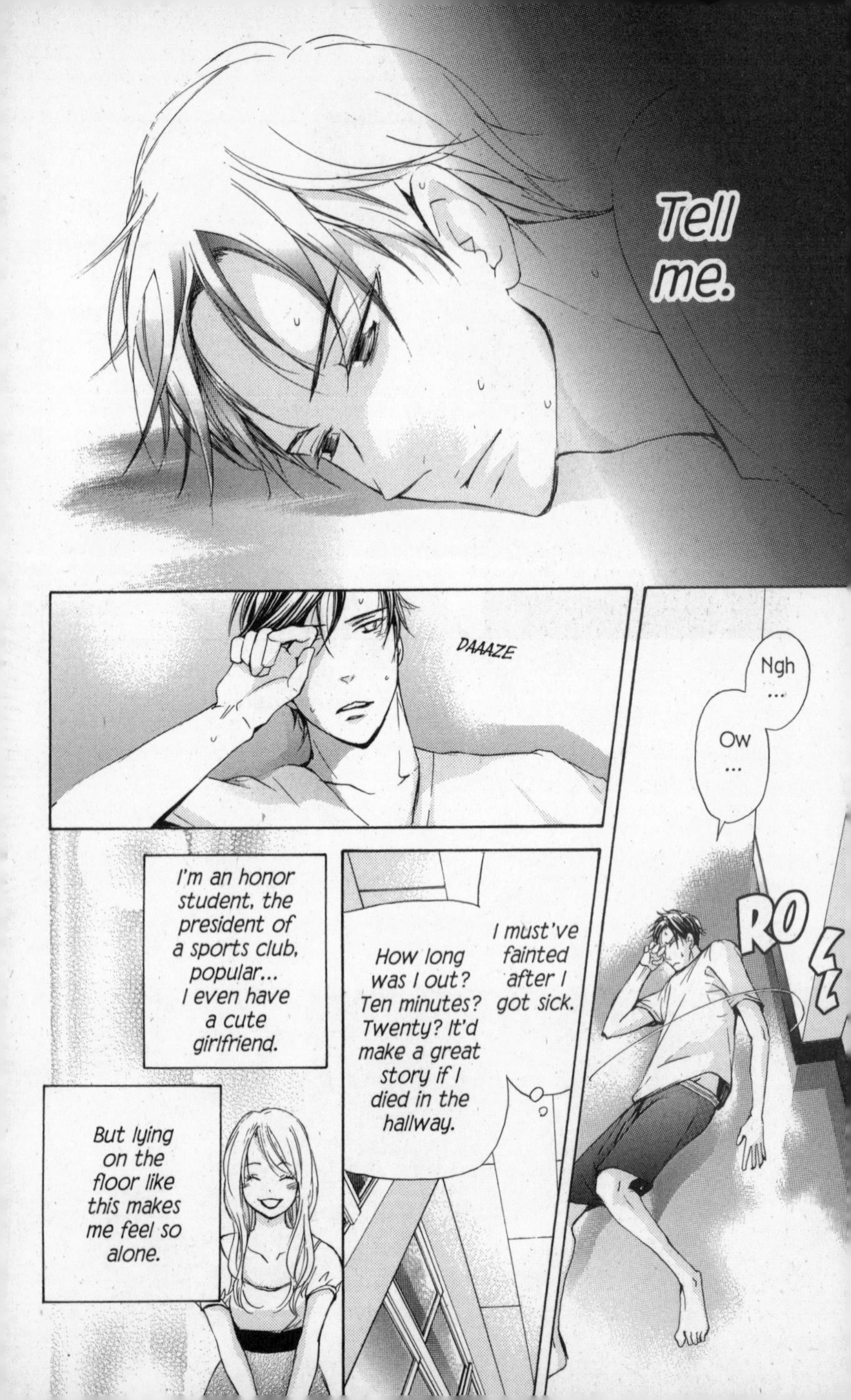
Tell me.
Ngh...
Ow...
ROLL
DAAAZE
I must've fainted after I got sick.
How long was I out? Ten minutes? Twenty? It'd make a great story if I died in the hallway.
I'm an honor student, the president of a sports club, popular... I even have a cute girlfriend.
But lying on the floor like this makes me feel so alone.

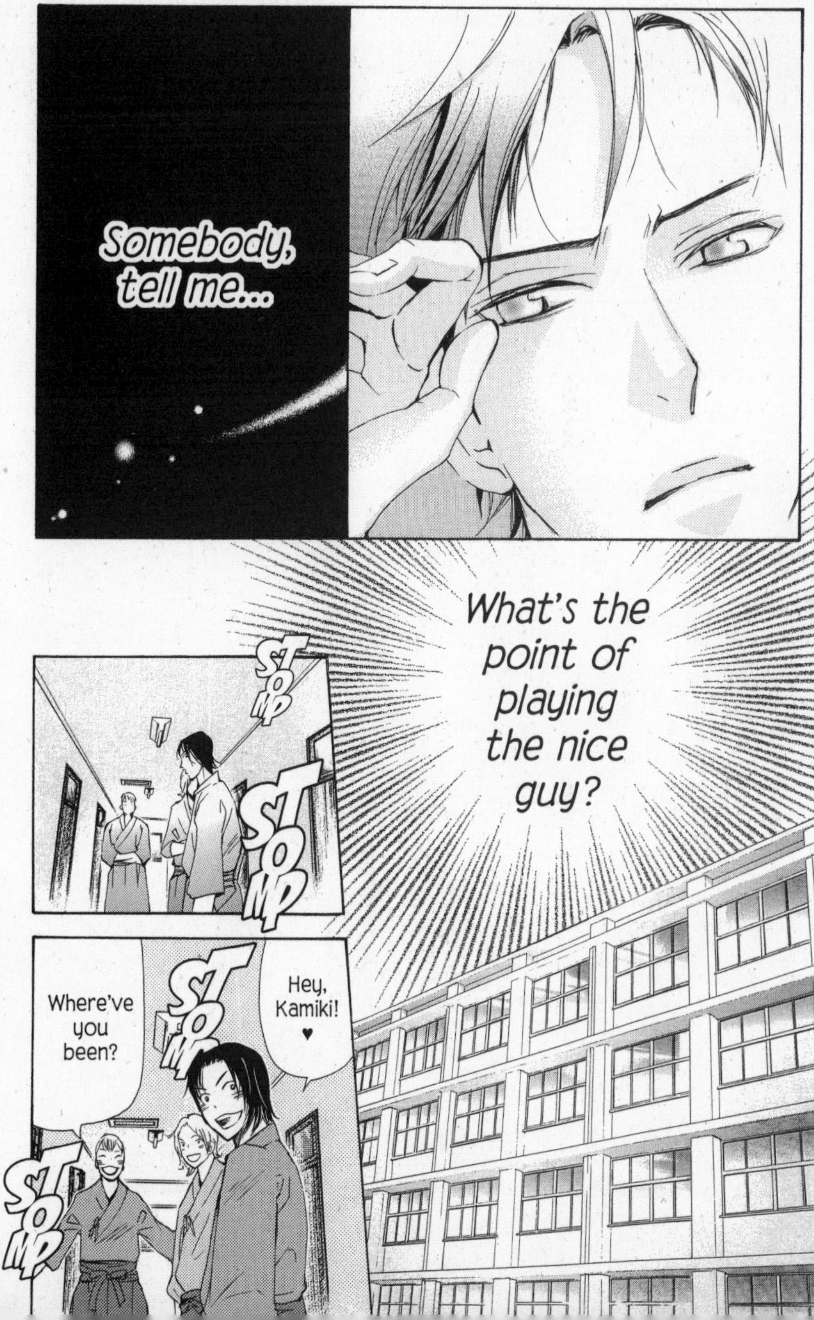
Somebody, tell me...
What's the point of playing the nice guy?
STOMP
STOMP
STOMP
Hey, Kamiki! ♥
Where've you been?
STOMP

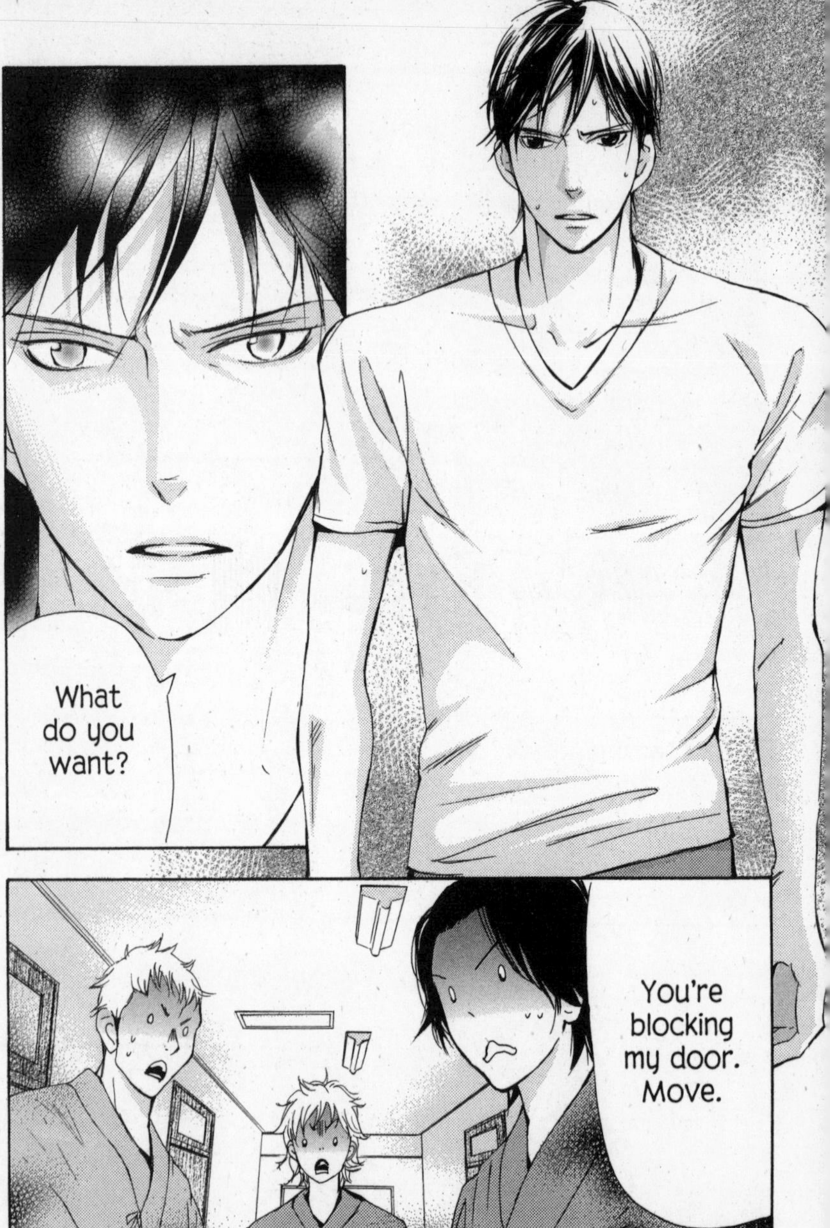
What do you want?
You're blocking my door. Move.

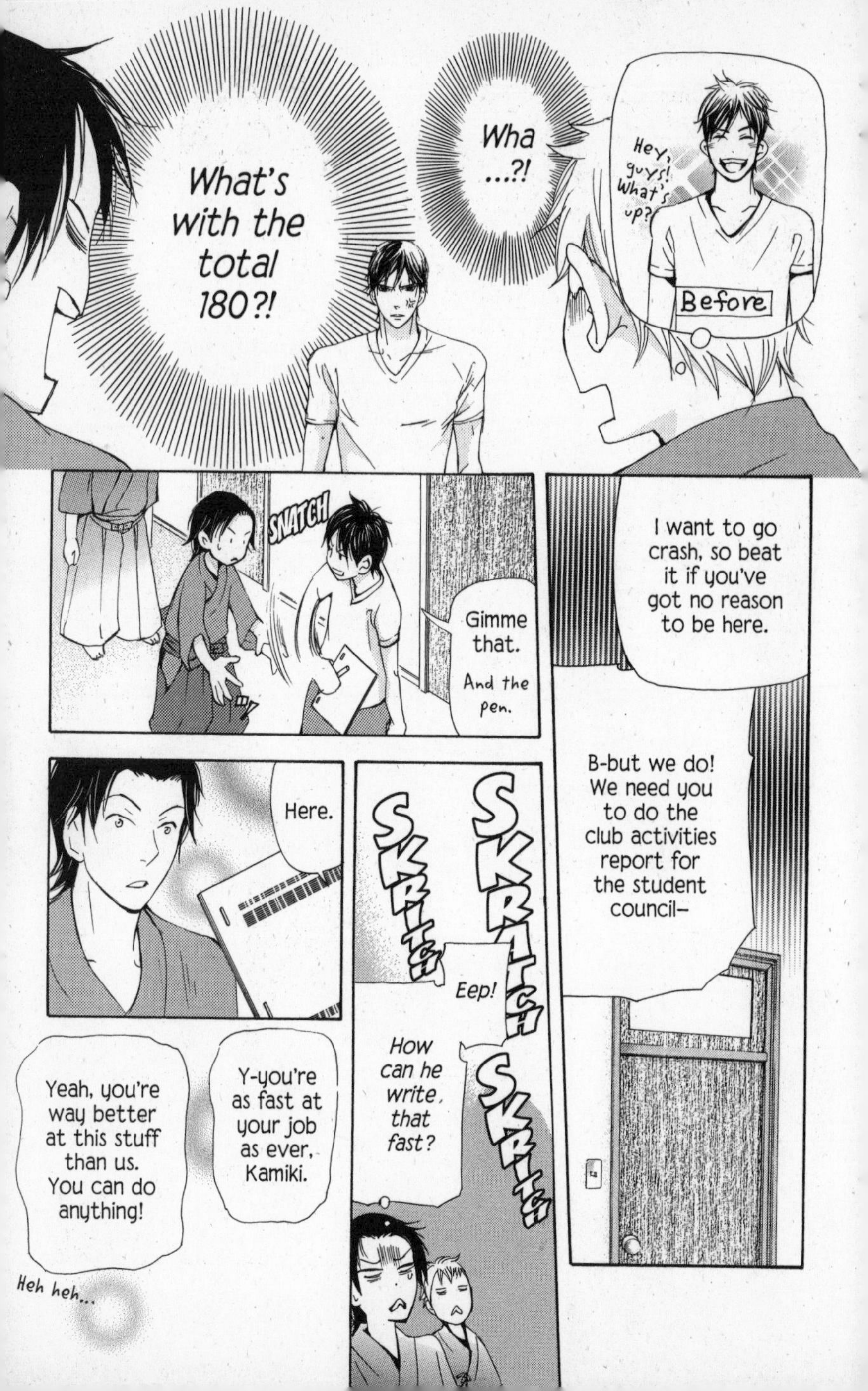
Hey, guys! What's up?!
Before
Wha ...?!
What's with the total 180?!
I want to go crash, so beat it if you've got no reason to be here.
B-but we do! We need you to do the club activities report for the student council–
SNATCH
Gimme that.
And the pen.
SKRATCH
SKRITCH
SKRITCH
Eep!
Here.
How can he write that fast?
Y-you're as fast at your job as ever, Kamiki.
Yeah, you're way better at this stuff than us. You can do anything!
Heh heh...

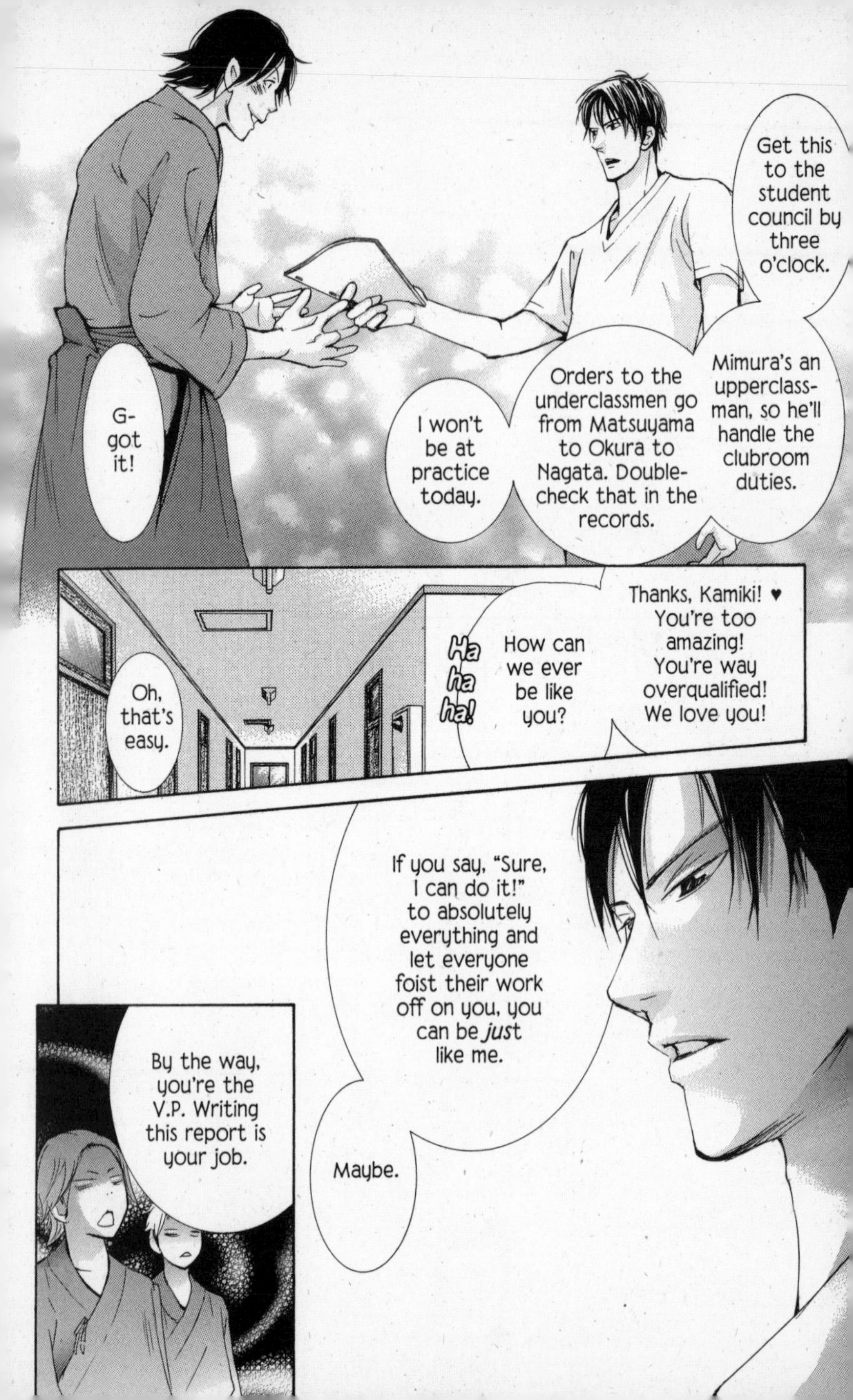
Get this to the student council by three o'clock.
Mimura's an upperclassman, so he'll handle the clubroom duties.
Orders to the underclassmen go from Matsuyama to Okura to Nagata. Double-check that in the records.
I won't be at practice today.
G-got it!
Thanks, Kamiki! ♥ You're too amazing! You're way overqualified! We love you!
How can we ever be like you?
Ha ha ha!
Oh, that's easy.
If you say, "Sure, I can do it!" to absolutely everything and let everyone foist their work off on you, you can be *just* like me.
Maybe.
By the way, you're the V.P. Writing this report is your job.

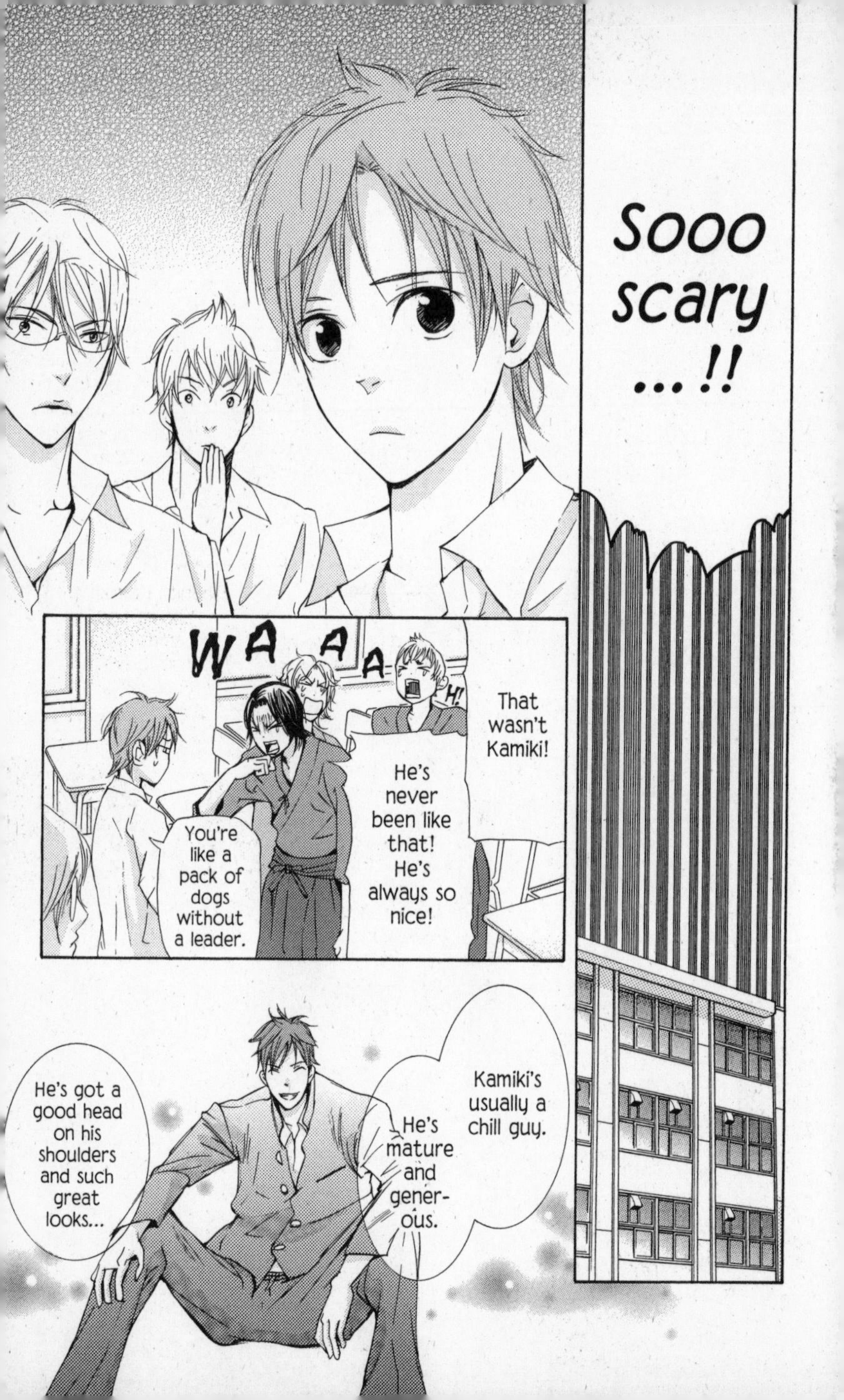
Sooo scary...!!
WAAAH!
That wasn't Kamiki!
He's never been like that! He's always so nice!
You're like a pack of dogs without a leader.
Kamiki's usually a chill guy.
He's mature and gener-ous.
He's got a good head on his shoulders and such great looks...

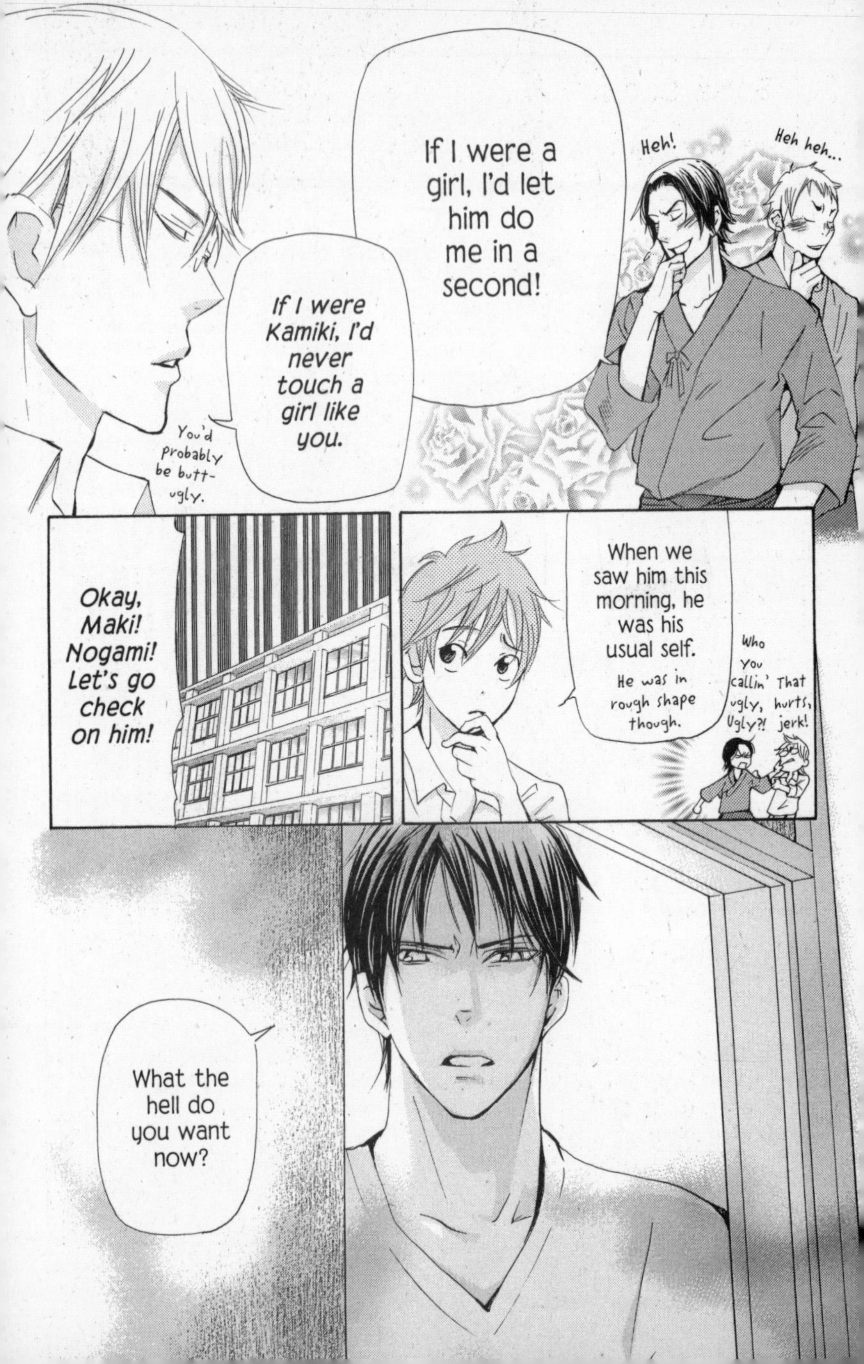
Heh heh...
Heh!
If I were a girl, I'd let him do me in a second!
If I were Kamiki, I'd never touch a girl like you.
You'd probably be butt-ugly.
When we saw him this morning, he was his usual self.
He was in rough shape though.
That hurts, jerk!
Who you callin' ugly, Ugly?!
Okay, Maki! Nogami! Let's go check on him!
What the hell do you want now?

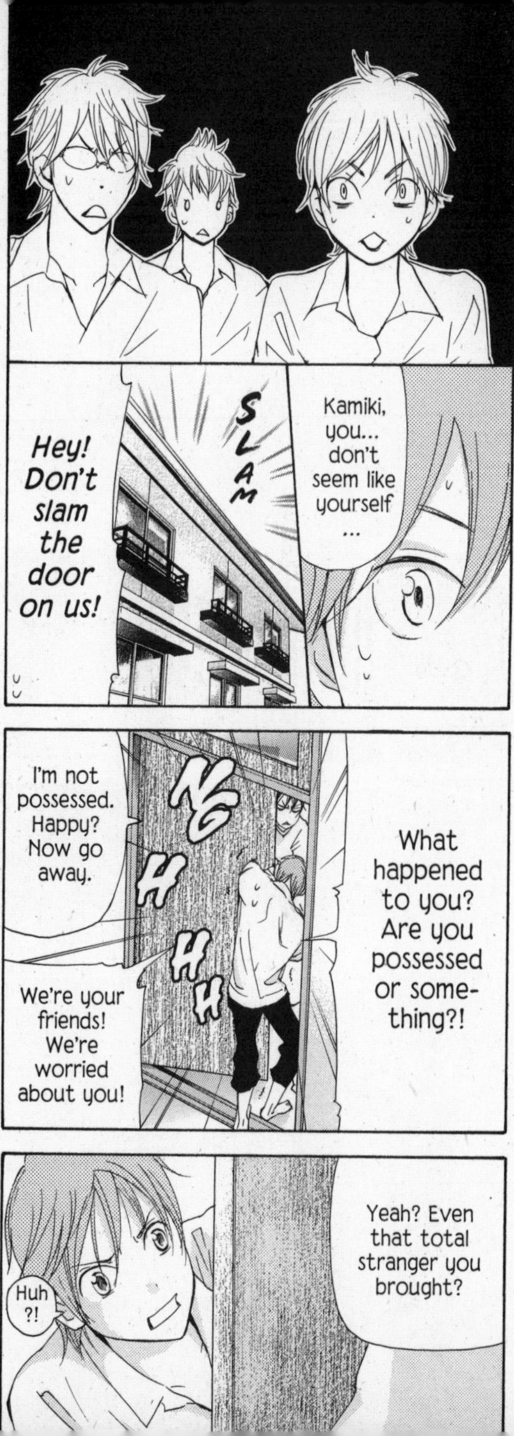
Kamiki, you... don't seem like yourself ...
SLAM
Hey! Don't slam the door on us!
What happened to you? Are you possessed or some-thing?!
I'm not possessed. Happy? Now go away.
NGHHH
We're your friends! We're worried about you!
Yeah? Even that total stranger you brought?
Huh ?!

Bonus Corner
Little Things ③

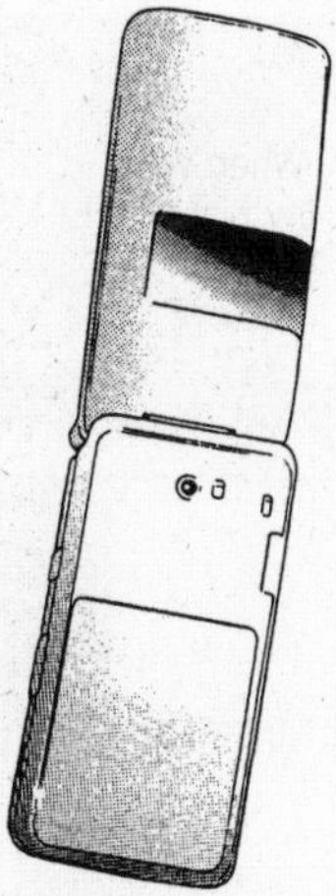

Genda's Cell Phone

I modeled this after an assistant's cell phone. It doesn't have any straps at all, like a real man's phone!!

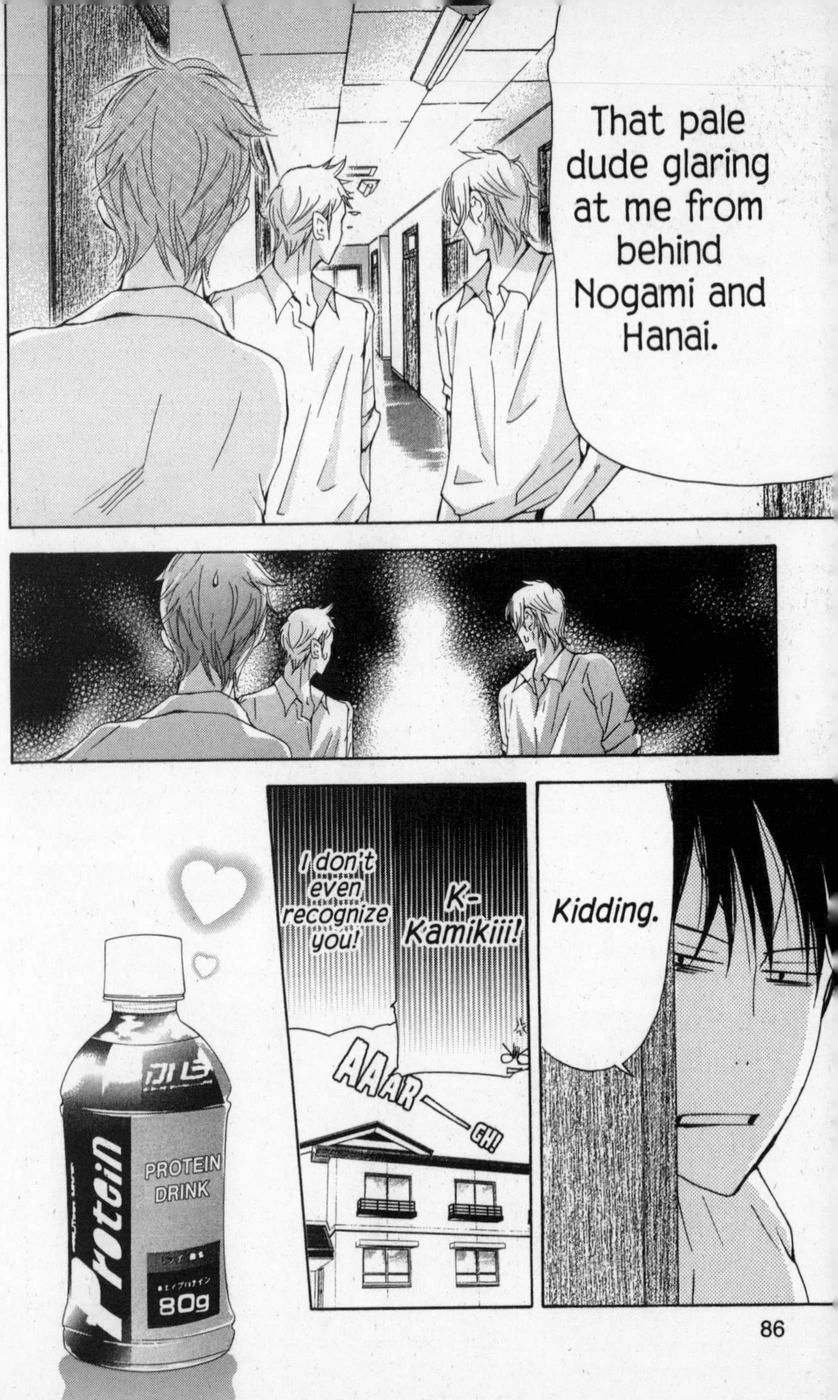
That pale dude glaring at me from behind Nogami and Hanai.
Kidding.
K-Kamikiii!
I don't even recognize you!
AAARGH!
Protein
PROTEIN DRINK
80g

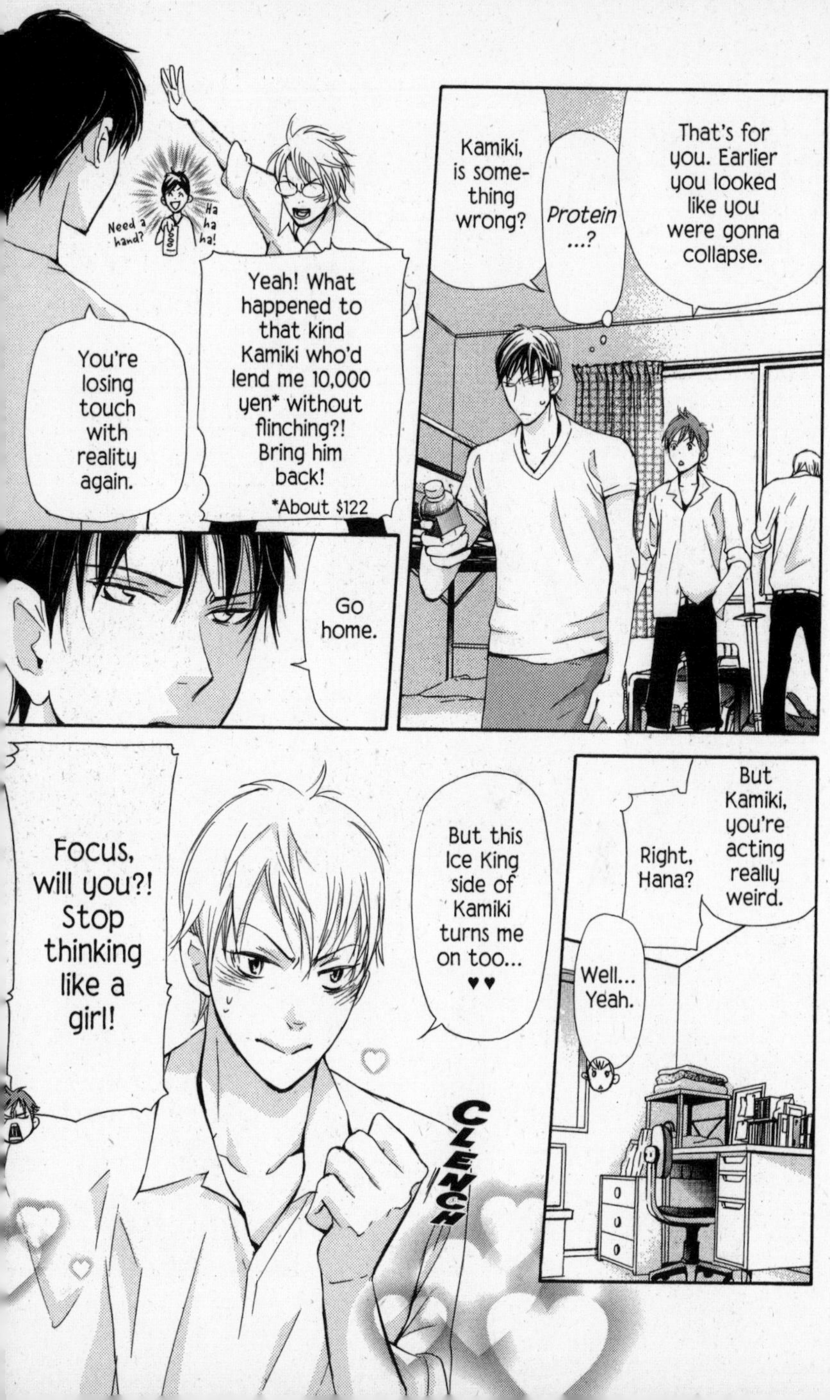
That's for you. Earlier you looked like you were gonna collapse.
Protein ...?
Kamiki, is some-thing wrong?
Need a hand?
Ha ha ha!
Yeah! What happened to that kind Kamiki who'd lend me 10,000 yen* without flinching?! Bring him back!
*About $122
You're losing touch with reality again.
Go home.
But Kamiki, you're acting really weird.
Right, Hana?
Well... Yeah.
But this Ice King side of Kamiki turns me on too... ♥♥
Focus, will you?! Stop thinking like a girl!
CLENCH

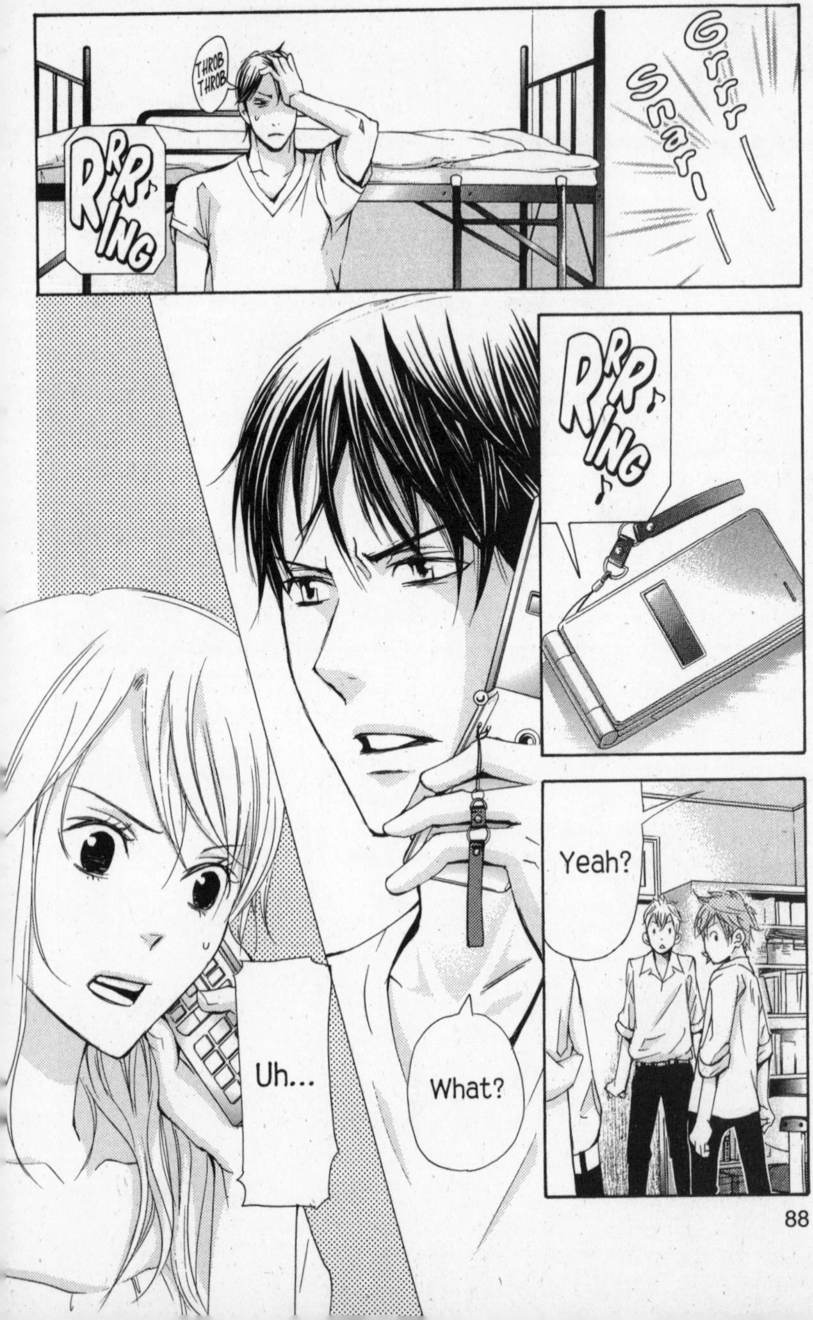
Grrr—
Snarl—
THROB THROB
RRRING
RRRING
Yeah?
What?
Uh...

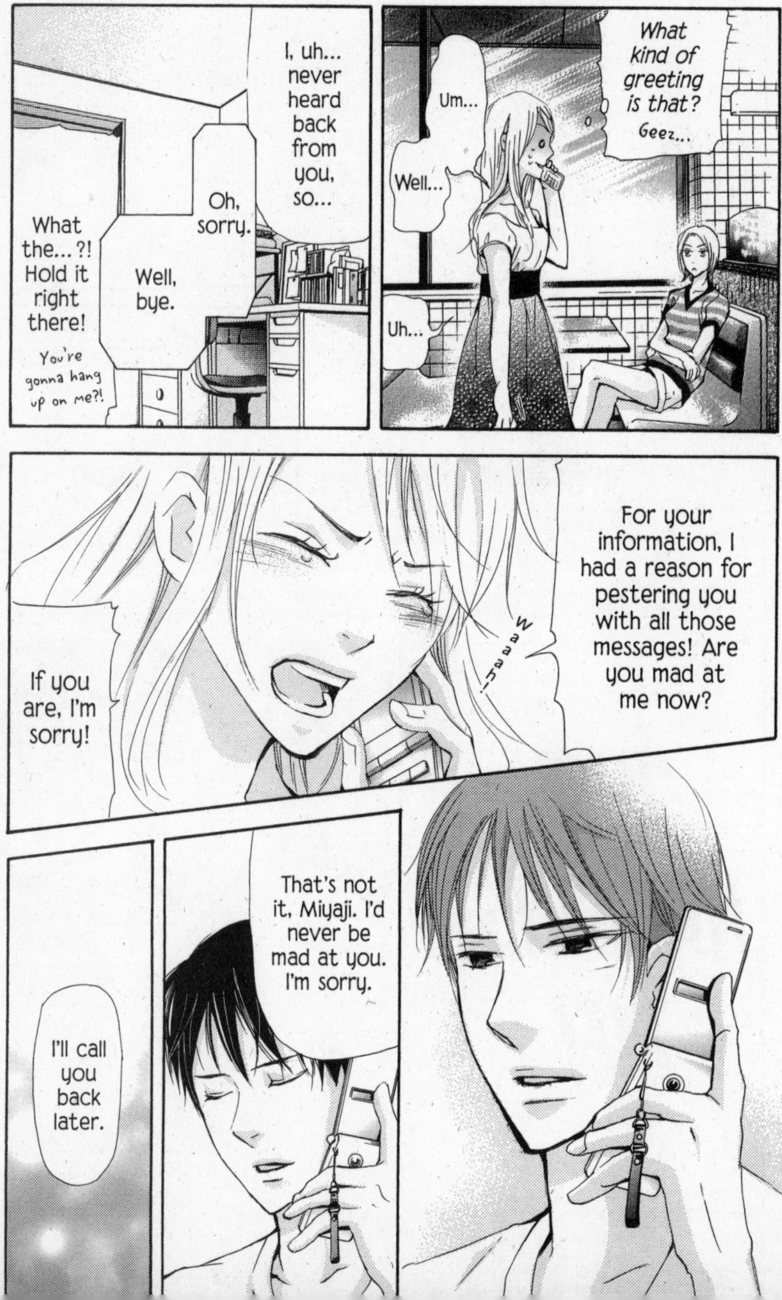
What kind of greeting is that? Geez...
Um...
Well...
Uh...
I, uh... never heard back from you, so...
Oh, sorry.
Well, bye.
What the...?! Hold it right there!
You're gonna hang up on me?!
For your information, I had a reason for pestering you with all those messages! Are you mad at me now?
Waaah!
If you are, I'm sorry!
That's not it, Miyaji. I'd never be mad at you. I'm sorry.
I'll call you back later.

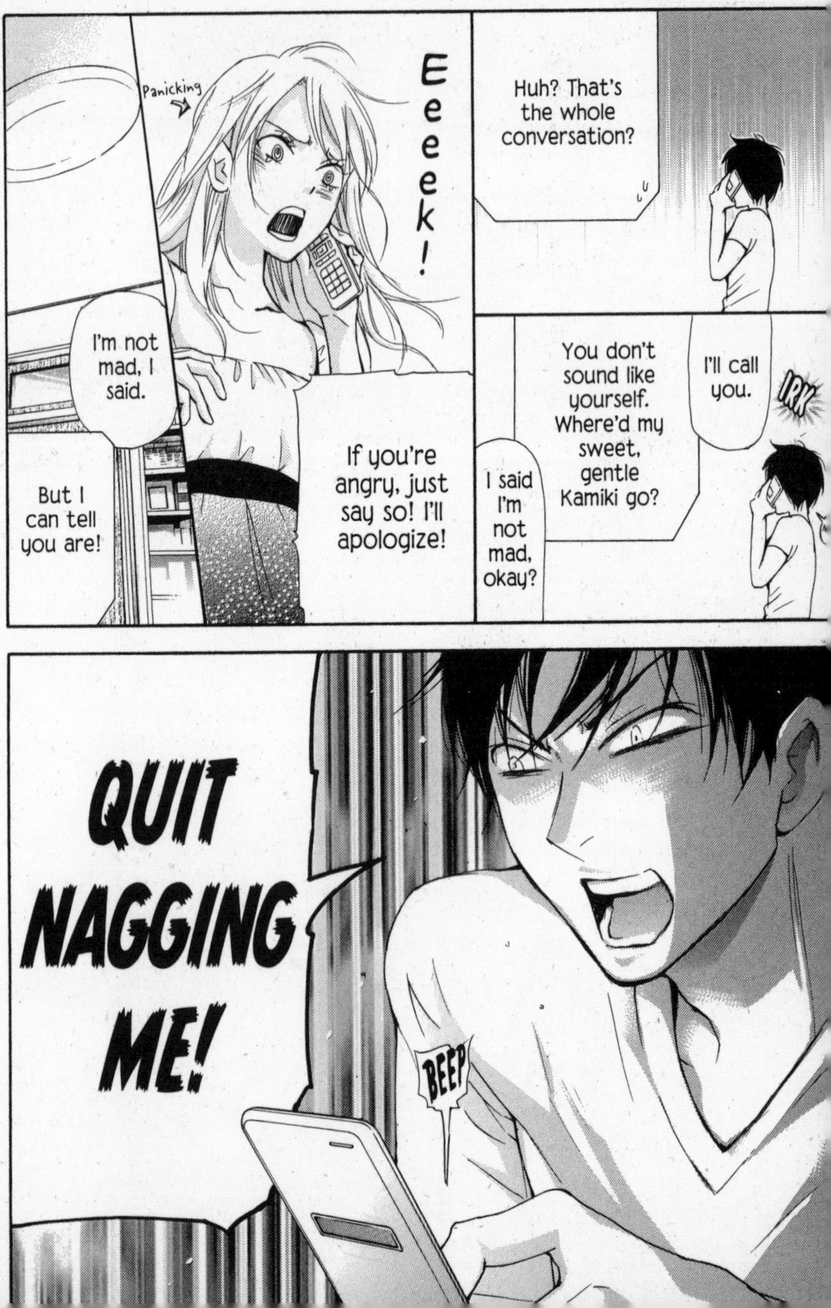

Huh? That's the whole conversation?
I'll call you.
IRK
You don't sound like yourself. Where'd my sweet, gentle Kamiki go?
I said I'm not mad, okay?
Eeeek!
Panicking
If you're angry, just say so! I'll apologize!
I'm not mad, I said.
But I can tell you are!
QUIT NAGGING ME!
BEEP

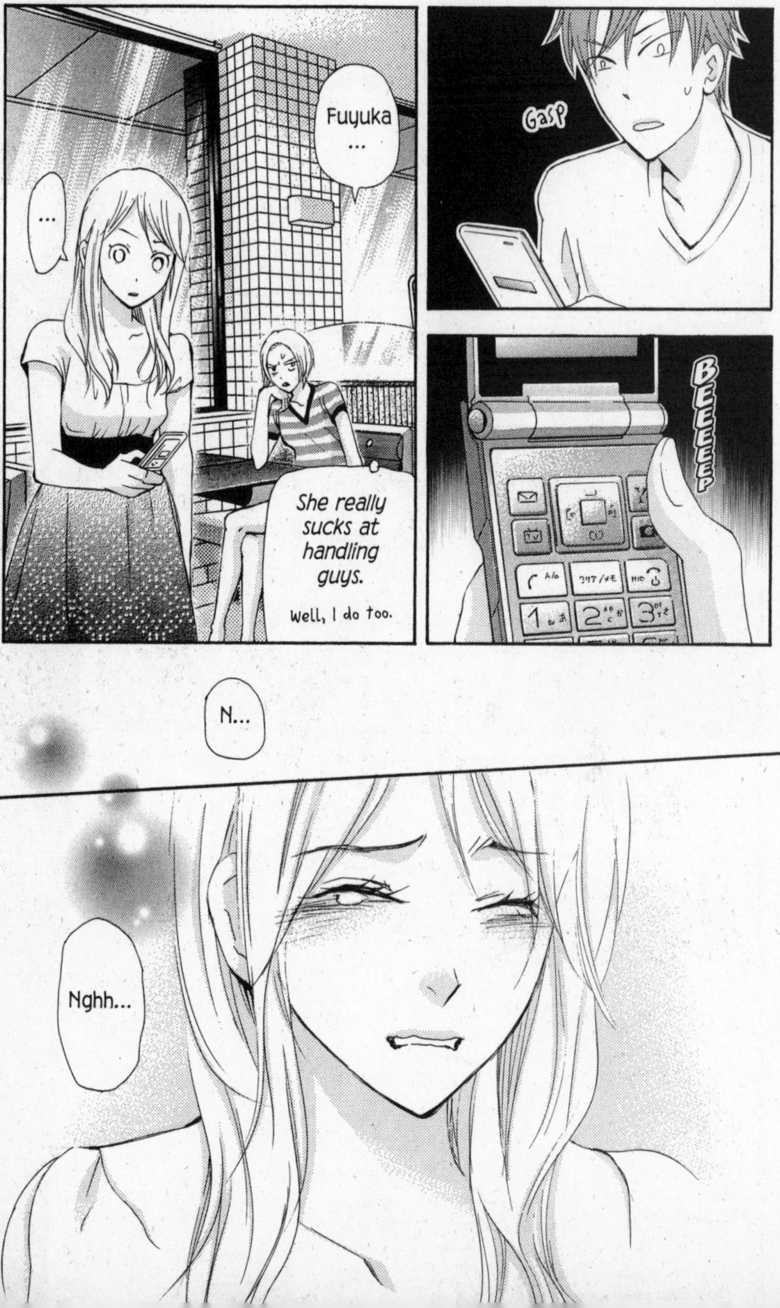
Gasp
BEEEEEP
Fuyuka ...
...
She really sucks at handling guys.
Well, I do too.
N...
Nghh...

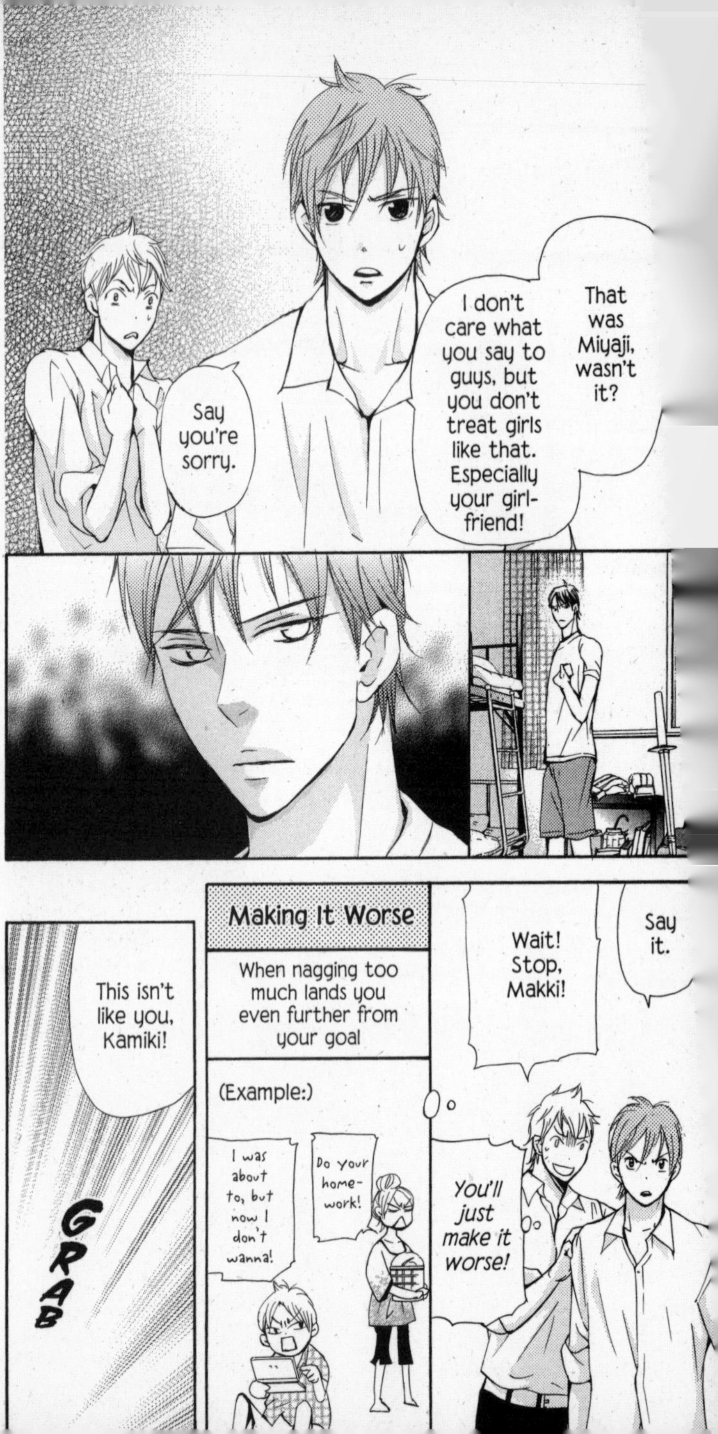
That was Miyaji, wasn't it?
I don't care what you say to guys, but you don't treat girls like that. Especially your girl-friend!
Say you're sorry.
Say it.
Wait! Stop, Makki!
You'll just make it worse!
Making It Worse
When nagging too much lands you even further from your goal
(Example:)
Do your home-work!
I was about to, but now I don't wanna!
This isn't like you, Kamiki!
GRAB

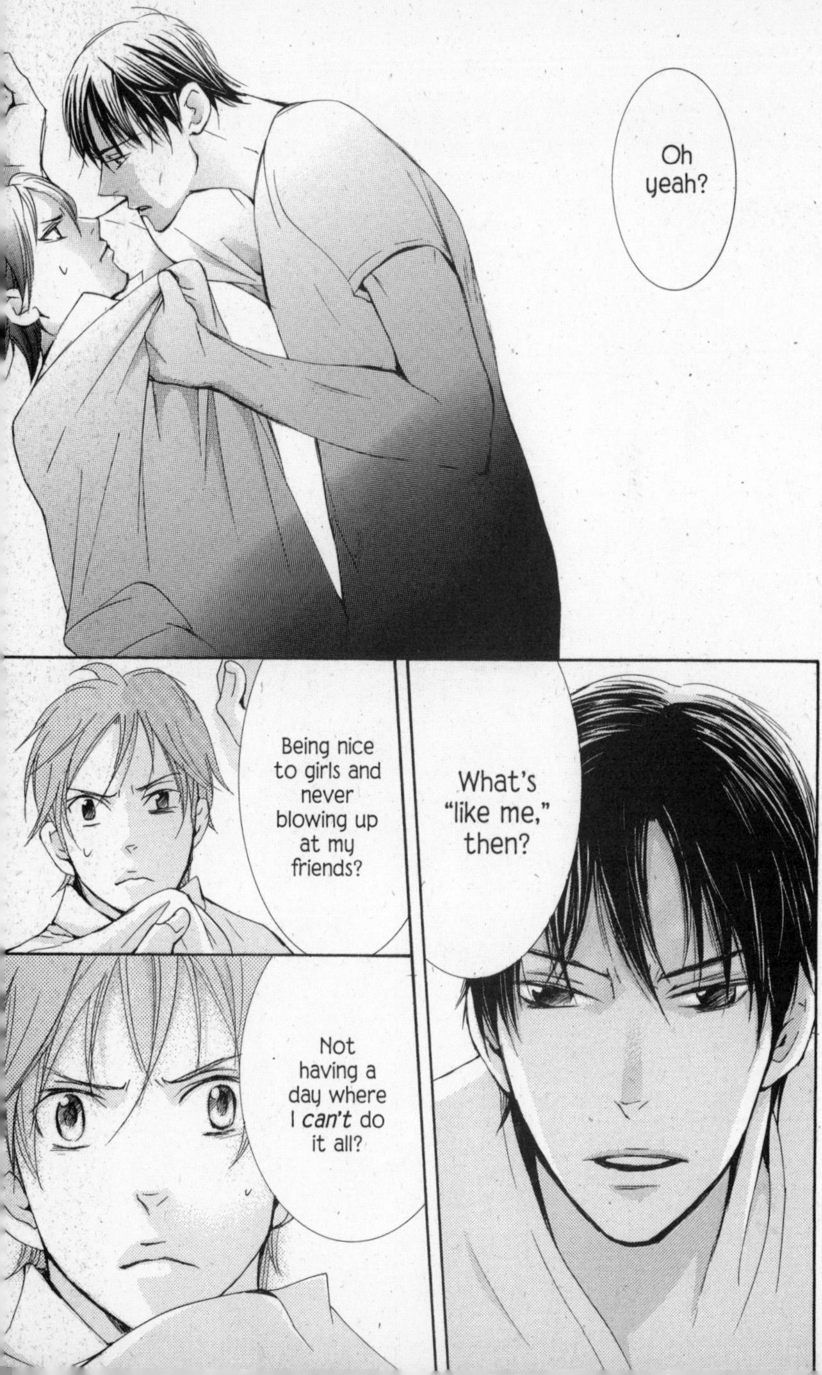
Oh yeah?
What's "like me," then?
Being nice to girls and never blowing up at my friends?
Not having a day where I *can't* do it all?

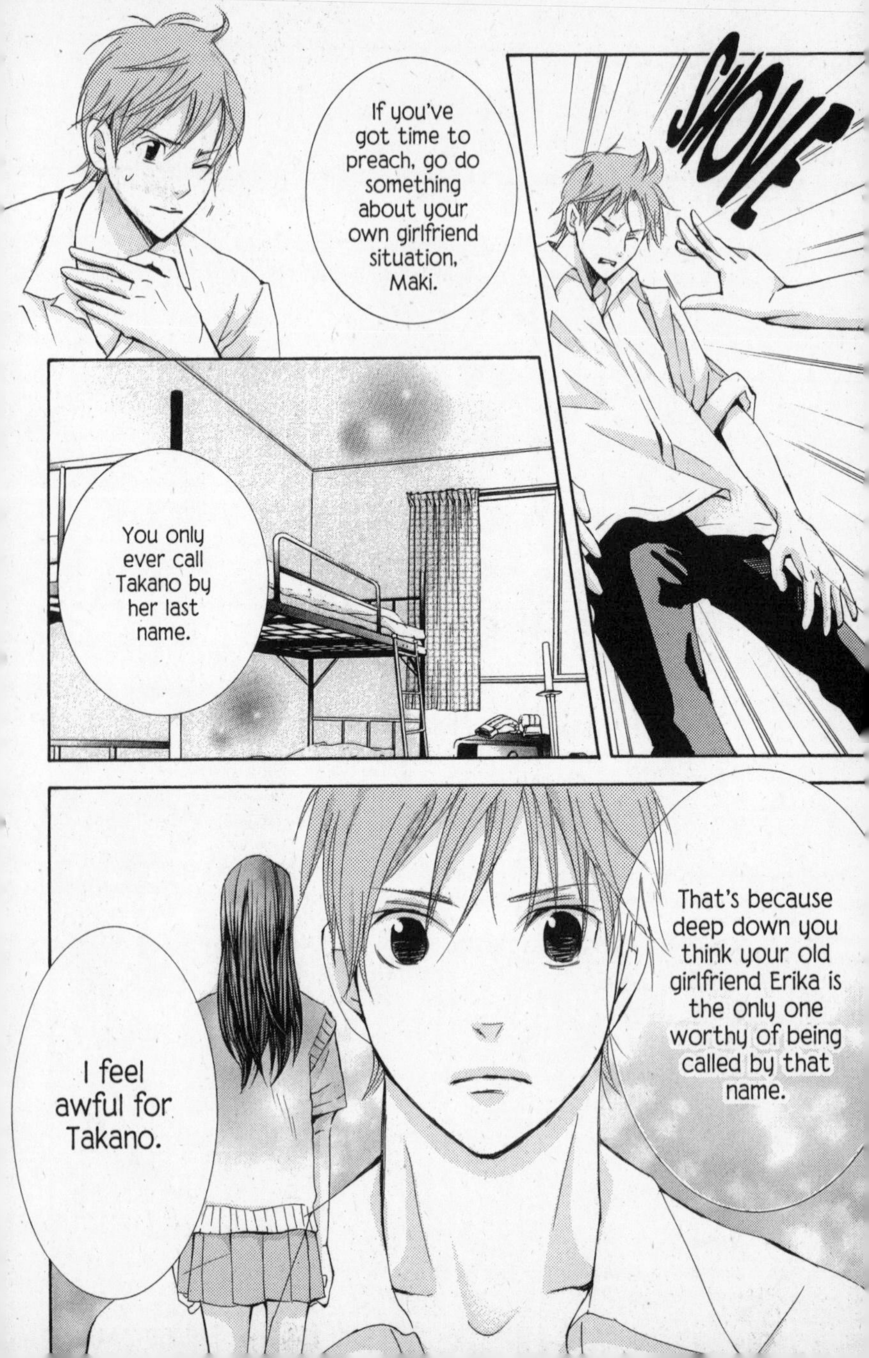
SHOVE!
If you've got time to preach, go do something about your own girlfriend situation, Maki.
You only ever call Takano by her last name.
That's because deep down you think your old girlfriend Erika is the only one worthy of being called by that name.
I feel awful for Takano.

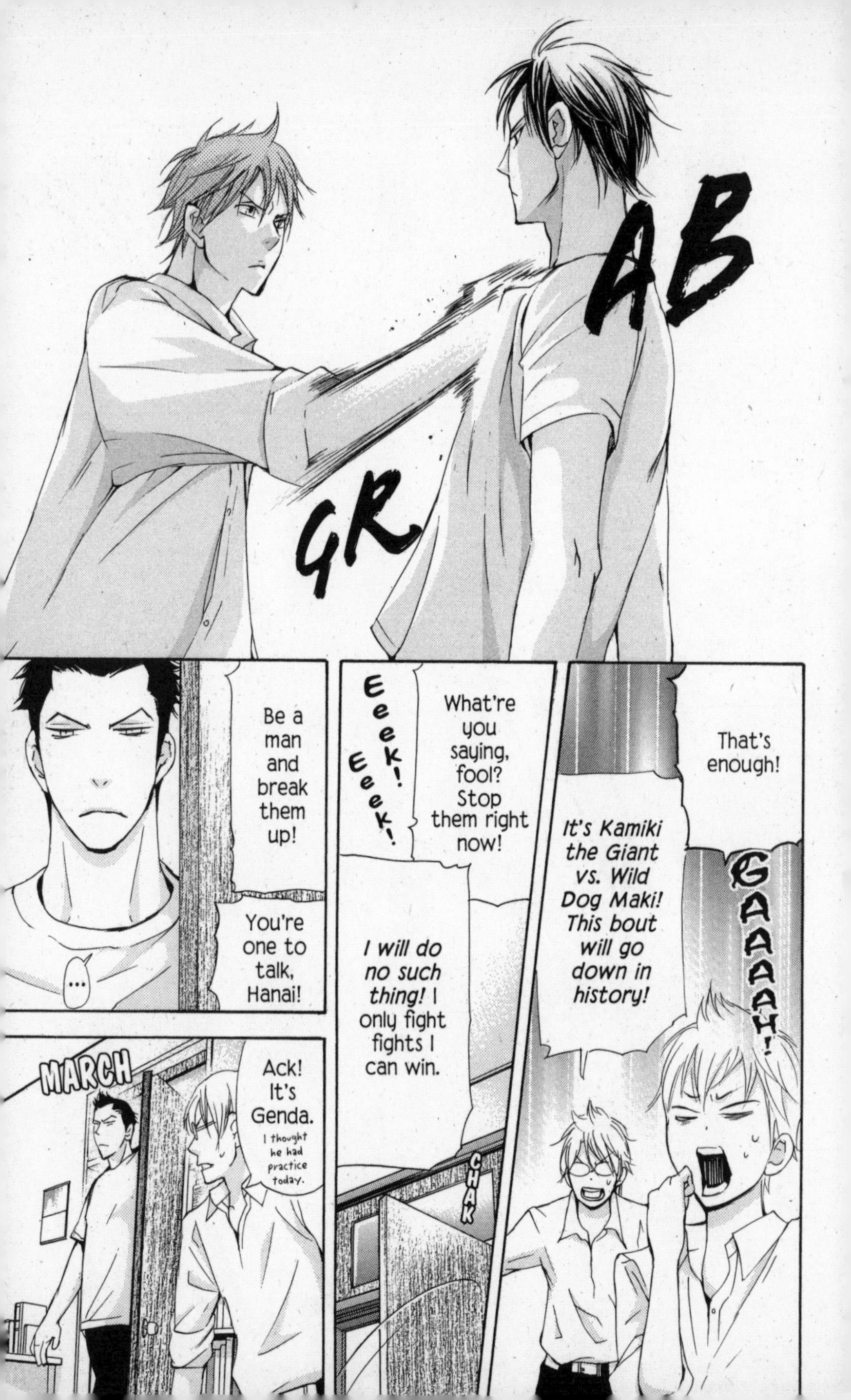

AB
GR
That's enough!
It's Kamiki the Giant vs. Wild Dog Maki! This bout will go down in history!
GAAAAAH!
What're you saying, fool? Stop them right now!
Eeeek! Eeeek!
I will do no such thing! I only fight fights I can win.
CHAK
Be a man and break them up!
You're one to talk, Hanai!
...
MARCH
Ack! It's Genda.
I thought he had practice today.

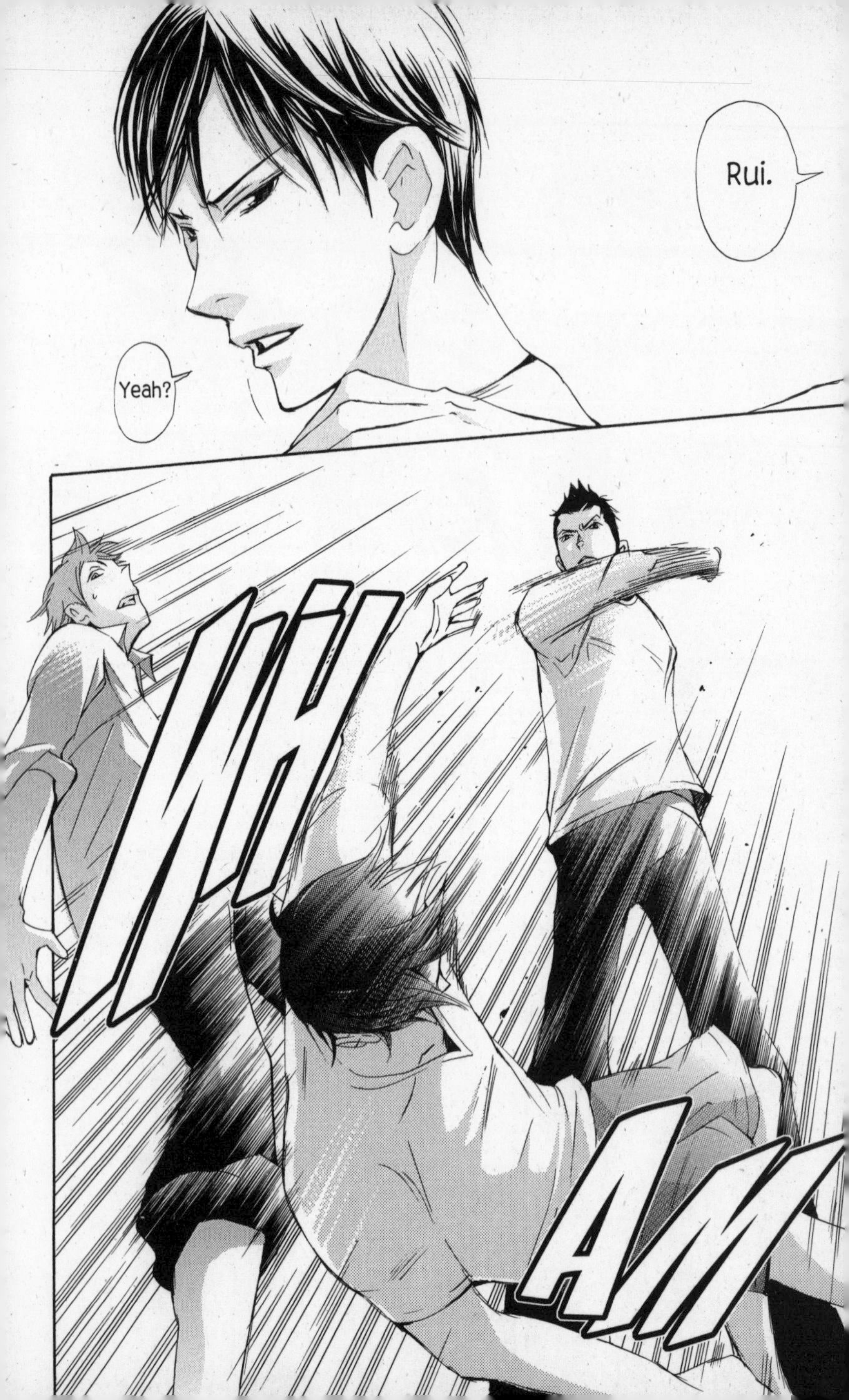
Rui.
Yeah?
WHAM

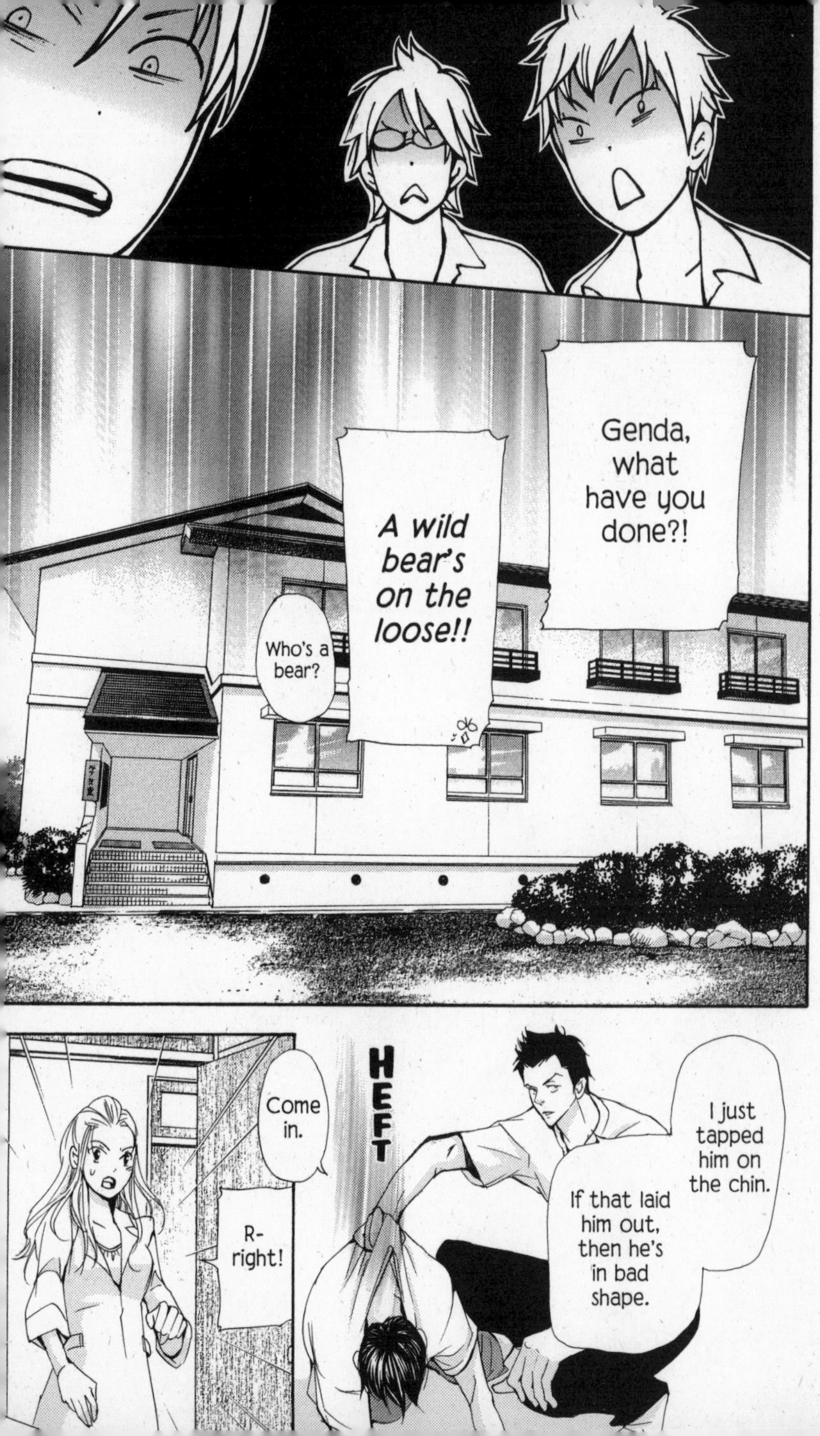
Genda, what have you done?!
A wild bear's on the loose!!
Who's a bear?
I just tapped him on the chin.
If that laid him out, then he's in bad shape.
HEFT
Come in.
R-right!

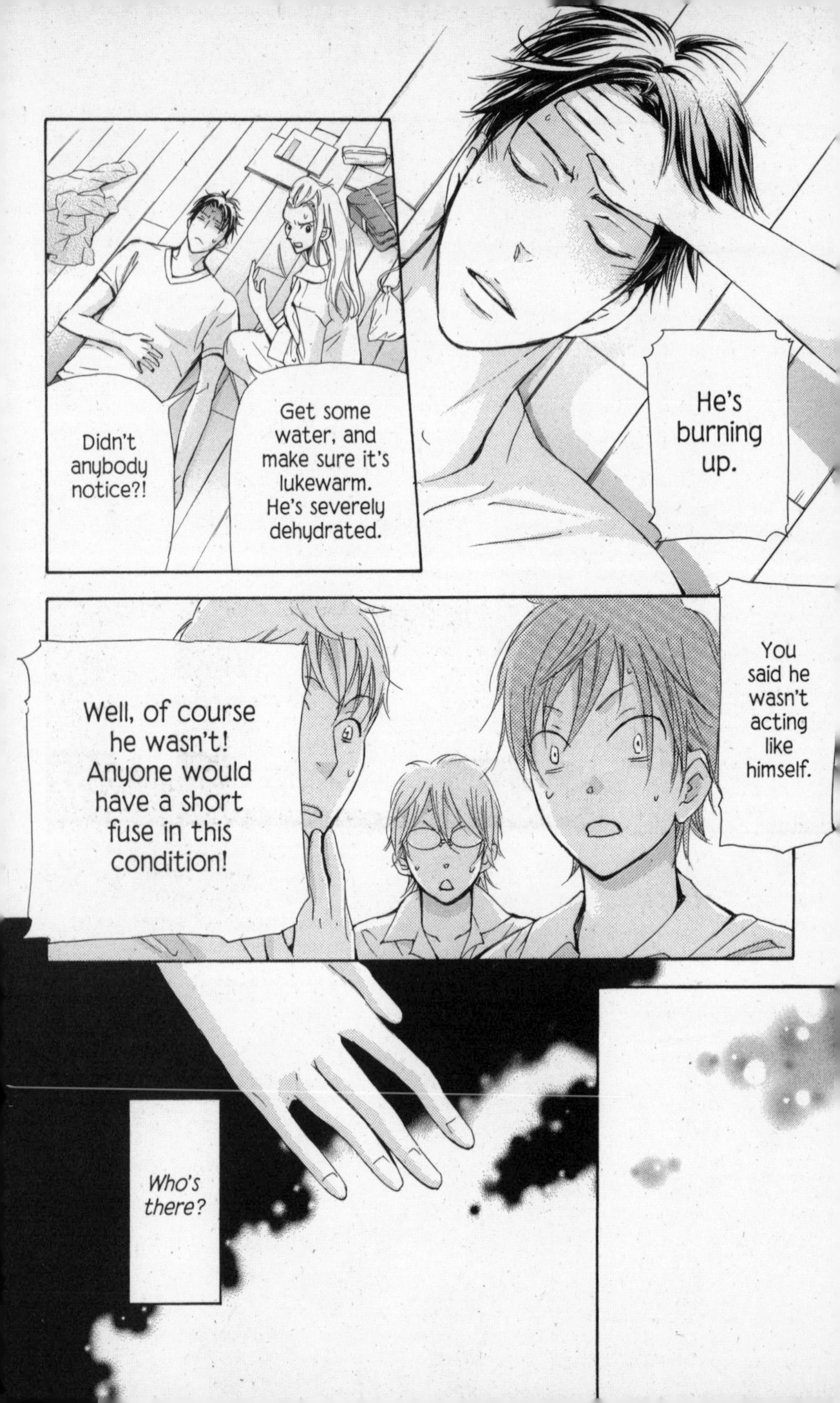
He's burning up.
Get some water, and make sure it's lukewarm. He's severely dehydrated.
Didn't anybody notice?!
You said he wasn't acting like himself.
Well, of course he wasn't! Anyone would have a short fuse in this condition!
Who's there?

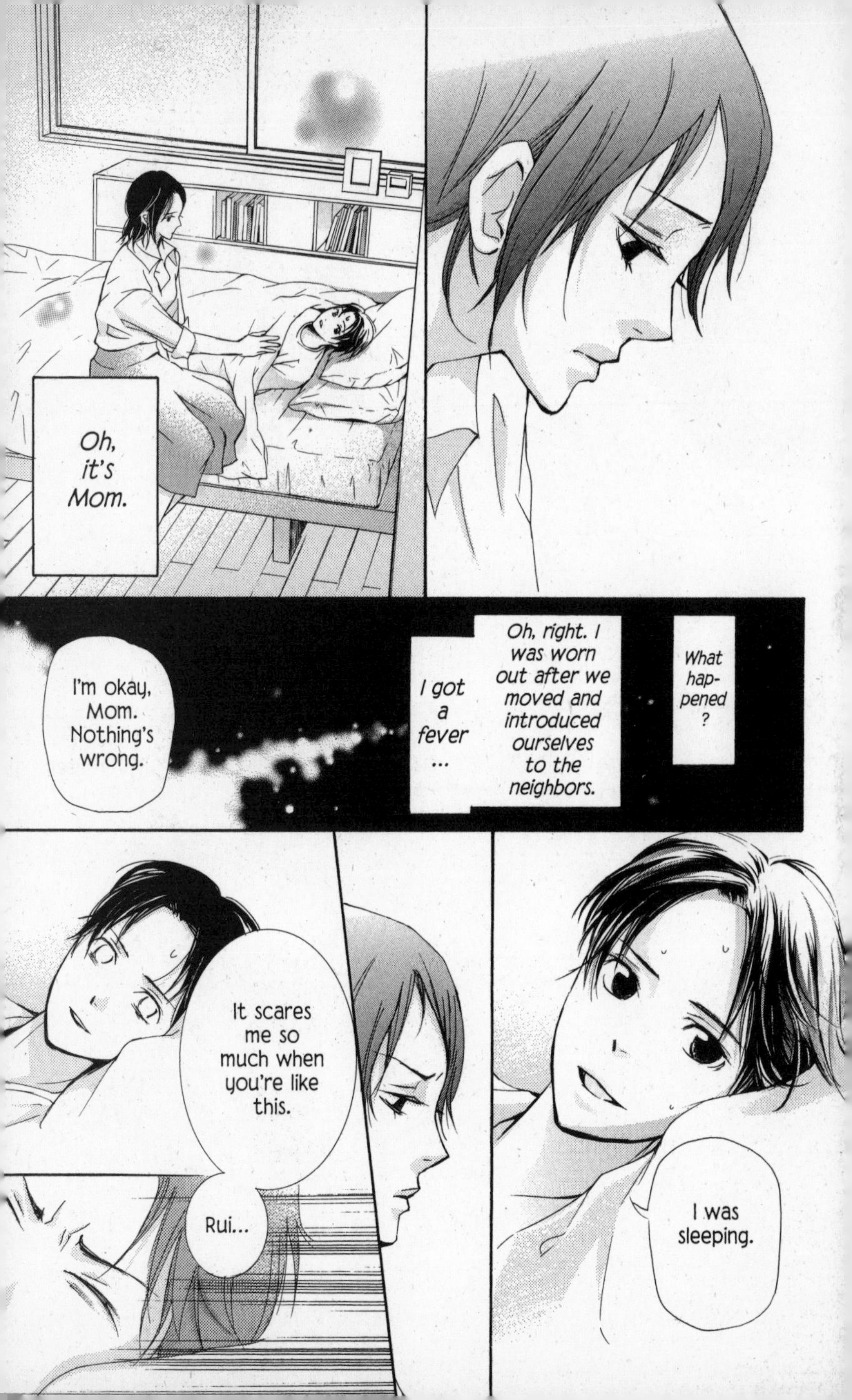
Oh, it's Mom.
What hap-pened?
Oh, right. I was worn out after we moved and introduced ourselves to the neighbors.
I got a fever...
I'm okay, Mom. Nothing's wrong.
I was sleeping.
It scares me so much when you're like this.
Rui...

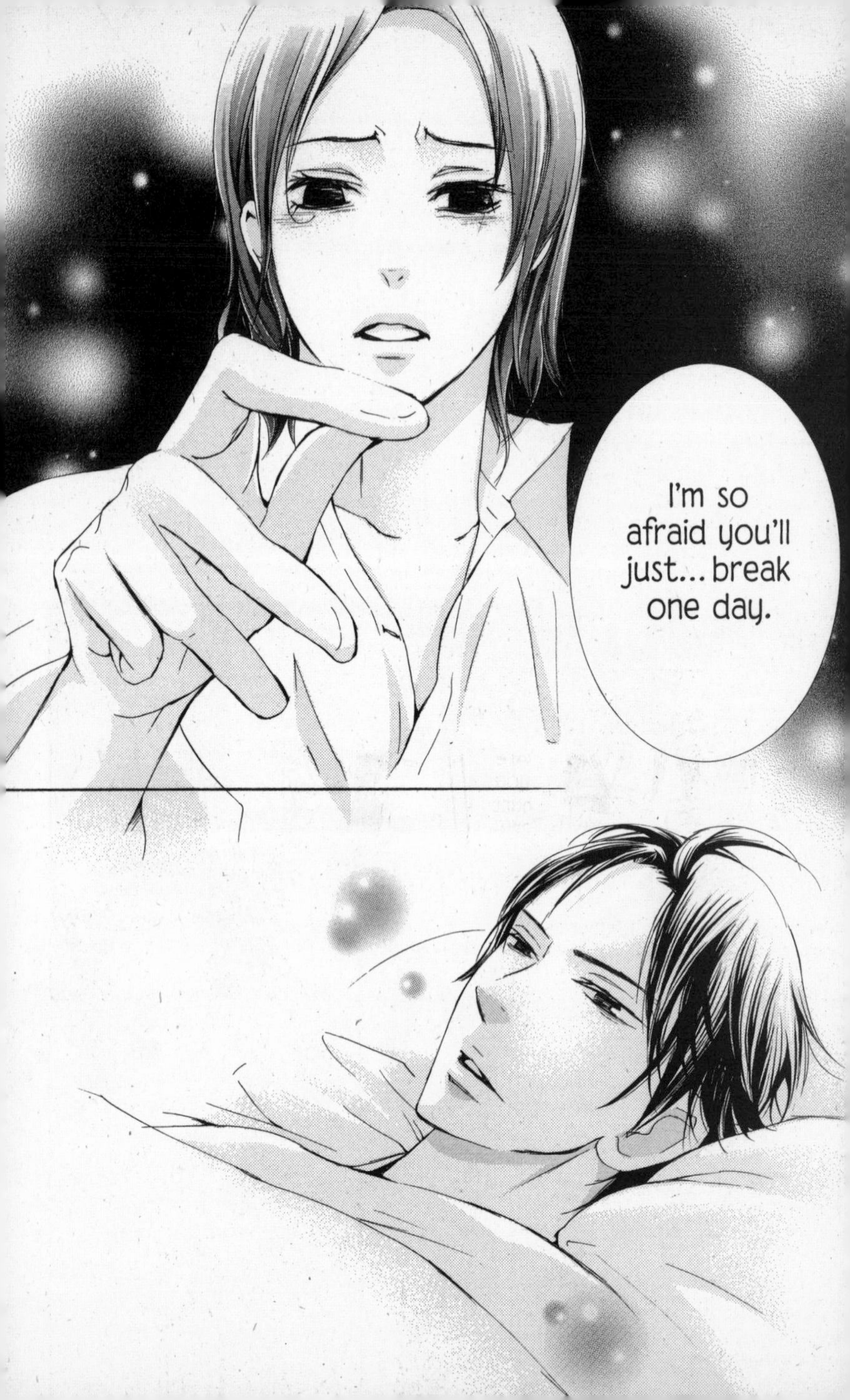
I'm so afraid you'll just... break one day.

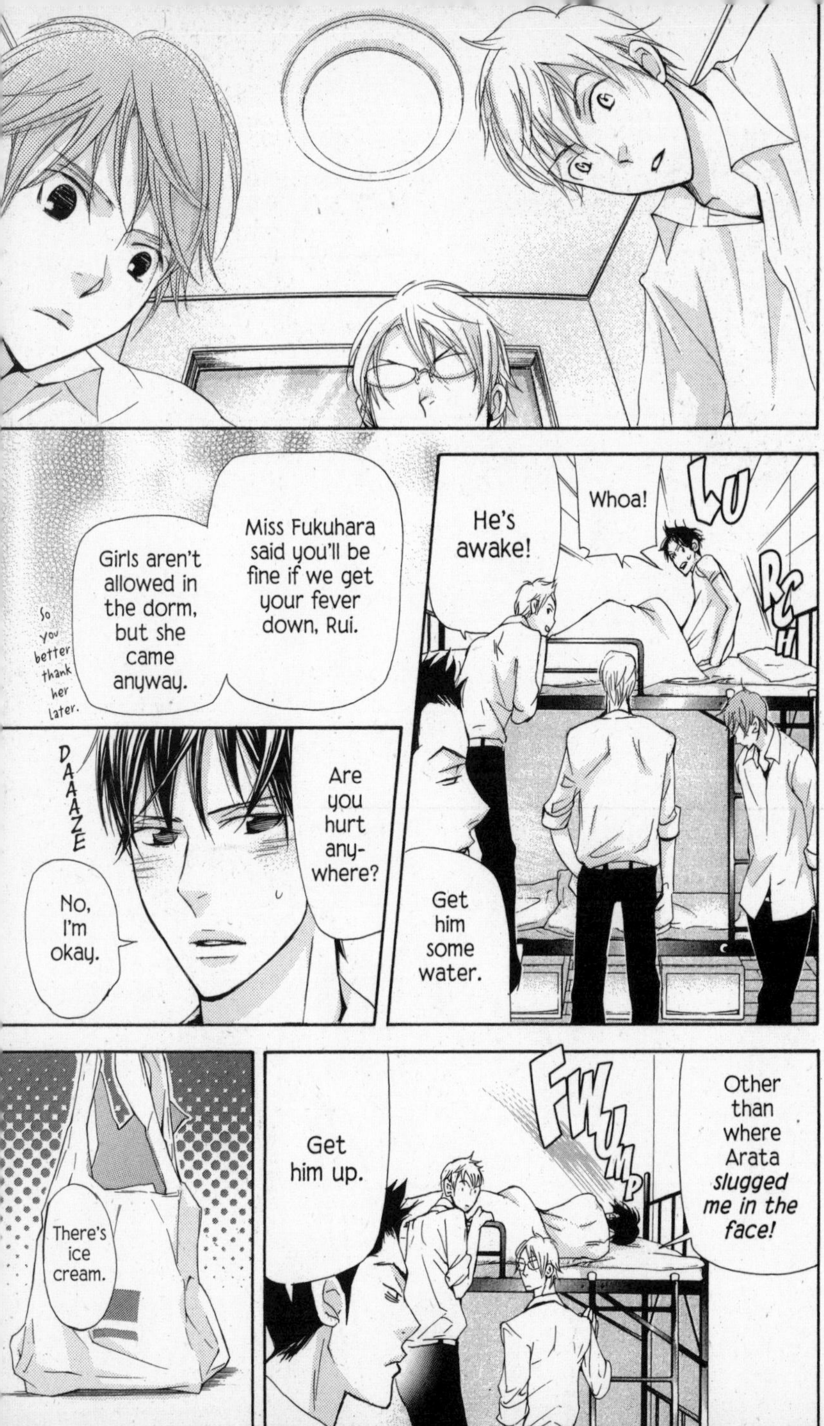
Whoa!
LURCH
He's awake!
Miss Fukuhara said you'll be fine if we get your fever down, Rui.
Girls aren't allowed in the dorm, but she came anyway.
So you better thank her later.
Get him some water.
Are you hurt anywhere?
DAAAZE
No, I'm okay.
Other than where Arata *slugged me in the face!*
FWUMP
Get him up.
There's ice cream.

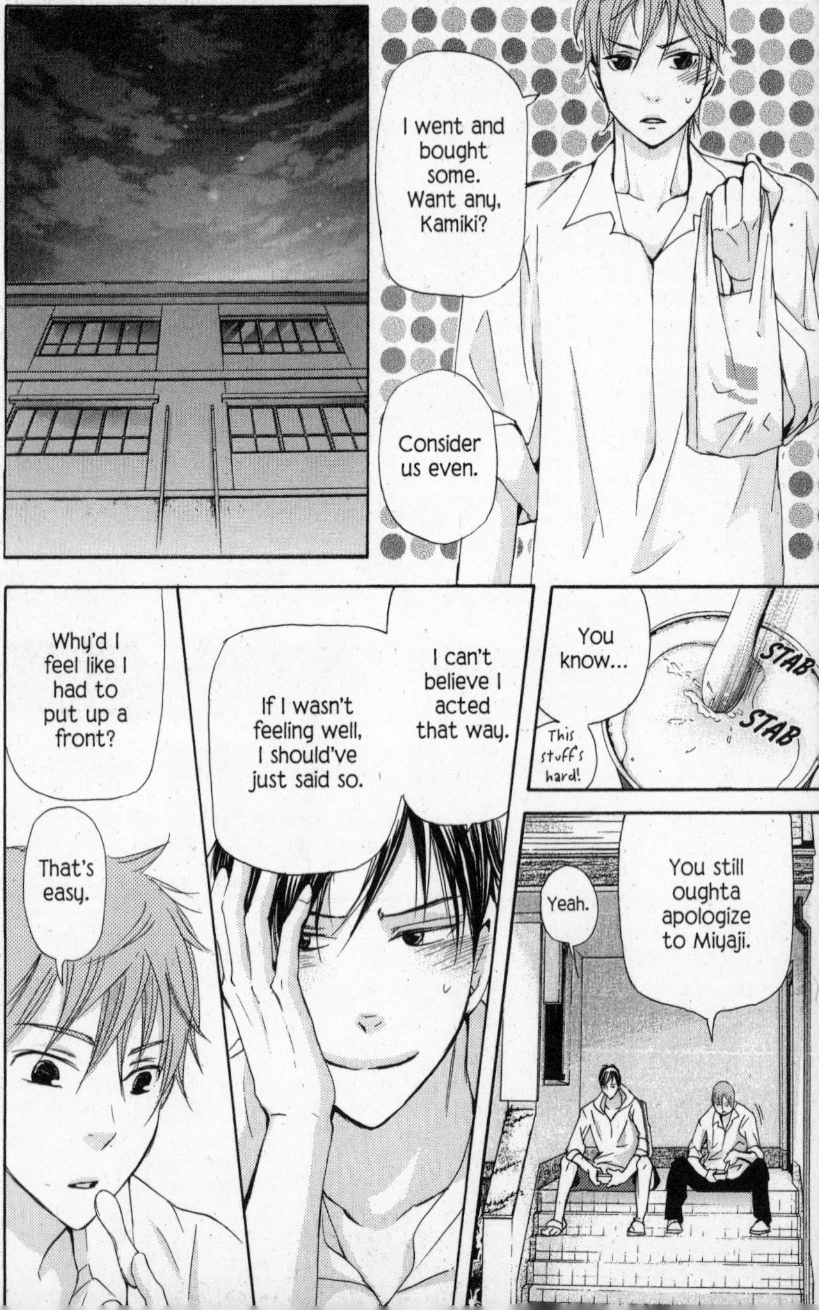
I went and bought some. Want any, Kamiki?
Consider us even.
You know...
STAB
STAB
This stuff's hard!
You still oughta apologize to Miyaji.
Yeah.
I can't believe I acted that way.
If I wasn't feeling well, I should've just said so.
Why'd I feel like I had to put up a front?
That's easy.

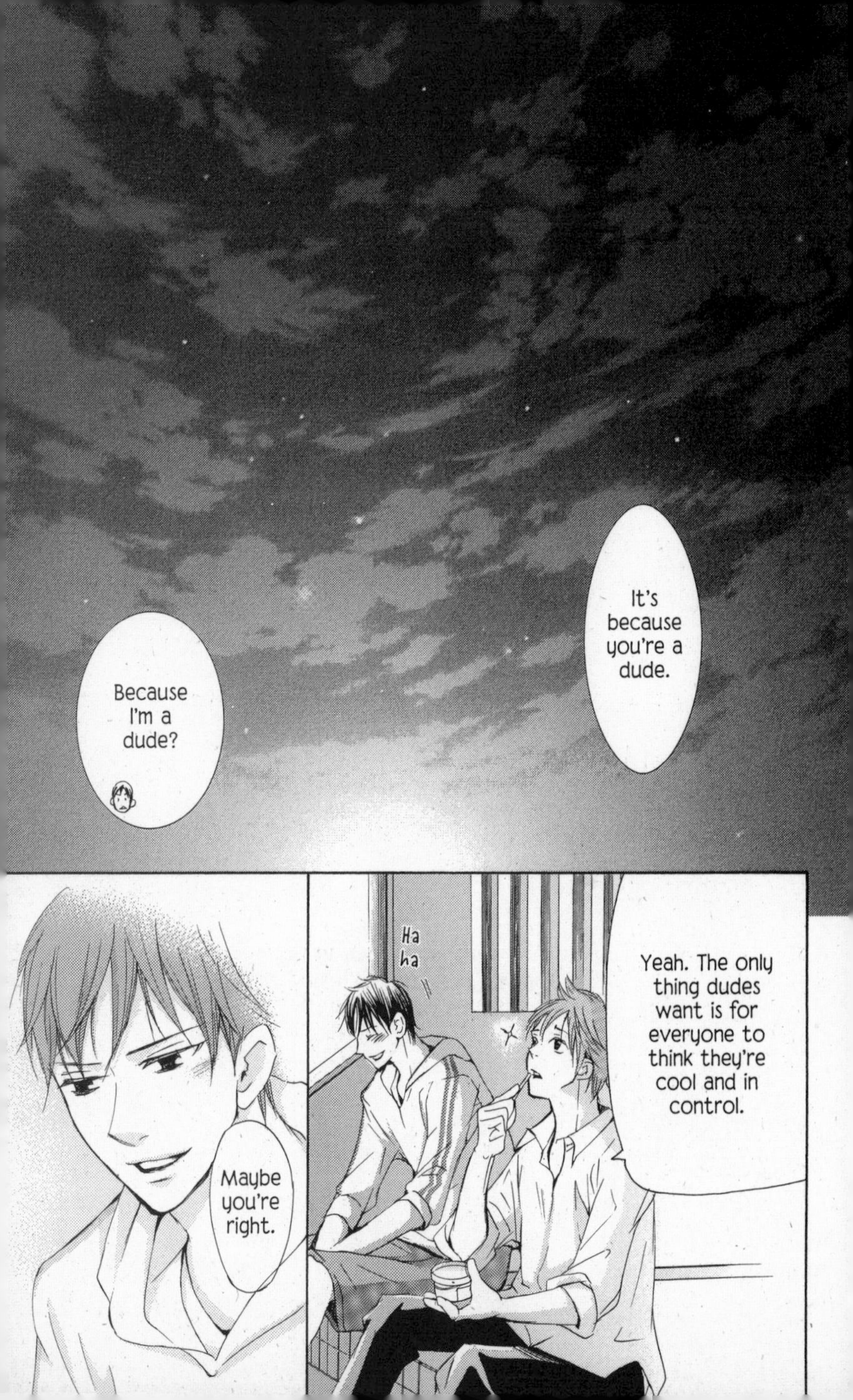
It's because you're a dude.
Because I'm a dude?
Yeah. The only thing dudes want is for everyone to think they're cool and in control.
Ha ha
Maybe you're right.

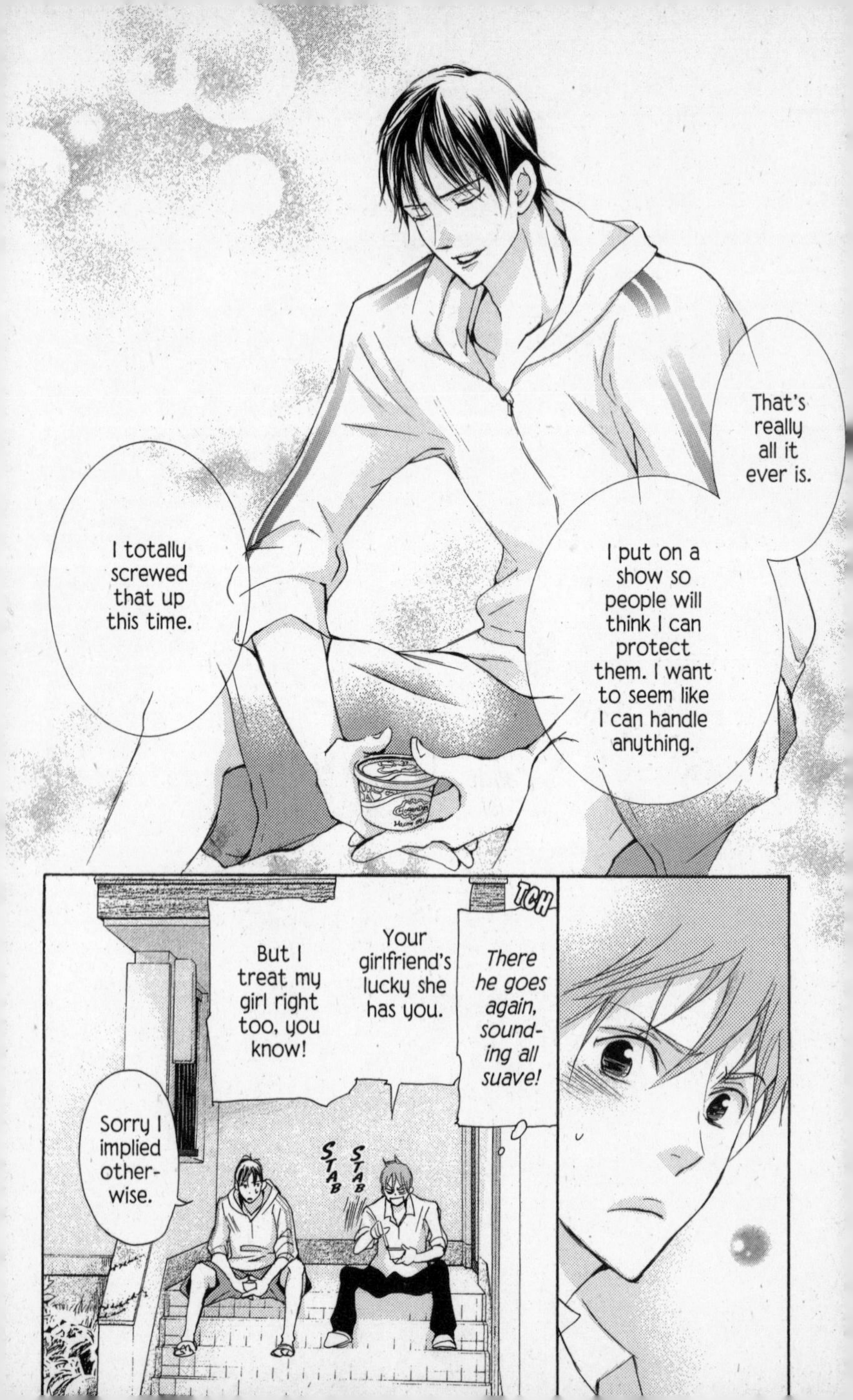
That's really all it ever is.
I put on a show so people will think I can protect them. I want to seem like I can handle anything.
I totally screwed that up this time.
Your girlfriend's lucky she has you.
There he goes again, sounding all suave!
TCH
But I treat my girl right too, you know!
STAB STAB
Sorry I implied otherwise.

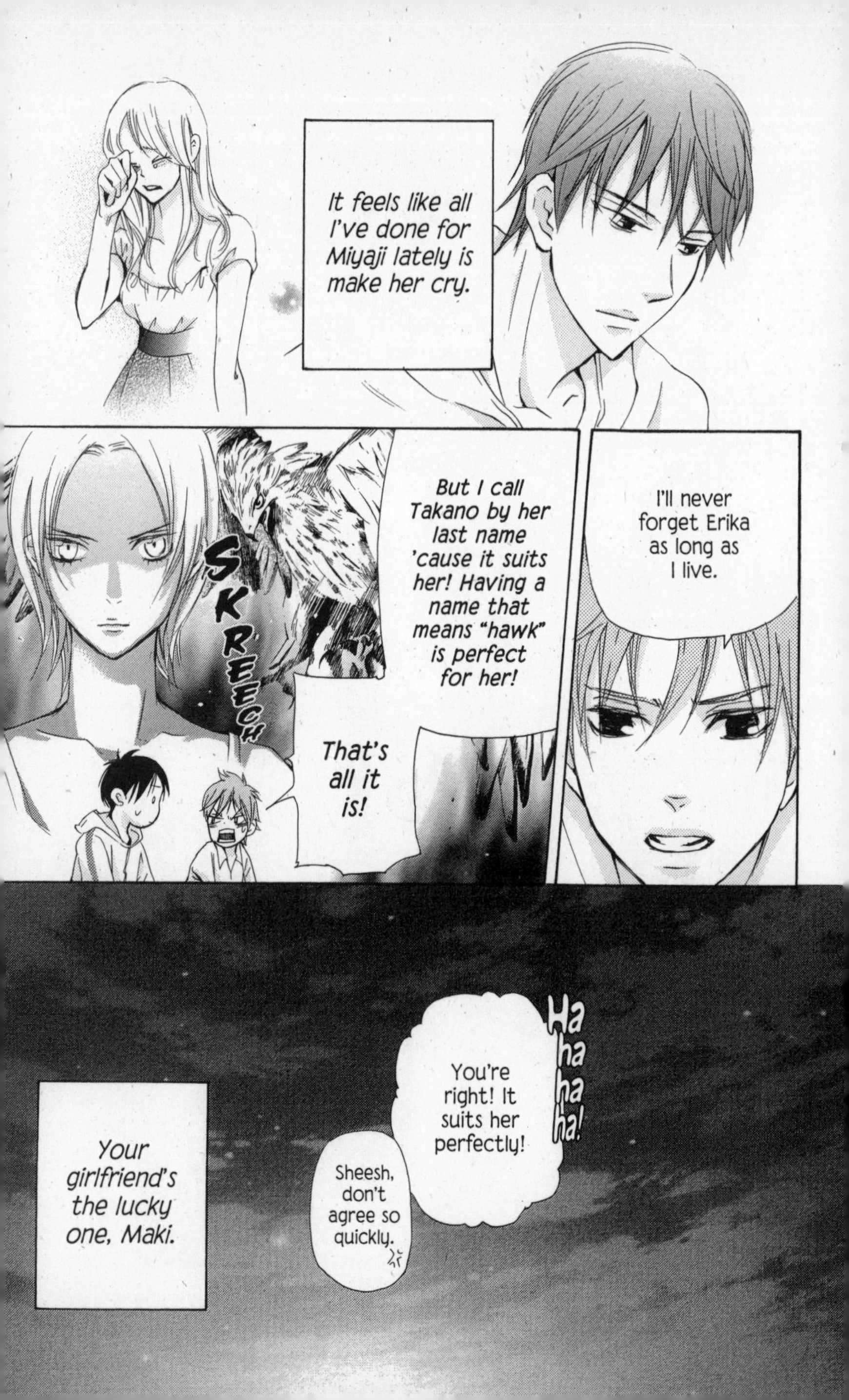
It feels like all I've done for Miyaji lately is make her cry.
I'll never forget Erika as long as I live.
But I call Takano by her last name 'cause it suits her! Having a name that means "hawk" is perfect for her!
SKREEECH
That's all it is!
Ha ha ha ha!
You're right! It suits her perfectly!
Sheesh, don't agree so quickly.
Your girlfriend's the lucky one, Maki.

Here's a bonus comic strip especially for readers of this manga volume! This is a scene that got cut in the magazine!

Operation: Cure Kamiki!

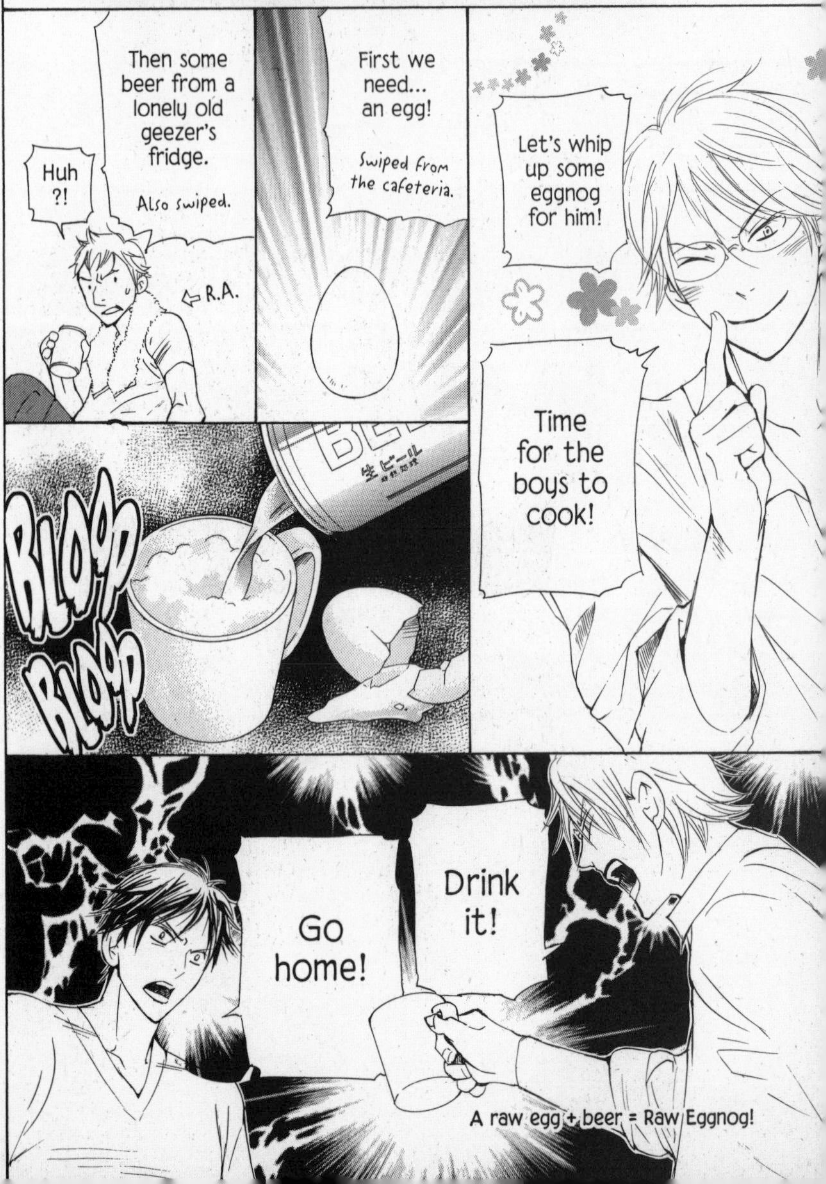
Let's whip up some eggnog for him!
Time for the boys to cook!
First we need... an egg!
Swiped from the cafeteria.
Then some beer from a lonely old geezer's fridge.
Also swiped.
Huh ?!
R.A.
BLOOP BLOOP
Drink it!
Go home!
A raw egg + beer = Raw Eggnog!

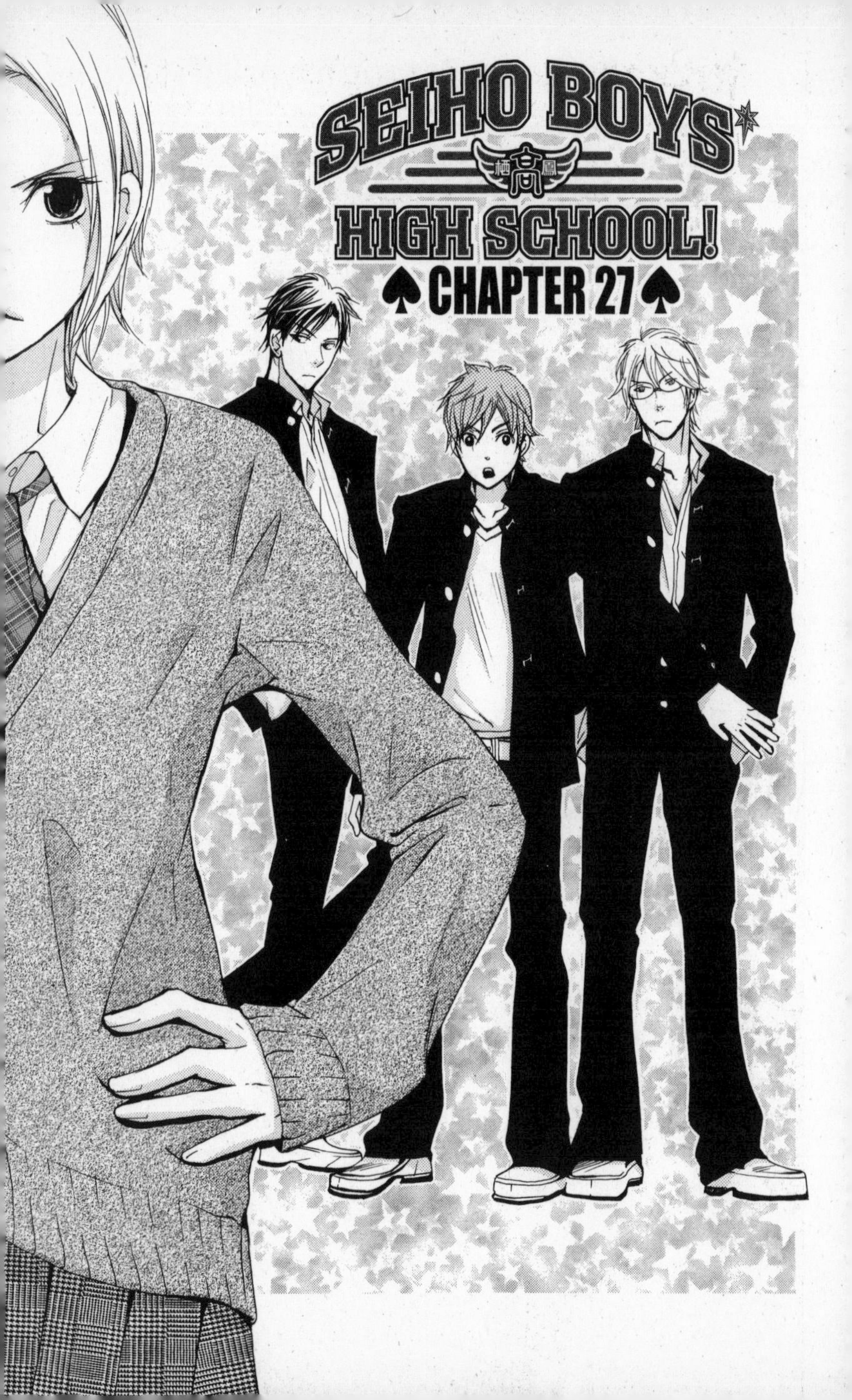
SEIHO BOYS' HIGH SCHOOL!
CHAPTER 27

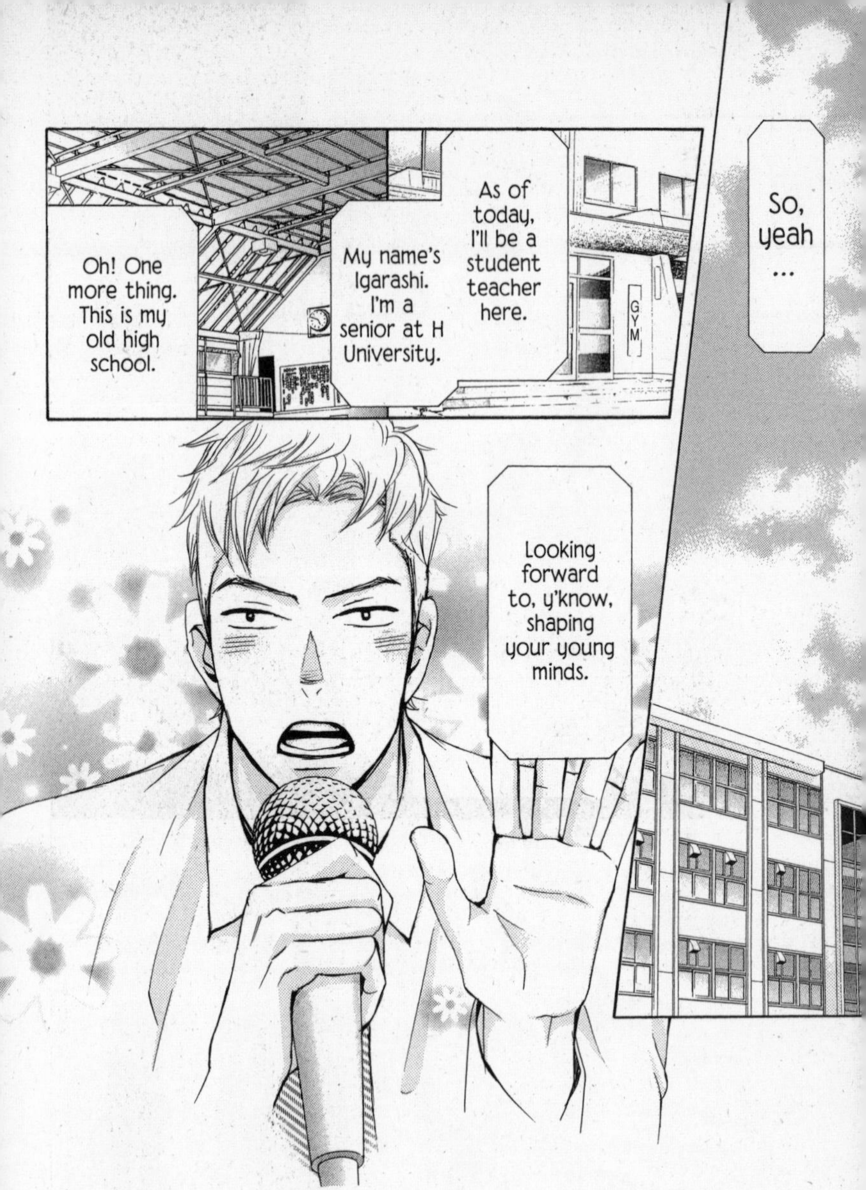
So, yeah ...
GYM
As of today, I'll be a student teacher here.
My name's Igarashi. I'm a senior at H University.
Oh! One more thing. This is my old high school.
Looking forward to, y'know, shaping your young minds.

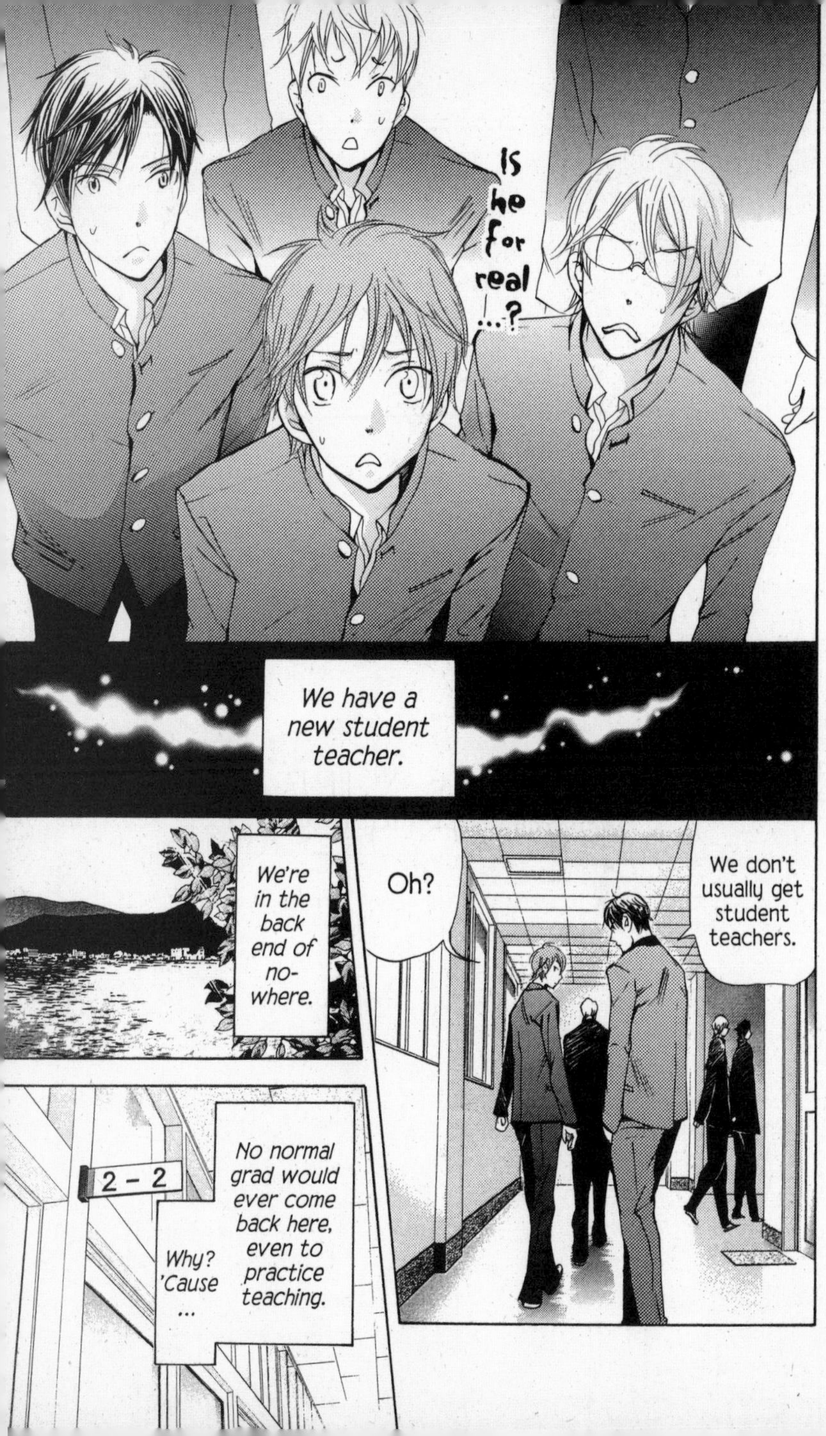

Is he for real...?
We have a new student teacher.
We don't usually get student teachers.
Oh?
We're in the back end of nowhere.
No normal grad would ever come back here, even to practice teaching.
Why? 'Cause ...
2 – 2

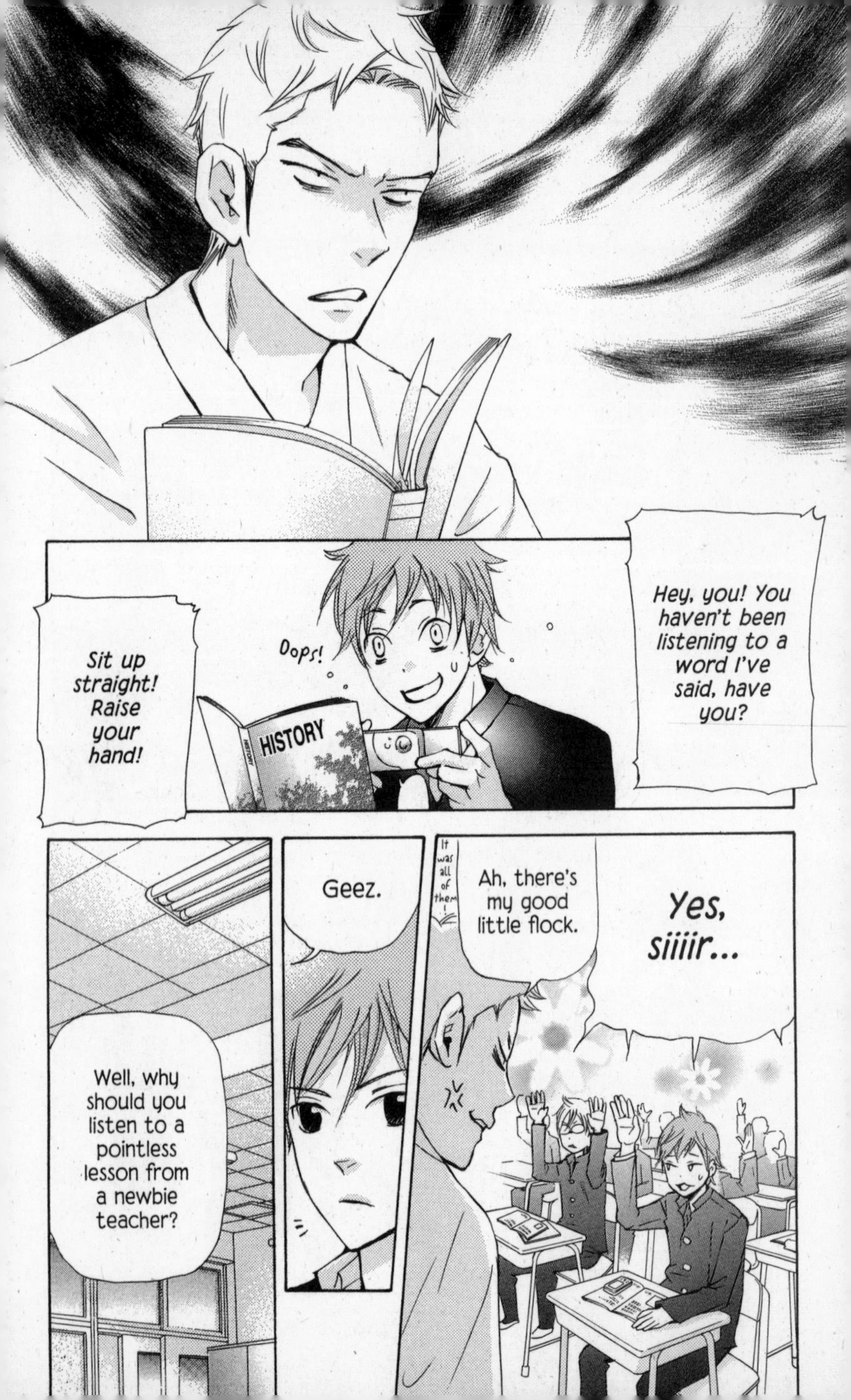
Hey, you! You haven't been listening to a word I've said, have you?
Oops!
Sit up straight! Raise your hand!
Yes, siiiir...
Ah, there's my good little flock.
It was all of them!
Geez.
Well, why should you listen to a pointless lesson from a newbie teacher?

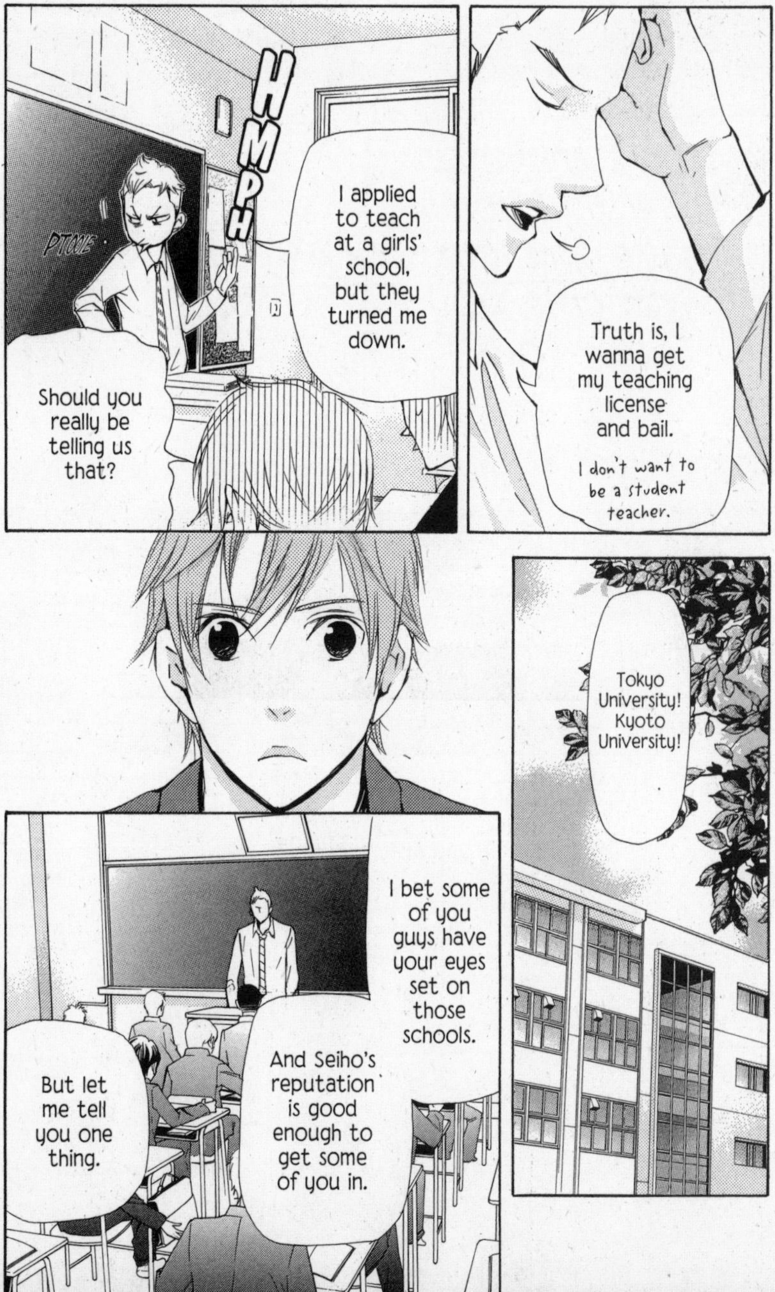
Truth is, I wanna get my teaching license and bail.
I don't want to be a student teacher.
HMPH
I applied to teach at a girls' school, but they turned me down.
PTOOIE
Should you really be telling us that?
Tokyo University! Kyoto University!
I bet some of you guys have your eyes set on those schools.
And Seiho's reputation is good enough to get some of you in.
But let me tell you one thing.

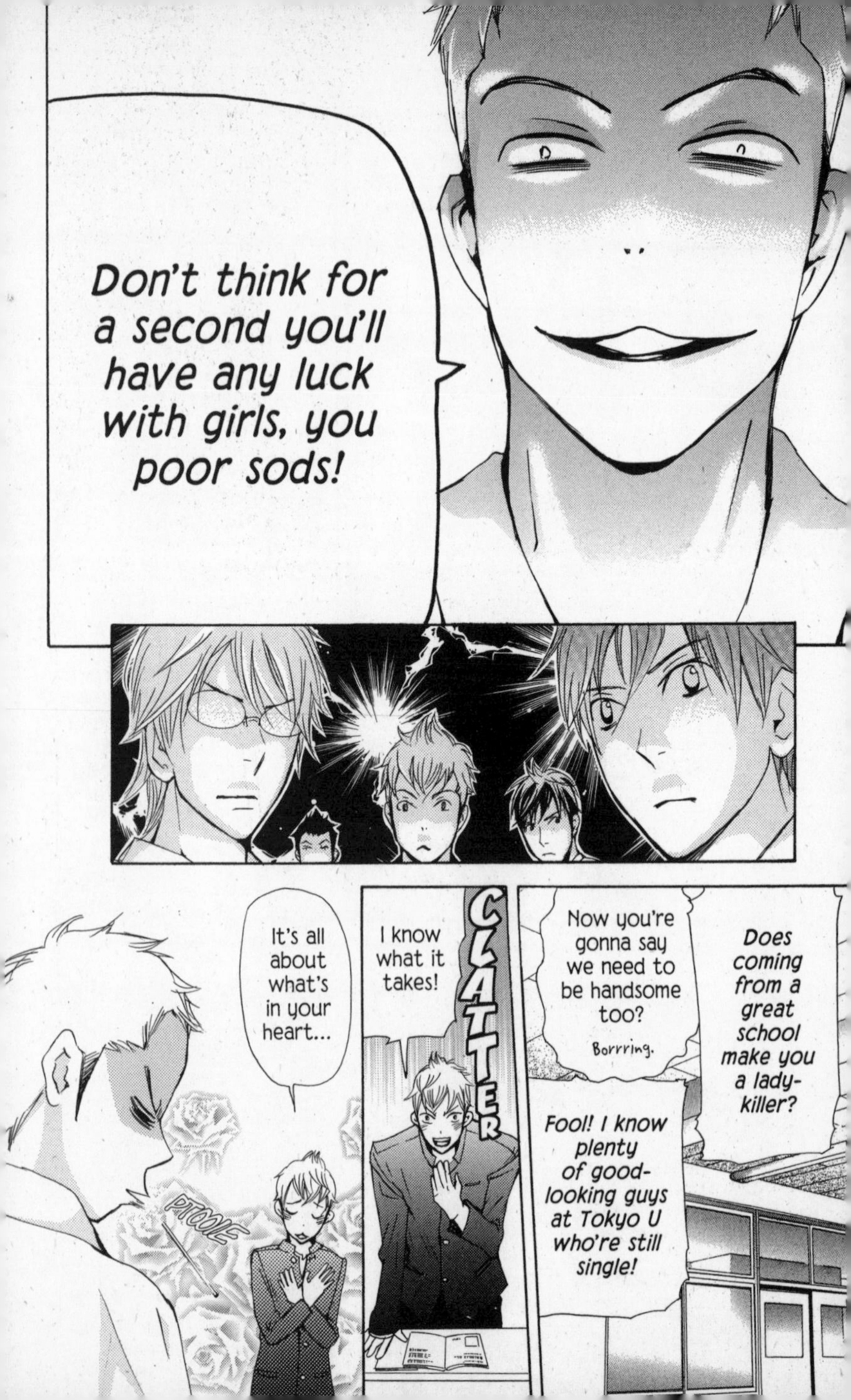
Don't think for a second you'll have any luck with girls, you poor sods!
Does coming from a great school make you a lady-killer?
Now you're gonna say we need to be handsome too?
Borrring.
Fool! I know plenty of good-looking guys at Tokyo U who're still single!
CLATTER
I know what it takes!
It's all about what's in your heart...
PTOOIE

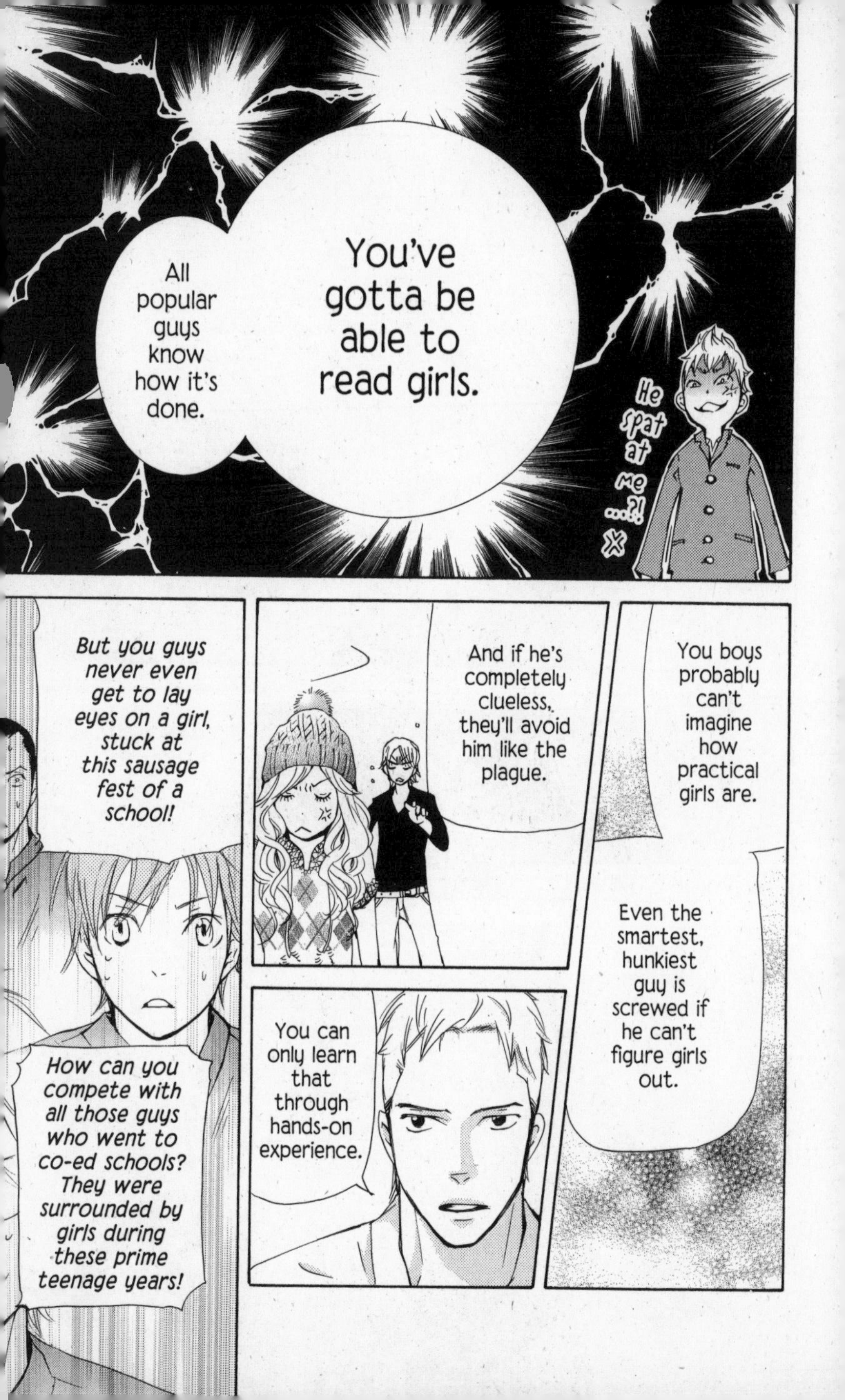
You've gotta be able to read girls.
All popular guys know how it's done.
He spat at me...?!
You boys probably can't imagine how practical girls are.
Even the smartest, hunkiest guy is screwed if he can't figure girls out.
And if he's completely clueless, they'll avoid him like the plague.
You can only learn that through hands-on experience.
But you guys never even get to lay eyes on a girl, stuck at this sausage fest of a school!
How can you compete with all those guys who went to co-ed schools? They were surrounded by girls during these prime teenage years!

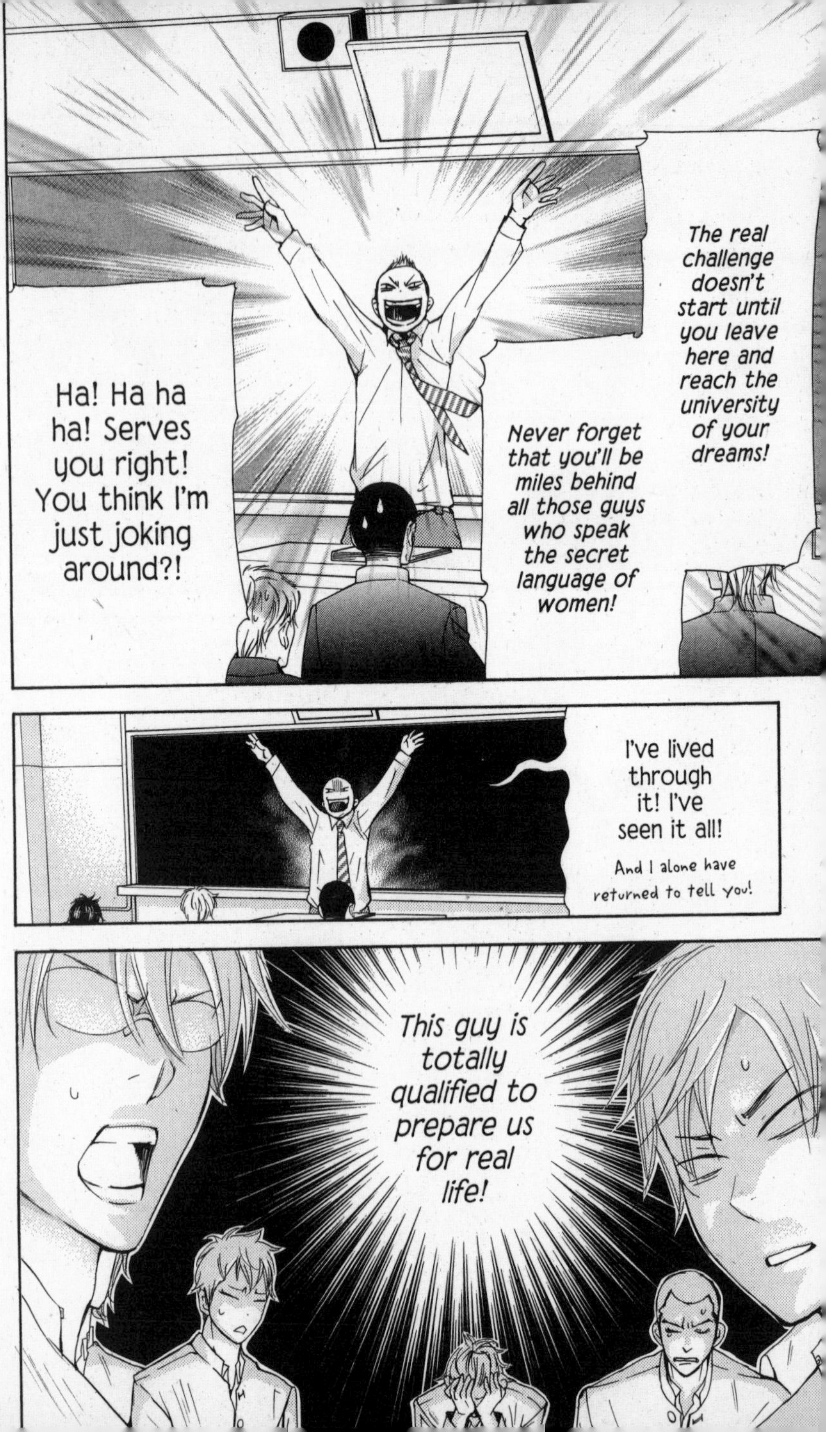
The real challenge doesn't start until you leave here and reach the university of your dreams!
Never forget that you'll be miles behind all those guys who speak the secret language of women!
Ha! Ha ha ha! Serves you right! You think I'm just joking around?!
I've lived through it! I've seen it all!
And I alone have returned to tell you!
This guy is totally qualified to prepare us for real life!

Bonus Corner

Little Things ④

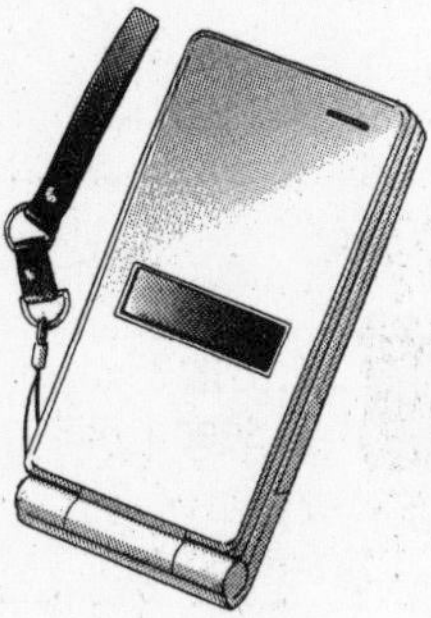

Kamiki's Cell Phone

I modeled this after my current cell phone.
I don't usually have my phone on me.
It might be rare in this day and age, but I don't like cell phones.

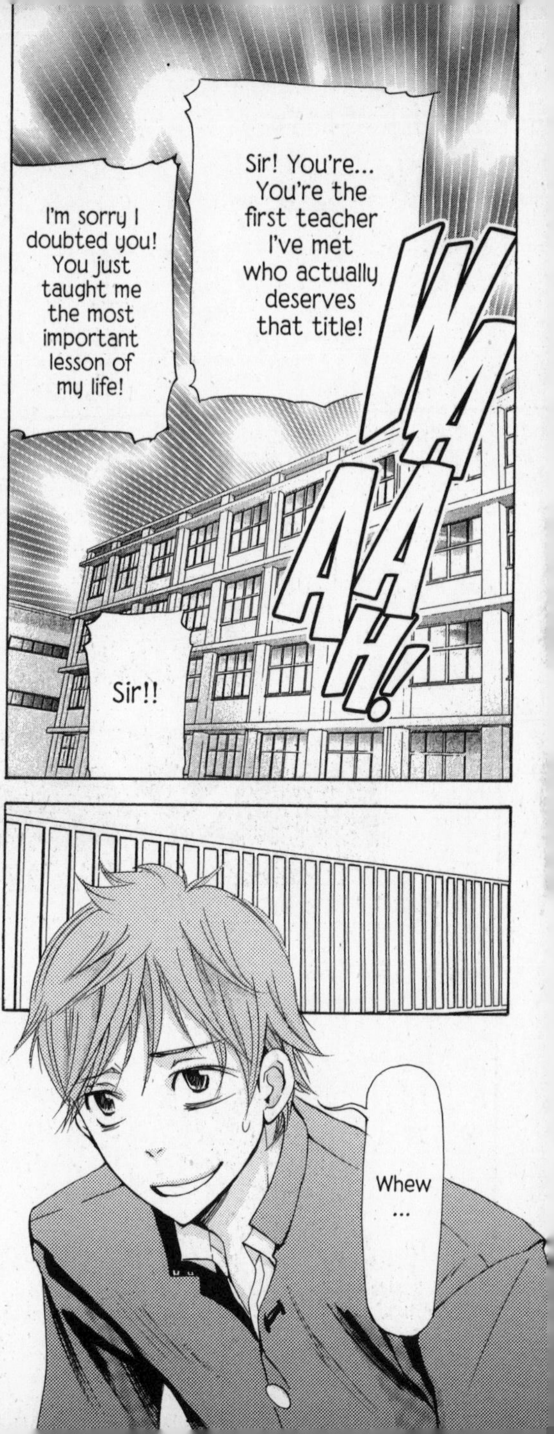

Sir! You're... You're the first teacher I've met who actually deserves that title!
I'm sorry I doubted you! You just taught me the most important lesson of my life!
WAAAH!
Sir!!
Whew ...

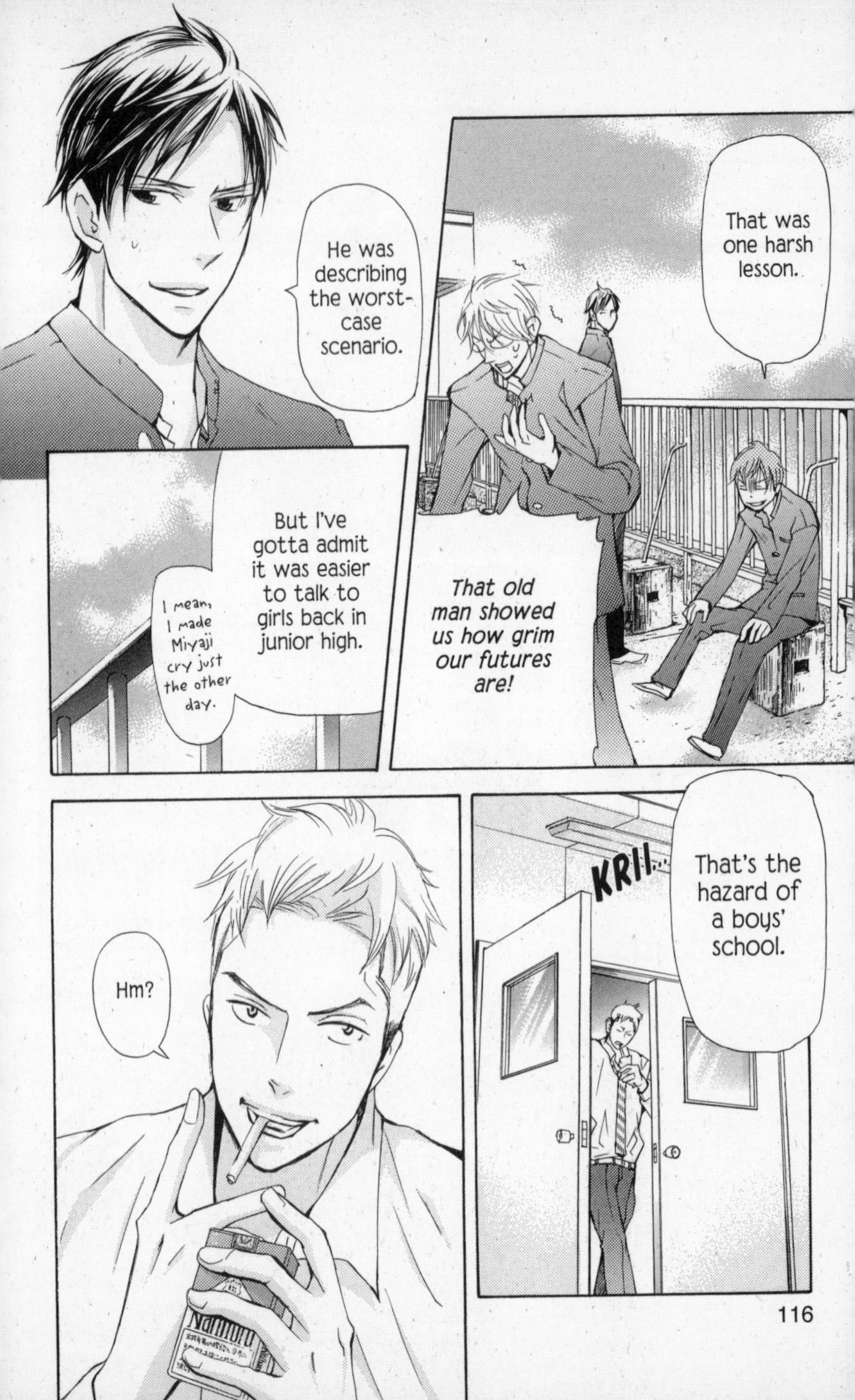
That was one harsh lesson.
That old man showed us how grim our futures are!
He was describing the worst-case scenario.
But I've gotta admit it was easier to talk to girls back in junior high.
I mean, I made Miyaji cry just the other day.
KRII...
That's the hazard of a boys' school.
Hm?

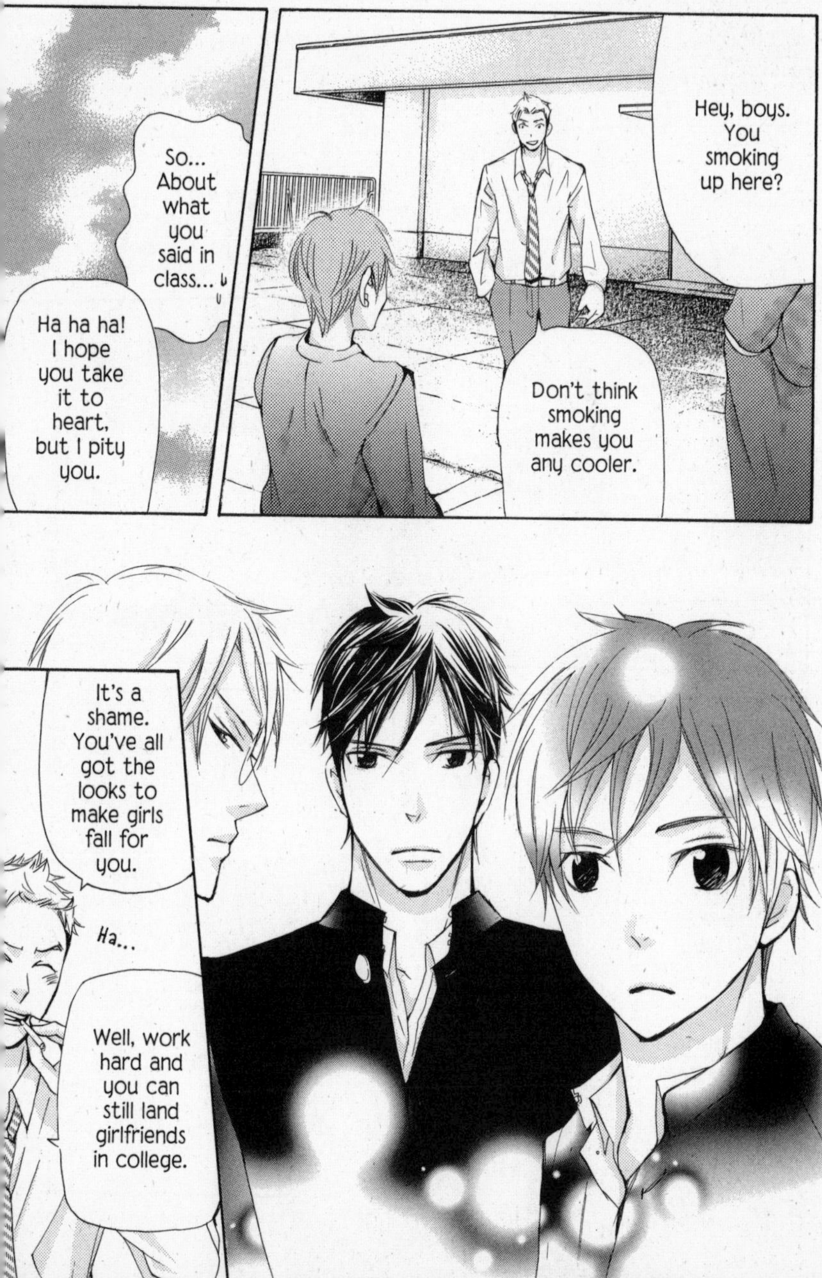
Hey, boys. You smoking up here?
Don't think smoking makes you any cooler.
So... About what you said in class...
Ha ha ha! I hope you take it to heart, but I pity you.
It's a shame. You've all got the looks to make girls fall for you.
Ha...
Well, work hard and you can still land girlfriends in college.

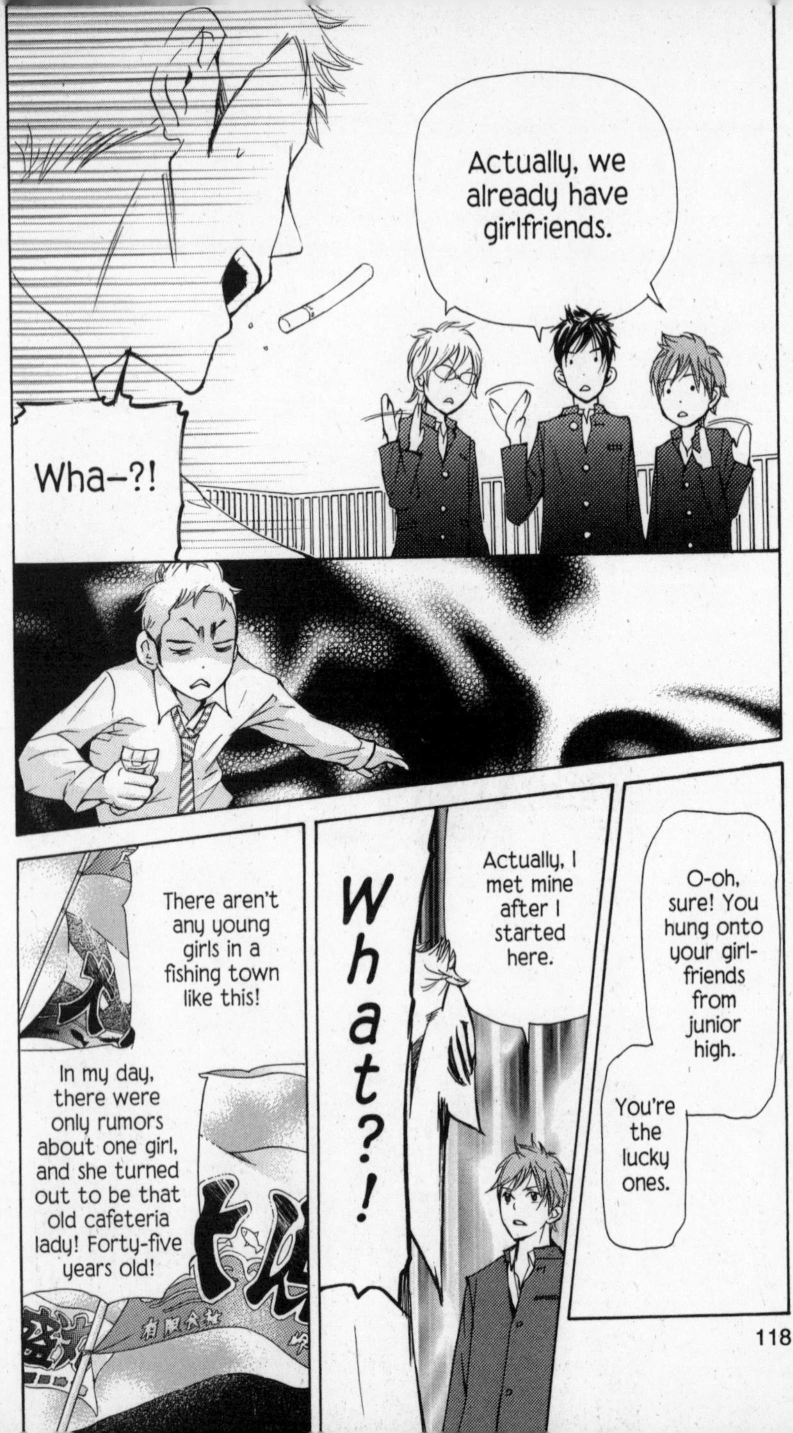
Actually, we already have girlfriends.
Wha–?!
O-oh, sure! You hung onto your girl-friends from junior high.
You're the lucky ones.
Actually, I met mine after I started here.
What?!
There aren't any young girls in a fishing town like this!
In my day, there were only rumors about one girl, and she turned out to be that old cafeteria lady! Forty-five years old!

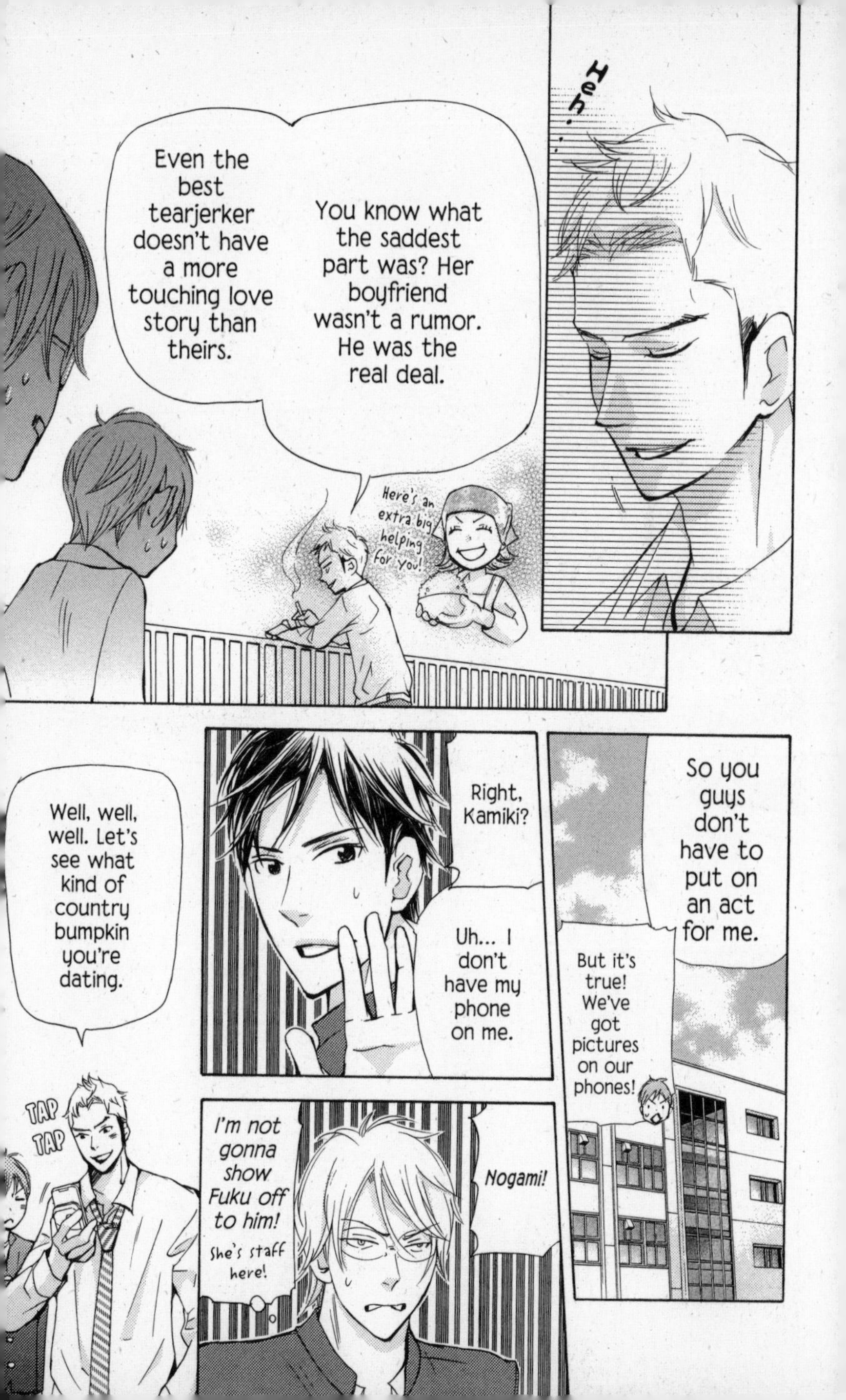
Heh...
You know what the saddest part was? Her boyfriend wasn't a rumor. He was the real deal.
Even the best tearjerker doesn't have a more touching love story than theirs.
Here's an extra big helping for you!
So you guys don't have to put on an act for me.
But it's true! We've got pictures on our phones!
Right, Kamiki?
Uh... I don't have my phone on me.
Nogami!
I'm not gonna show Fuku off to him!
She's staff here!
Well, well, well. Let's see what kind of country bumpkin you're dating.
TAP TAP

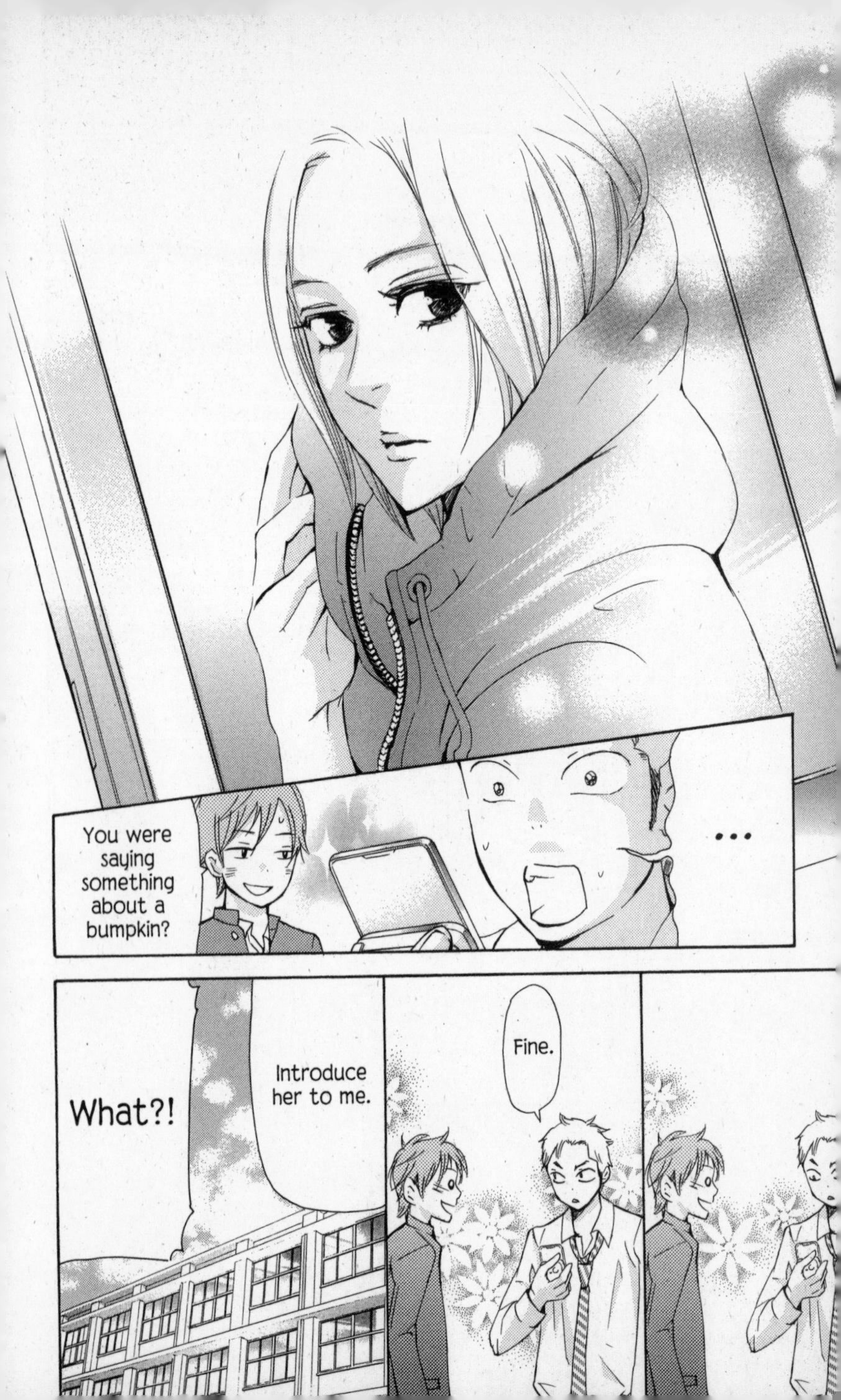
...
You were saying something about a bumpkin?
Fine.
Introduce her to me.
What?!

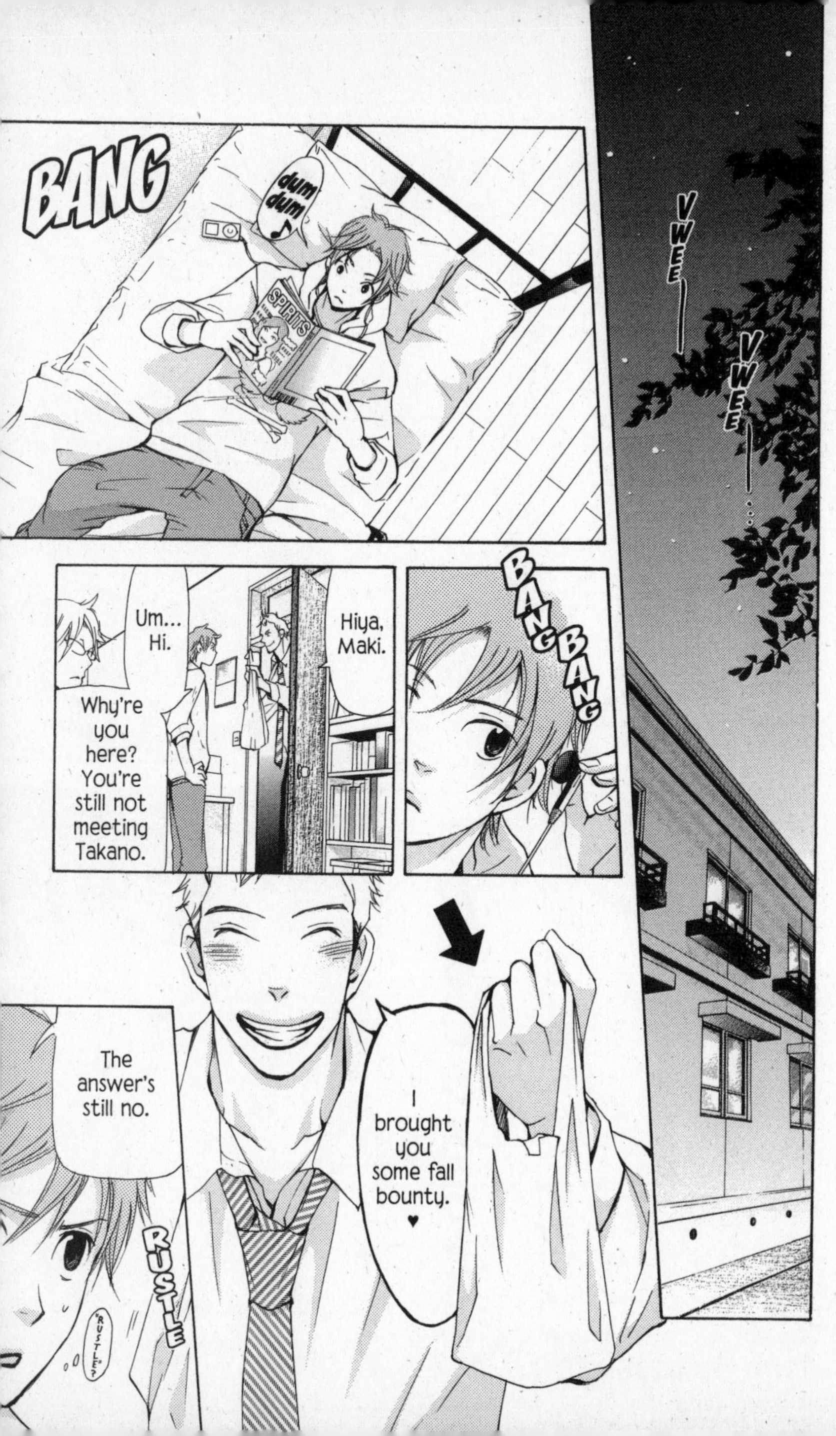
VWEE—
VWEE—...
BANG
dum dum ♪
BANG BANG
Hiya, Maki.
Um... Hi.
Why're you here? You're still not meeting Takano.
I brought you some fall bounty. ♥
The answer's still no.
RUSTLE
RUSTLE?

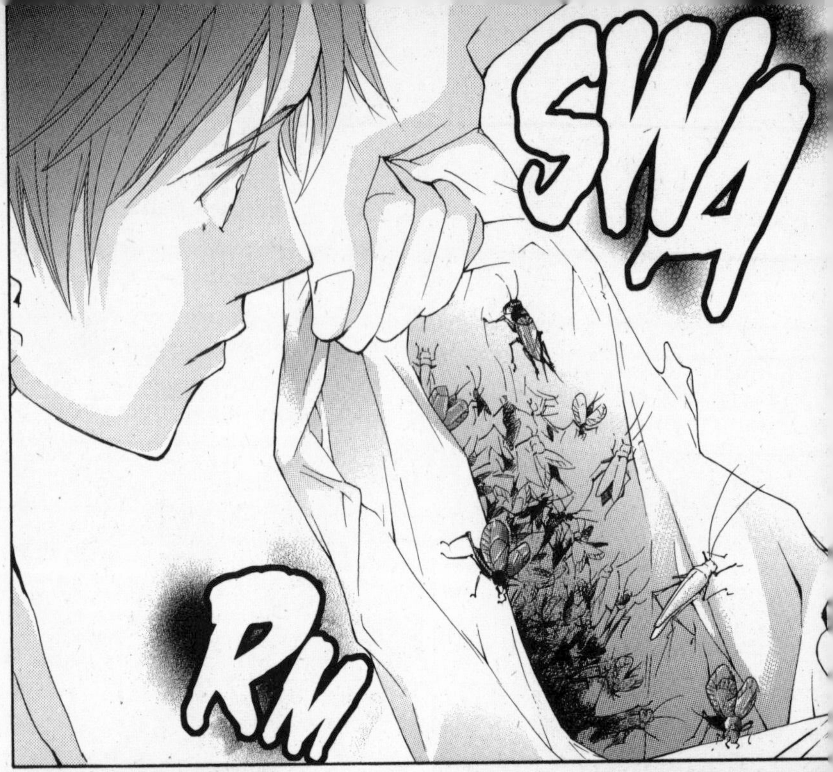
SWA
RM

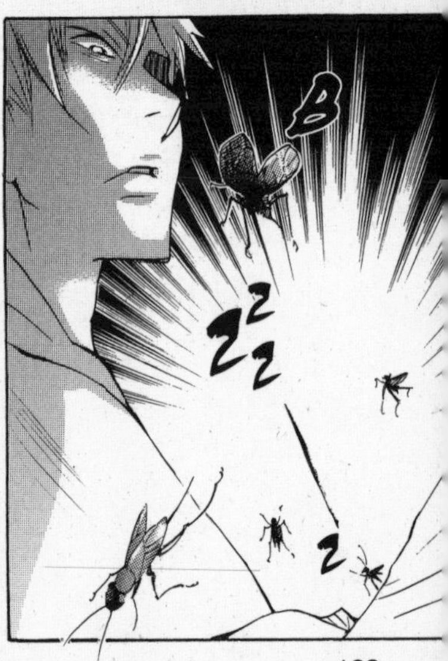
B
ZZZ
Z

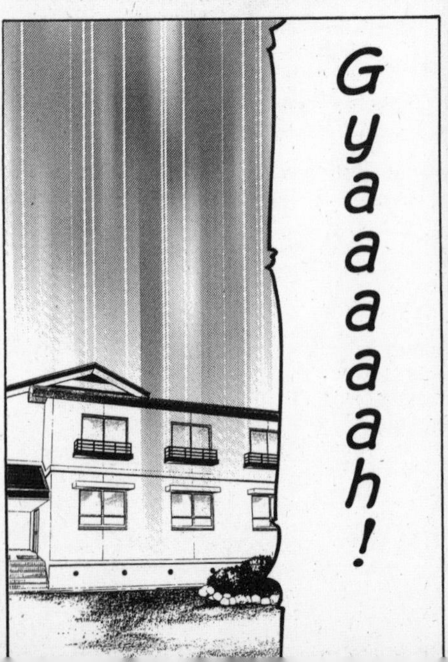
Gyaaaaah!

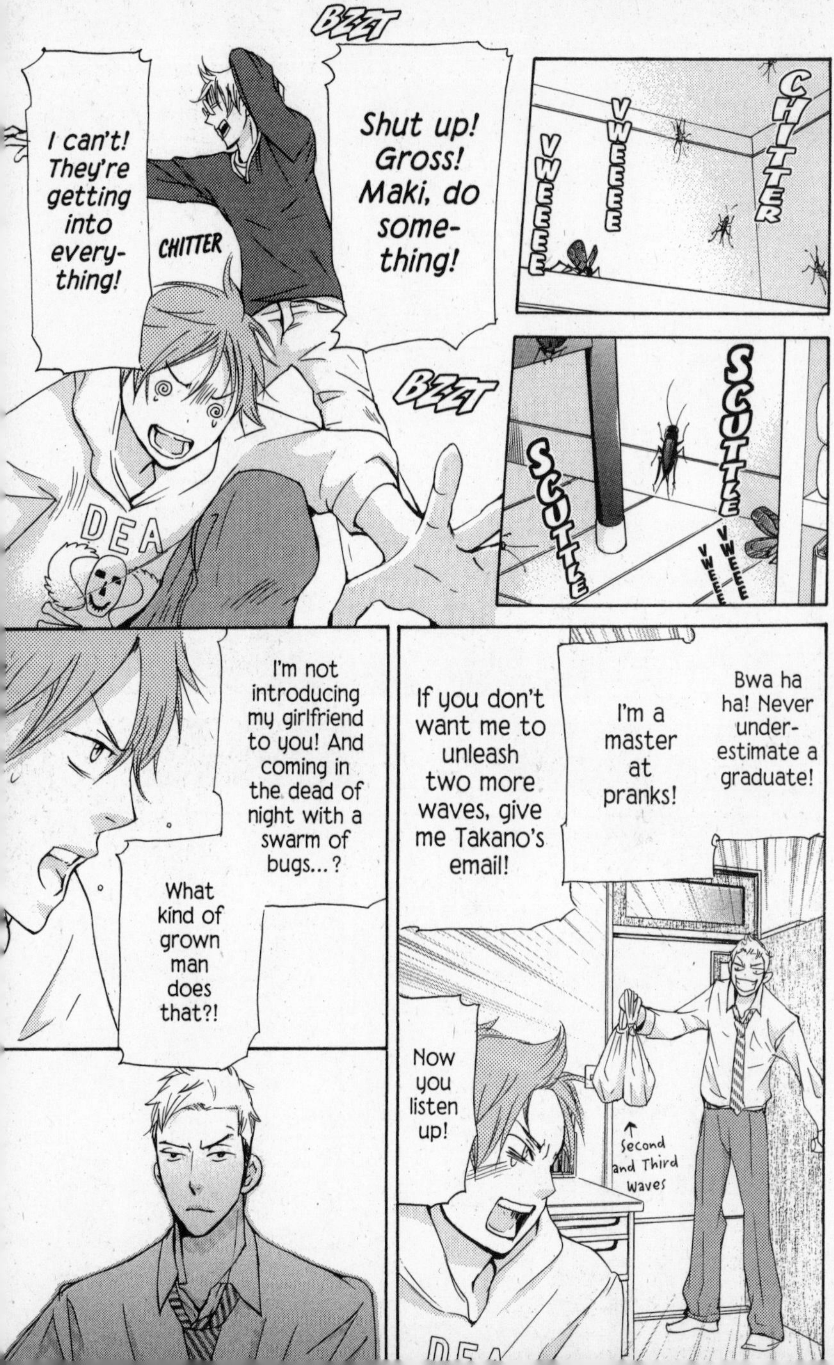
CHITTER
VWEEEE
VWEEEEE
SCUTTLE
VWEEE
VWEEE
SCUTTLE
BZZT
Shut up! Gross! Maki, do something!
I can't! They're getting into everything!
CHITTER
BZZT
Bwa ha ha! Never underestimate a graduate!
I'm a master at pranks!
If you don't want me to unleash two more waves, give me Takano's email!
Second and Third Waves
Now you listen up!
I'm not introducing my girlfriend to you! And coming in the dead of night with a swarm of bugs...?
What kind of grown man does that?!

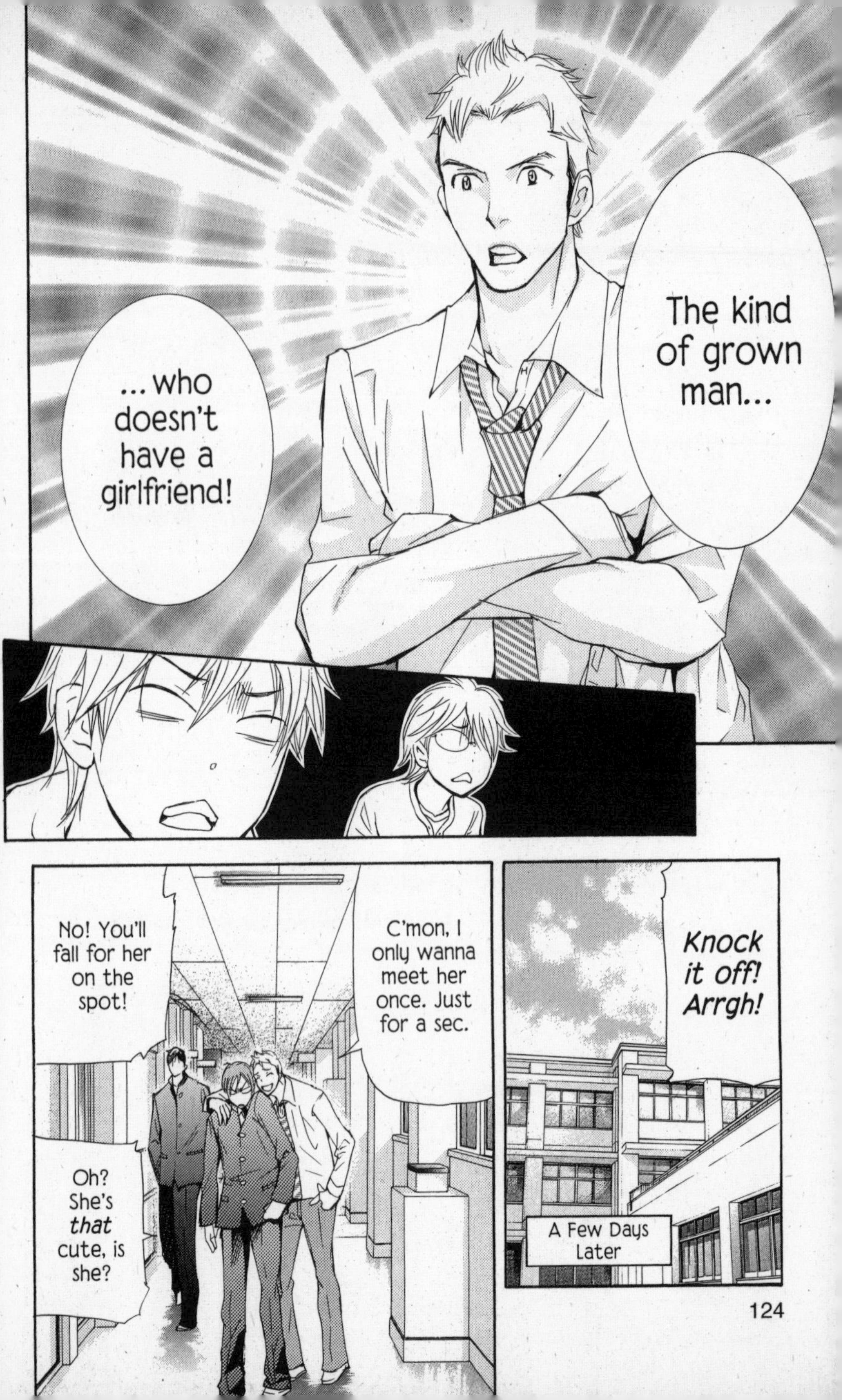
The kind of grown man...
...who doesn't have a girlfriend!
Knock it off! Arrgh!
A Few Days Later
C'mon, I only wanna meet her once. Just for a sec.
No! You'll fall for her on the spot!
Oh? She's *that* cute, is she?

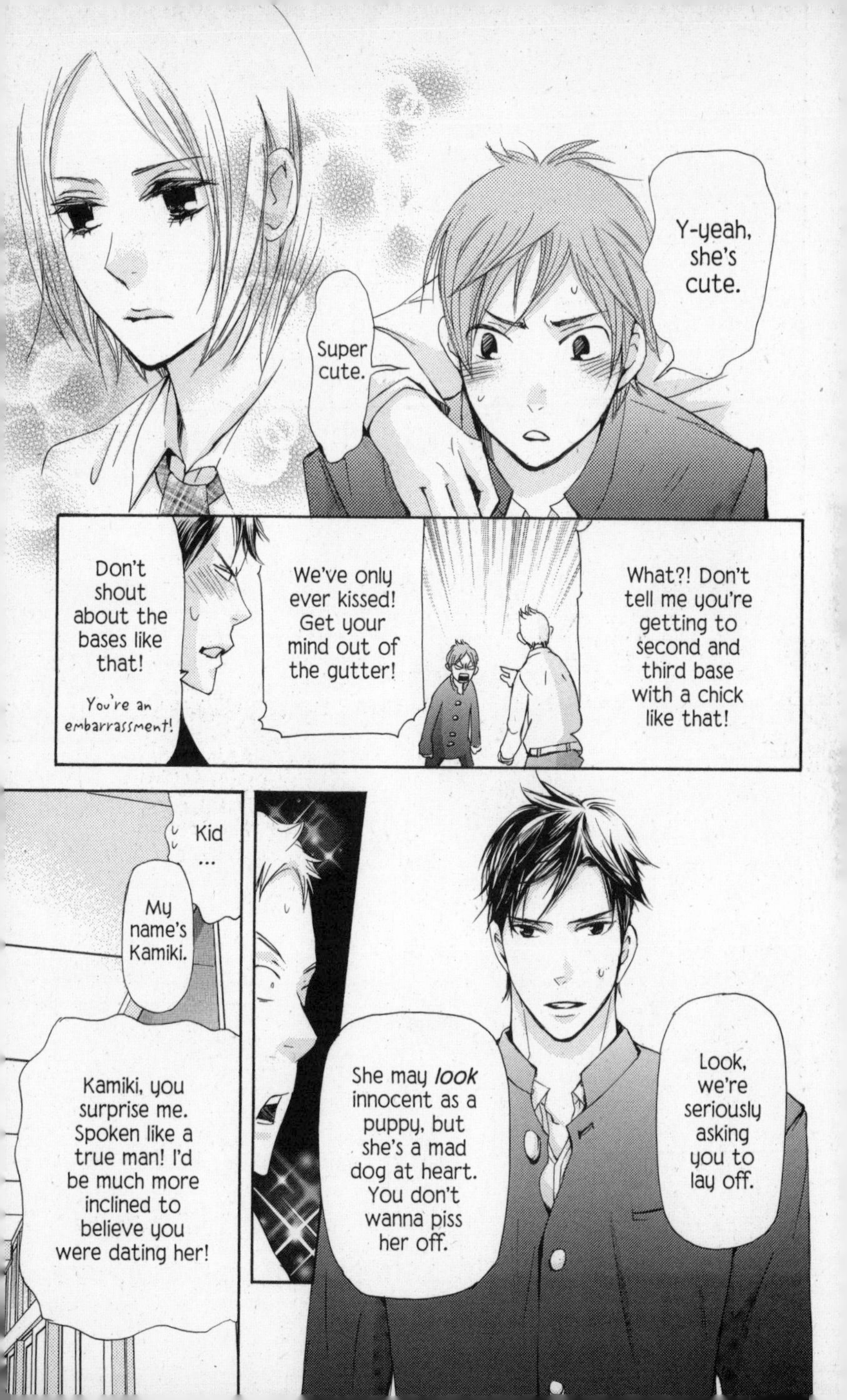
Y-yeah, she's cute.
Super cute.
What?! Don't tell me you're getting to second and third base with a chick like that!
We've only ever kissed! Get your mind out of the gutter!
Don't shout about the bases like that!
You're an embarrassment!
Look, we're seriously asking you to lay off.
She may *look* innocent as a puppy, but she's a mad dog at heart. You don't wanna piss her off.
Kid...
My name's Kamiki.
Kamiki, you surprise me. Spoken like a true man! I'd be much more inclined to believe you were dating her!

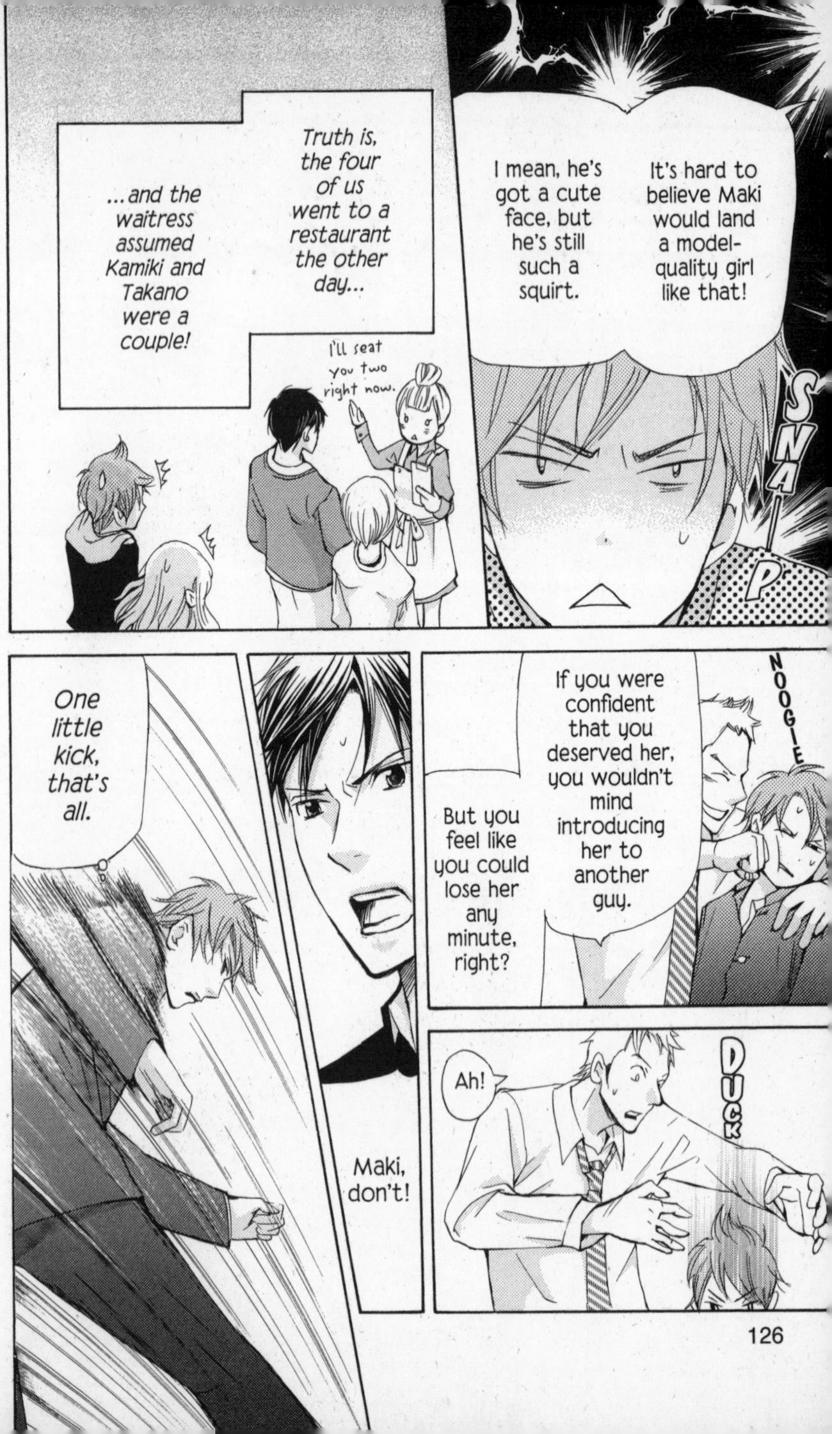

It's hard to believe Maki would land a model-quality girl like that!
I mean, he's got a cute face, but he's still such a squirt.
SNAP
Truth is, the four of us went to a restaurant the other day...
...and the waitress assumed Kamiki and Takano were a couple!
I'll seat you two right now.
NOOGIE
If you were confident that you deserved her, you wouldn't mind introducing her to another guy.
But you feel like you could lose her any minute, right?
DUCK
Ah!
Maki, don't!
One little kick, that's all.

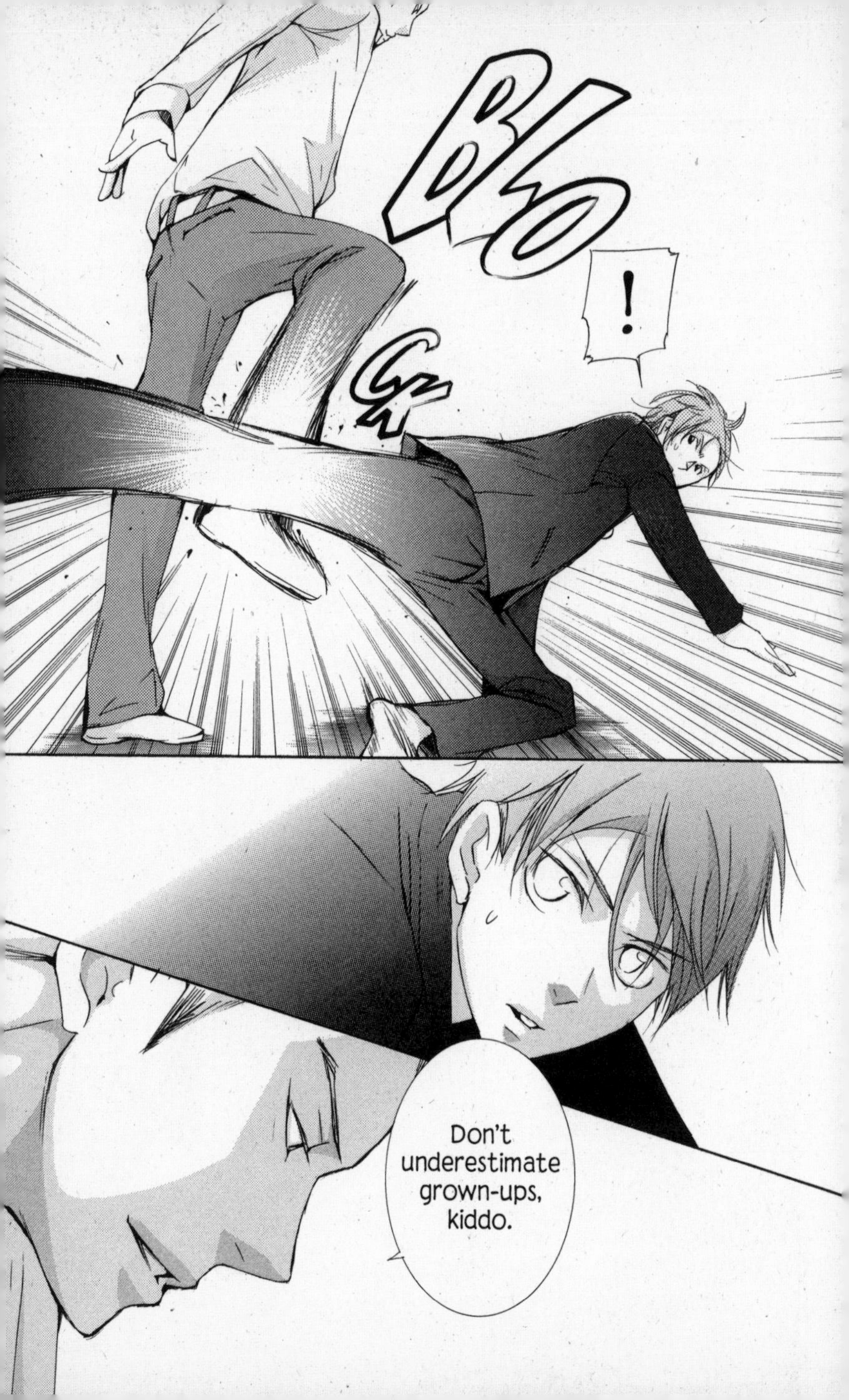
BLO
!
Don't underestimate grown-ups, kiddo.

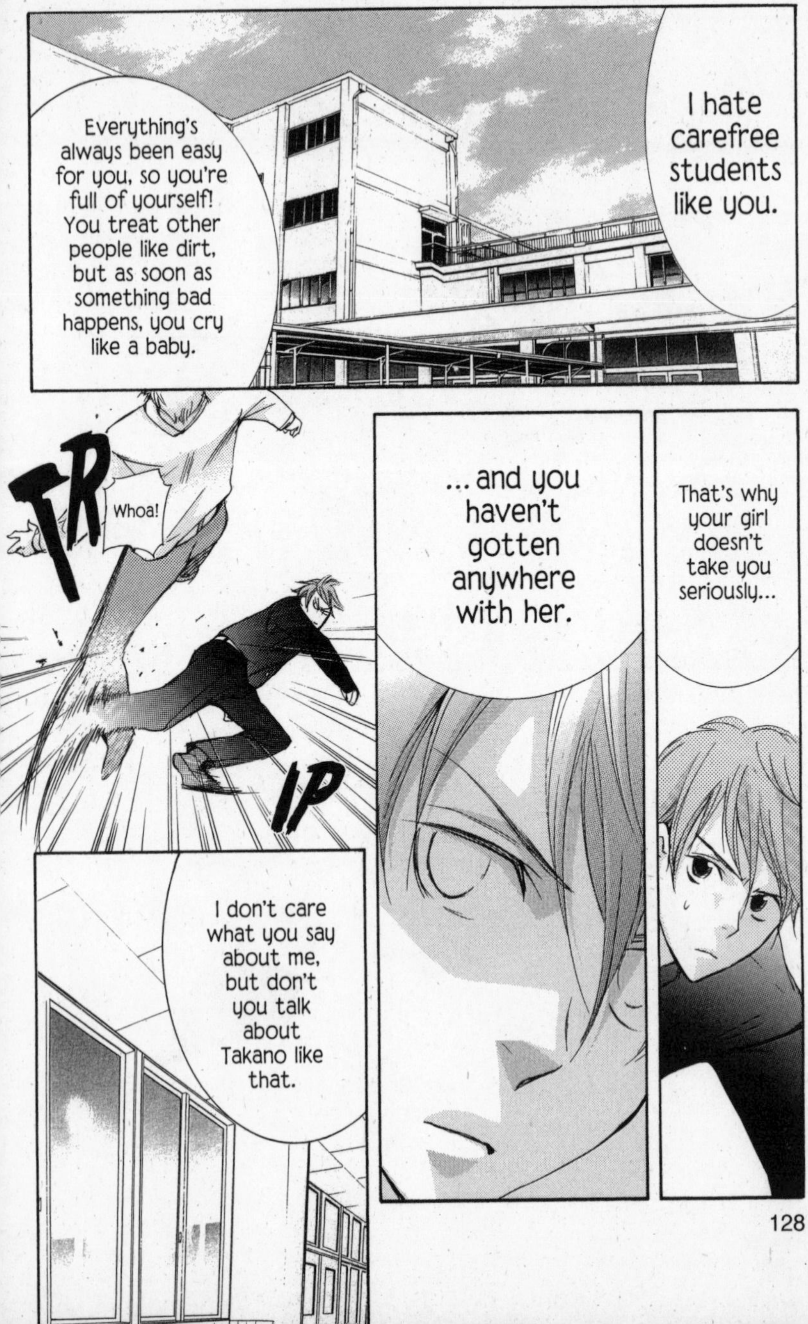
I hate carefree students like you.
Everything's always been easy for you, so you're full of yourself! You treat other people like dirt, but as soon as something bad happens, you cry like a baby.
That's why your girl doesn't take you seriously...
...and you haven't gotten anywhere with her.
TR
Whoa!
IP
I don't care what you say about me, but don't you talk about Takano like that.

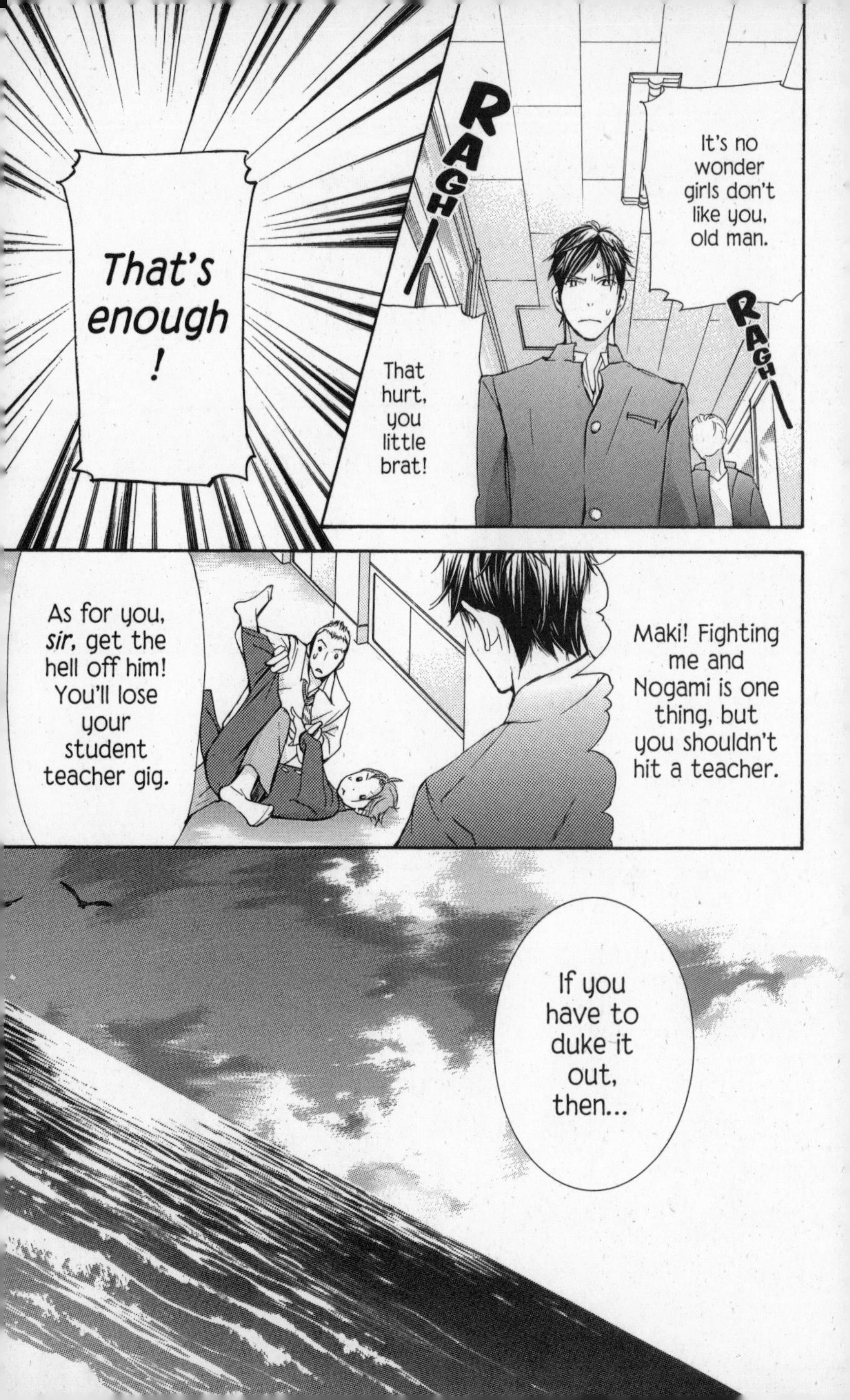

It's no wonder girls don't like you, old man.
RAGH
RAGH
That hurt, you little brat!
That's enough!
Maki! Fighting me and Nogami is one thing, but you shouldn't hit a teacher.
As for you, *sir*, get the hell off him! You'll lose your student teacher gig.
If you have to duke it out, then...

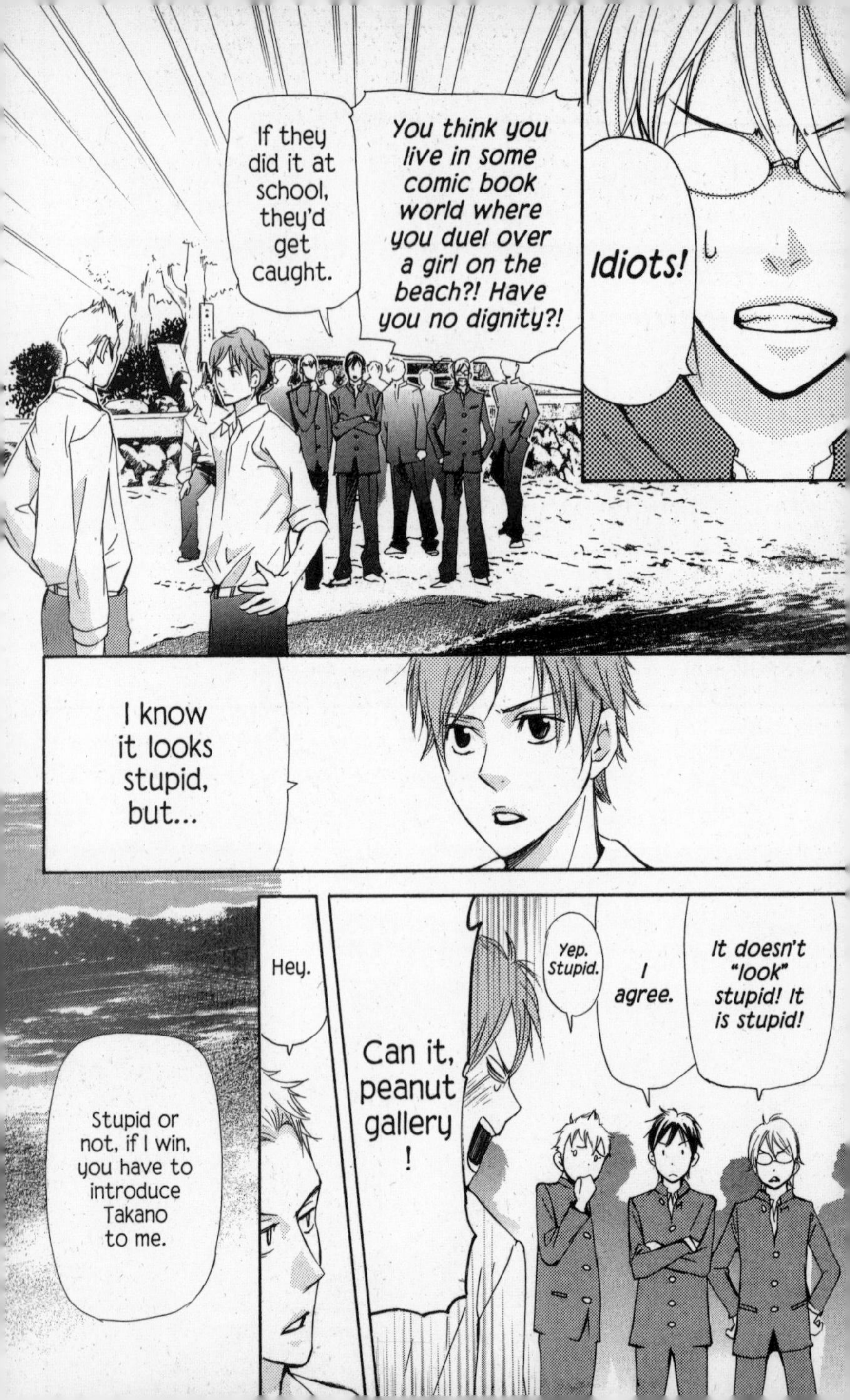
Idiots!
You think you live in some comic book world where you duel over a girl on the beach?! Have you no dignity?!
If they did it at school, they'd get caught.
I know it looks stupid, but...
It doesn't "look" stupid! It is stupid!
I agree.
Yep. Stupid.
Can it, peanut gallery!
Hey.
Stupid or not, if I win, you have to introduce Takano to me.

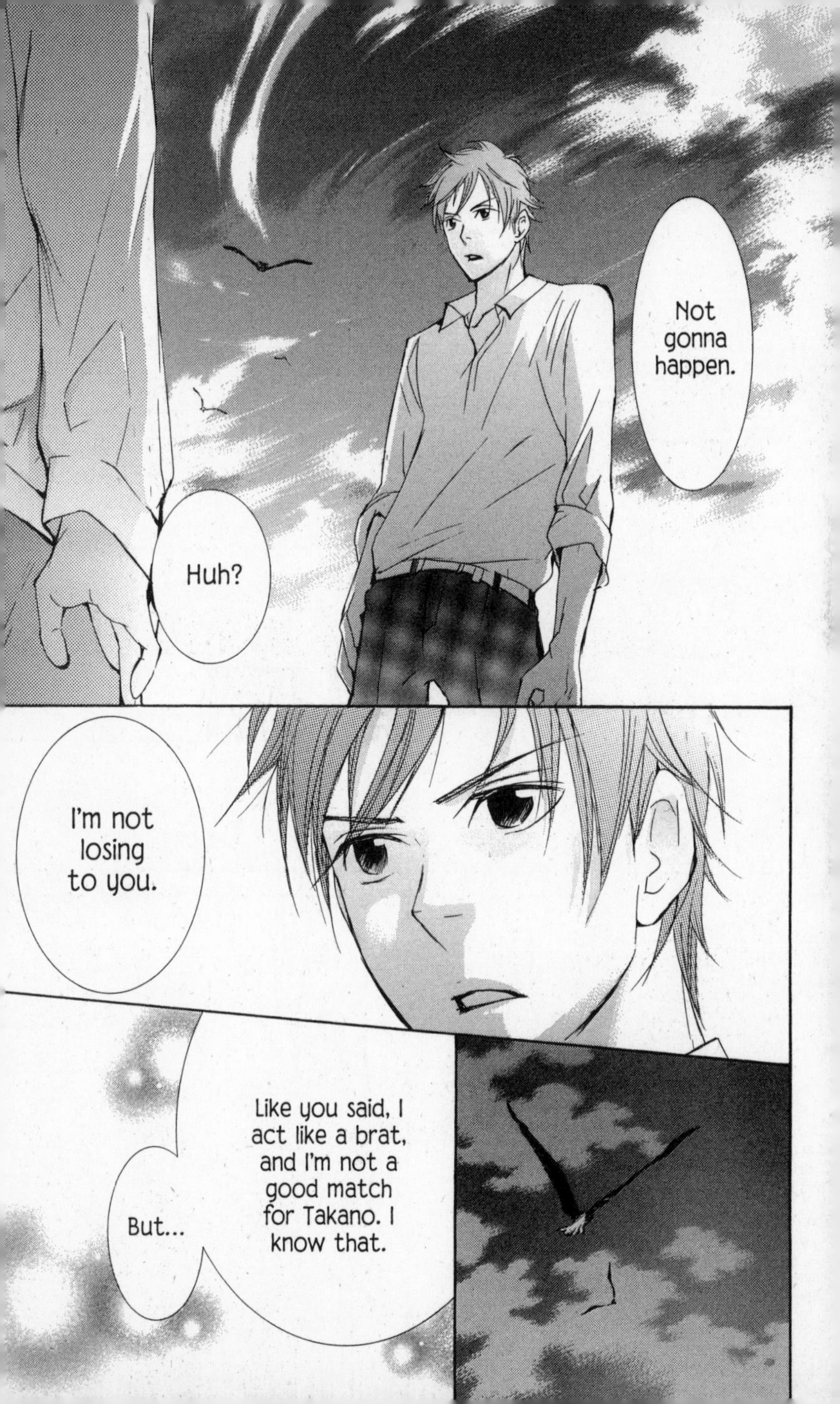
Not gonna happen.
Huh?
I'm not losing to you.
Like you said, I act like a brat, and I'm not a good match for Takano. I know that.
But...

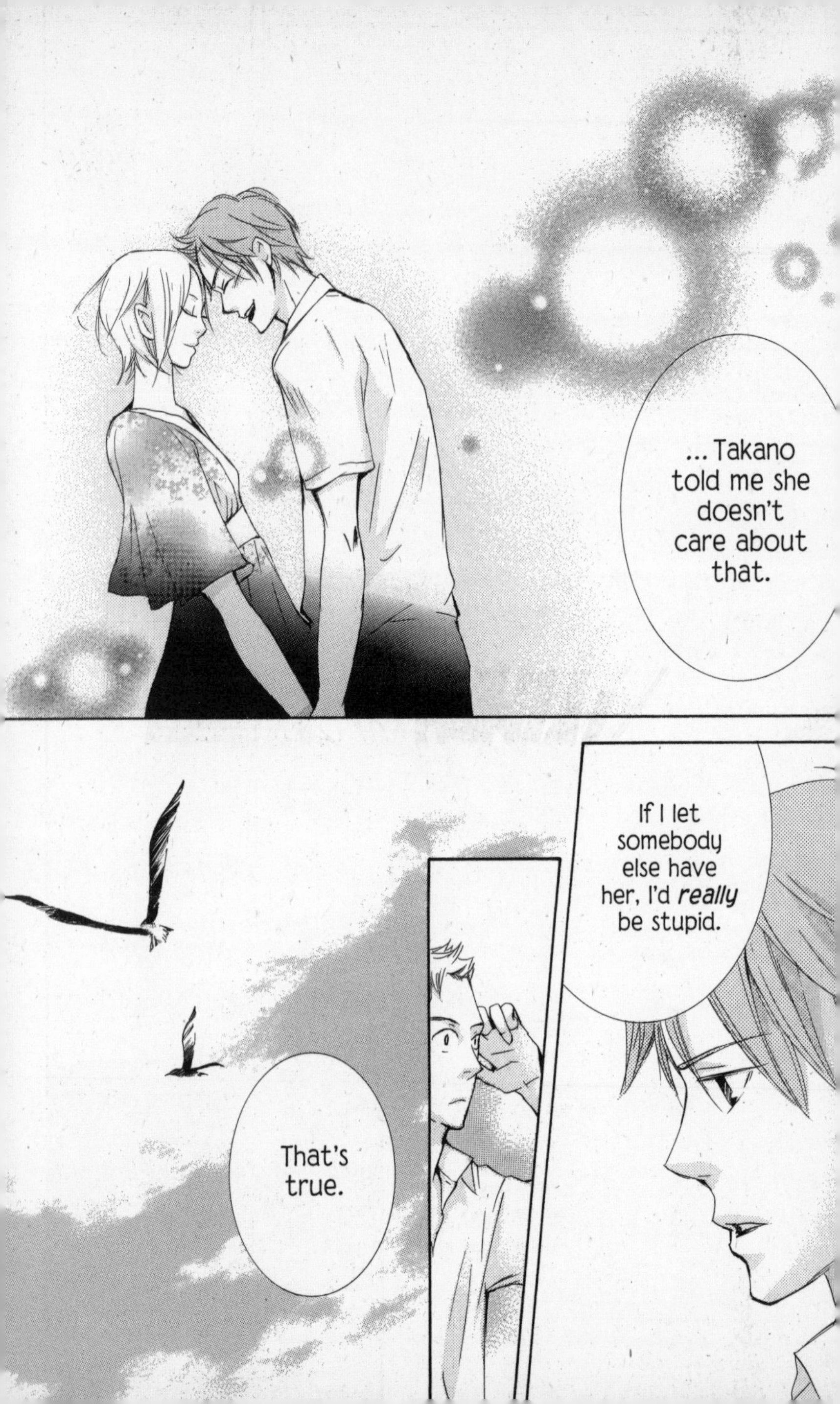
...Takano told me she doesn't care about that.
If I let somebody else have her, I'd *really* be stupid.
That's true.

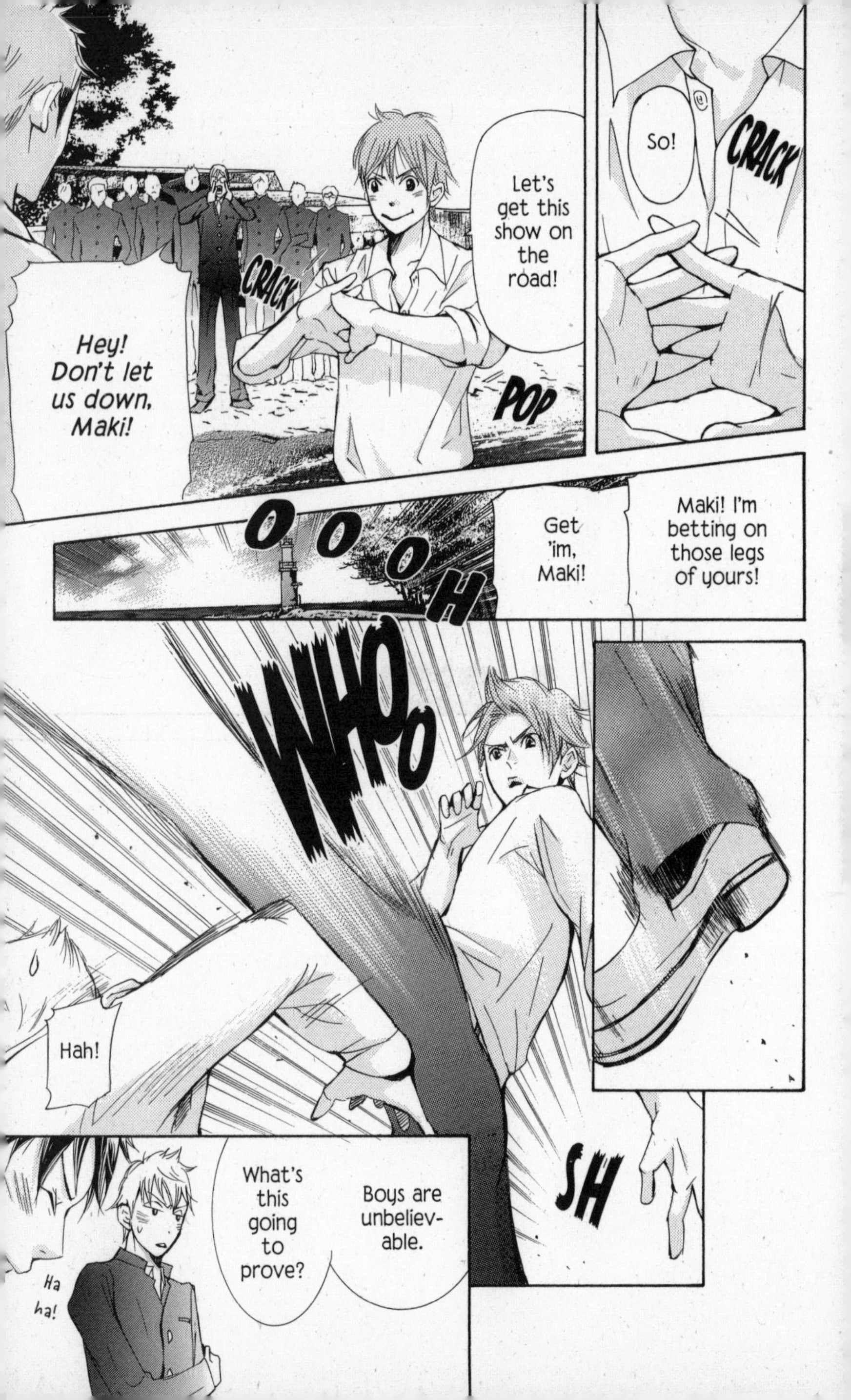
So!
CRACK
Let's get this show on the road!
CRACK
POP
Hey! Don't let us down, Maki!
Maki! I'm betting on those legs of yours!
Get 'im, Maki!
OOOOH
WHOO
Hah!
SH
Boys are unbelievable.
What's this going to prove?
Ha ha!

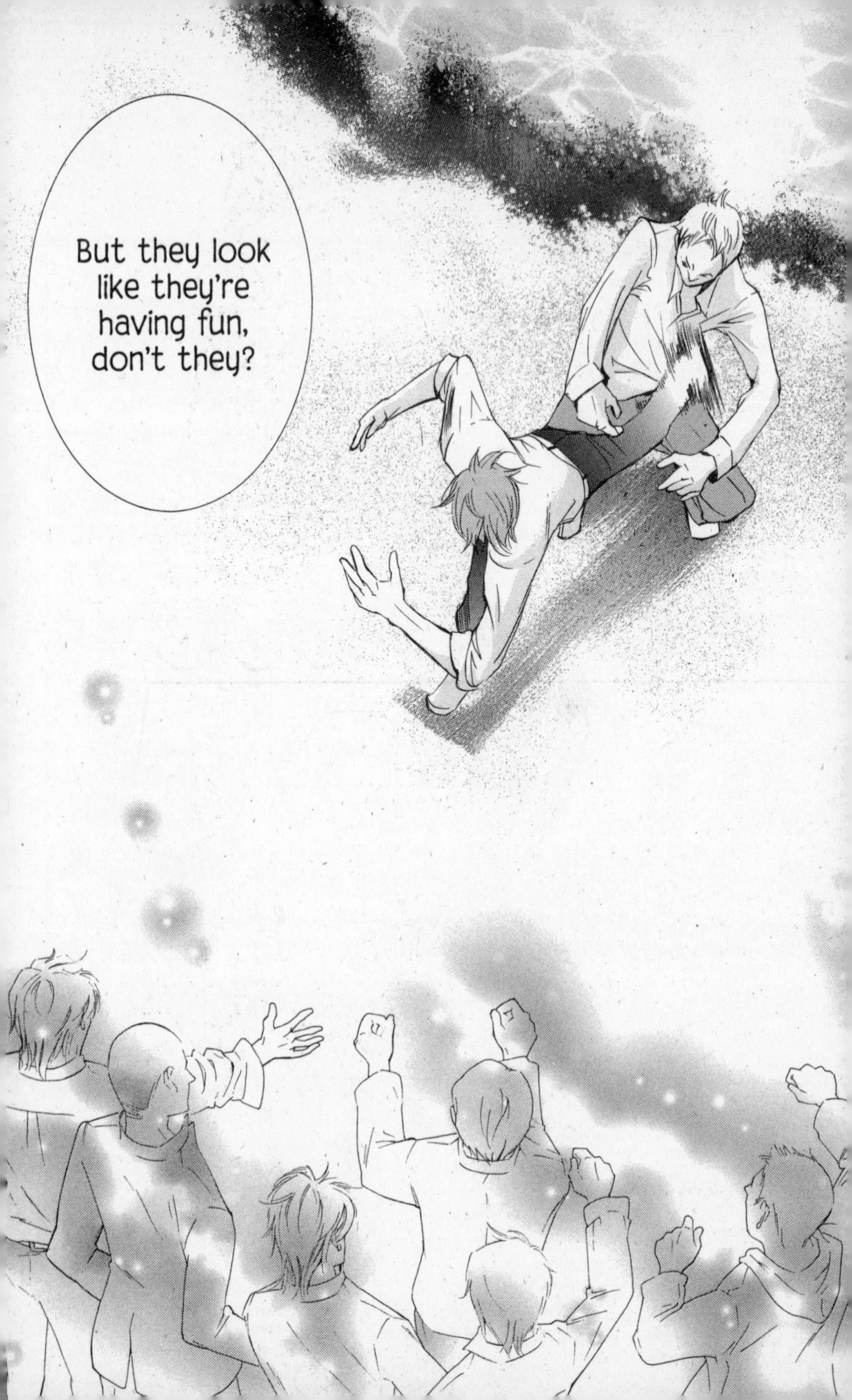
But they look like they're having fun, don't they?

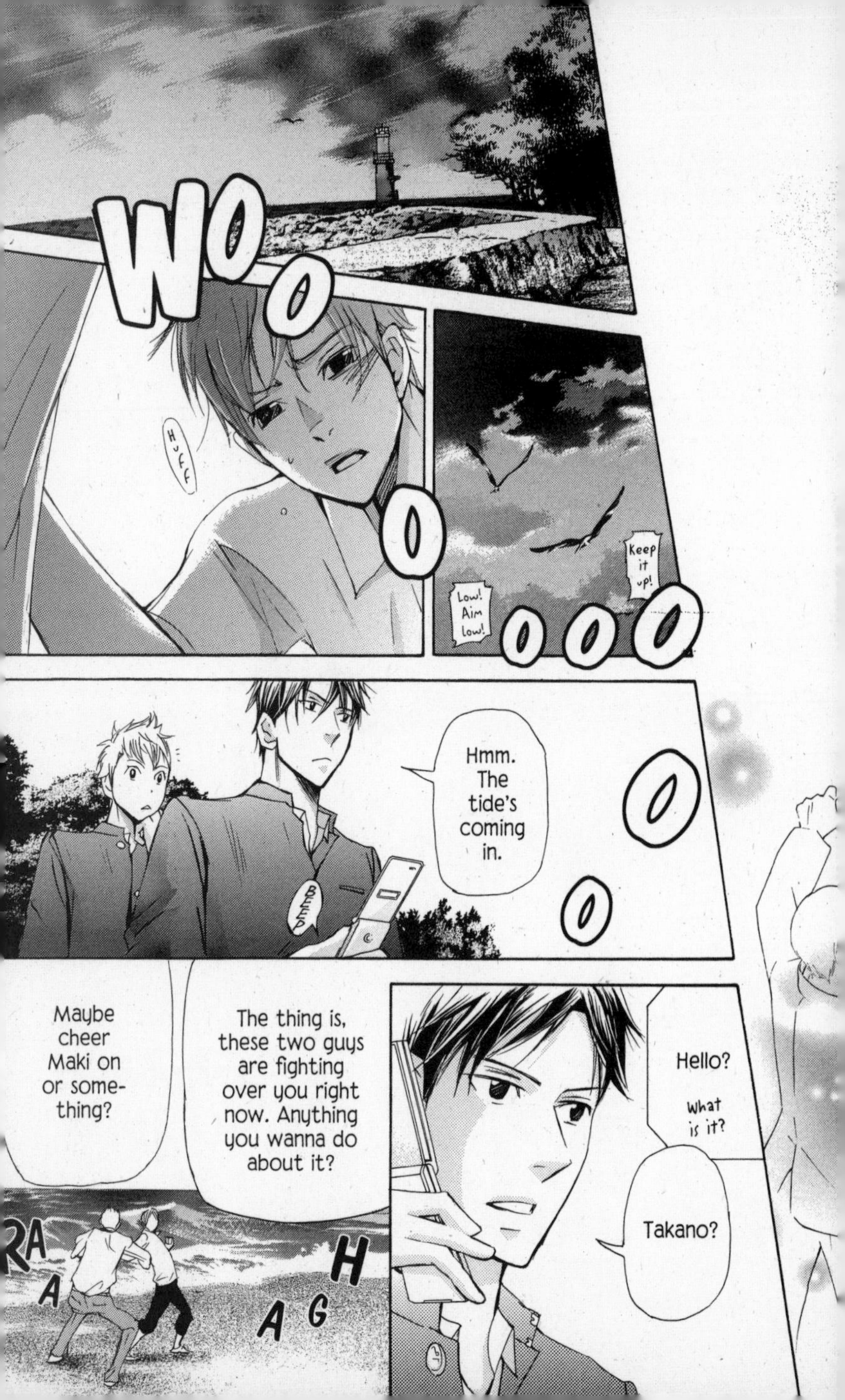
WOOOOOOOOO
Keep it up!
Low! Aim low!
Huff
Hmm. The tide's coming in.
BEEP
Hello?
What is it?
Takano?
The thing is, these two guys are fighting over you right now. Anything you wanna do about it?
Maybe cheer Maki on or some-thing?
RAAGH

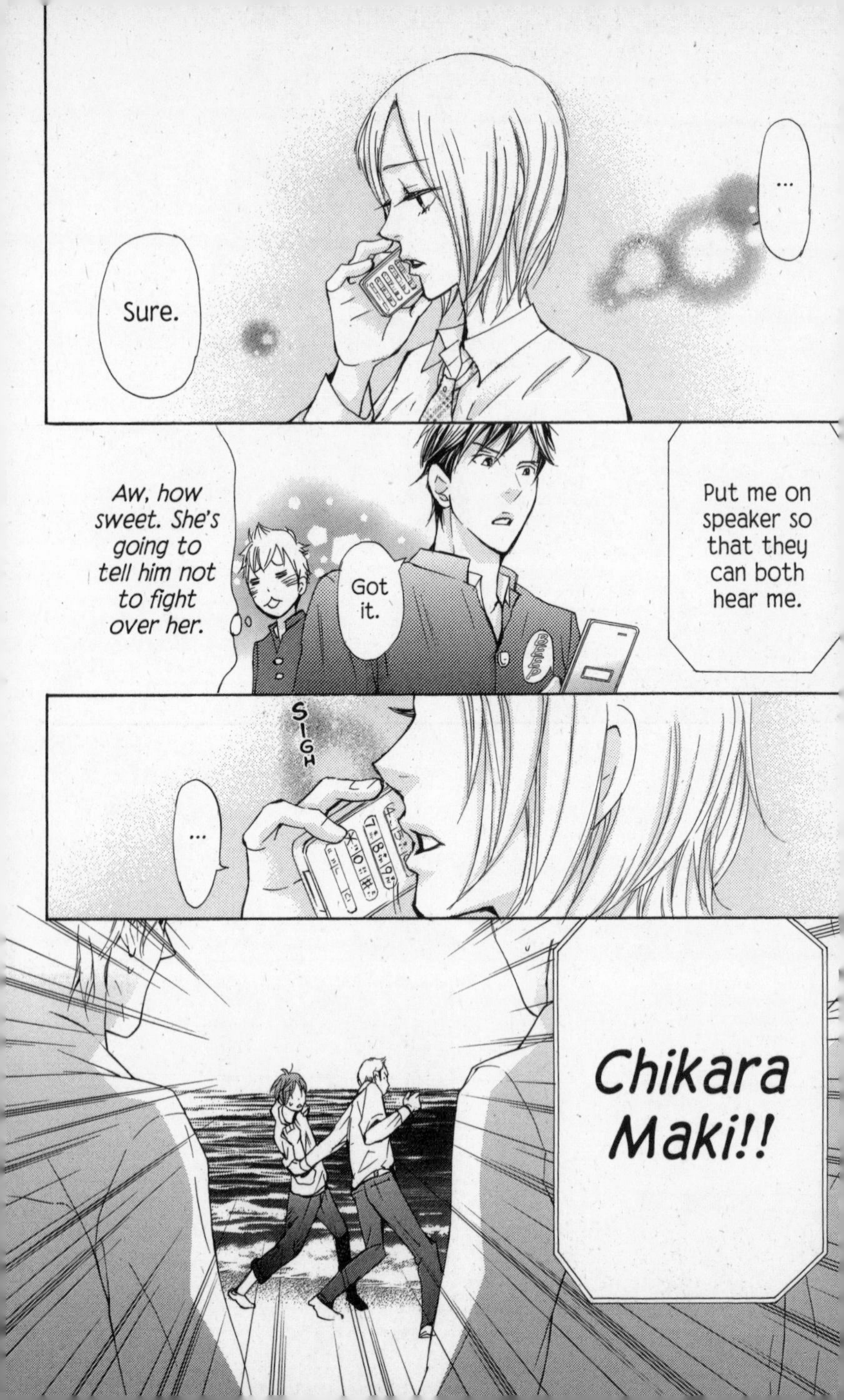
...
Sure.
Put me on speaker so that they can both hear me.
Got it.
Aw, how sweet. She's going to tell him not to fight over her.
SIGH
...
Chikara Maki!!

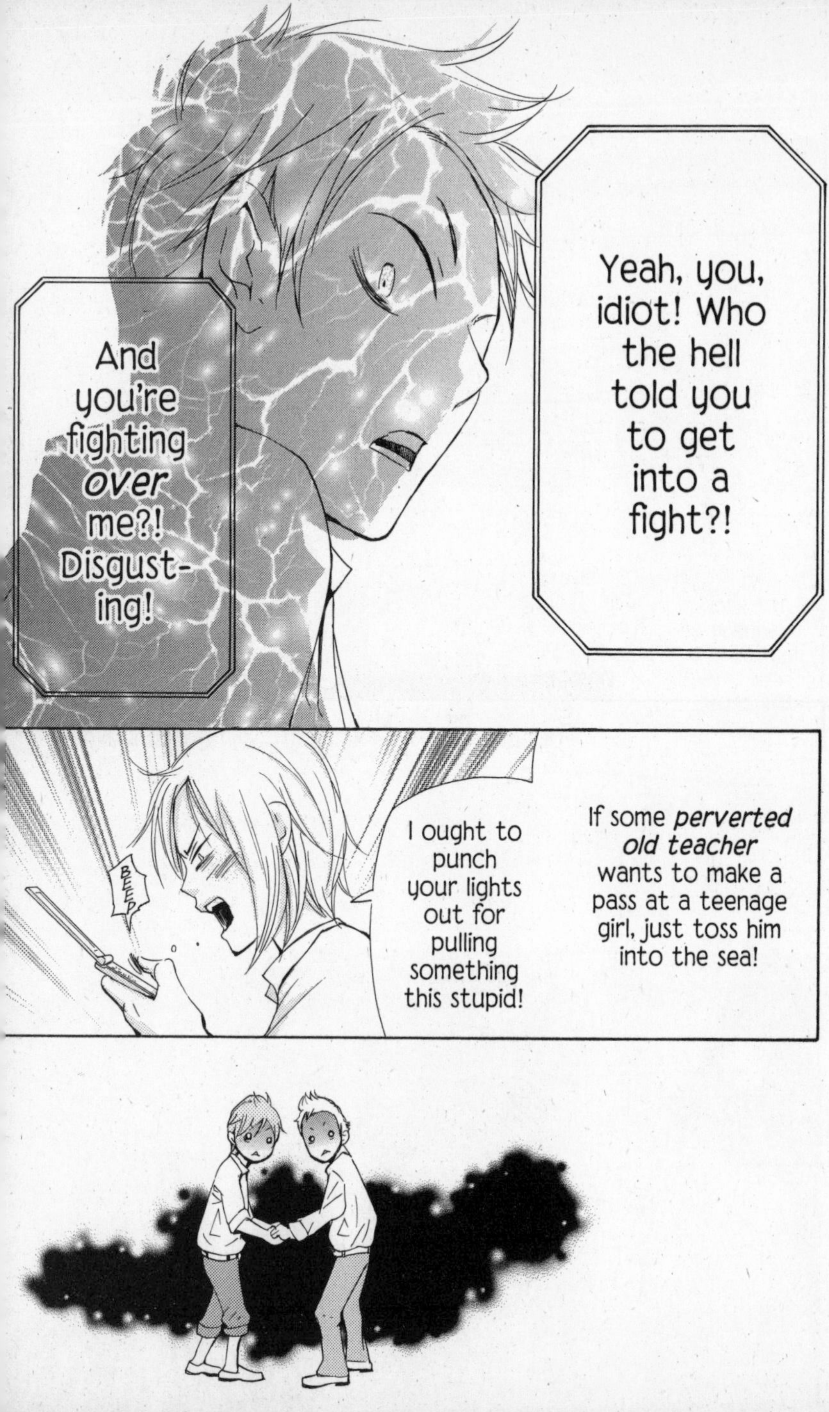
Yeah, you, idiot! Who the hell told you to get into a fight?!
And you're fighting *over* me?! Disgust-ing!
If some *perverted old teacher* wants to make a pass at a teenage girl, just toss him into the sea!
I ought to punch your lights out for pulling something this stupid!
BEEP

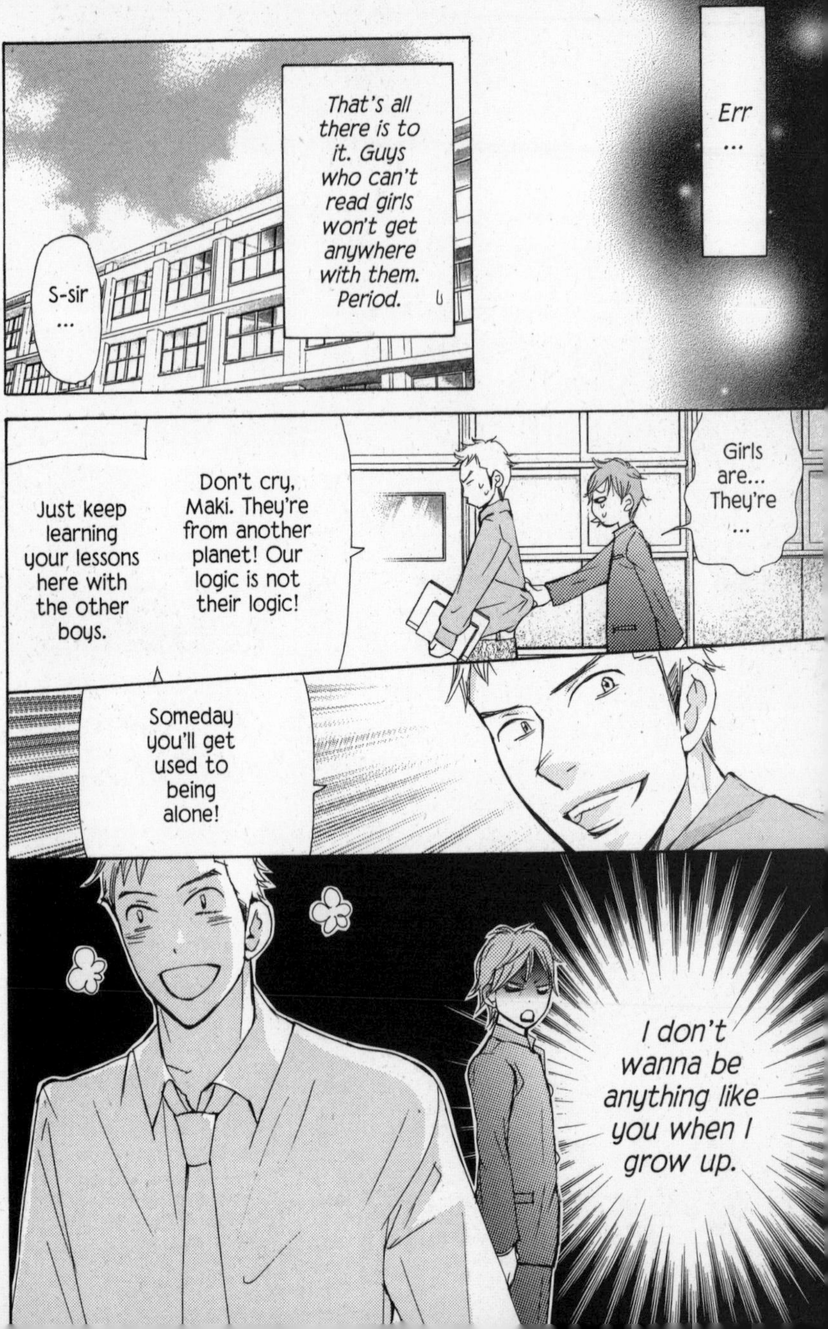
Err ...
That's all there is to it. Guys who can't read girls won't get anywhere with them. Period.
S-sir ...
Girls are... They're ...
Don't cry, Maki. They're from another planet! Our logic is not their logic!
Just keep learning your lessons here with the other boys.
Someday you'll get used to being alone!
I don't wanna be anything like you when I grow up.

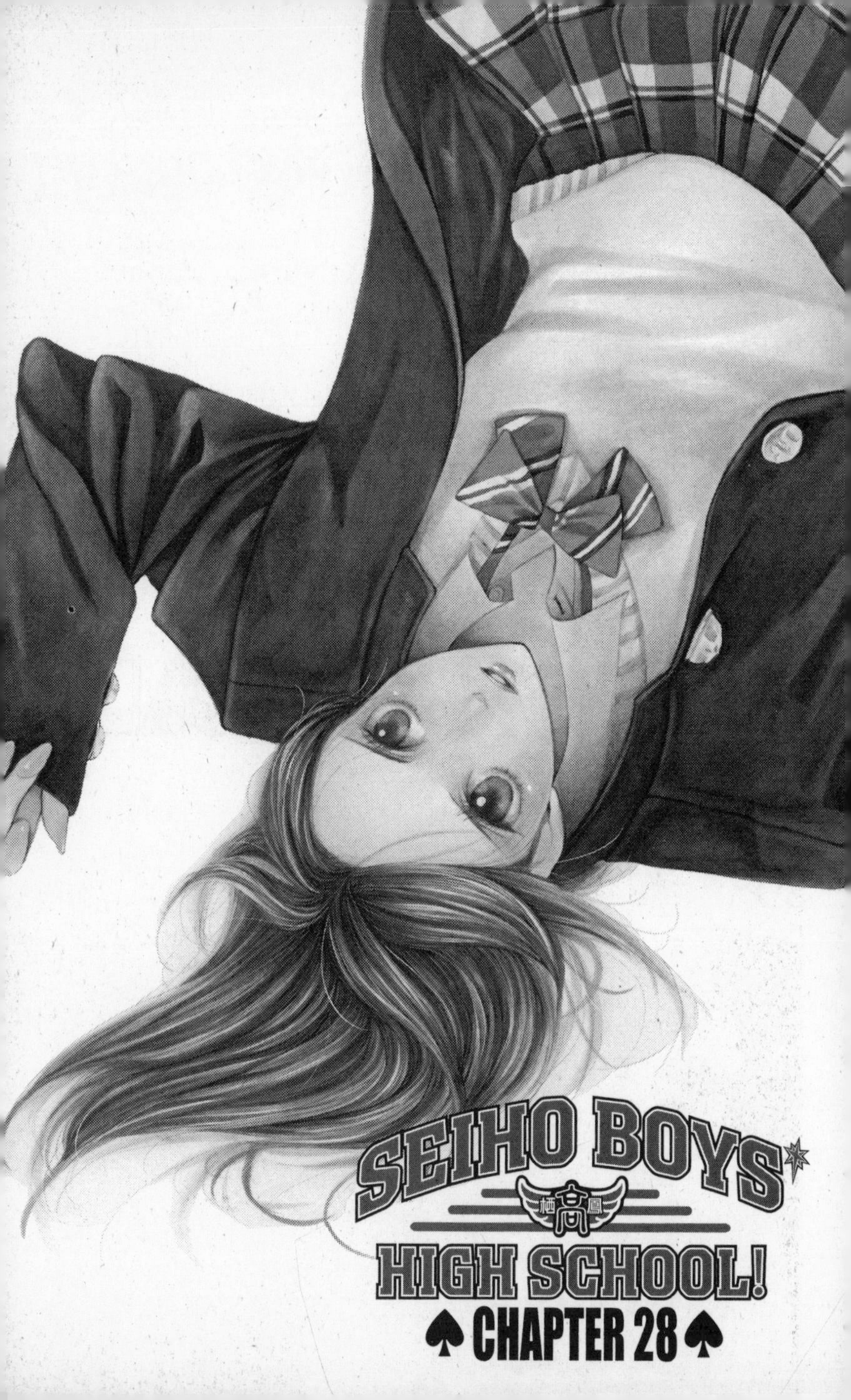
SEIHO BOYS
HIGH SCHOOL!
CHAPTER 28

Bonus Page Plan

Presenting Izumi's Sketches!!

Sometimes when I draw a rough sketch, I realize that it'll never capture my idea for the final product. Since I sometimes hand in my art without drawing in all the details, my inkers often have to work with some approximate fuzzy lines. Right now, we're in the coloring stage. Since I can't go back and change anything, I thought I'd take this opportunity to show you some behind-the-scenes shots.

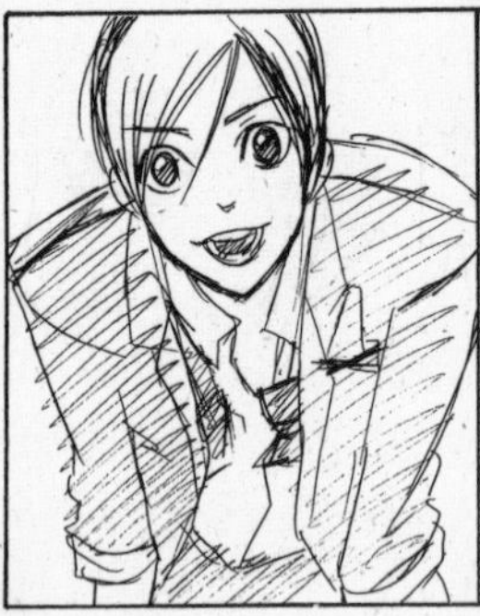

①Almost-final version. After this, I made little corrections to the clothes and the pose.

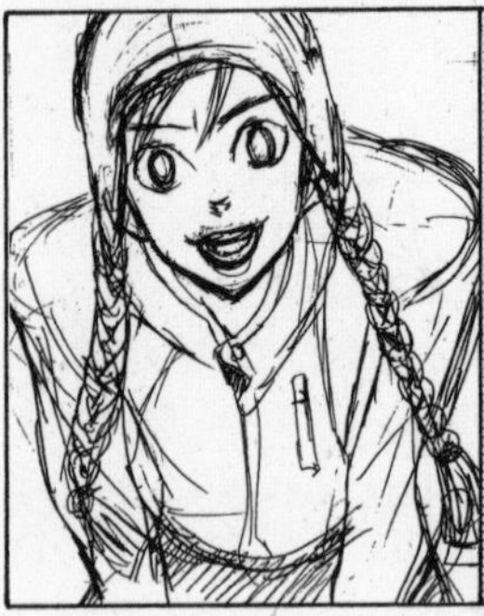

②I was told the clothes look too casual, so I toned it down to look like image①.

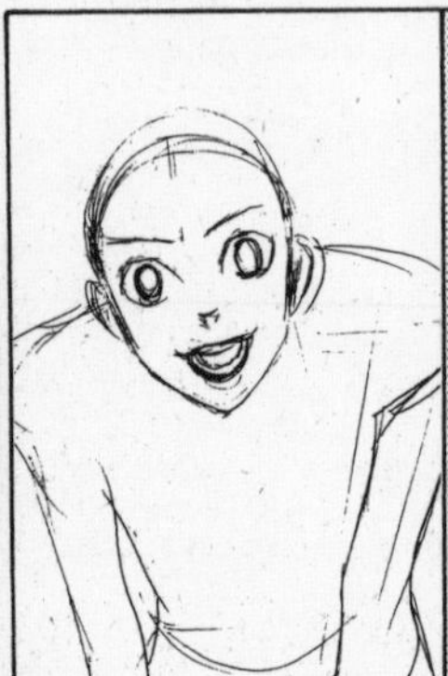

③Before reaching step②, I sketched in the main character from the waist up, starting with his head.

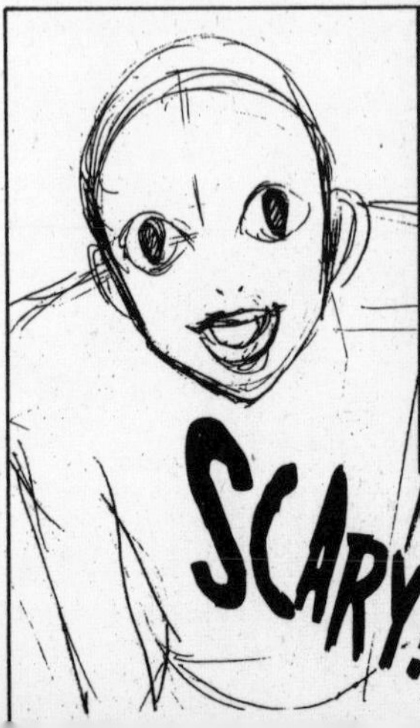
SCARY!!

④The first rough sketch I made. I'm not sure how I feel about it, actually.

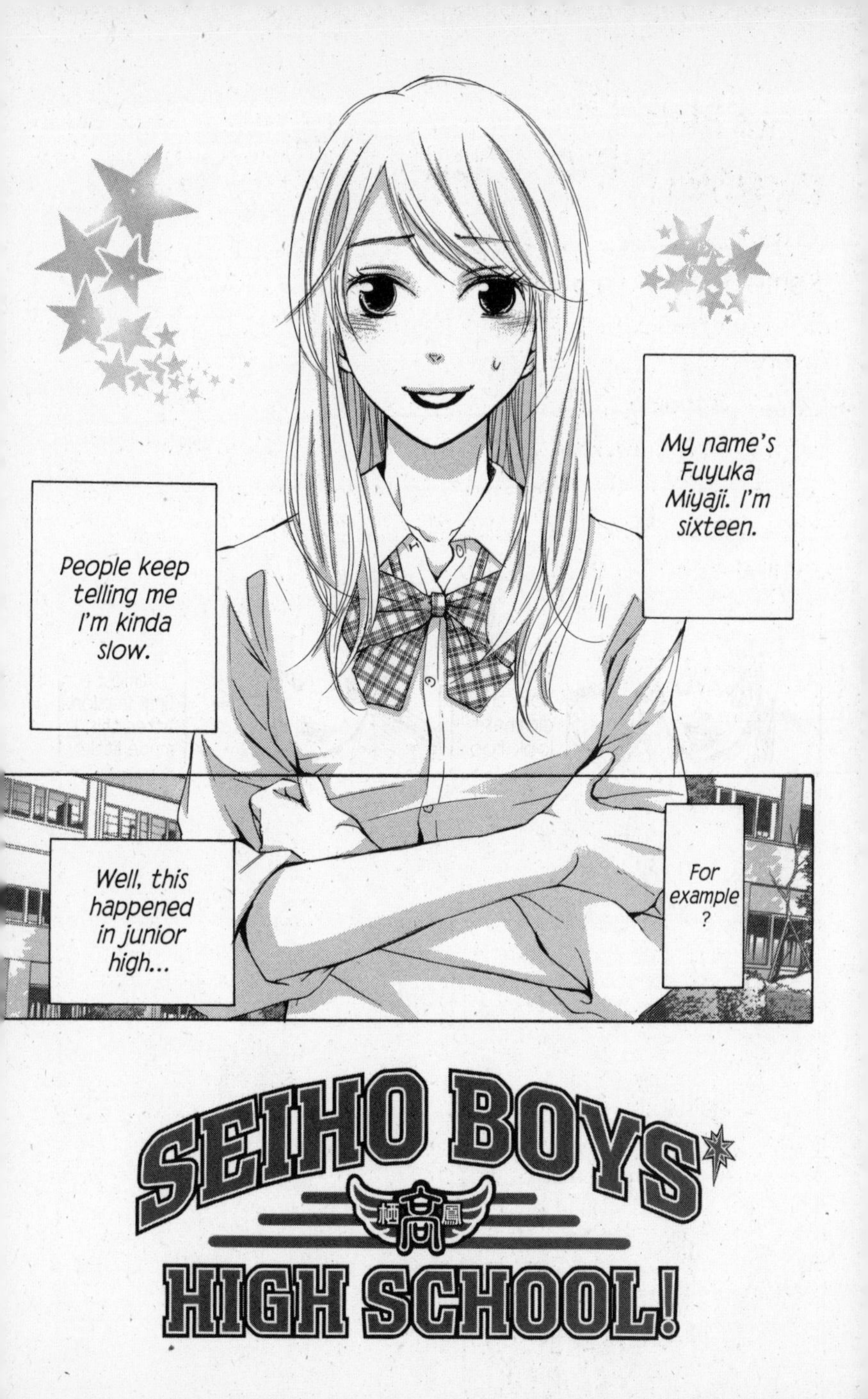
My name's Fuyuka Miyaji. I'm sixteen.
People keep telling me I'm kinda slow.
For example?
Well, this happened in junior high...
SEIHO BOYS HIGH SCHOOL!

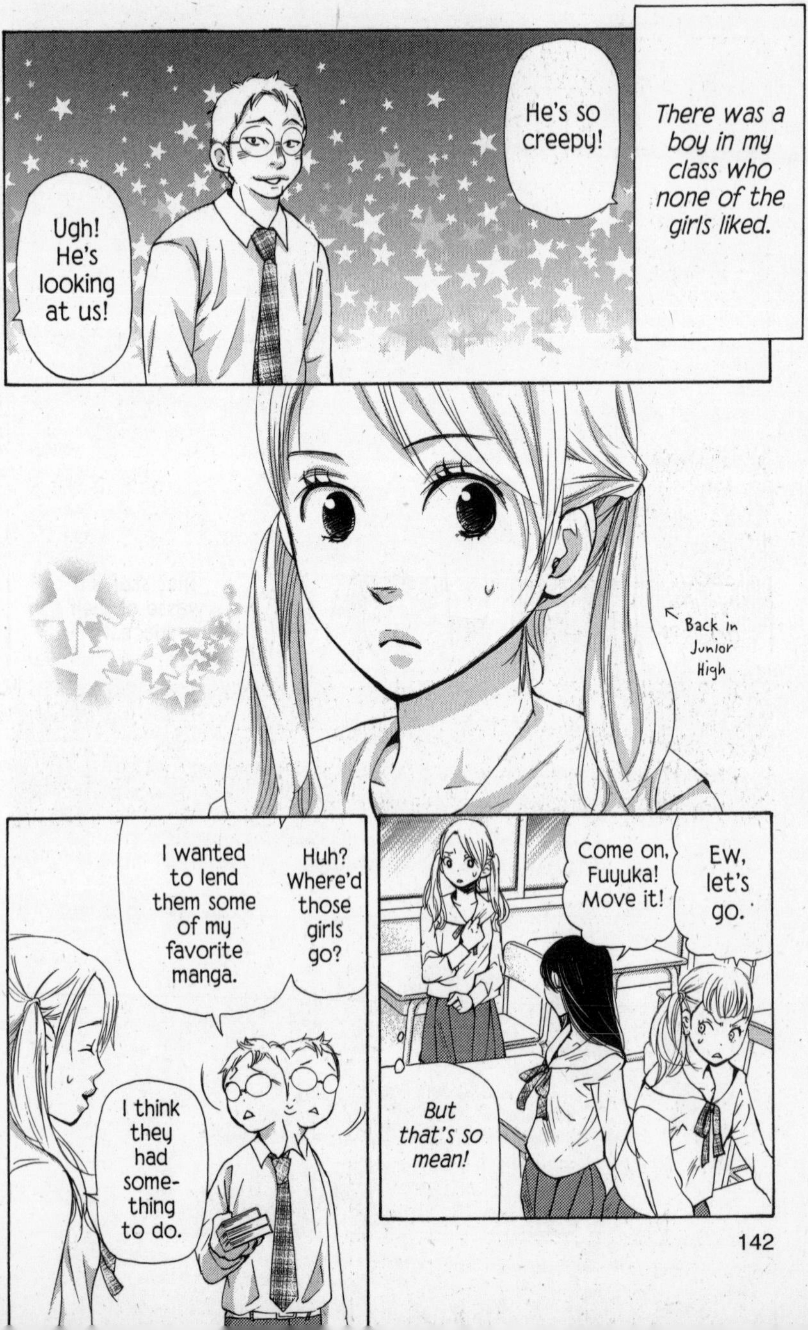
There was a boy in my class who none of the girls liked.
He's so creepy!
Ugh! He's looking at us!
Back in Junior High
Ew, let's go.
Come on, Fuyuka! Move it!
But that's so mean!
Huh? Where'd those girls go?
I wanted to lend them some of my favorite manga.
I think they had some-thing to do.

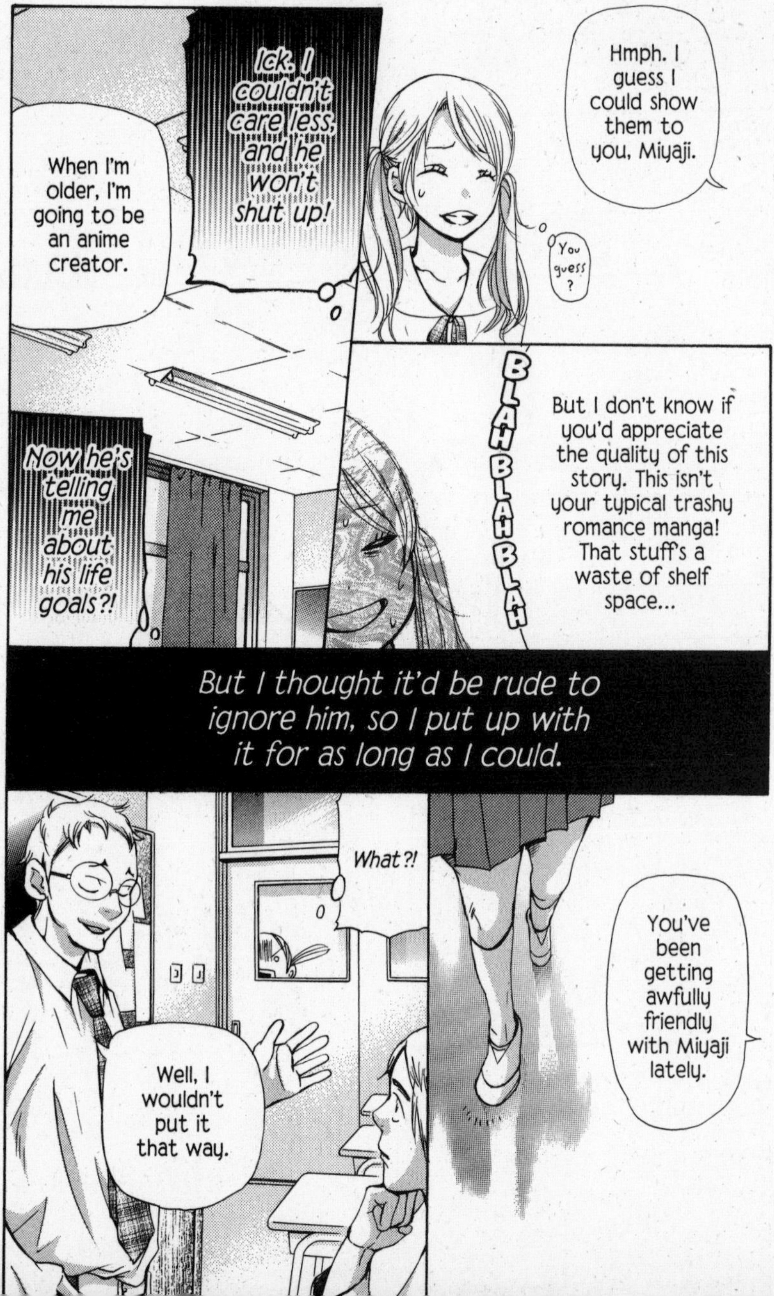
Hmph. I guess I could show them to you, Miyaji.
You guess?
But I don't know if you'd appreciate the quality of this story. This isn't your typical trashy romance manga! That stuff's a waste of shelf space...
BLAH BLAH BLAH
When I'm older, I'm going to be an anime creator.
Ick. I couldn't care less, and he won't shut up!
Now he's telling me about his life goals?!
But I thought it'd be rude to ignore him, so I put up with it for as long as I could.
You've been getting awfully friendly with Miyaji lately.
What?!
Well, I wouldn't put it that way.

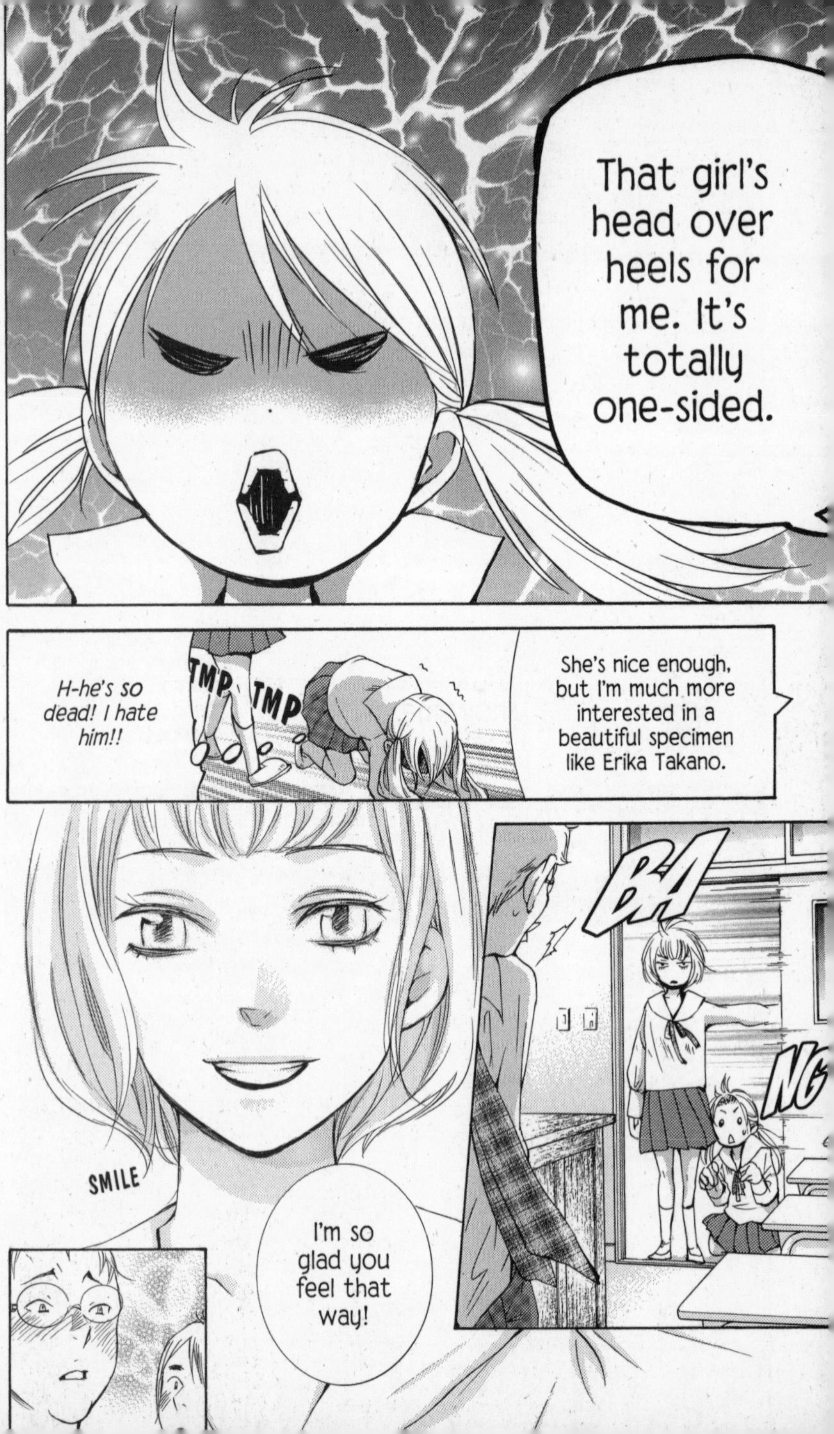
That girl's head over heels for me. It's totally one-sided.
She's nice enough, but I'm much more interested in a beautiful specimen like Erika Takano.
TMP TMP
H-he's so dead! I hate him!!
BANG
SMILE
I'm so glad you feel that way!

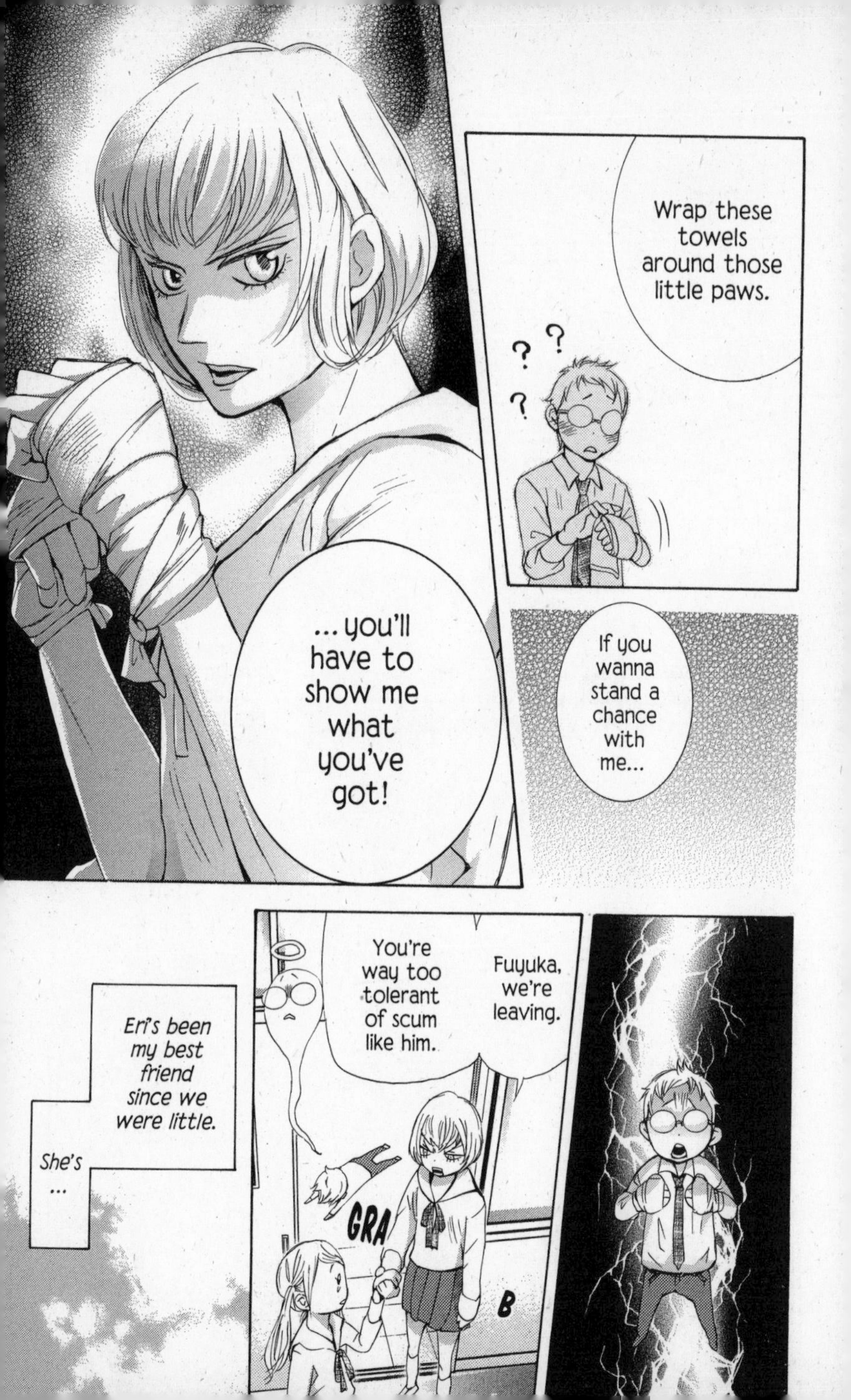
Wrap these towels around those little paws.
If you wanna stand a chance with me...
...you'll have to show me what you've got!
Fuyuka, we're leaving.
You're way too tolerant of scum like him.
GRA
B
Eri's been my best friend since we were little.
She's ...

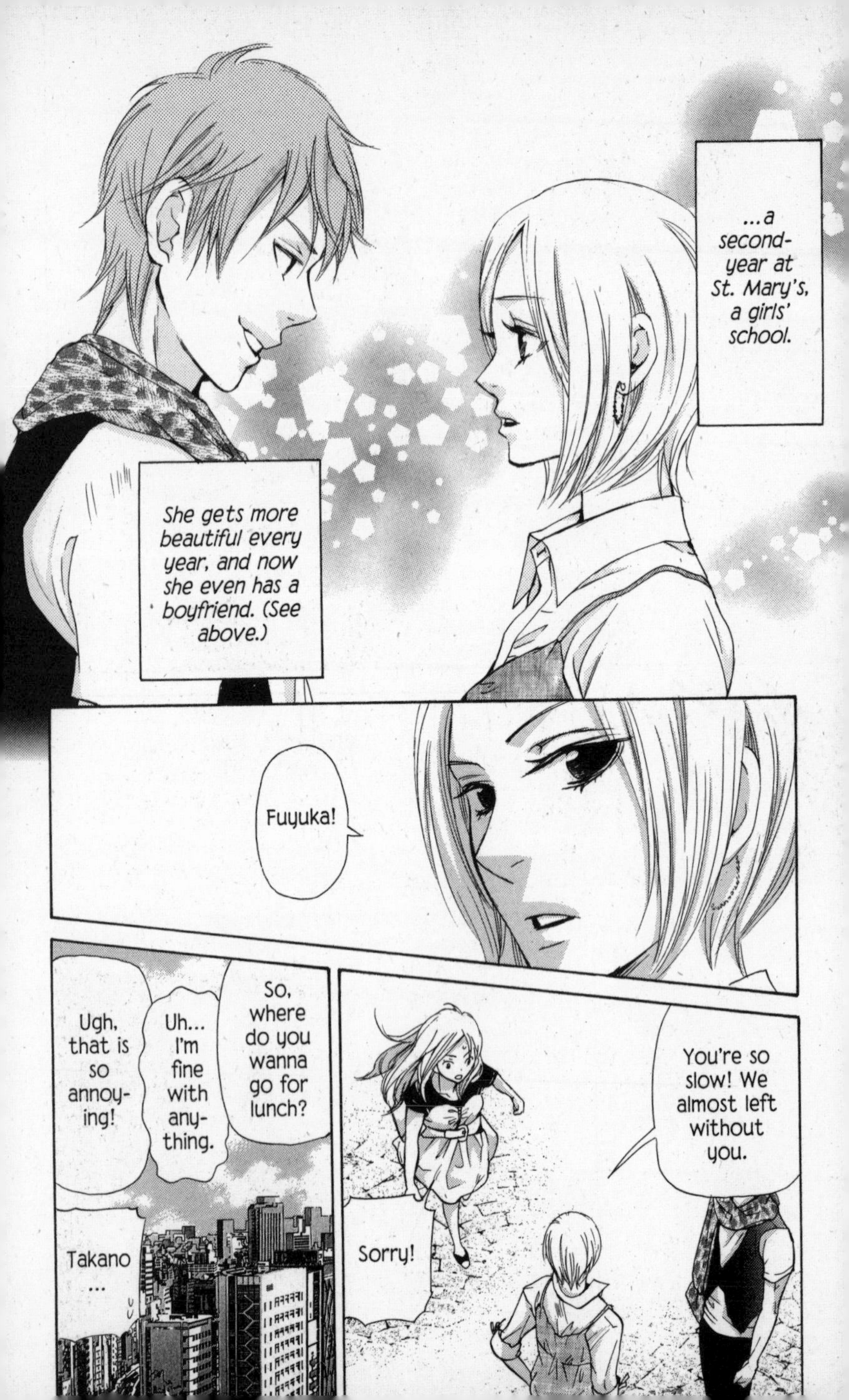
...a second-year at St. Mary's, a girls' school.
She gets more beautiful every year, and now she even has a boyfriend. (See above.)
Fuyuka!
You're so slow! We almost left without you.
Sorry!
So, where do you wanna go for lunch?
Uh... I'm fine with anything.
Ugh, that is so annoying!
Takano ...

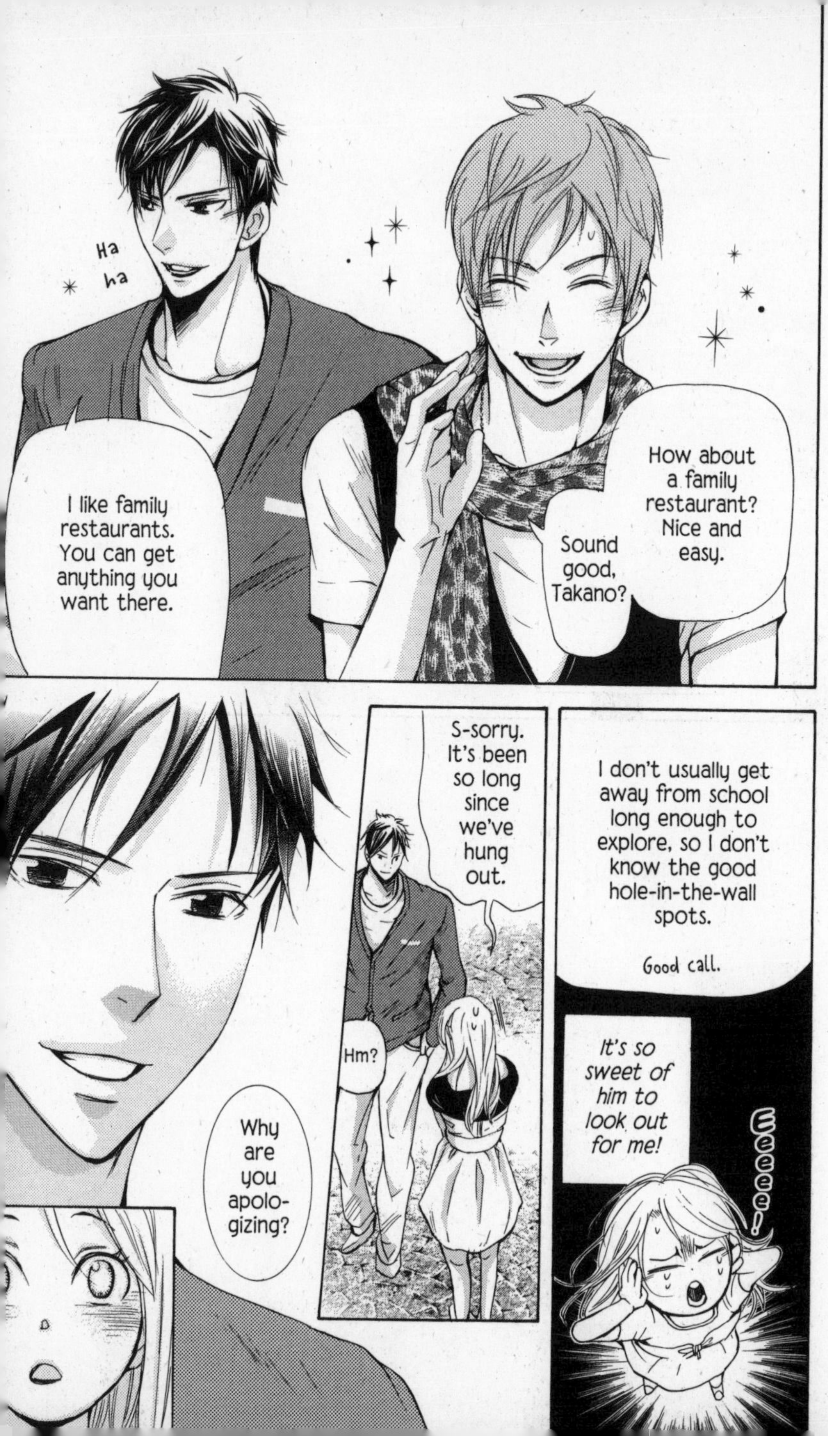
How about a family restaurant? Nice and easy.
Sound good, Takano?
Ha ha
I like family restaurants. You can get anything you want there.
I don't usually get away from school long enough to explore, so I don't know the good hole-in-the-wall spots.
Good call.
It's so sweet of him to look out for me!
Eeeeee!
S-sorry. It's been so long since we've hung out.
Hm?
Why are you apologizing?

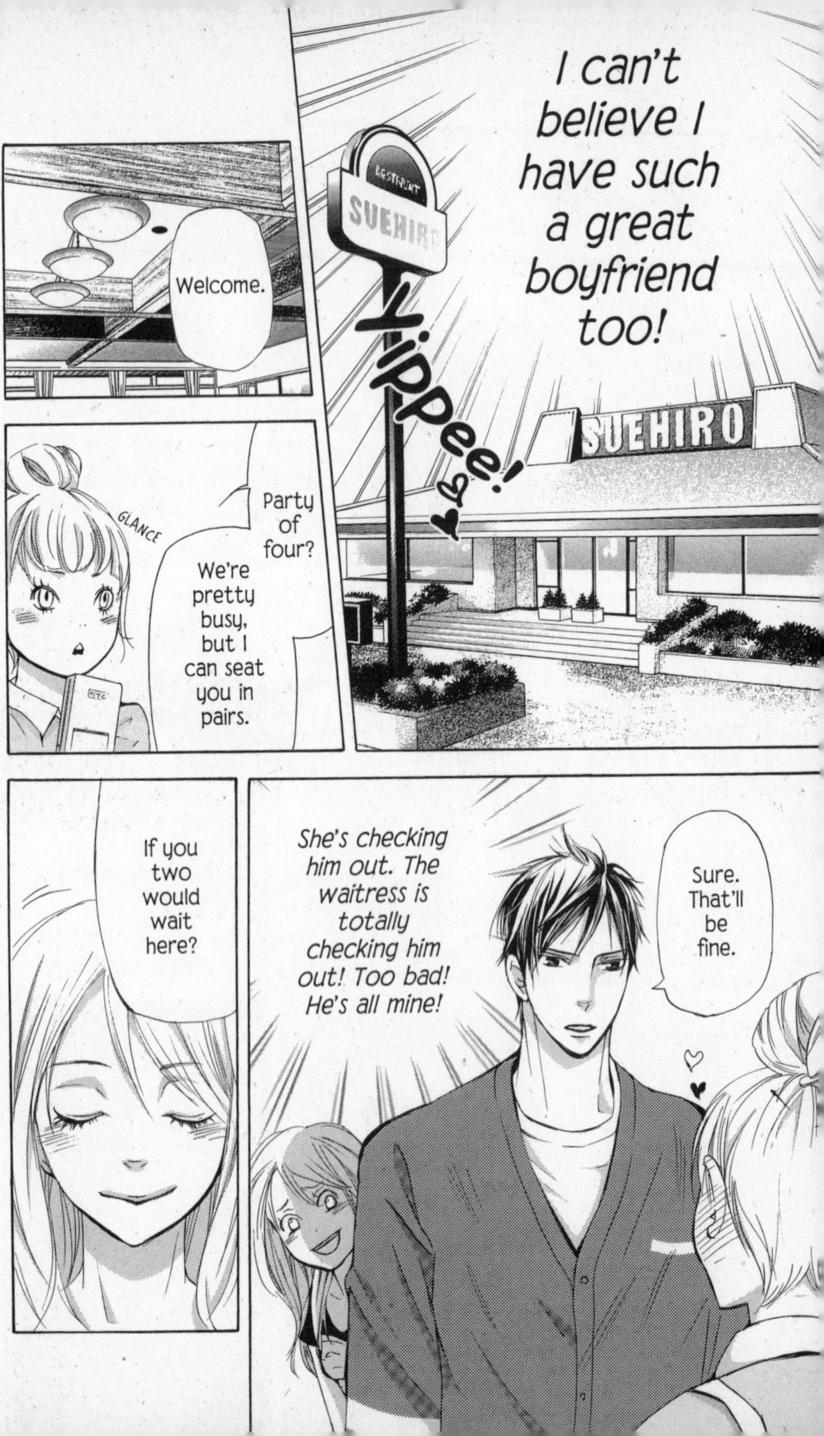
I can't believe I have such a great boyfriend too!
Yippee!
SUEHIRO
Welcome.
GLANCE
Party of four?
We're pretty busy, but I can seat you in pairs.
Sure. That'll be fine.
She's checking him out. The waitress is totally checking him out! Too bad! He's all mine!
If you two would wait here?

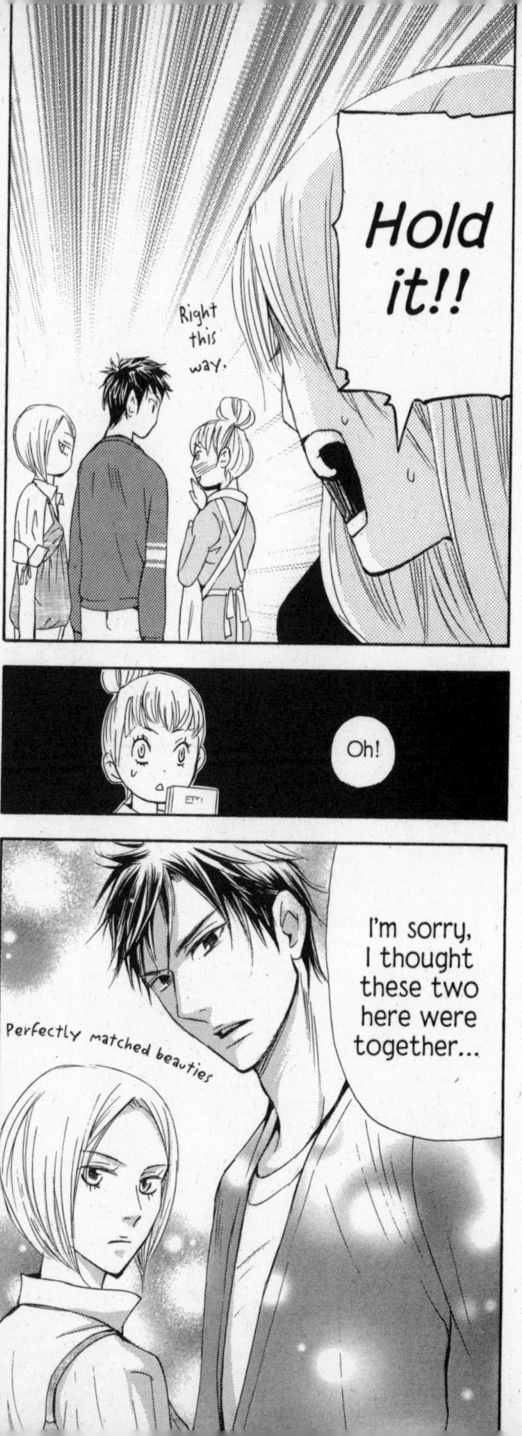
Hold it!!
Right this way.
Oh!
I'm sorry, I thought these two here were together...
Perfectly matched beauties

Seiho Boys' High School! Drama CD ①~④

Sorry to have to cram this into such a small space, but I have an announcement!

The CD is being released by Cyber Phase and features very impressive voice actors, so if you're interested, **by all means**, pick up a copy.

<Cast>
Maki = Jun Fukuyama
Kamiki = Daisuke Ono
Nogami = Takehito Koyasu
Hanai = Wataru Hatano
Genda = Kenta Miyake

They even let me visit their dubbing once, and the performances of the voice actors was truly incredible.

WOW

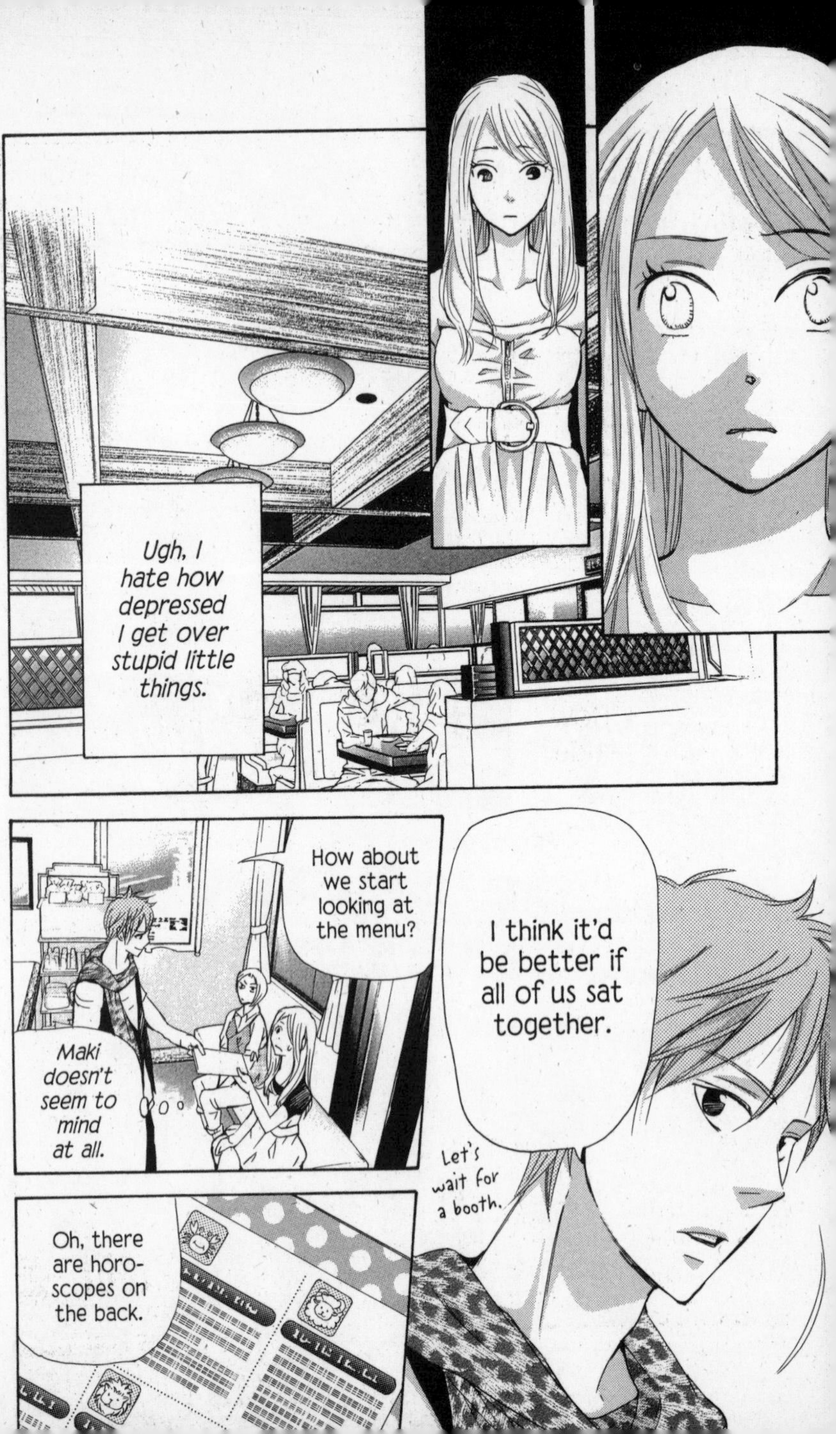
Ugh, I hate how depressed I get over stupid little things.
I think it'd be better if all of us sat together.
Let's wait for a booth.
How about we start looking at the menu?
Maki doesn't seem to mind at all.
Oh, there are horoscopes on the back.

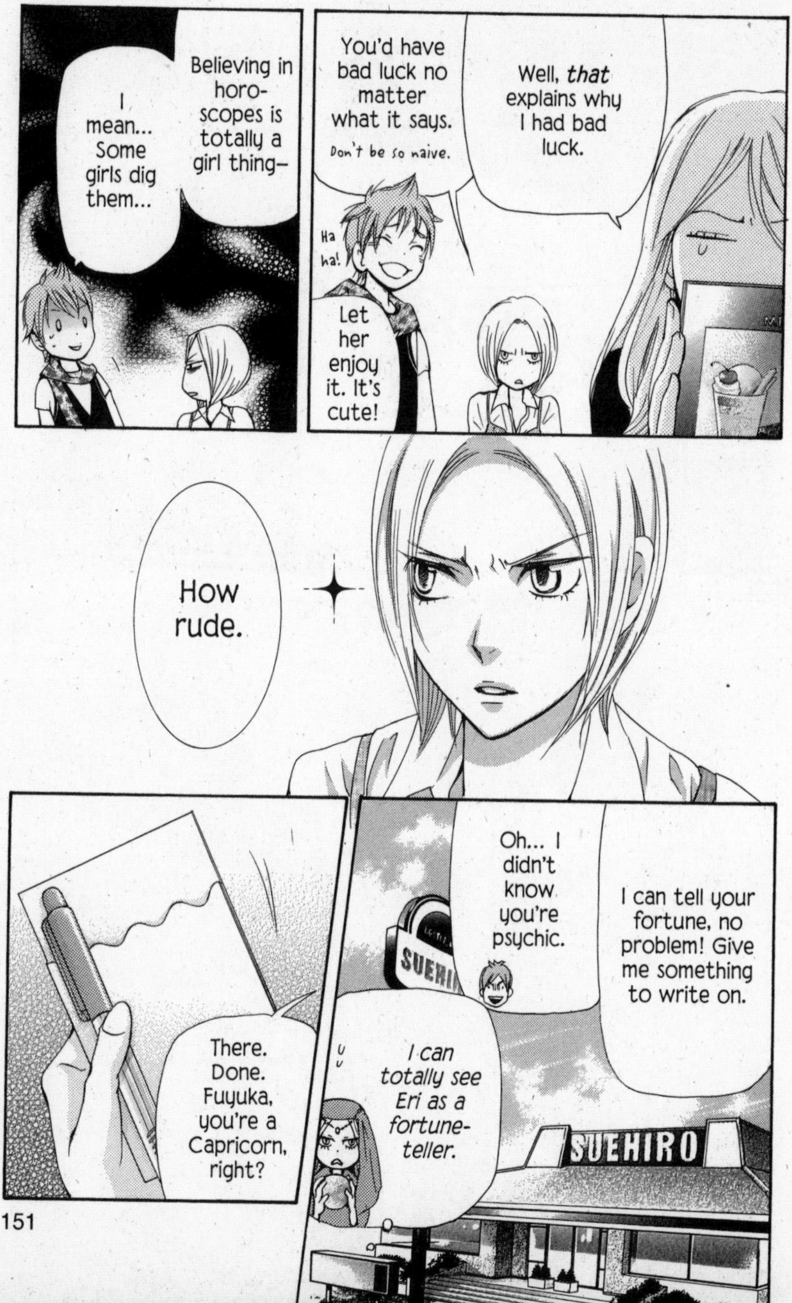
Well, *that* explains why I had bad luck.
You'd have bad luck no matter what it says.
Don't be so naive.
Ha ha!
Let her enjoy it. It's cute!
Believing in horoscopes is totally a girl thing–
I mean... Some girls dig them...
How rude.
I can tell your fortune, no problem! Give me something to write on.
Oh... I didn't know you're psychic.
SUEHIRO
I can totally see Eri as a fortune-teller.
SUEHIRO
There. Done. Fuyuka, you're a Capricorn, right?

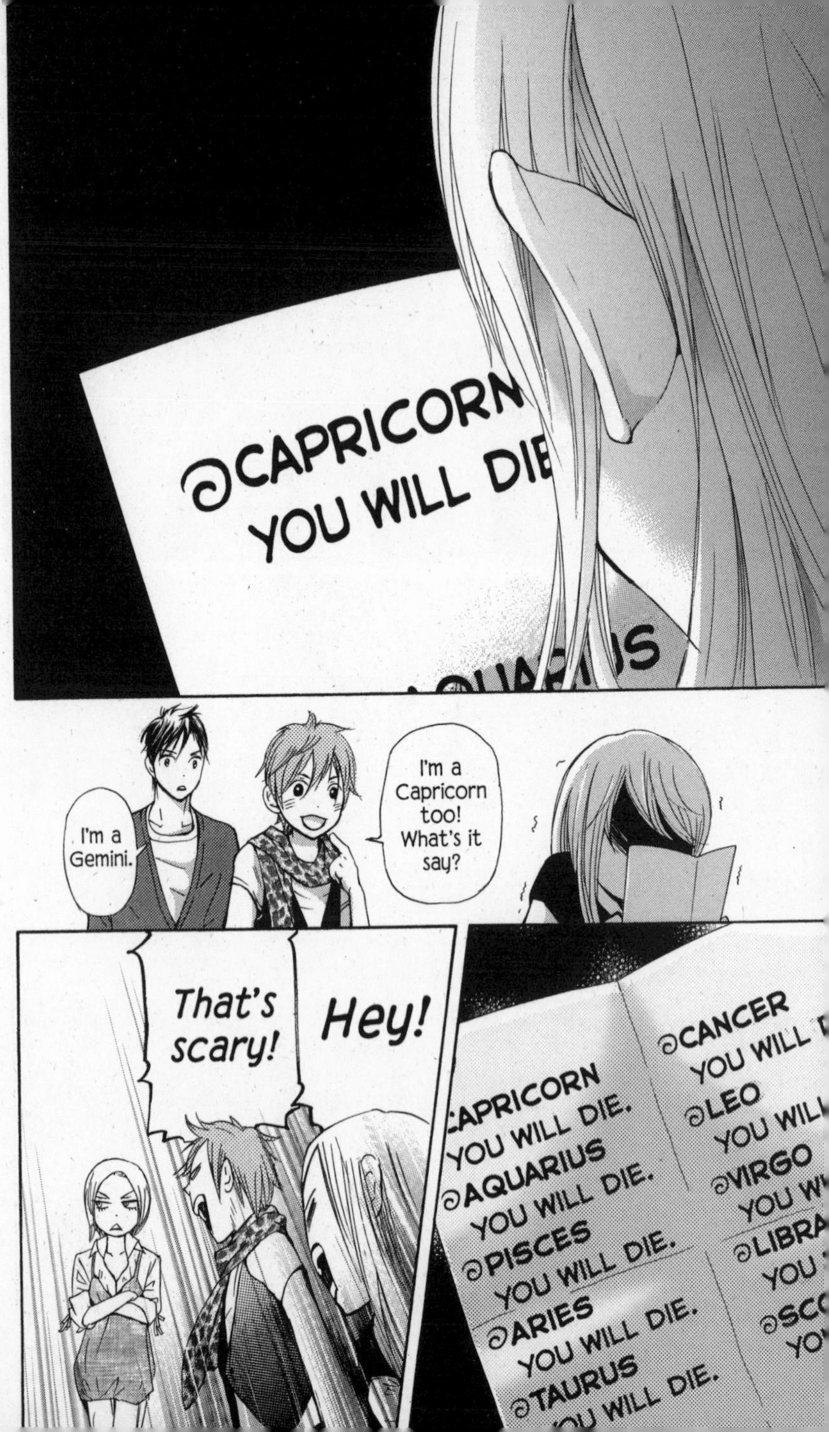
CAPRICORN
YOU WILL DIE
I'm a Capricorn too! What's it say?
I'm a Gemini.
CAPRICORN
YOU WILL DIE.
AQUARIUS
YOU WILL DIE.
PISCES
YOU WILL DIE.
ARIES
YOU WILL DIE.
TAURUS
CANCER
LEO
VIRGO
Hey!
That's scary!

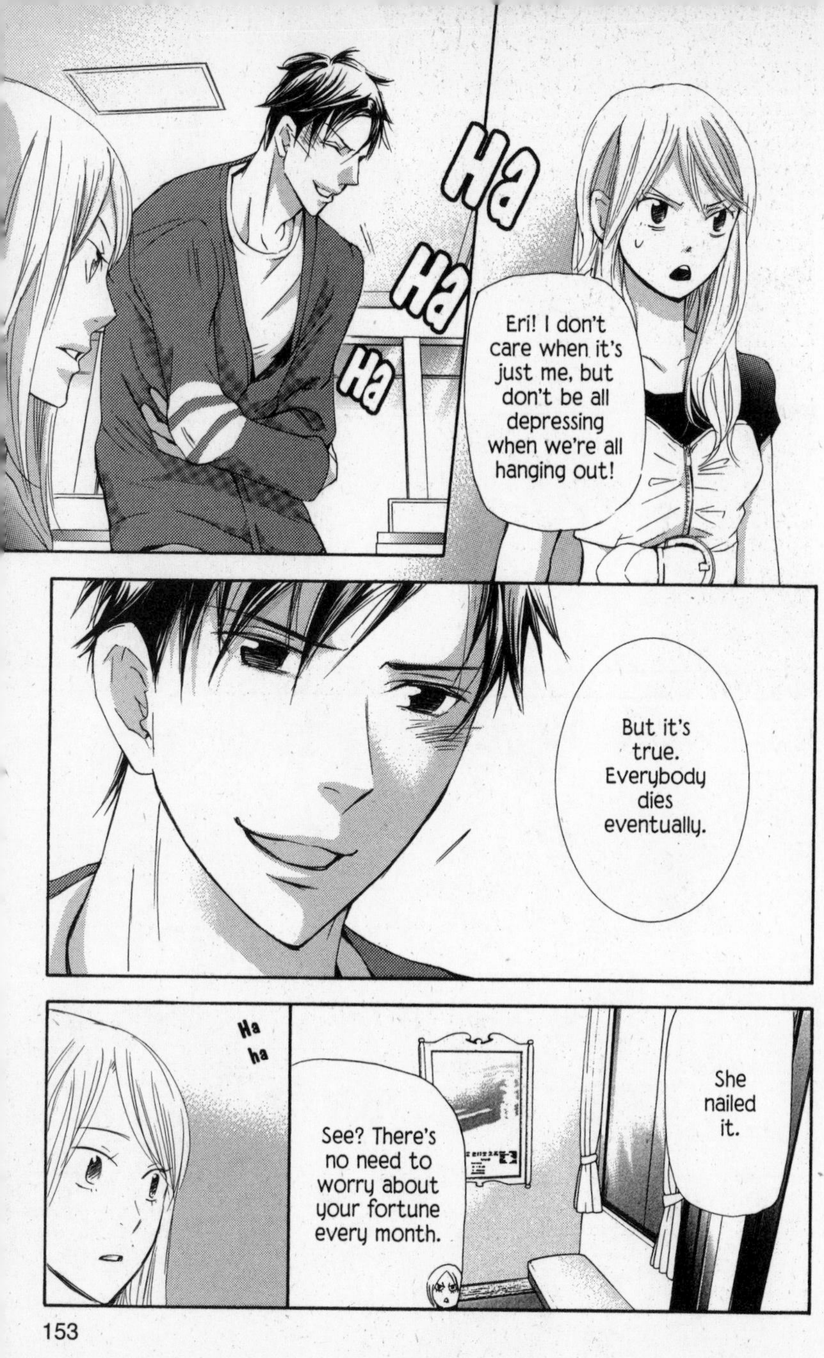
Eri! I don't care when it's just me, but don't be all depressing when we're all hanging out!
Ha
Ha
Ha
But it's true. Everybody dies eventually.
She nailed it.
See? There's no need to worry about your fortune every month.
Ha ha

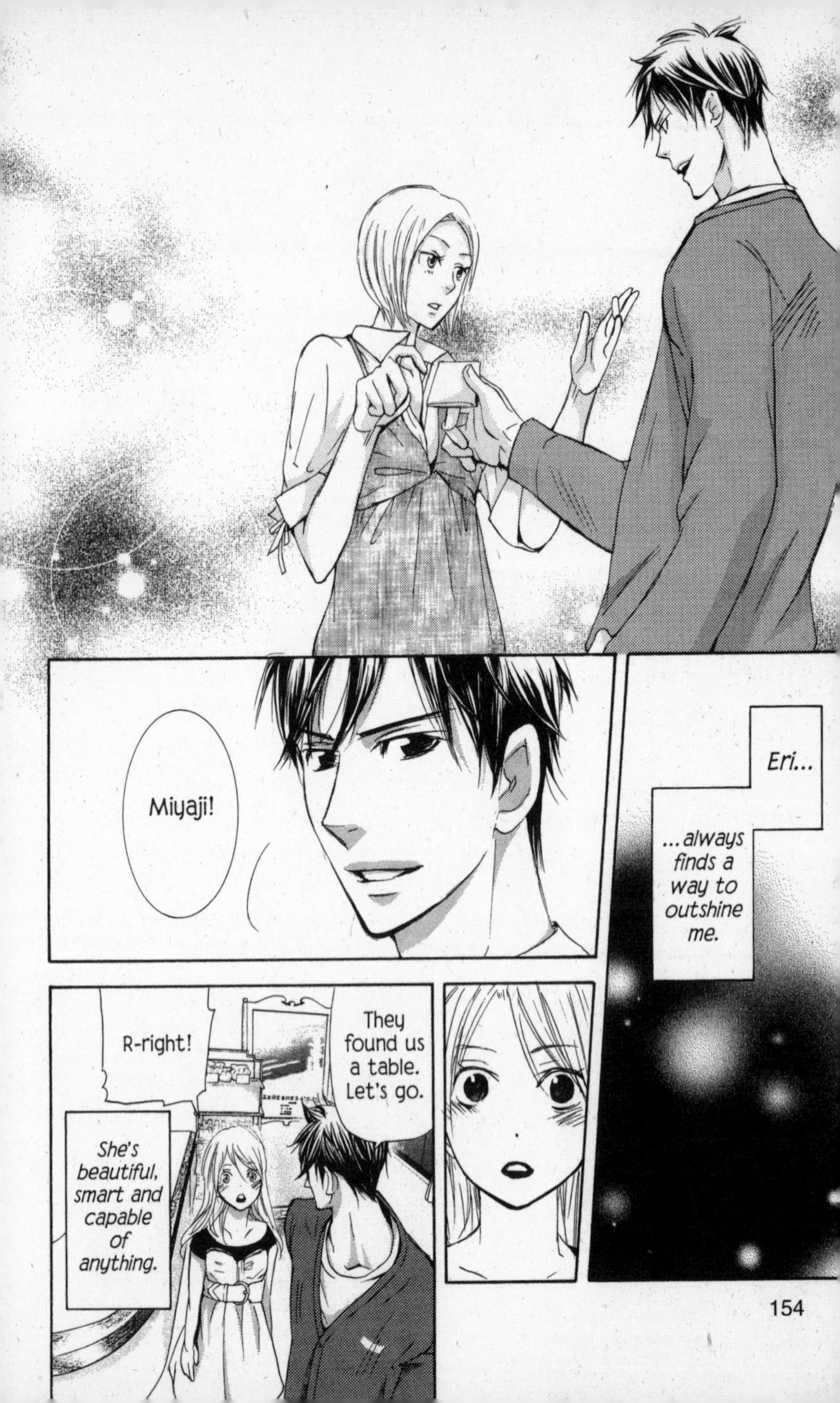
Eri...
...always finds a way to outshine me.
Miyaji!
They found us a table. Let's go.
R-right!
She's beautiful, smart and capable of anything.

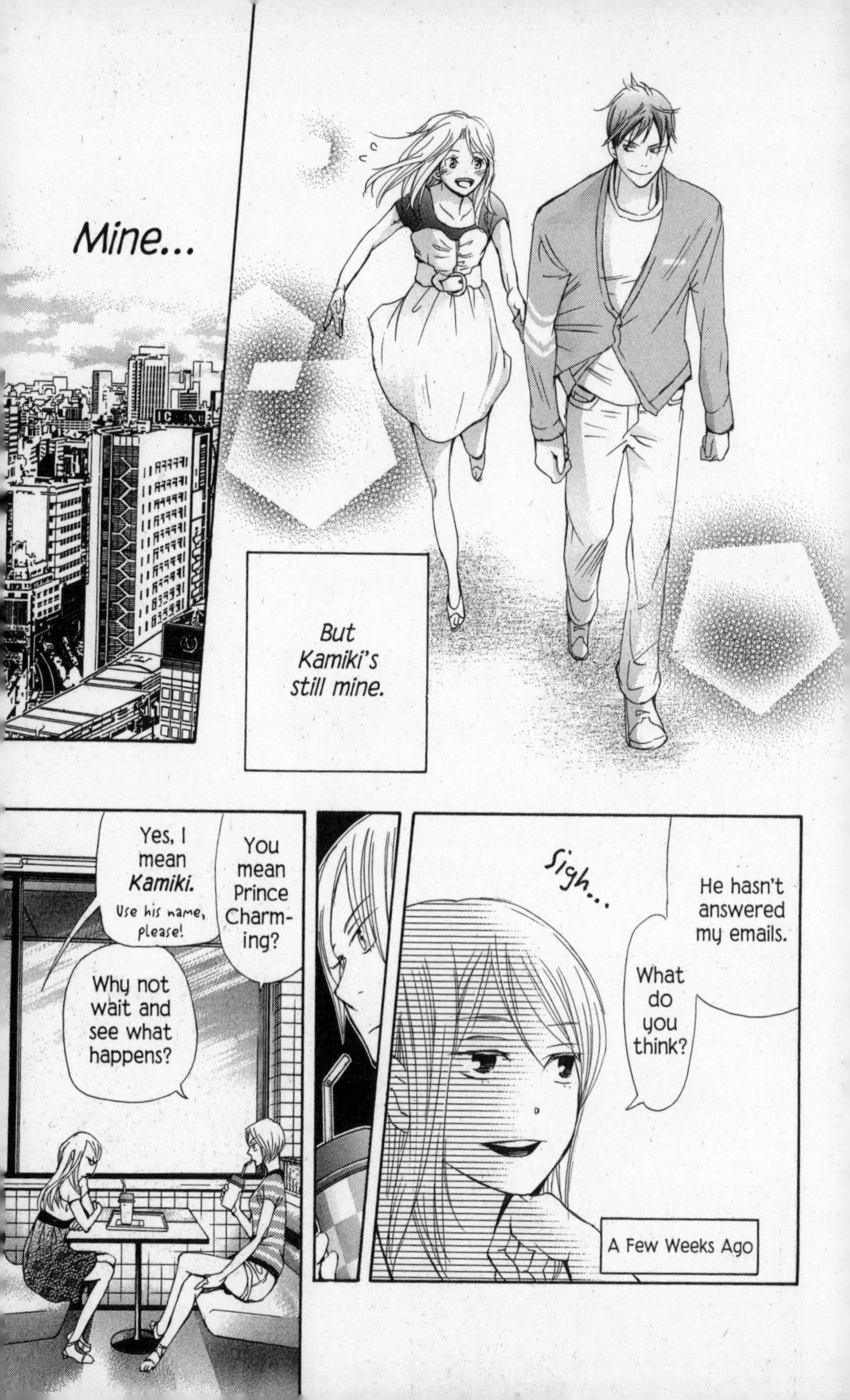
But Kamiki's still mine.
Mine...
Sigh...
He hasn't answered my emails.
What do you think?
A Few Weeks Ago
You mean Prince Charming?
Yes, I mean *Kamiki.* Use his name, please!
Why not wait and see what happens?

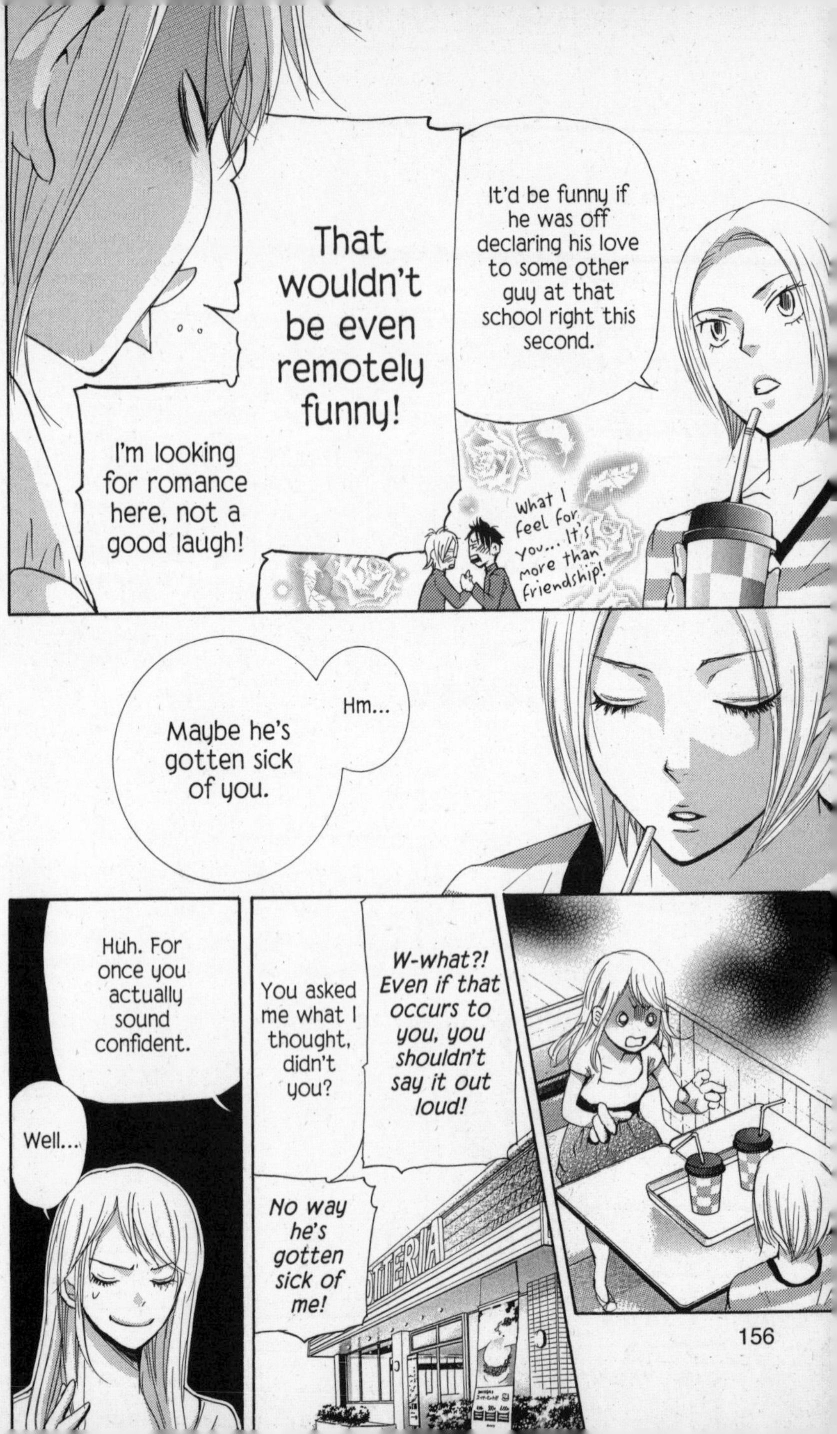
It'd be funny if he was off declaring his love to some other guy at that school right this second.
What I feel for you... It's more than friendship!
That wouldn't be even remotely funny!
I'm looking for romance here, not a good laugh!
Hm...
Maybe he's gotten sick of you.
W-what?! Even if that occurs to you, you shouldn't say it out loud!
You asked me what I thought, didn't you?
No way he's gotten sick of me!
Huh. For once you actually sound confident.
Well...

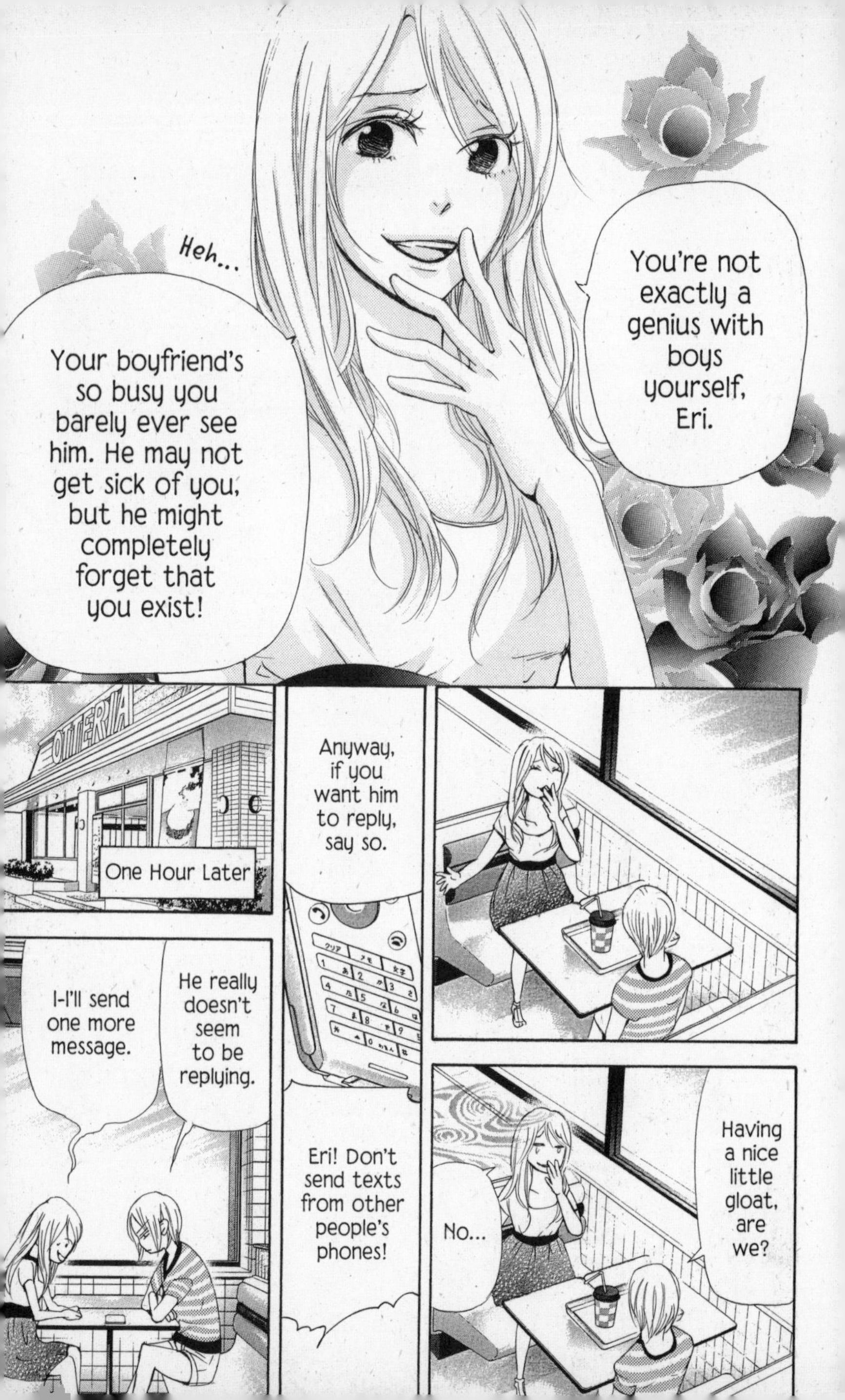
You're not exactly a genius with boys yourself, Eri.
Heh...
Your boyfriend's so busy you barely ever see him. He may not get sick of you, but he might completely forget that you exist!
Having a nice little gloat, are we?
No...
Anyway, if you want him to reply, say so.
Eri! Don't send texts from other people's phones!
OTTERIA
One Hour Later
He really doesn't seem to be replying.
I-I'll send one more message.

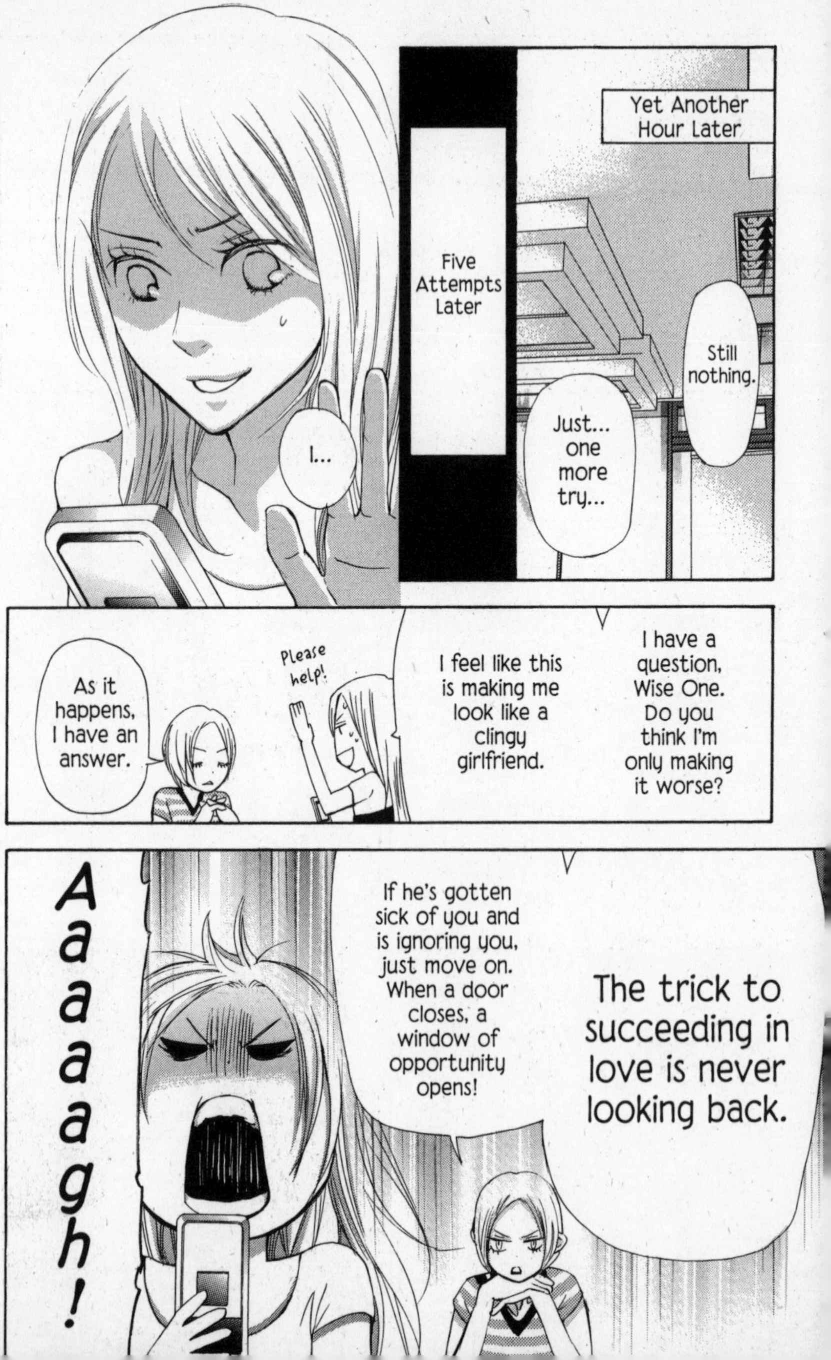
Yet Another Hour Later
Still nothing.
Just... one more try...
Five Attempts Later
I...
I have a question, Wise One. Do you think I'm only making it worse?
I feel like this is making me look like a clingy girlfriend.
Please help!
As it happens, I have an answer.
The trick to succeeding in love is never looking back.
If he's gotten sick of you and is ignoring you, just move on. When a door closes, a window of opportunity opens!
Aaaaagh!

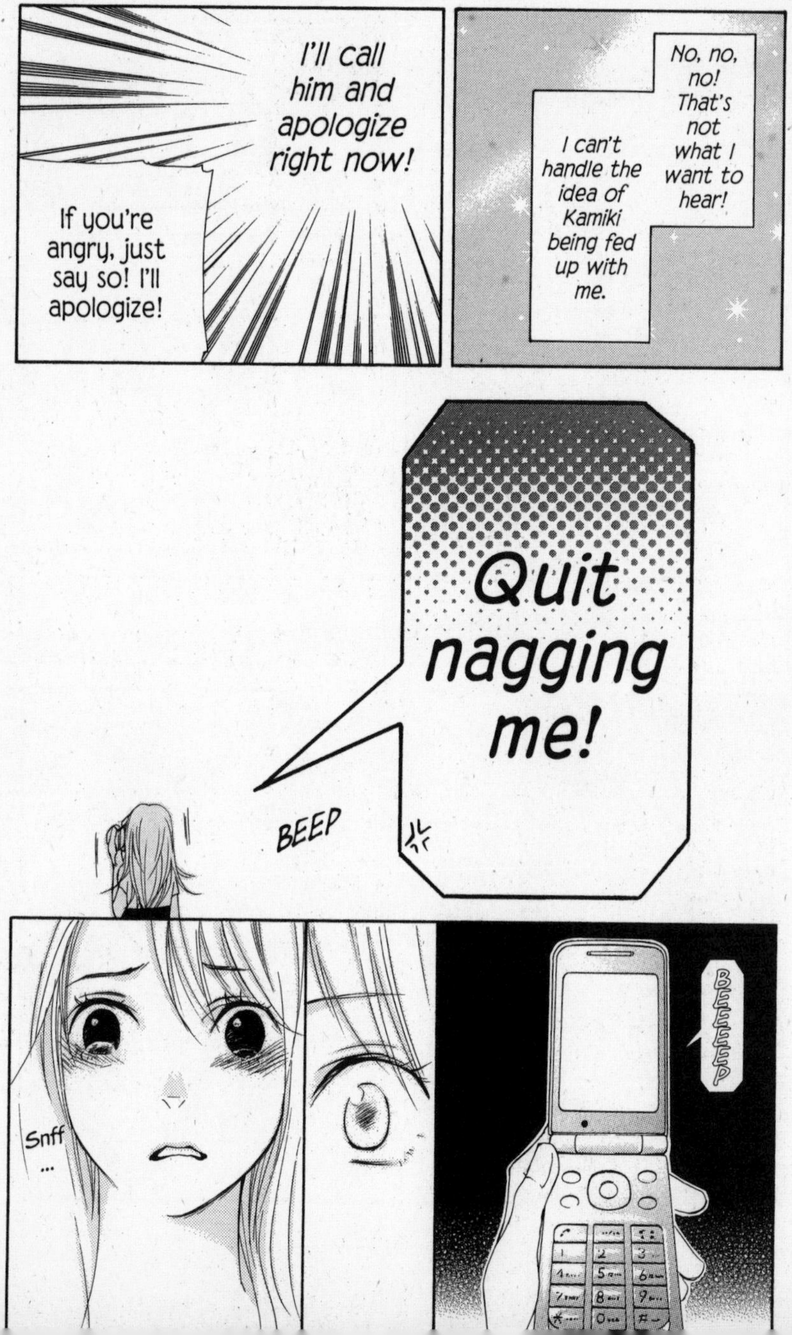
No, no, no! That's not what I want to hear!
I can't handle the idea of Kamiki being fed up with me.
I'll call him and apologize right now!
If you're angry, just say so! I'll apologize!
Quit nagging me!
BEEP
BEEEEEP
Snff ...

Sigh...
What?
You just sighed.
You're sitting there being irritated, aren't you?
No, I'm not.
But I think crying over some guy is pathetic. I don't want to see a single tear out of you.
Eri doesn't understand.

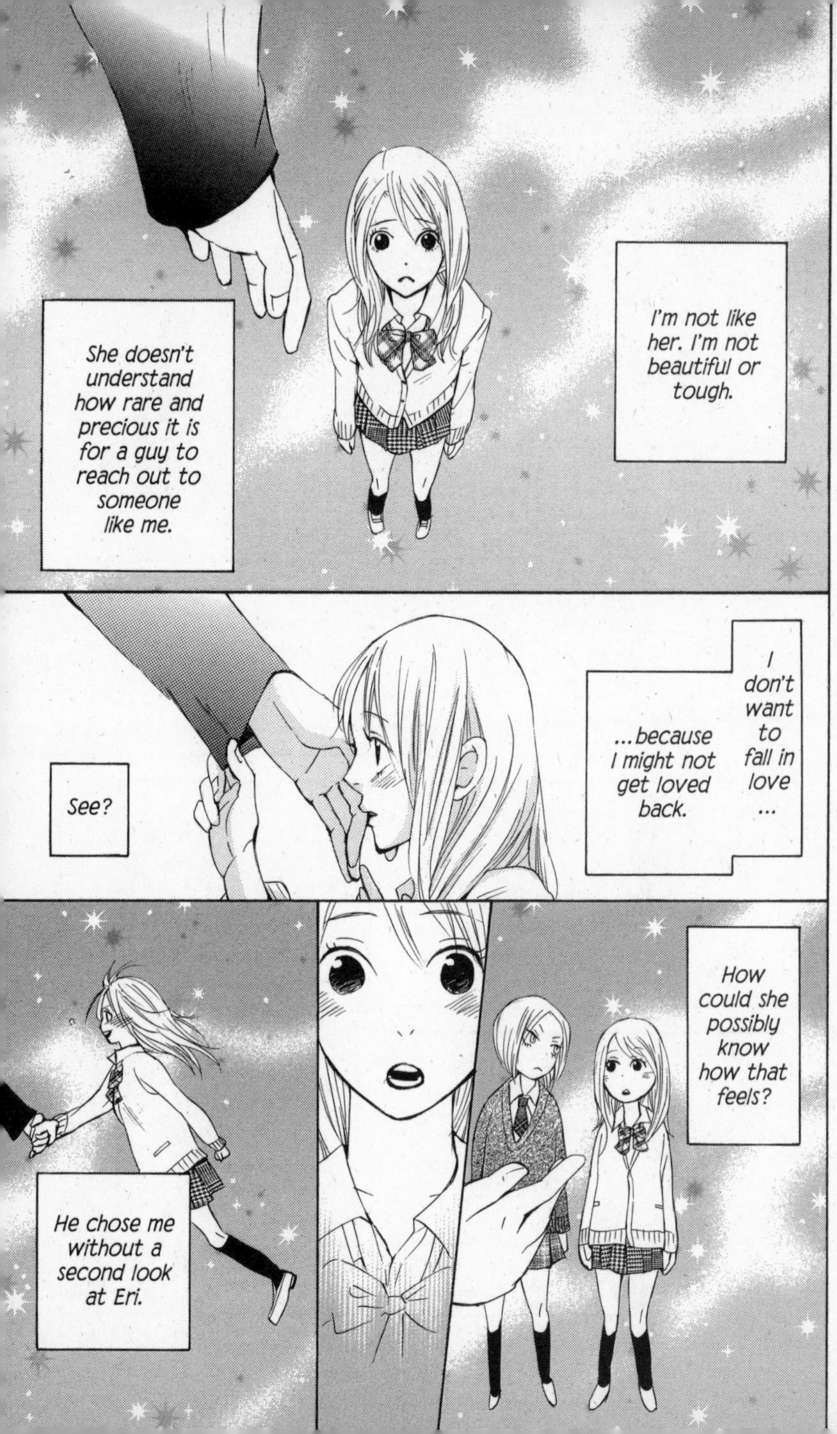
I'm not like her. I'm not beautiful or tough.
She doesn't understand how rare and precious it is for a guy to reach out to someone like me.
I don't want to fall in love ...
...because I might not get loved back.
See?
How could she possibly know how that feels?
He chose me without a second look at Eri.

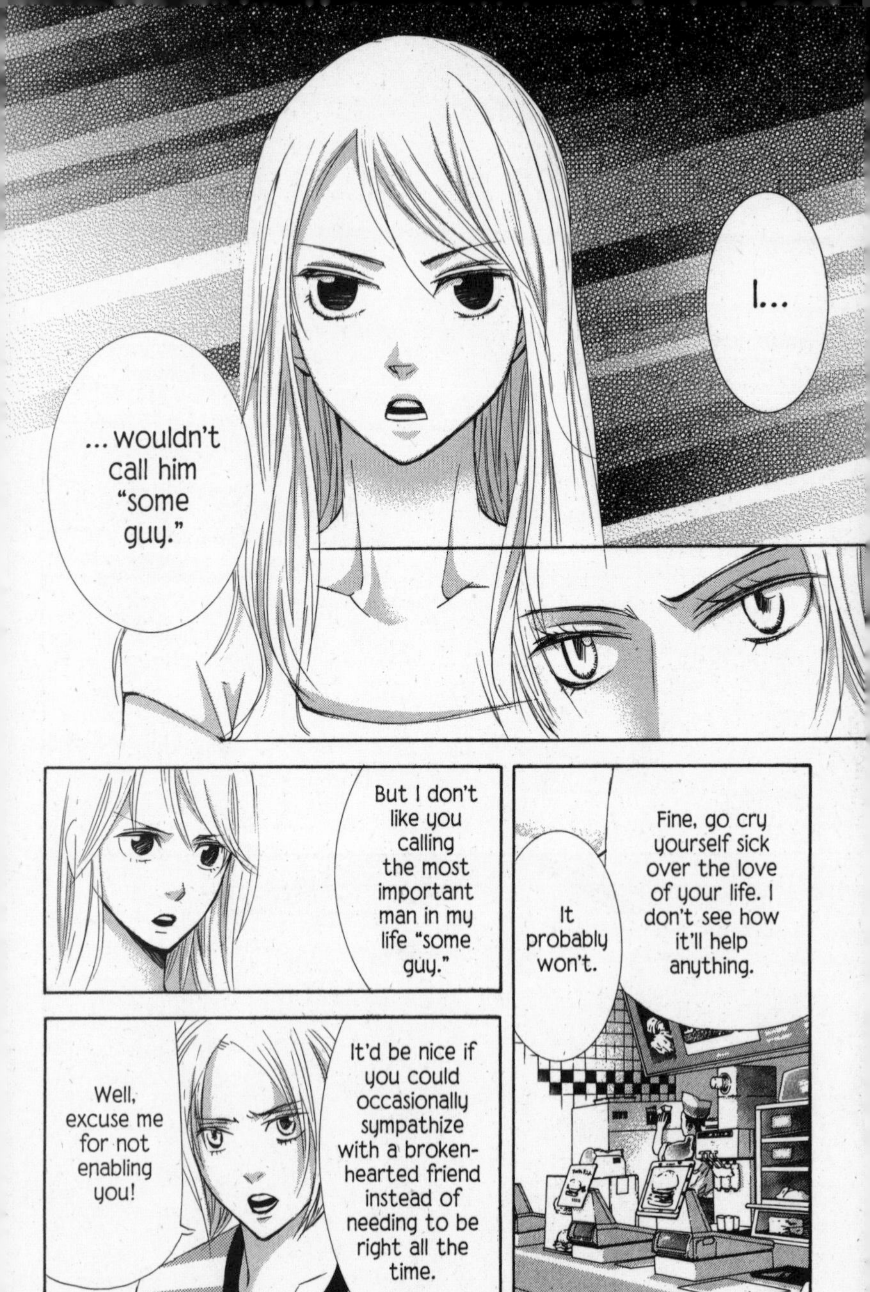
I...
...wouldn't call him "some guy."
But I don't like you calling the most important man in my life "some guy."
Fine, go cry yourself sick over the love of your life. I don't see how it'll help anything.
It probably won't.
It'd be nice if you could occasionally sympathize with a broken-hearted friend instead of needing to be right all the time.
Well, excuse me for not enabling you!

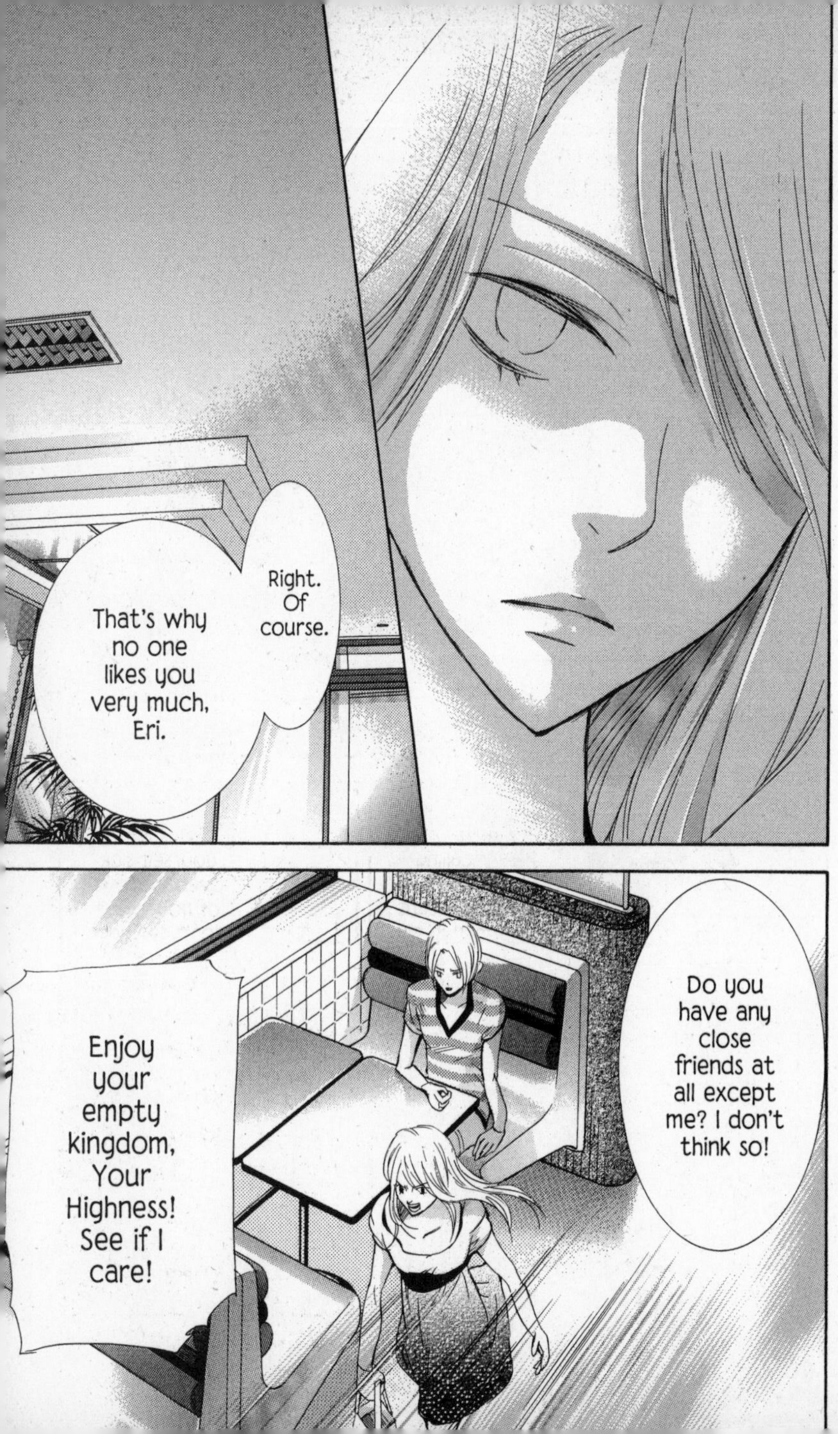
Right. Of course.
That's why no one likes you very much, Eri.
Do you have any close friends at all except me? I don't think so!
Enjoy your empty kingdom, Your Highness! See if I care!

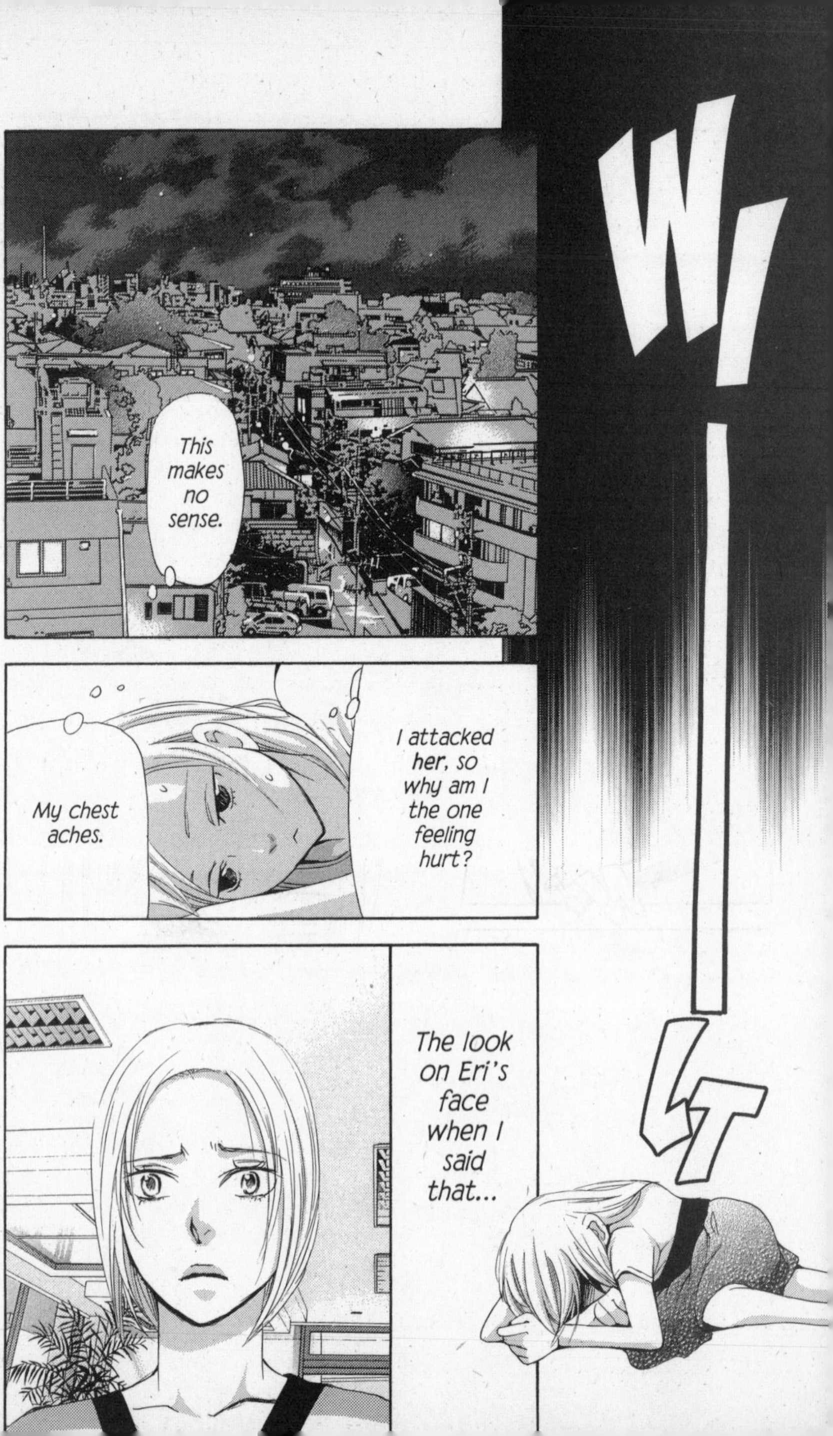
WI—LT
This makes no sense.
I attacked her, so why am I the one feeling hurt?
My chest aches.
The look on Eri's face when I said that...

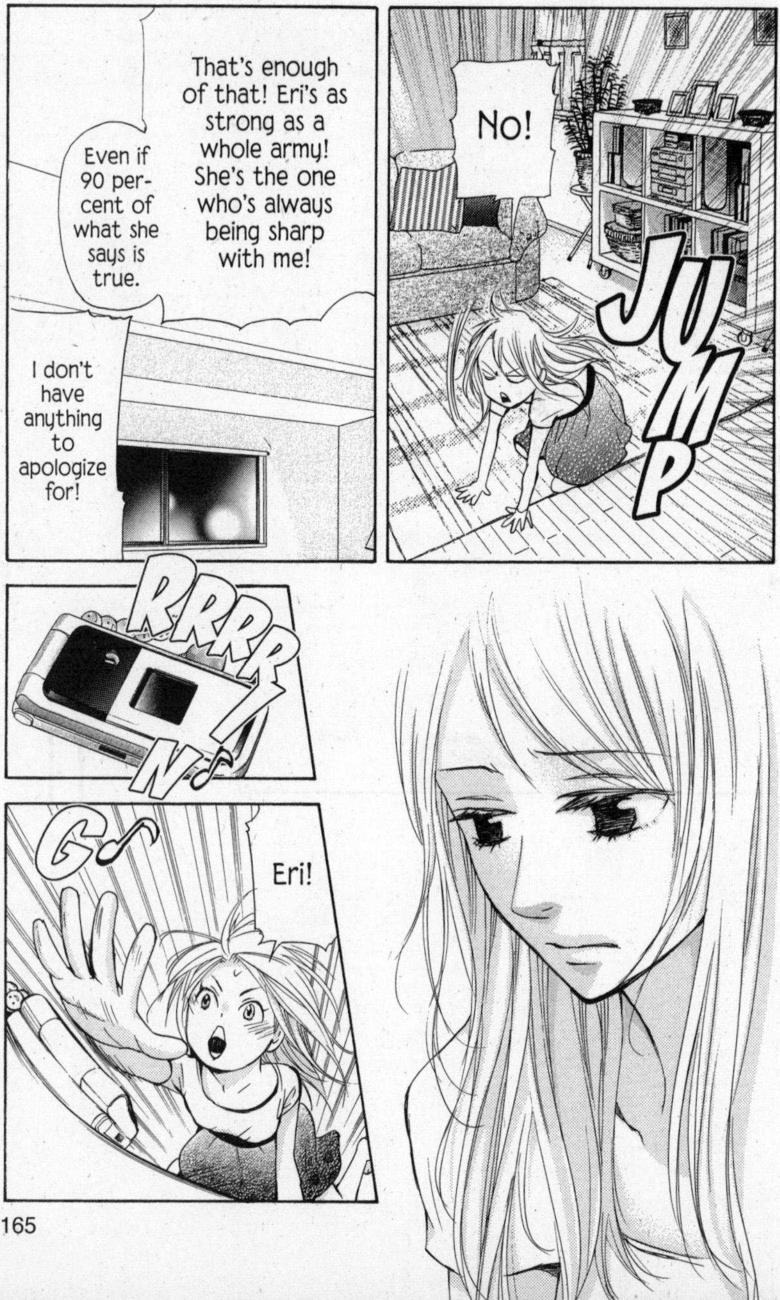
No!
JUMP
That's enough of that! Eri's as strong as a whole army! She's the one who's always being sharp with me!
Even if 90 percent of what she says is true.
I don't have anything to apologize for!
RRRRN
G
Eri!

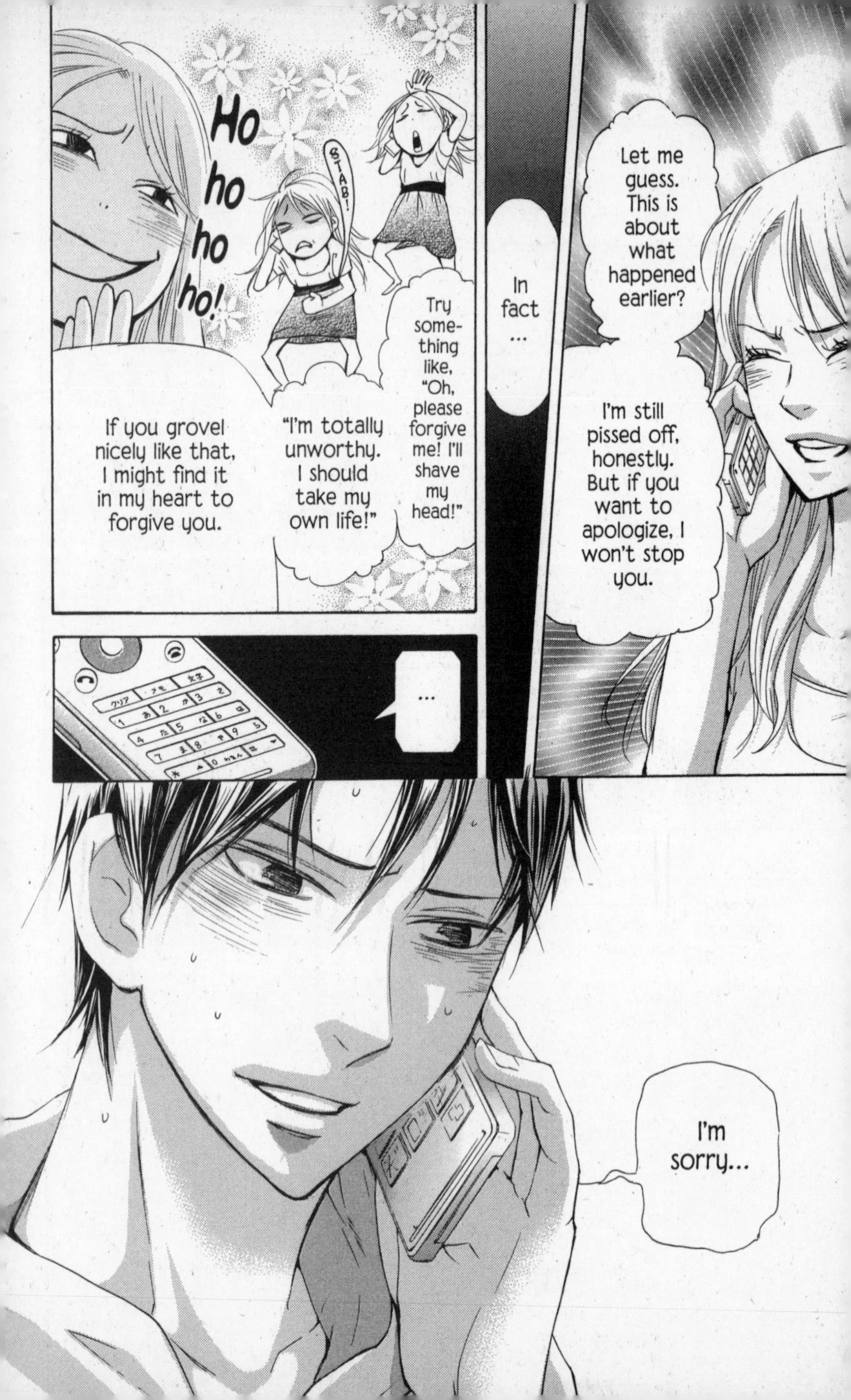
Let me guess. This is about what happened earlier?
I'm still pissed off, honestly. But if you want to apologize, I won't stop you.
In fact ...
Try something like, "Oh, please forgive me! I'll shave my head!"
"I'm totally unworthy. I should take my own life!"
STAB!
Ho ho ho ho!
If you grovel nicely like that, I might find it in my heart to forgive you.
...
I'm sorry...

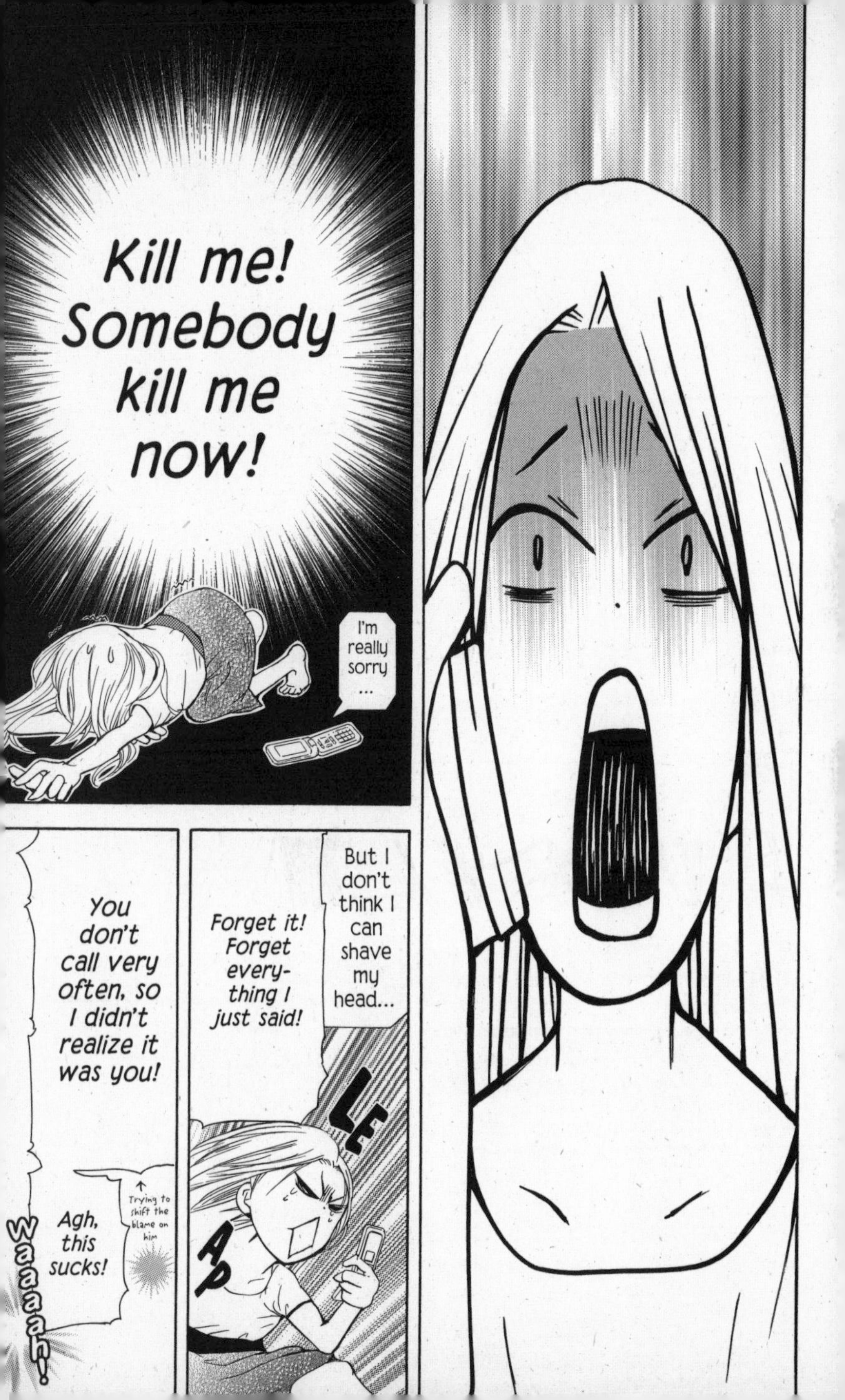
Kill me! Somebody kill me now!
I'm really sorry ...
But I don't think I can shave my head...
Forget it! Forget every-thing I just said!
LEAP
You don't call very often, so I didn't realize it was you!
↑ Trying to shift the blame on him
Agh, this sucks!
Waaaah!

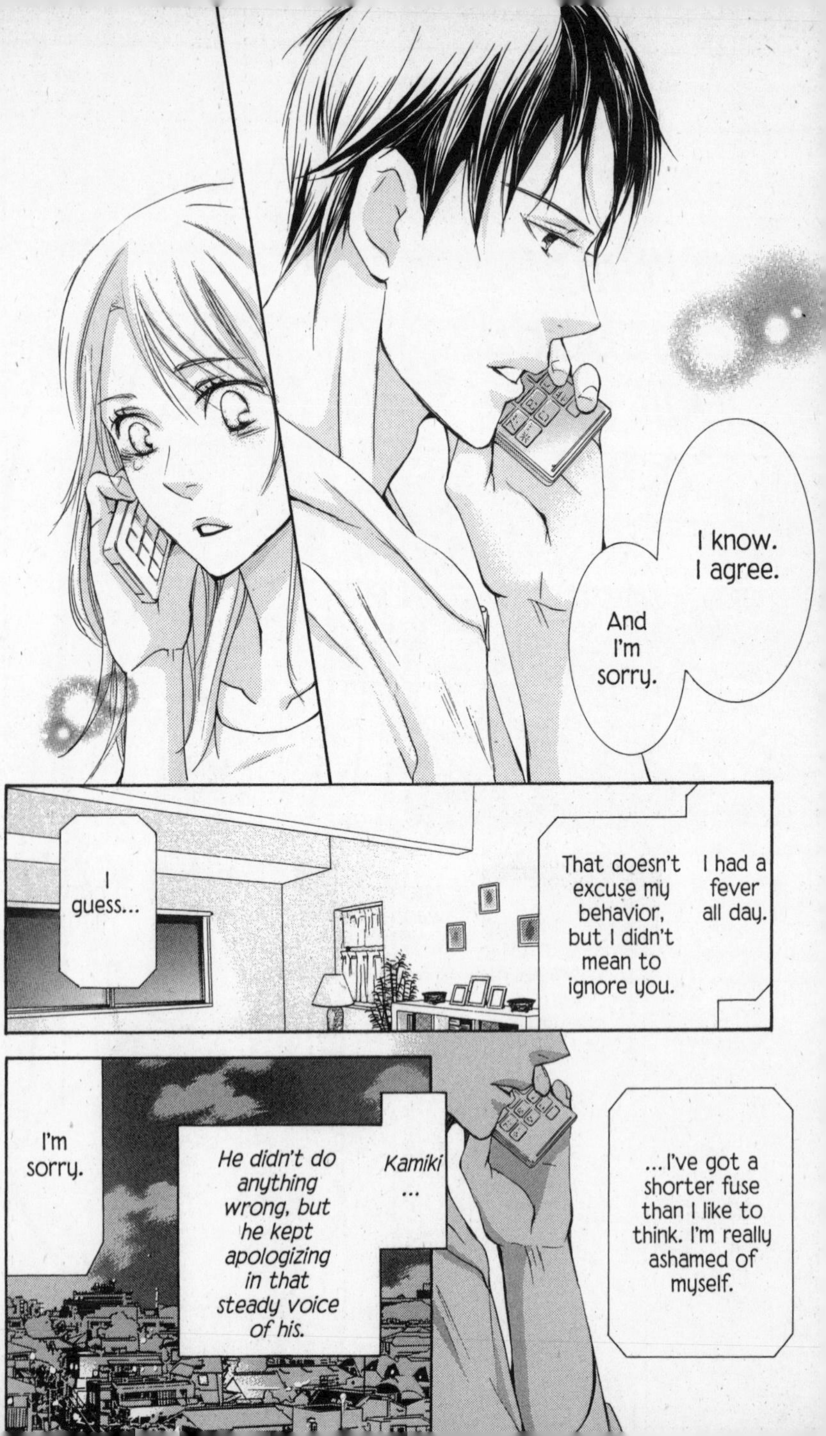
I know. I agree.
And I'm sorry.
I had a fever all day.
That doesn't excuse my behavior, but I didn't mean to ignore you.
I guess...
...I've got a shorter fuse than I like to think. I'm really ashamed of myself.
Kamiki ...
He didn't do anything wrong, but he kept apologizing in that steady voice of his.
I'm sorry.

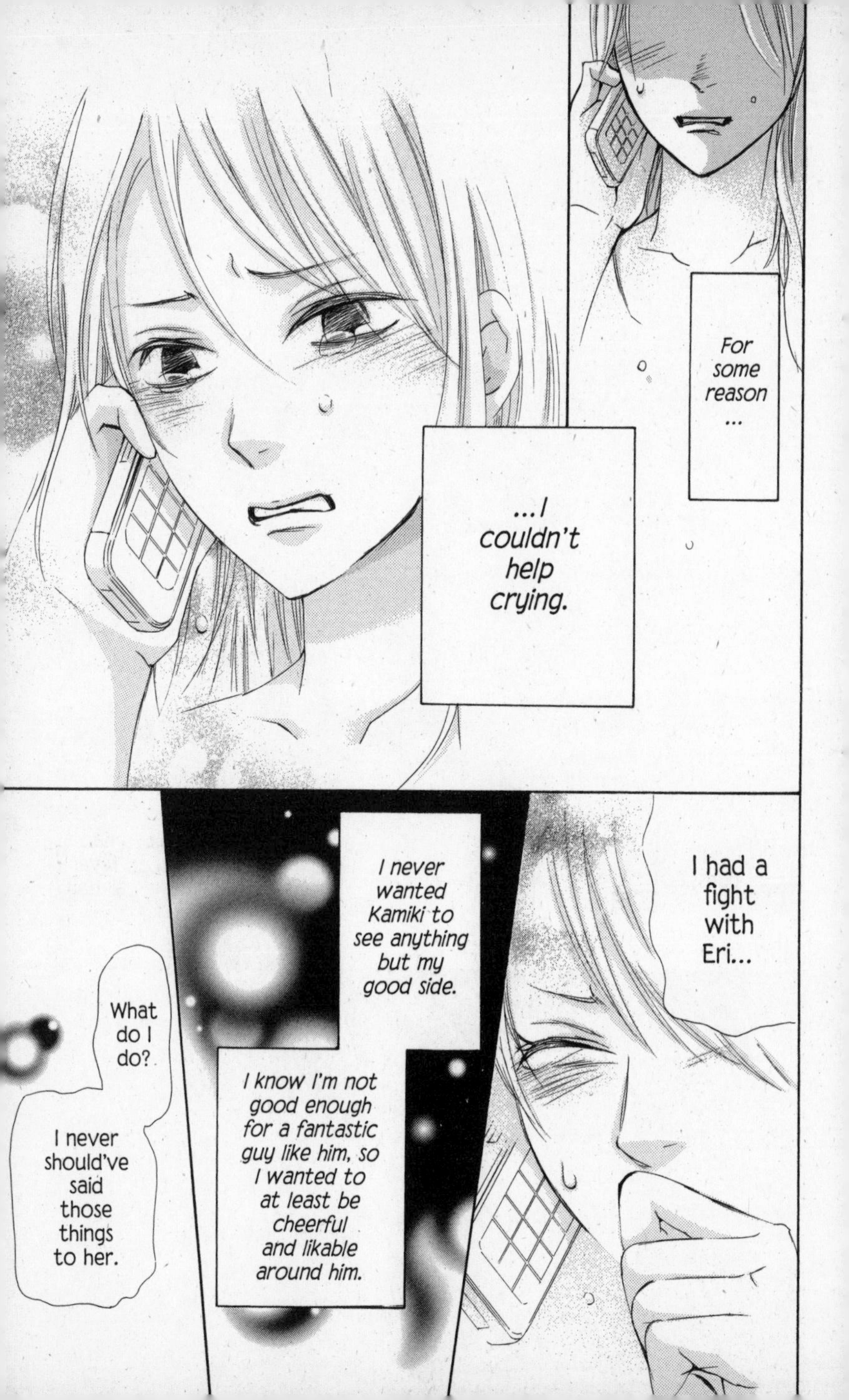
For some reason...
...I couldn't help crying.
I had a fight with Eri...
I never wanted Kamiki to see anything but my good side.
I know I'm not good enough for a fantastic guy like him, so I wanted to at least be cheerful and likable around him.
What do I do?
I never should've said those things to her.

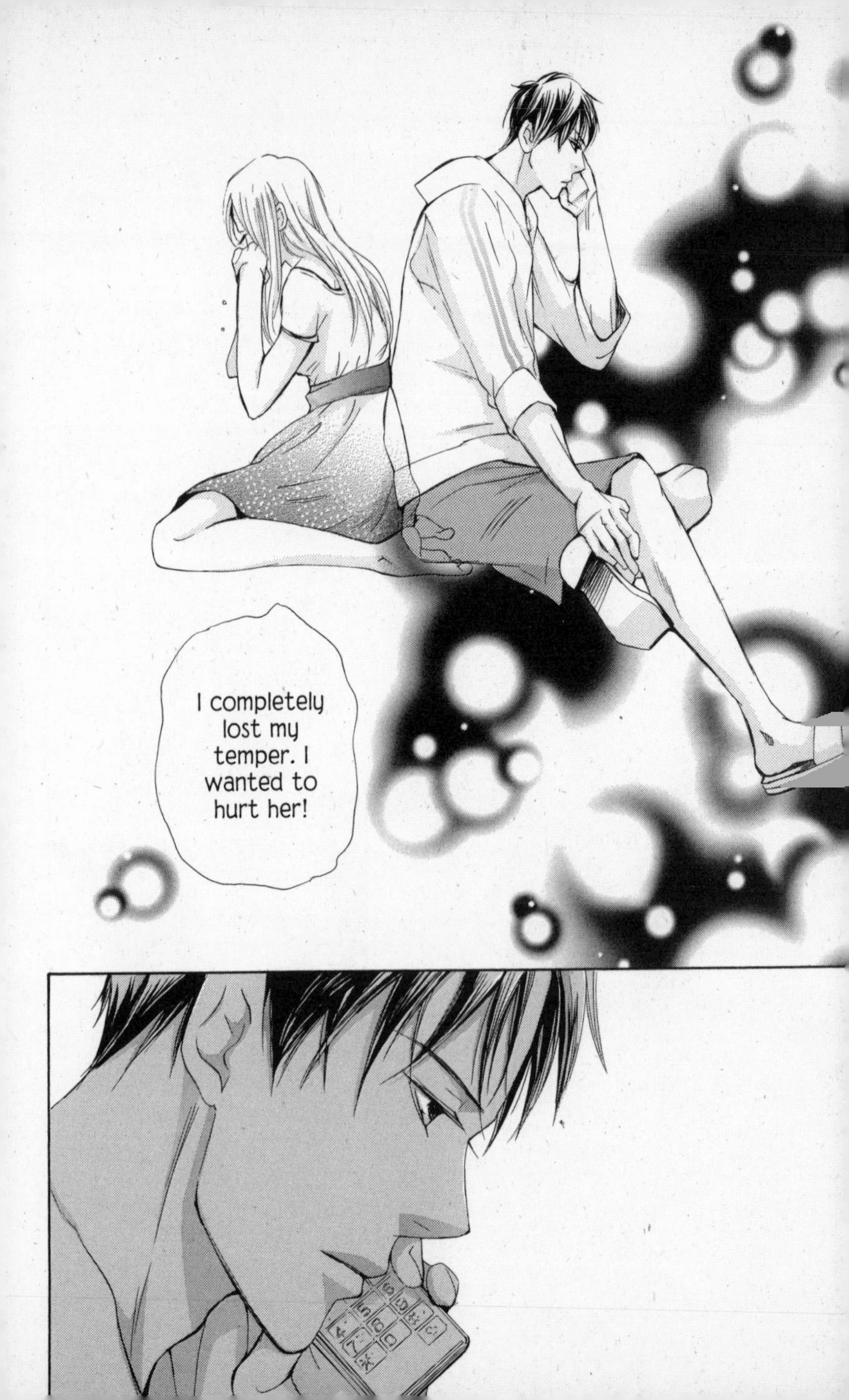
I completely lost my temper. I wanted to hurt her!

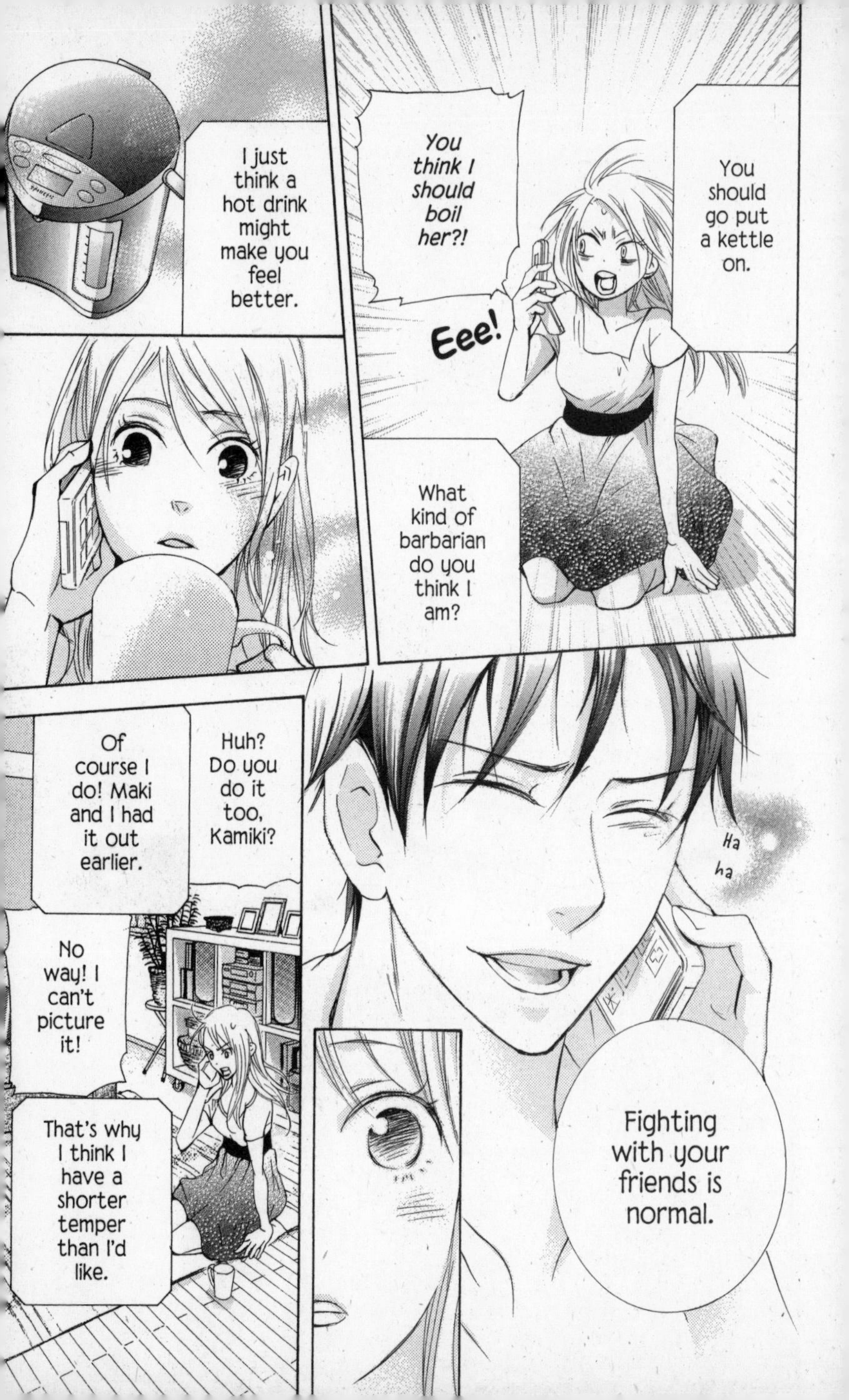

You should go put a kettle on.
You think I should boil her?!
Eee!
What kind of barbarian do you think I am?
I just think a hot drink might make you feel better.
Ha ha
Fighting with your friends is normal.
Huh? Do you do it too, Kamiki?
Of course I do! Maki and I had it out earlier.
No way! I can't picture it!
That's why I think I have a shorter temper than I'd like.

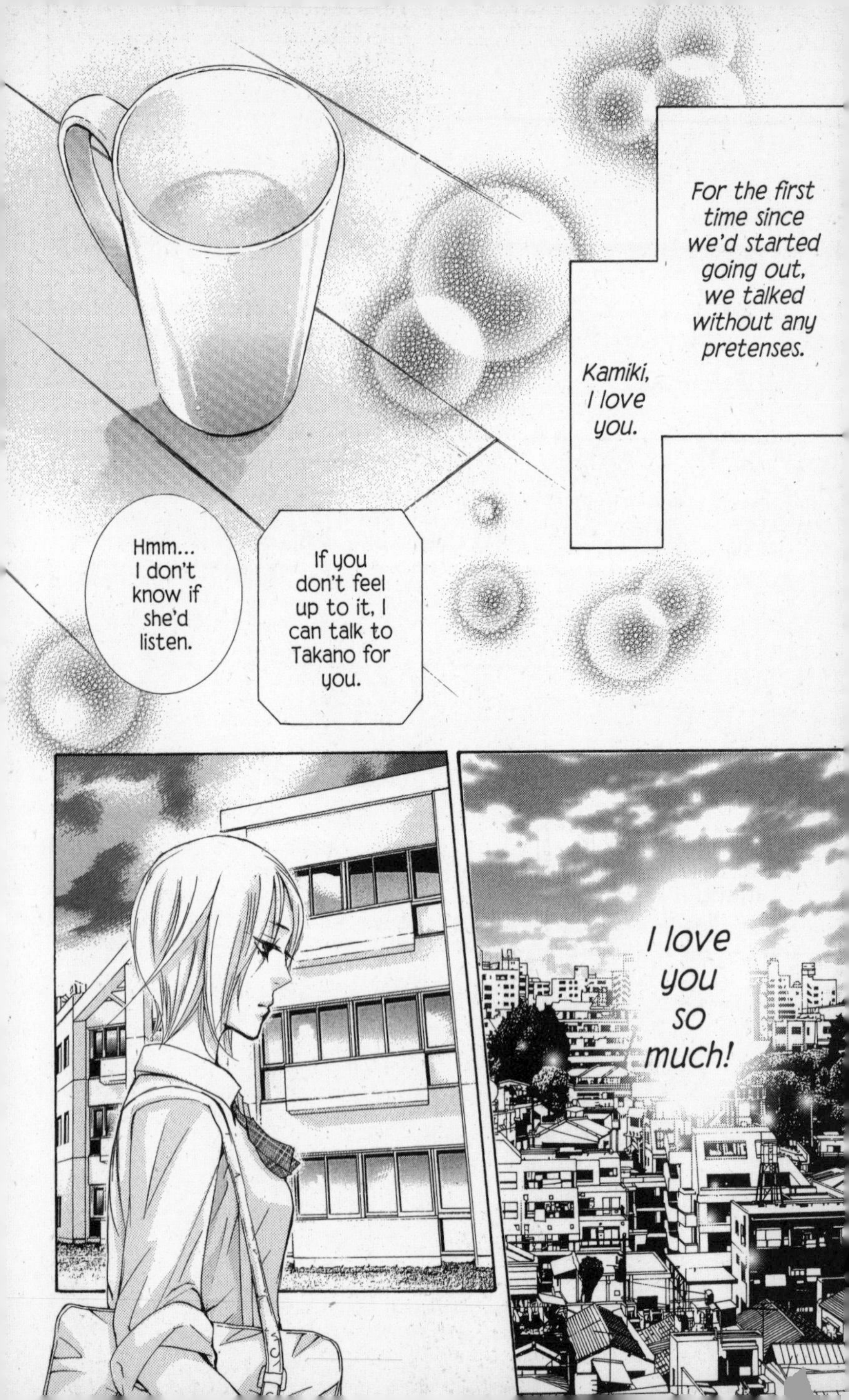
For the first time since we'd started going out, we talked without any pretenses.
Kamiki, I love you.
If you don't feel up to it, I can talk to Takano for you.
Hmm... I don't know if she'd listen.
I love you so much!

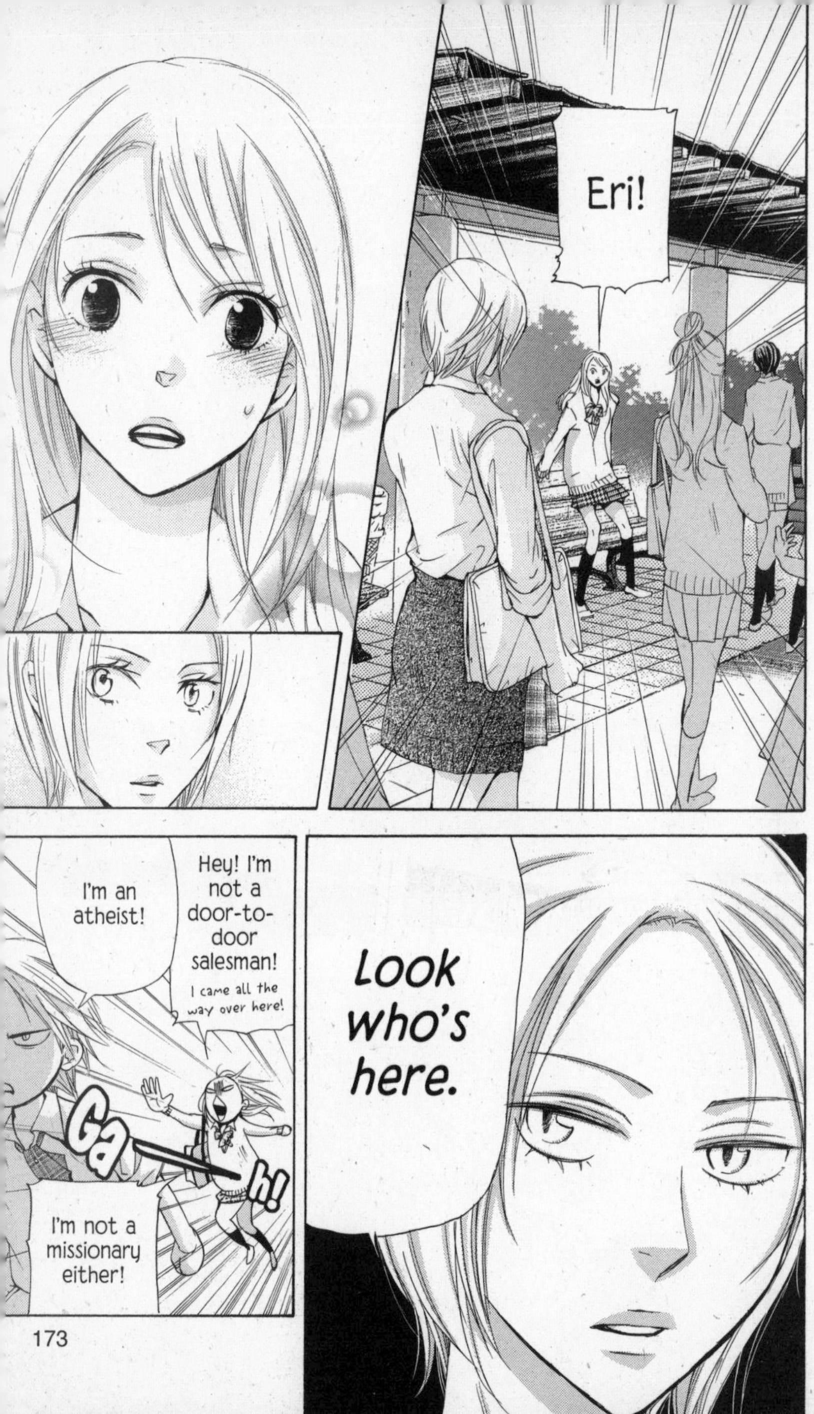
Eri!
Look who's here.
Hey! I'm not a door-to-door salesman!
I came all the way over here!
I'm an atheist!
Ga h!
I'm not a missionary either!

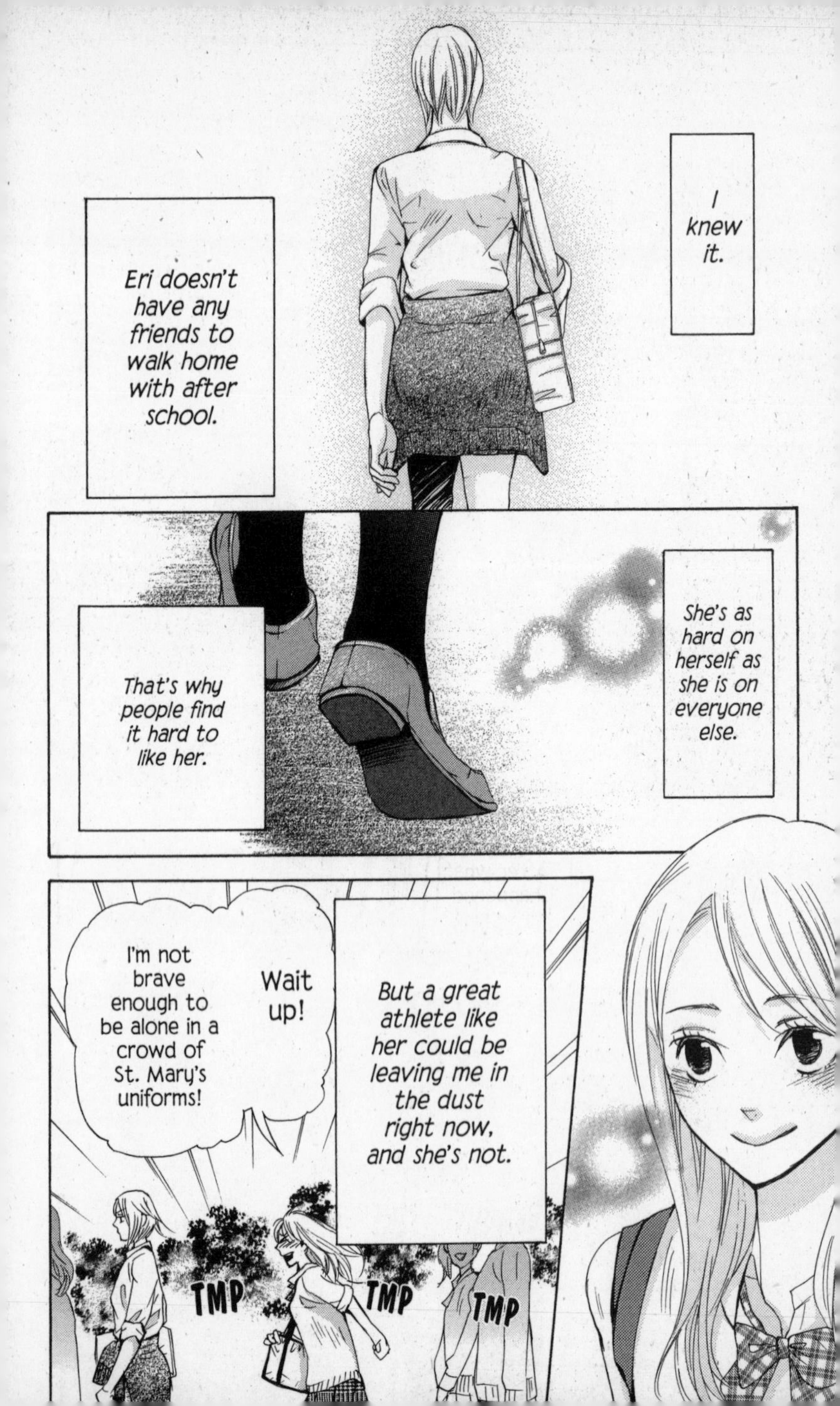
I knew it.
Eri doesn't have any friends to walk home with after school.
She's as hard on herself as she is on everyone else.
That's why people find it hard to like her.
But a great athlete like her could be leaving me in the dust right now, and she's not.
Wait up!
I'm not brave enough to be alone in a crowd of St. Mary's uniforms!
TMP
TMP
TMP

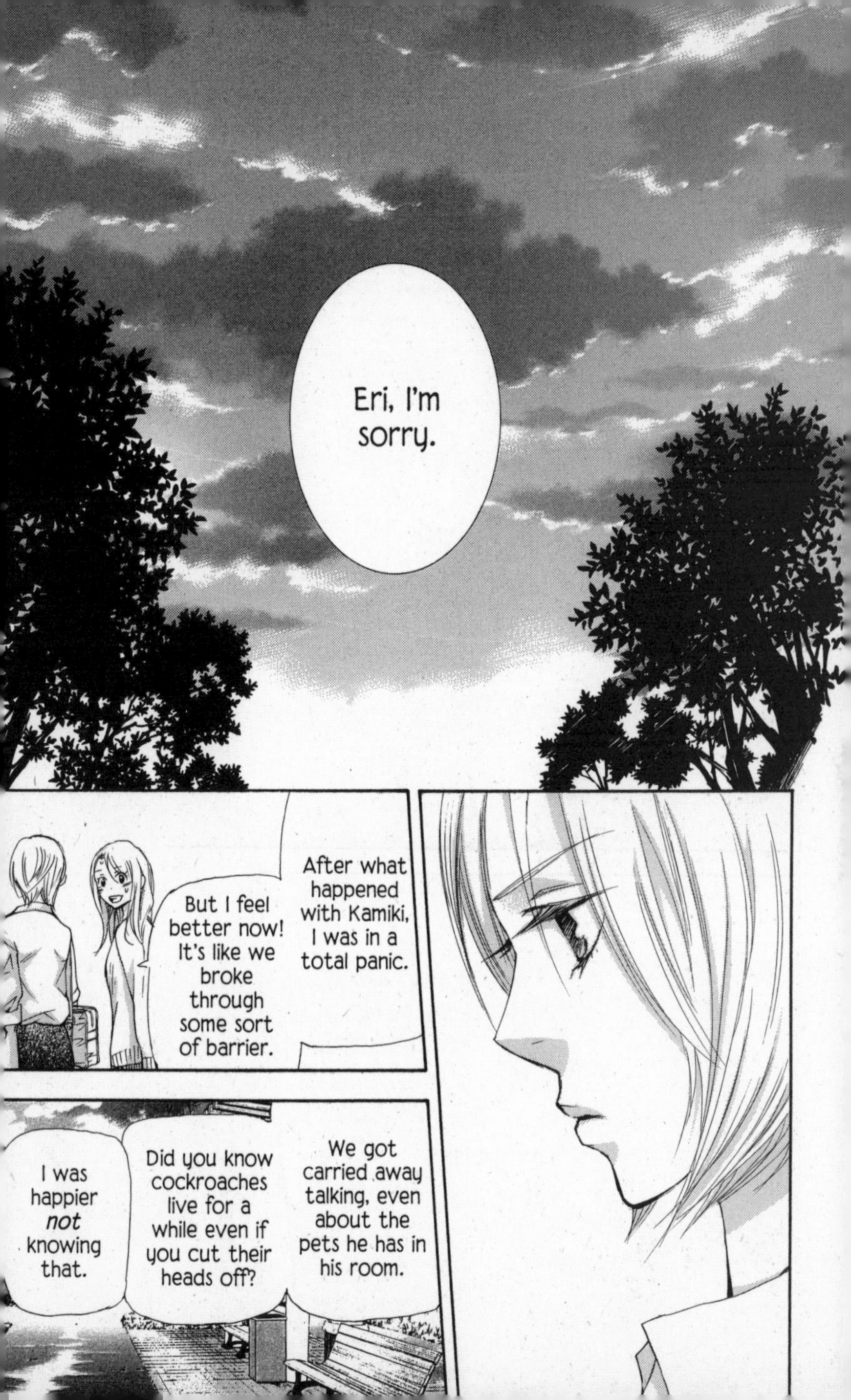
Eri, I'm sorry.
After what happened with Kamiki, I was in a total panic.
But I feel better now! It's like we broke through some sort of barrier.
We got carried away talking, even about the pets he has in his room.
Did you know cockroaches live for a while even if you cut their heads off?
I was happier *not* knowing that.

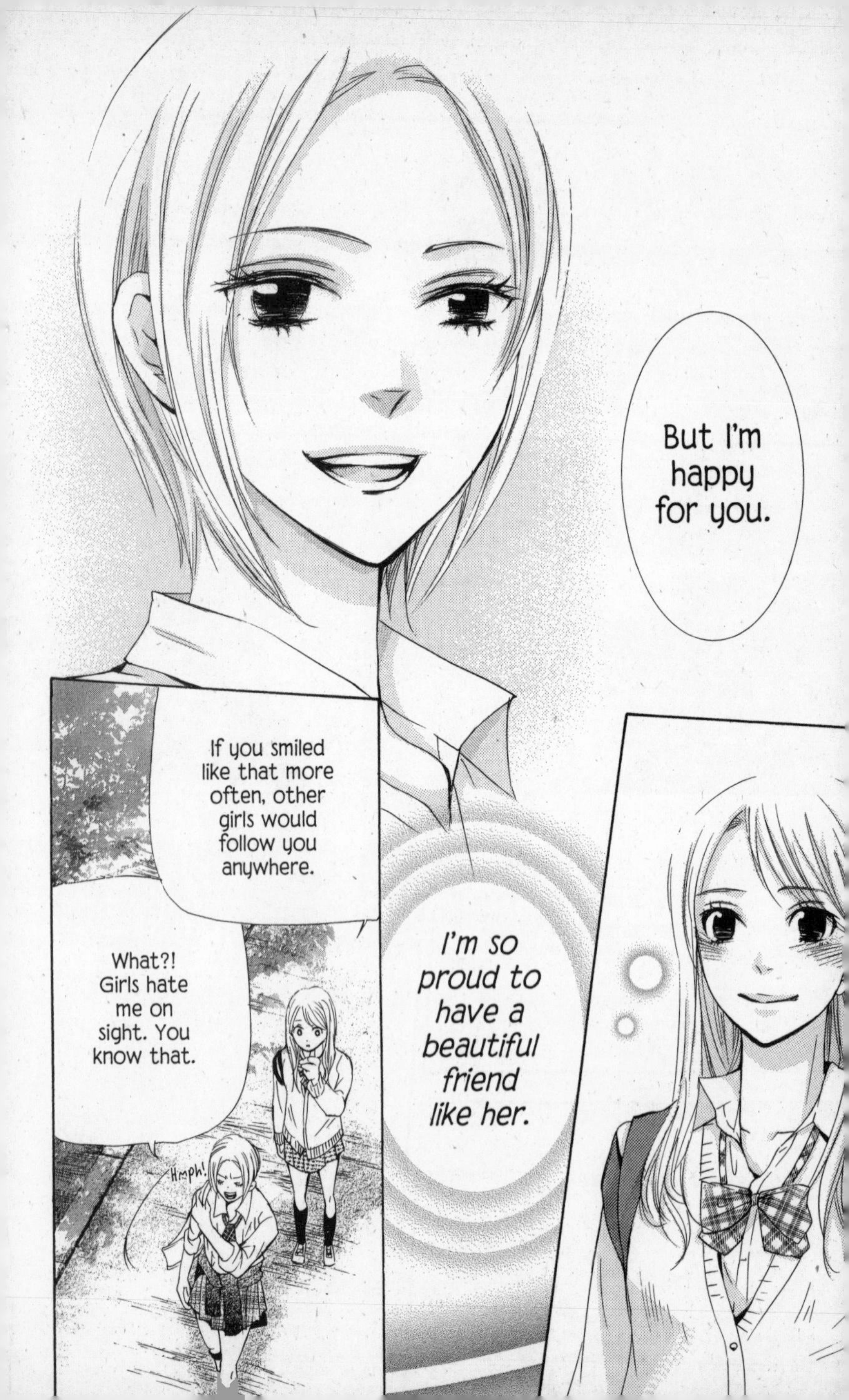
But I'm happy for you.
I'm so proud to have a beautiful friend like her.
If you smiled like that more often, other girls would follow you anywhere.
What?! Girls hate me on sight. You know that.
Hmph!

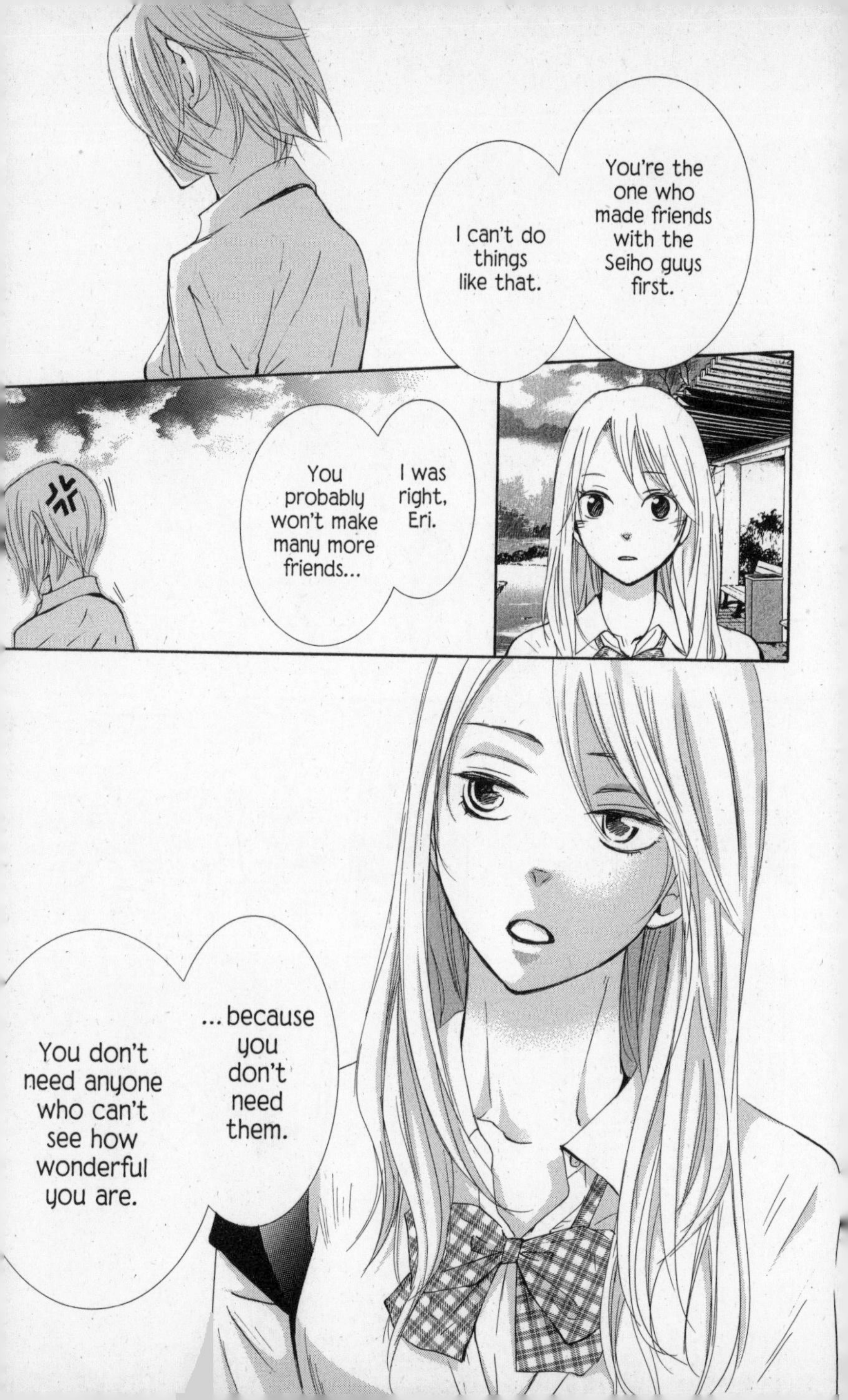
You're the one who made friends with the Seiho guys first.
I can't do things like that.
I was right, Eri.
You probably won't make many more friends...
...because you don't need them.
You don't need anyone who can't see how wonderful you are.

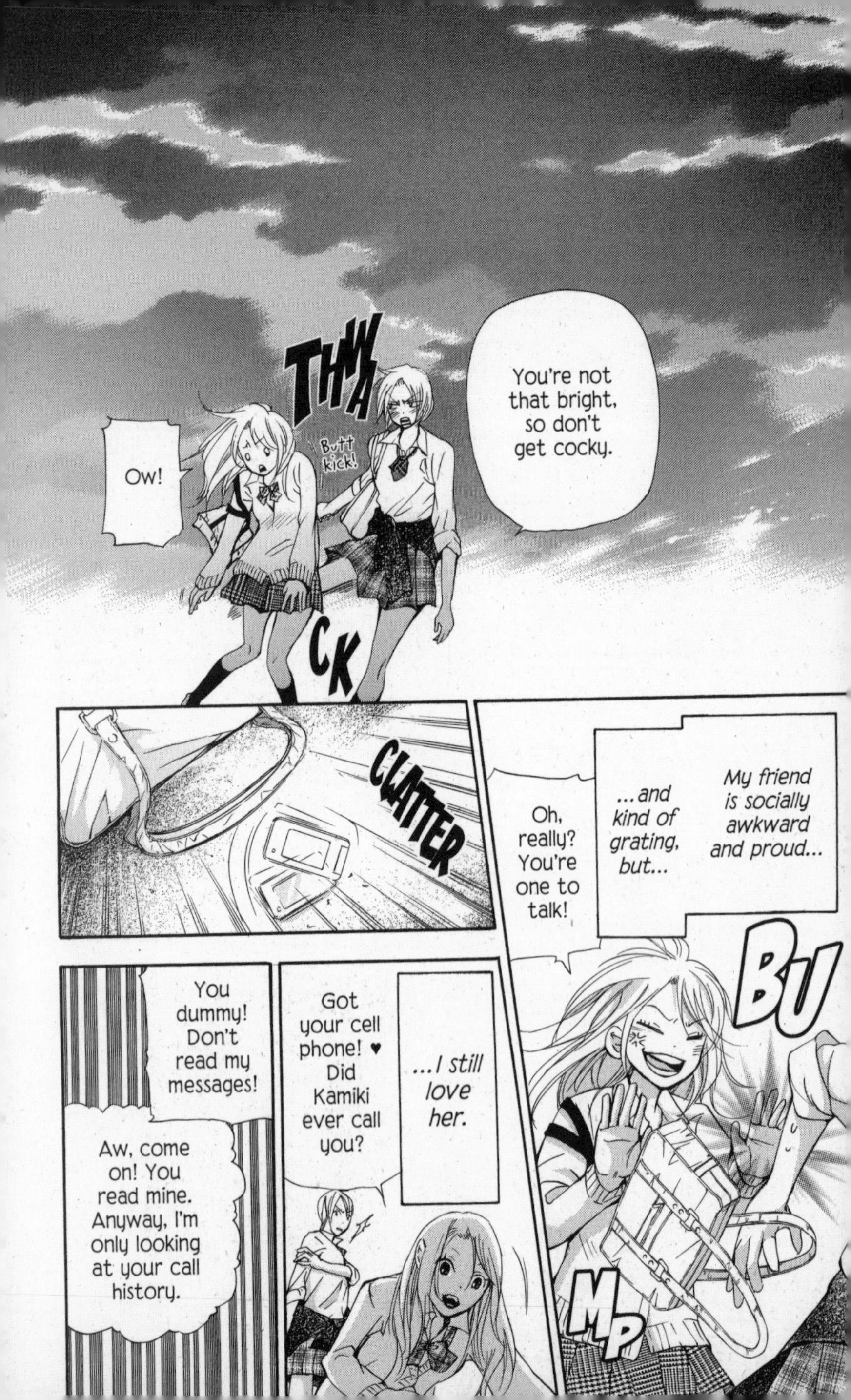
You're not that bright, so don't get cocky.
THWA
Butt kick!
Ow!
CK
My friend is socially awkward and proud...
...and kind of grating, but...
Oh, really? You're one to talk!
BU
MP
CLATTER
...I still love her.
Got your cell phone! ♥ Did Kamiki ever call you?
You dummy! Don't read my messages!
Aw, come on! You read mine. Anyway, I'm only looking at your call history.

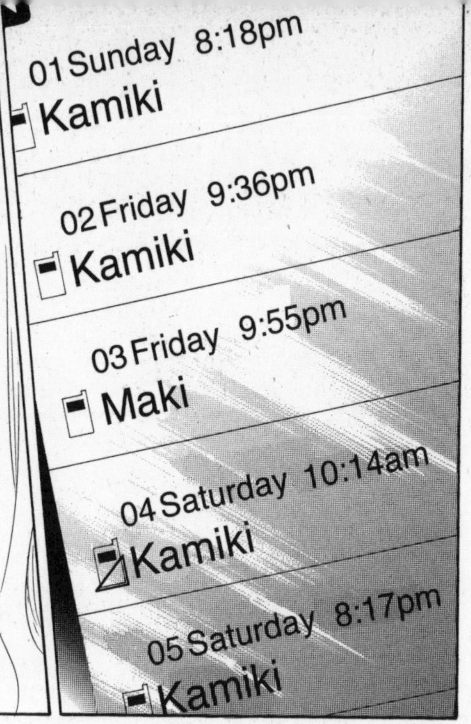
01 Sunday 8:18pm
Kamiki
02 Friday 9:36pm
Kamiki
03 Friday 9:55pm
Maki
04 Saturday 10:14am
Kamiki
05 Saturday 8:17pm
Kamiki
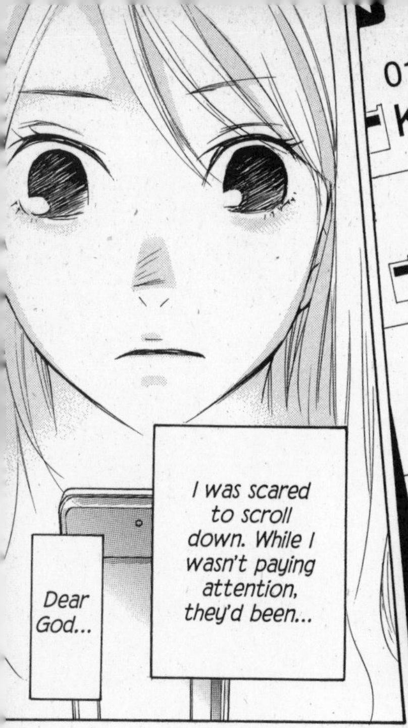
I was scared to scroll down. While I wasn't paying attention, they'd been...
Dear God...
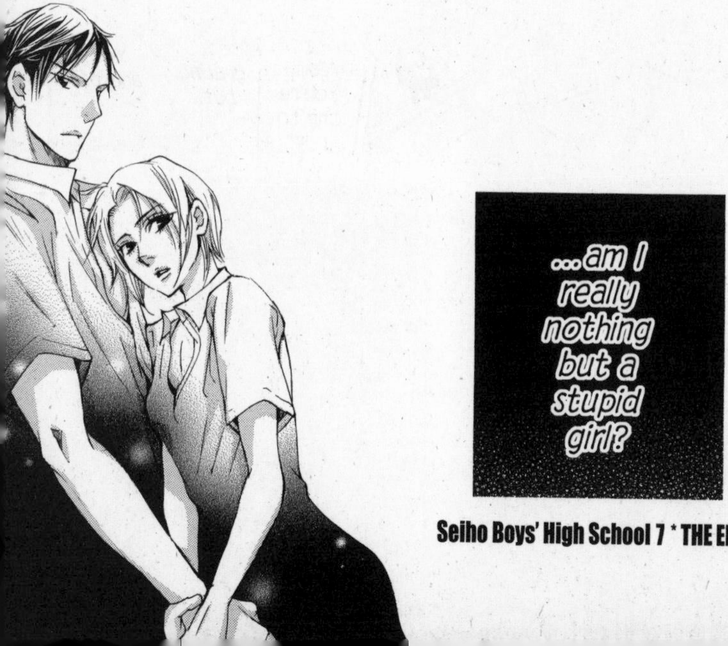
...am I really nothing but a stupid girl?

Seiho Boys' High School 7 * THE END *

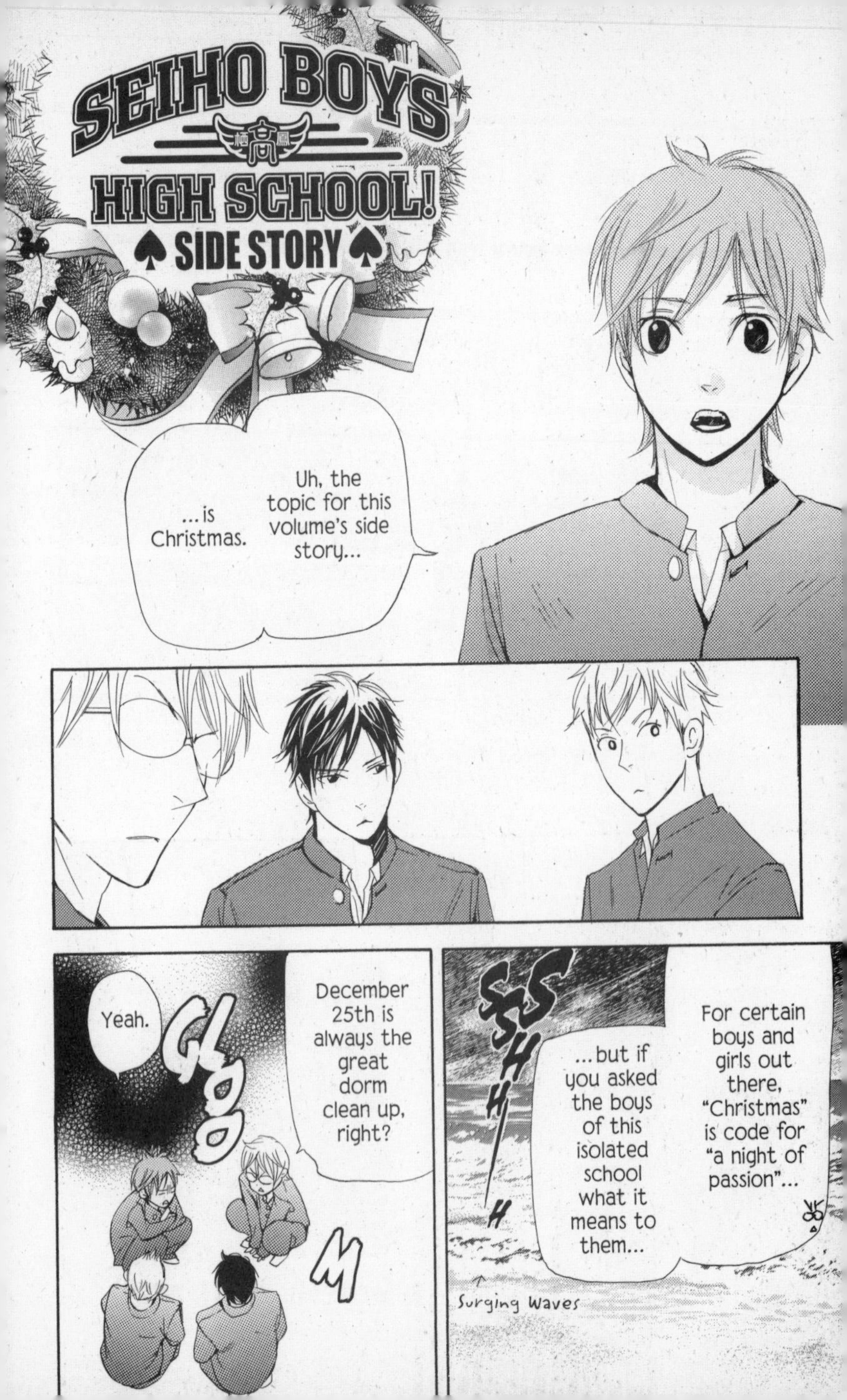
SEIHO BOYS' HIGH SCHOOL!
♠ SIDE STORY ♠
Uh, the topic for this volume's side story...
...is Christmas.
For certain boys and girls out there, "Christmas" is code for "a night of passion"...
...but if you asked the boys of this isolated school what it means to them...
SSHHH
Surging Waves
December 25th is always the great dorm clean up, right?
Yeah.
GLOOM

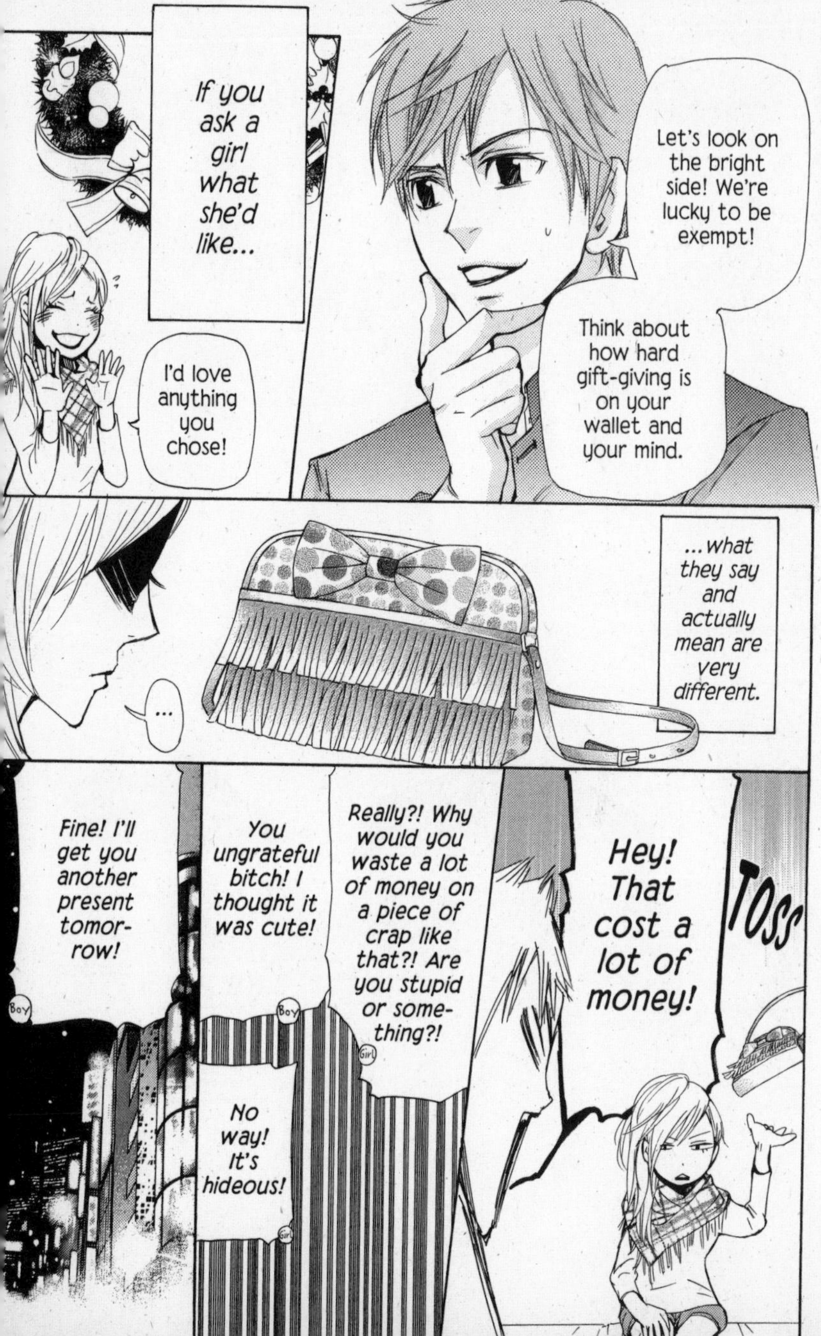
Let's look on the bright side! We're lucky to be exempt!
Think about how hard gift-giving is on your wallet and your mind.
If you ask a girl what she'd like...
I'd love anything you chose!
...what they say and actually mean are very different.
...
TOSS
Hey! That cost a lot of money!
Really?! Why would you waste a lot of money on a piece of crap like that?! Are you stupid or something?!
You ungrateful bitch! I thought it was cute!
No way! It's hideous!
Fine! I'll get you another present tomorrow!

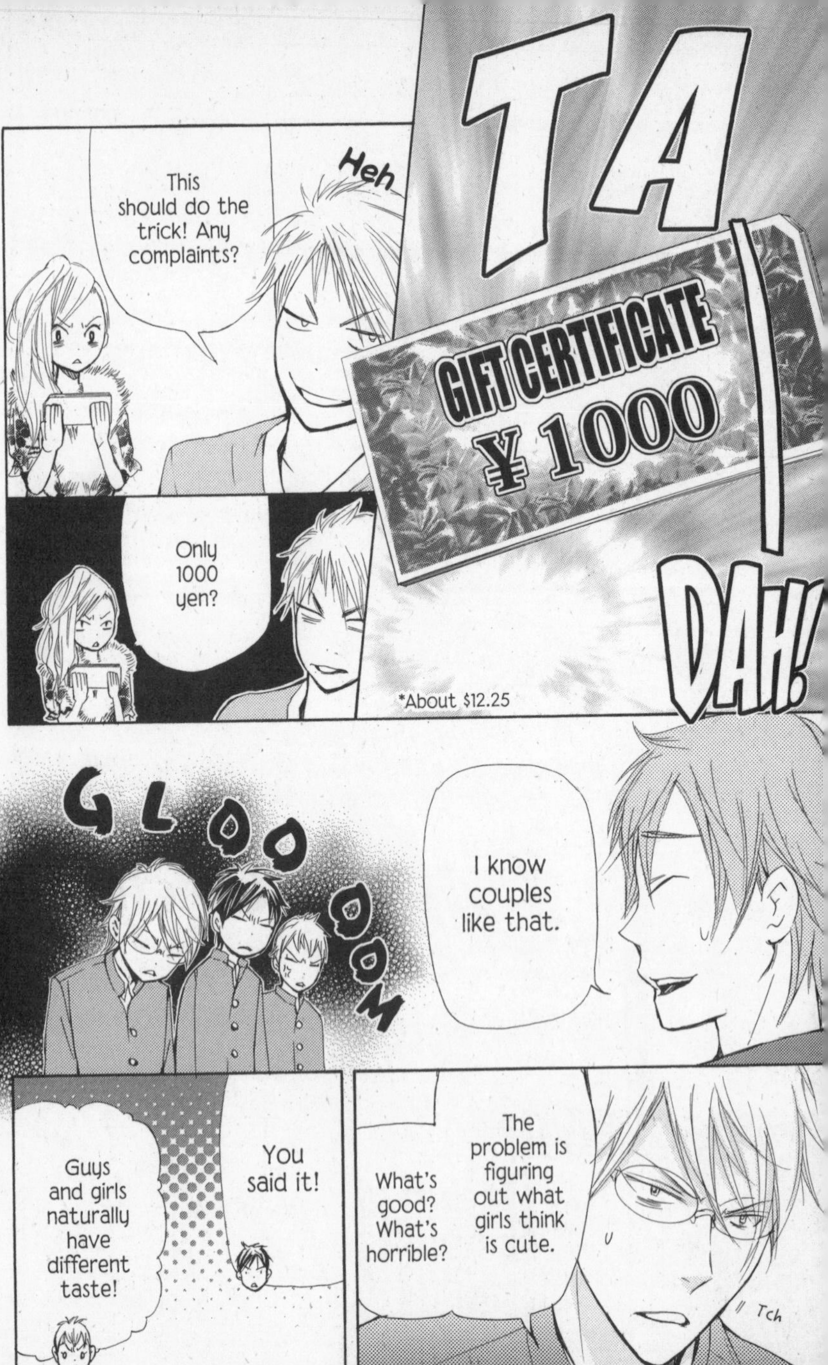
TA
GIFT CERTIFICATE ¥1000
DAH!
Heh
This should do the trick! Any complaints?
Only 1000 yen?
*About $12.25
I know couples like that.
GLOOOOM
The problem is figuring out what girls think is cute.
What's good? What's horrible?
Tch
You said it!
Guys and girls naturally have different taste!

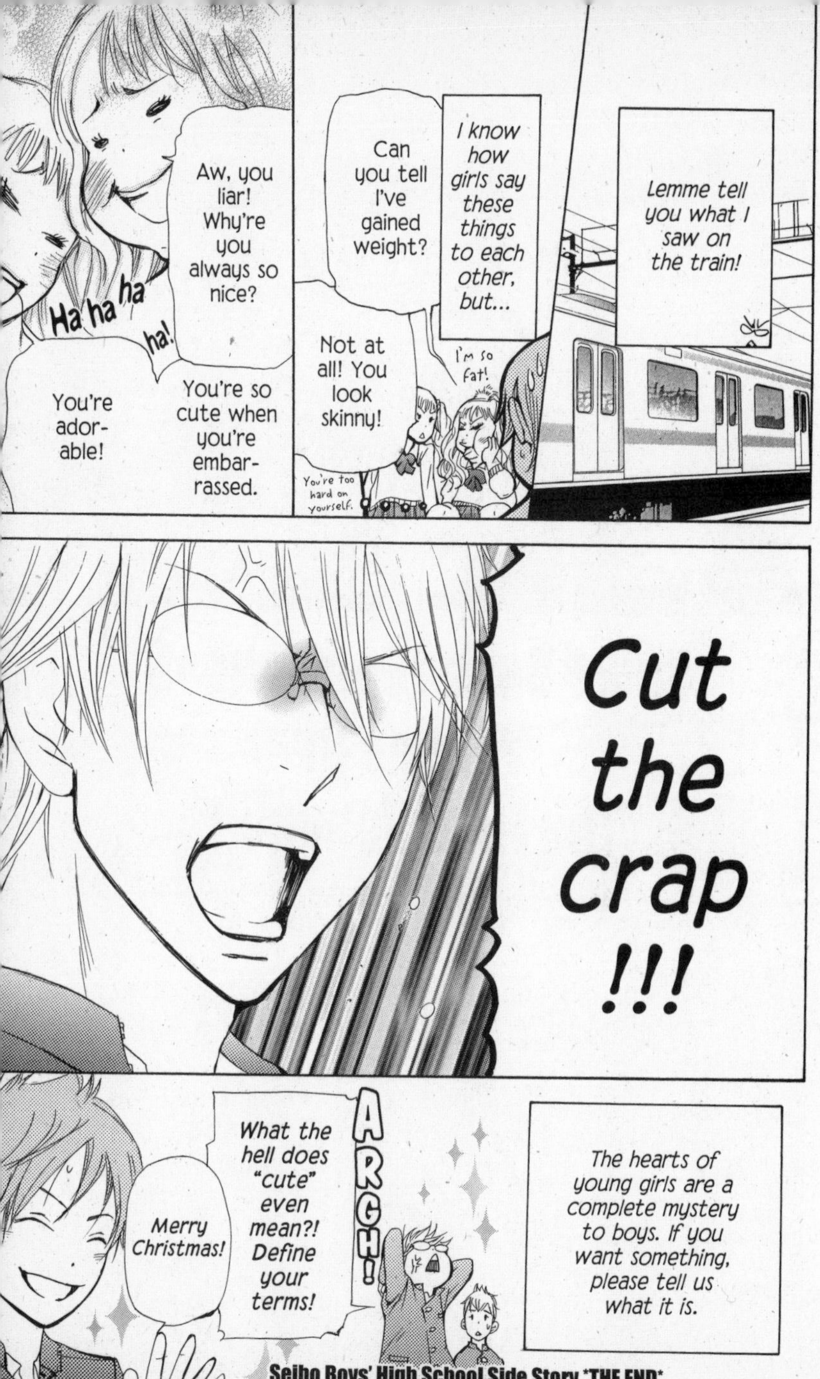
Lemme tell you what I saw on the train!
I know how girls say these things to each other, but...
Can you tell I've gained weight?
I'm so fat!
Not at all! You look skinny!
You're too hard on yourself.
Aw, you liar! Why're you always so nice?
Ha ha ha ha!
You're so cute when you're embarrassed.
You're adorable!
Cut the crap!!!
The hearts of young girls are a complete mystery to boys. If you want something, please tell us what it is.
ARGH!
What the hell does "cute" even mean?! Define your terms!
Merry Christmas!

Seiho Boys' High School Side Story *THE END*

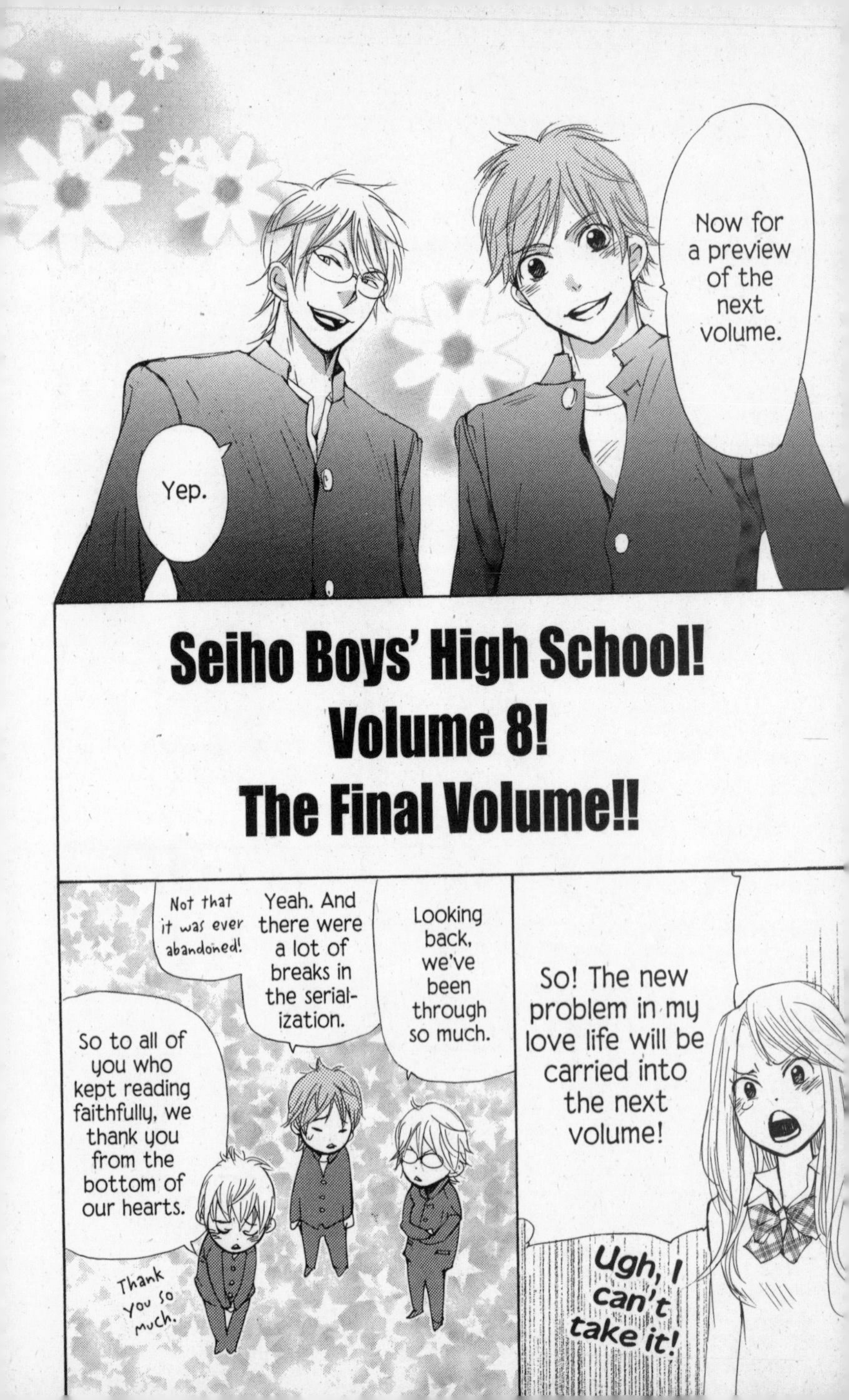
Now for a preview of the next volume.
Yep.
Seiho Boys' High School! Volume 8! The Final Volume!!
So! The new problem in my love life will be carried into the next volume!
Ugh, I can't take it!
Looking back, we've been through so much.
Yeah. And there were a lot of breaks in the serial-ization.
Not that it was ever abandoned!
So to all of you who kept reading faithfully, we thank you from the bottom of our hearts.
Thank you so much.

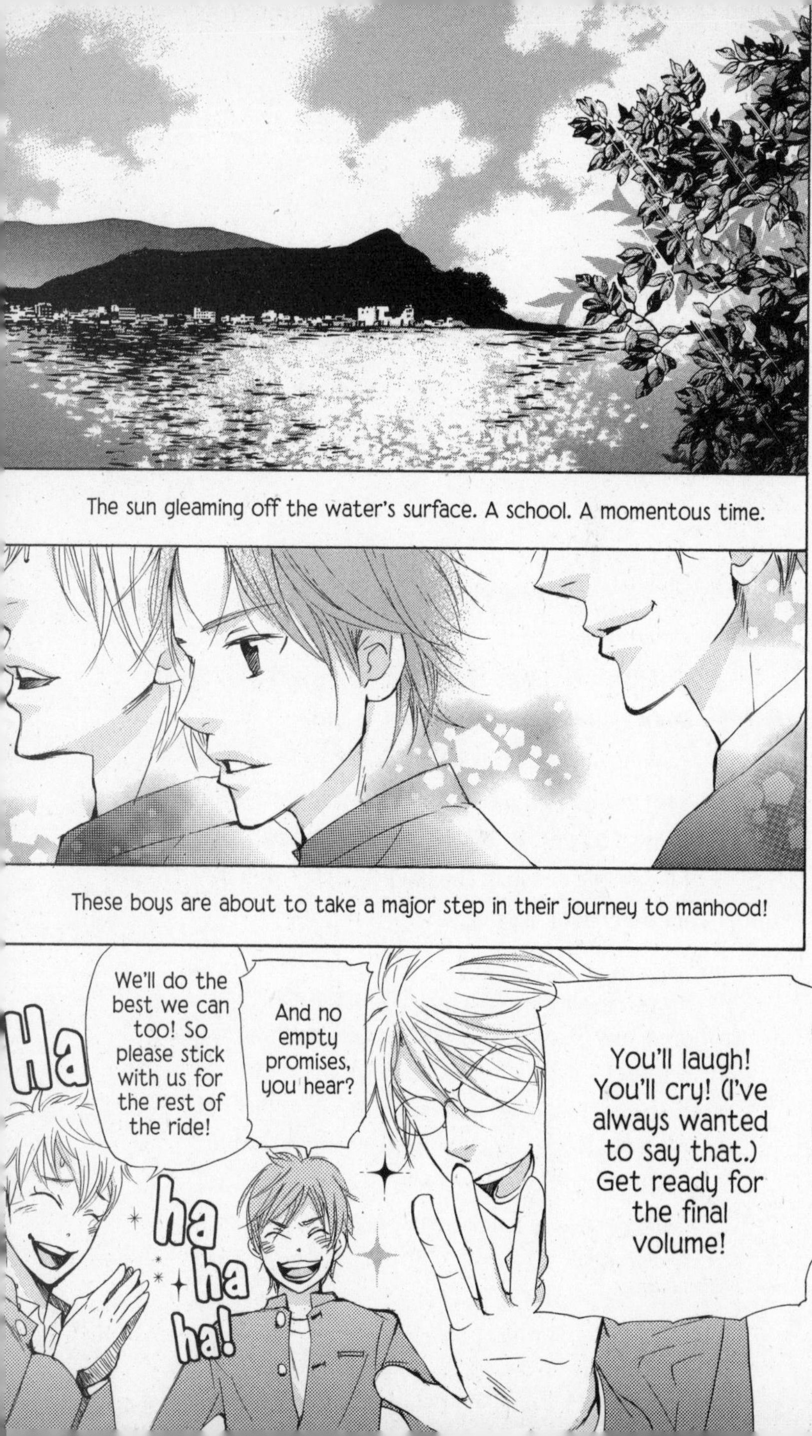
The sun gleaming off the water's surface. A school. A momentous time.
These boys are about to take a major step in their journey to manhood!
You'll laugh! You'll cry! (I've always wanted to say that.) Get ready for the final volume!
And no empty promises, you hear?
We'll do the best we can too! So please stick with us for the rest of the ride!
Ha ha ha ha!

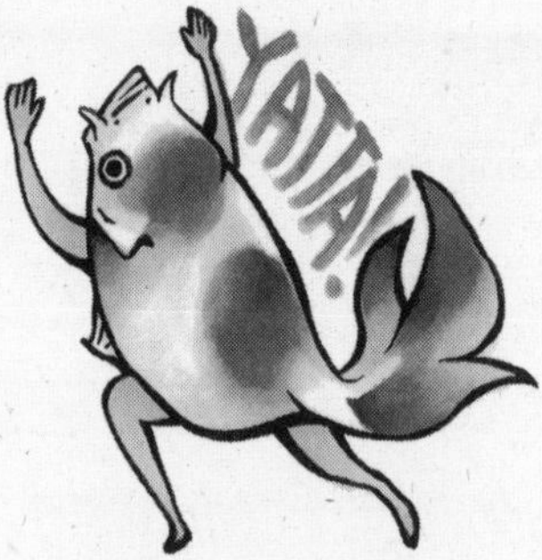
YATTA!

Kaneyoshi Izumi

Here we are at volume 7. Without my noticing, there wound up being a time lag between this volume and the previous one... All of you readers who always remember to buy a copy are angels to me. I don't plan to take any more breaks until I finish this series, so I hope you'll stay with me for the rest of the ride.

Kaneyoshi Izumi's birthday is April 1, and her blood type is probably type A (but she hasn't actually had it checked yet). Her debut story *Tenshi* (Angel) appeared in the September 1995 issue of *Bessatsu Shojo Comic* and won the 36th Shogakukan Shinjin (newbie) Comics Award. Her hobbies include riding motorcycles, playing the piano and feeding stray cats, and she continues to work as an artist for *Betsucomi.*

SEIHO BOYS' HIGH SCHOOL

Volume 7
Shojo Beat Edition

STORY AND ART BY
KANEYOSHI IZUMI

Original Japanese edition "MEN'S KOU"
published by SHOGAKUKAN Inc.

English Adaptation/Ysabet MacFarlane
Translation/Katherine Schilling
Touch-up Art & Lettering/Maui Girl
Cover Design/Julie Behn
Interior Design/Ronnie Casson
Editor/Amy Yu

Printed in Canada

Published by VIZ Media, LLC
P.O. Box 77010
San Francisco, CA 94107

10 9 8 7 6 5 4 3 2 1
First printing, August 2011

www.viz.com

RATED T+ FOR OLDER TEEN
PARENTAL ADVISORY
SEIHO BOYS' HIGH SCHOOL is rated T+ for Older Teen and is recommended for ages 16 and up. This volume contains suggestive themes and adult situations.
ratings.viz.com

www.shojobeat.com

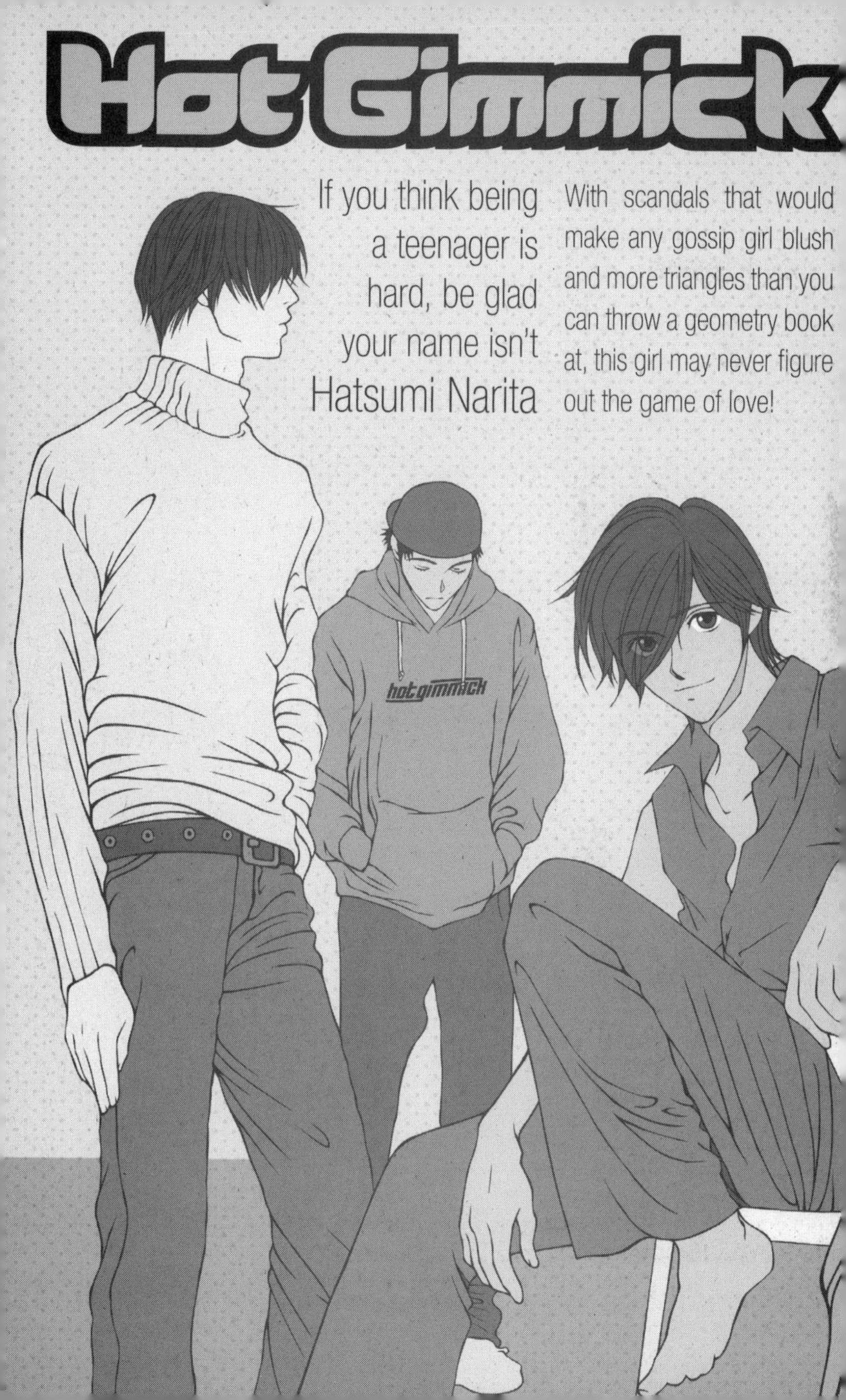
Hot Gimmick
If you think being a teenager is hard, be glad your name isn't Hatsumi Narita
With scandals that would make any gossip girl blush and more triangles than you can throw a geometry book at, this girl may never figure out the game of love!
hotgimmick

Monkey High! SB

By Shouko Akira

After her politician father is disgraced in scandal, Haruna Aizawa transfers to a new school. But school life, with all its cliques, fights and drama, reminds her of a monkey mountain! Will she ever fit in?

Find out in the *Monkey High!* manga series

Now Available!!